EXCEPTION TAKEN

Film and Culture

FILM AND CULTURE
A series of Columbia University Press
Edited by John Belton

For the list of titles in this series, see pages 395–398.

EXCEPTION TAKEN

How France Has Defied
Hollywood's New World Order

JONATHAN BUCHSBAUM

Columbia University Press
New York

Columbia University Press

Publishers Since 1893

New York   Chichester, West Sussex

cup.columbia.edu

Copyright © 2017 Columbia University Press

All rights reserved

ISBN 978-0-231-17066-6 (cloth: alk. paper)

ISBN 978-0-231-17067-3 (paperback: alk. paper)

ISBN 978-0-231-54307-1 (e-book)

Cataloging-in-Publication Data is on file at the Library of Congress.

Columbia University Press books are printed on permanent
and durable acid-free paper.

Printed in the United States of America

COVER DESIGN: Michael Nagin

FOR AÏCHA CHEHIDA, 1959–2012

CONTENTS

6. *BILAN(S)* 120

7. FROM CULTURAL EXCEPTION TO CULTURAL DIVERSITY 149

8. WAS THE EXPERIENCE BENEFICIAL? 181

CONCLUSION 213

FIGURES

PREFACE

An imaginative leap will benefit most readers of this book in the United States. Imagine a capitalist country that has preserved a safety net for residents. However frayed, that safety net still receives the financial and political support of most politicians in France. In the United States, a long tradition of individualist ideology deprecates so-called losers in a market that reaches increasingly into public goods. Things once thought of as services to be provided to residents, from education to health care and even national security, are now outsourced to private companies. With the free market as the model, U.S. government at all levels tries to privatize those public goods and services. Witness the complaisance with which the press treats the oxymoron "for-profit schools."

On one level, this book tries to consider the viability of cinema in the world today. While some, especially Hollywood pitch people, maintain that the spoils belong to the victors, the vanquished may not want to surrender their ability to continue making films. In most cases, that means developing policies to defend filmmaking, and those policies are largely national ones, though few writers on cinema concentrate on policy. In most countries, however, film industries cannot survive without state support policies.

Randal Johnson took on the challenge of understanding state support for film thirty years ago in *The Film Industry in Brazil: Culture and the State*

(Pittsburgh: University of Pittsburgh Press, 1987). His attempt to make sense of cinema policy, not to mention his lucid writing, has served as an inspiration for this book. More recently, European scholars have written about policy. France offers an exemplary case for study, for France has a long history of a state cinema policy, one that has become especially sophisticated and complex since 1980, the period covered in these pages. The French film industry consequently has maintained the most successful European film industry during those years.

In the most recent phase of globalization, developed countries have tried to reduce national trade barriers for goods and services. This is the central goal of the World Trade Organization, formed in 1995. Yet France objected to including cinema in the new rules, threatening to withhold its signature from the largest trade agreement in history, the General Agreement on Tariffs and Trade in 1993 (GATT). Cinema occupies a privileged place in French culture, and the French did not want to subject their carefully constructed cultural policies to the same rules being applied to other goods and services. Over time, other countries recognized the potential dangers to their own national cultures. Thus, cinema ended up triggering widespread opposition to the march of globalization just as the United States sought to strengthen its superpower position in the new world order. It seemed that culture, improbably, provided an alternative terrain for resistance, and France has articulated that rationale most persuasively and consistently.

I could not have completed this book without the constant support of the staff at the Documentation Center at the Centre national de la cinématographie (CNC) in Paris. I would like to thank all of them for their unstinting generosity: Susane Rodes, Sébastien Magnier Ariane Nouvet, Marielle Fernandez, Magali Jammet, and the late Estelle Baïche. I would also like to express my appreciation to people who were kind enough to share their knowledge and grant me interviews: Karim Amellal, Pierre Chevalier, Malik Chibane, Pascal Ferran, Stéphane Goudet, François Hurard, Cédric Klapisch, Florent Lamare, Claude Miller, Gérard Mordillat, Emmanuel Rufi, and Michelle Soulignac. In New York, two friends at the French Cultural Services, Delphine Selles-Alvarez and Sandrine Butteau, arranged many of the interviews and provided other valuable support.

French colleagues offered their hospitality and the opportunity to present some of the work in progress: Michel Marie, Laurent Creton, Laurent Jullier, and Jean-Pierre Bertin-Maghit. British colleagues Martin O'Shaughnessy and Graeme Hayes provided encouragement and venues for some of the work. Other friends and colleagues have helped in many and varied ways over the years: Maguy Alziari, Viviane Alziari, Ali Akika, Nejma Akika, Yacine Akika, Henry Bean, Jean-Jacques Birgé, Barbara Bowen, Arthur Chitty, Mark Jacobson, Stuart Liebman, Richard Maxwell, Charles Molesworth, Roopali Mukherjee, Laura Mulvey, Françoise Romand, and Don Siegel. My apologies to those whose names I have overlooked.

I would like to thank John Belton, my first film teacher and editor of the Film and Culture series at Columbia University Press, for his early interest in the book, and Jennifer Crewe, the director of Columbia University Press, for her support of the project. Others at CUP ensured the steady and careful guidance of this book through production to publication, including Philip Leventhal, Miriam Grossman, Kathryn Jorge, and the excellent design department. Glenn Perkins executed skillful copyediting and Cynthia Savage produced a robust index.

This book benefited from a PSC-CUNY Award, jointly funded by the Professional Staff Congress and the City University of New York.

Doris Lee never hesitated to help in small and large ways.

As ever, my friend Joel Haycock served as an intellectual compass throughout.

I decided long ago, before her death, to dedicate this book to Aïcha Chehida. Stricken with two serious maladies, each treated entirely at state expense in France, she used to refer to herself as having two 100 percenters. Her spirit pervades this book.

ABBREVIATIONS

ACID	Association of Independent Cinema for Its Distribution
ADRC	Agence pour le développement régional du cinéma
AFCAE	Association française des cinémas d'art et essai
AMI/MAI	multilateral agreement on investment
ARP	Association des réalisateurs et producteurs
ASR	avance sur recettes
BLAC	Bureau de liaison de l'action culturelle
BLIC	Bureau de liaison des industries cinématographiques
BLOC	Bureau de liaison des organisations du cinéma
CGE	Compagnie générale des eaux
CNC	Centre national du cinéma (now Centre national du cinéma et de l'image animée)
COE	Council of Europe
COIC	Comité d'organisation de l'industrie cinématographique
COSIP	Compte de soutien financier de l'industrie cinématographique et de l'industrie des programmes audiovisuels
CSA	Conseil supérieur de l'audiovisuel
CUSFTA	Canada–United States Free Trade Agreement

DG	Direction Générale (General Directorate of the European Commission)
EC	European Commission
ECJ	European Court of Justice
EEC	European Economic Community
ENA	École nationale d'administration
EU	European Union
FIF	French-initiative (entirely or majority-financed) film
GATT	General Agreement on Tariffs and Trade
GNCR	Groupement national des cinémas de recherche
IFCIC	Institut de financement du cinéma et des industries culturelles
INCP	International Network for Cultural Policy
MAI	multilateral agreement on investment
MFN	most favored nation
MPA/MPAA	Motion Picture Association of America
NT	national treatment
NWICO	New World Information and Communication Order
OECD	Organization for Economic Cooperation and Development
PME	petites et moyennes entreprises (small and medium [size] enterprises)
SOFICAs	Sociétés pour le financement de l'industrie cinématographique et audiovisuel
SRF	Society of Film Directors
TPS	television by satellite
TRIPS	Trade-Related Aspects of Industrial Property Rights
TSA	taxe spéciale additionelle
TWF	Television Without Frontiers
UNESCO	United Nations Educational, Scientific, and Cultural Organization
VU	Vivendi Universal
WTO	World Trade Organization

INTRODUCTION

A s recently as the 1970s, films from most major foreign filmmaking industries drew more domestic spectators than Hollywood films. With the ascendance of neoliberalism during the 1980s, many of those foreign industries shriveled and were no longer able to compete with Hollywood products on their home turfs. According to one astonishing estimate, 80 percent of all money spent worldwide for films went to U.S. films.[1] France initially experienced a similar erosion of its film industry during those years but designed a strategy to nurture its own film industry and developed a rhetorical argument to defend cinema beyond its borders. That strategy entailed a plethora of new cinema policies domestically and extensive lobbying in regional and international venues for a recognition of the "cultural exception" of film and television production in trade agreements, contesting the unconditional free trade demands of the United States.

These developments served as the background to the defining confrontation between France and the United States over the conclusion of the seven-year negotiations for the General Agreement on Tariffs and Trade (GATT) in the last months of 1993. In those negotiations, France threatened to withhold its signature from—and potentially derail—the largest trade pact in history if the United States did not accept the European Union's demand for a "cultural exception." The few U.S. news reports of that battle failed to recognize the larger significance of this standoff.[2] Subsequent U.S. commentary, concentrated in law journals, tended to debate minutiae of official texts, concluding that France and the EU, flouting the Washington Consensus, violated the putative imperatives of free trade principles. In fact, France had drawn a line in the sand over cultural sovereignty. Despite the accession of neoliberal governments and their pressures to remove restrictions on trade internationally, France rallied other countries to resist the application of liberalization to cultural production. Despite what Laurent Creton has called the "Lilliputian" economic weight of cinema, the perception of film's imbrication with national identity conferred a disproportionately public importance on the cinema industry as a key catalyst for resistance to globalization.[3] In that sense, the years since 1993 are "exceptional times."

During the 1980s, the audiovisual landscape was changing radically in Europe and the rest of the world, just as paeans to the virtues of globalization exercised a tightening hegemony over global economic policies, promulgated primarily by the United States. In country after country, state-owned television began to privatize, responding to political and technological changes and finally addressing pent-up demand. In 1989, the European Economic Community (EEC), following several years of difficult negotiations, approved the first European policy document on television, even though the EEC's founding document, the Treaty of Rome (1957), made no mention of cultural matters. France argued with only partial success that cultural goods were not like other goods and deserved special treatment. The Directive on Television Without Frontiers called for a minimum quota (50 percent) of European films to be shown on national television (though that requirement was weakened by the compromise phrase "where practicable"). Nevertheless, France had forced the question of culture, specifically audiovisual production, onto the European agenda.

Three years later, the Maastricht Treaty brought the European Union into existence, and that treaty did, for the first time, include provisions on culture. The new regional treaty accepted promotion and preservation of culture as criteria for approval when evaluating the legality of cultural policies adopted by member states. The European regional debate over the Directive on Television Without Frontiers pitted free trade liberals against interventionist dirigistes, but when faced with the ongoing international negotiations over GATT, France convinced its European partners to refuse to sign any agreement that would prevent countries from setting their own cultural policies, above all policies to preserve national film industries.

In the tense final days of the GATT face-off, the United States blinked. Though details were complicated and the outcome of the battle over the "cultural exception" was inconclusive, the very public debate in France placed culture at the center of emerging discourses of globalization, carving out a space for alter-globalization movements. After GATT, replaced in 1995 by the World Trade Organization (WTO), other countries, and many nongovernmental organizations (NGOs) joined a larger struggle to resist the free trade mantra, most dramatically at the meltdown of the WTO meeting in Seattle in 1999. As a domestic struggle began with the design of an audiovisual strategy encompassing both film and television, France was simultaneously developing its strategy regionally within the EU, internationally within GATT and then the WTO, and finally outside the WTO within UNESCO, culminating in the overwhelming vote in 2005 in favor of UNESCO's Convention on Cultural Diversity (barely covered in the *New York Times*), when only two countries (the United States and Israel) cast dissenting votes. After passage of the convention, the French minister of culture called it "one of the essential conditions for attaining a more tractable and humane globalization."[4]

In the 1980s, cinema attendance, production, and domestic market share in France began to slip, following a decade of relative stability. In the fateful year of 1986, the French market share taken by U.S. product caught up with the market share taken by French film (43 percent), and the U.S. share climbed at the expense of French films throughout the decade and into the 1990s. The state of French cinema continued to decline further in the 1990s, with domestic market share reaching a low of 28 percent in 1994 (and again in 1998). Other European countries fared far worse. Once-thriving national film industries in Germany, Spain, and Great Britain saw their domestic market shares hover around 10 percent (see figure 0.1).

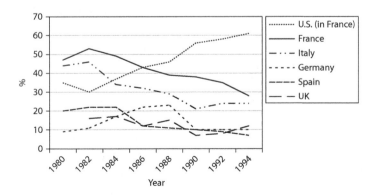

FIGURE 0.1 Percentage of domestic market share, 1980–1994

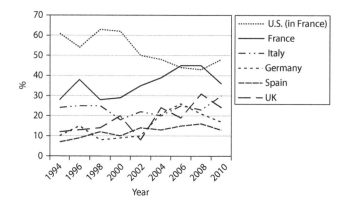

FIGURE 0.2 Percentage of domestic market share, 1994–2010

Since that time, however, French film production has doubled, attendance has revived, and the number of screens has continued to rise. Perhaps most important for the health of an alternative to Hollywood, French market share has stabilized between 35 and 45 percent, even topping U.S. market share in France in 2006 for the first time since 1986; other European industries have also improved, but lag well behind (see figure 0.2).

The key element in this successful French resistance has been the role of the state. When they saw the dangers to the film industry mounting in the 1980s, Minister of Culture Jack Lang and others made a concerted effort to save it, including the decision to tap the rising revenues of newly privatized television to replenish investment resources lost at the shrinking box office. While the government tried to satisfy competing sectors of the film industry, the country presented a united front outside its borders, and that front included filmmakers, producers, exhibitors, and politicians from across the political spectrum able to maintain unity in the face of intense pressure from the United States in multiple venues.

Designing policies required careful examination of the structure of the film and television industries. In order to guide the many new initiatives, the Centre national du cinéma (CNC), the national film office, vastly expanded its gathering of data, making more and more figures available in print and on the Internet.[5] To take only one example among many, the national film office publishes an annual report on the film industry, known as the *Bilan*. In 1980, the *Bilan* contained thirty-two pages; the 2013 *Bilan* ran to two hundred pages.[6] French officials and scholars have drawn on this trove of information to limn many details of how the film industry actually functions, in contrast to the dearth of information about the U.S. film industry attested to by virtually all U.S. scholars.[7] Thus, the French data and studies present a rich portrait of the stress points and trade-offs in the modern film industry, for policy measures crafted to solve immediate problems often open breaches in other parts of the industry.[8]

These kinds of stresses arise in any country trying to preserve its film industry. The closing of art cinemas and the migration of art films to festivals can give the misleading impression that smaller countries (Taiwan, Romania) maintain thriving industries. In fact, critically acclaimed films from such countries mask the withering of national industries as local audiences flock to heavily promoted U.S. exports, which dominate local markets (with the two very different exceptions of India and China).[9]

Although Hollywood has succeeded in maintaining, and often enlarging upon, its "major presence in all the world markets,"[10] other countries have pulled their own film industries back from the abyss of the 1990s. They have done so in their own ways, with no single model predominating, but most often after having rejected the free trade dogma that the United States has sought to impose through international trade agreements. France has led that resistance at three different levels—national, regional, global—showing how national film industries can intervene to preserve their existence in each of three concentric circles. After a survey of the international context in chapter 1, with especial consideration of the domination of U.S. cinema, chapter 2 traces the first concerted efforts to respond to the crisis. France first sought to shore up its domestic industry as the great transformation of privatized television took off in the 1980s. At the same time, the EEC was mutating and expanding into the EU, which grew from the original six founding EEC members in 1956 to the twenty-eight members of the EU today. Fitfully, but on a continuing basis, the EU has stood up to the pressures of the United States over culture. Chapter 3 follows the European debates over television during the 1980s. Chapter 4 examines the dramatic confrontation over the "cultural exception" that almost scuttled the seven-year Uruguay GATT round in 1993. Chapter 5 looks at the rise and fall of Canal+, the "banker" of French cinema and a central player in the new audiovisual configuration in France. Chapter 6 considers French attempts to assess the efficacy of the measures it had taken to rescue its film industry. After the formation of the WTO, in 1995, gave more favorable ground on which the United

States could exert its commercial might, France and Canada led the mission to find safer refuge from that agreement in a different international organization, UNESCO. Chapter 7 explicates the genesis of the term "cultural diversity" as a less controversial replacement in international negotiations and covers efforts to establish an alternative venue for pursuing cultural diversity within UNESCO, an avowedly cultural institution where the United States traditionally has had a less dominant position. Those efforts culminated with the passage by UNESCO of the Convention on Cultural Diversity in 2005. Chapter 8 takes on the conundrum of quality. Sustaining a vibrant national film industry in the current global environment is already a difficult challenge. But perhaps there would be little benefit in a film industry that produced few works of value. How can one identify quality films? To break the unacceptable yardstick that measures quality exclusively by box office performance, France has tried to rebuild demand for quality cinema. Chapter 9 looks at a recent case history in Paris, pitting a dynamic art cinema in a Paris suburb against a large Parisian art circuit, a battle that illustrates some of the basic tensions of French national cinema policy.

What lessons can then be drawn from the strife-ridden past thirty years over the "cultural exception"? Ultimately, the future of filmmaking for the foreseeable future will depend on the commitment of countries to defend their national cultural prerogatives and interests against Hollywood and its immense financial resources. Taking France as the most effective model, this book shows how countries can at least mitigate the losses imposed by relentless Hollywood hegemony.

The French model hinges on two related stories. First, like most European countries during the 1980s, France relaxed its controls over television, opening the airwaves to private companies and privatizing formerly state-owned stations. Throughout Europe, the number of new stations exploded. Television prospered as national cinemas went into free fall. With theatrical attendance and revenues plummeting, France initiated new policies to counteract these trends, most notably by mandating the transfer of funds from television to cinema to replace dwindling theatrical receipts. Given the unusually high status accorded film as a national cultural asset in France, the new policies also entailed careful monitoring of the health of the film industry, generating a wealth of data needed to assess the effectiveness of these measures. Those data, and the discussions attending them, reveal the real functioning of one of the largest and most successful contemporary film industries. Because the government has played an active role in supporting the film industry, a researcher can answer basic questions about French film that are rarely even asked in studies of other film industries, including such issues as the number of new filmmakers each year as a measure of resources devoted to research and development, the geographical distribution of theaters by population density (to gauge the access of the population to theaters), and the activity of distributors (to trace patterns of concentration in the key sector controlling the supply of films to theaters).

Second, how did cultural questions assume such seminal importance in international trade agreements? Beginning with the first GATT agreement, in 1947, negotiations concentrated exclusively on manufactured goods. Cultural production of books and film represented a minor economic aspect of industrial production and did not clearly qualify as goods. For various reasons, films received a special exemption in the 1947 agreement and barely figured in subsequent negotiations. The project of European integration did not include culture at all in its founding documents. That situation began to change during the 1980s, just as the U.S. film industry was strengthening its international reach and the European national cinemas entered a decline. In the years leading up to the final GATT agreement, France sought to alert and rally its European partners to the dangers threatening national film industries. On the international level it waged an analogous struggle to preserve national cultural prerogatives with the 1993 GATT agreement. The Maastricht Treaty of 1992, ushering in the formation of the European Union, included culture for the first time. While films had retained their special excluded status since 1947, television had been categorized for the most part as a service, and the GATT battle, though popularly associated with the film industry, actually revolved around the EU preservation of broadcast quotas for television. The arguments mounted by France during the European debate over television programming quotas eventually took shape as the "cultural exception" in 1993. In that year, the final GATT round, precursor to the creation of the WTO, included for the first time an agreement on services in addition to the traditional agreement on goods. Television audiences already dwarfed viewership in theaters. Film had only a marginal economic significance in these regional and international exchanges, yet its defenders catalyzed resistance to free trade orthodoxy. That gathering of forces helped articulate a nascent vision of an alternative globalization that would surface dramatically in the violent demonstrations in Seattle in 1999.

The economic logic driving the current form of globalization may bring efficiencies in the production of many goods and services, but France has fought to apply a different logic to cultural production, one that seeks to preserve and foment diversity, even if it has not resolved the tensions at the intersection of what Jean-Michel Baer calls "the capitalist logic and the logic of creation."[11] This book attempts to explain and critically assess this success story during a period of accelerated globalization, from the gestation of the cultural exception in France during the 1980s through battles beyond its borders in the 1990s to the metamorphosis of those questions into the struggle over "cultural diversity" internationally in the first years of the twenty-first century.

The often-heralded death of cinema may yet arrive, but more people watch films today than ever before, even if they are watching most of them on smaller screens (though the number of theatrical screens has also risen significantly since 1990).[12] The export pressure of the U.S. industry continues to threaten the survival of once vibrant national industries. More successfully than other countries, France has managed to resuscitate a declining national film industry over the last thirty years. While attendance and production were falling throughout Europe, the French government intervened to reverse those trends in France, applying an increasingly sophisticated set of measures in favor of cinema. As globalization has indeed reduced national trade barriers, efforts to eliminate national prerogatives over cultural production hit the sensitive nerve of national identity in many countries.

But France has done more than defend its national cinema. It has financed and promoted a "certain idea of cinema" that made it the art form of the twentieth century.[13] Despite the current academic interest in films that contest narrow notions of national identity, called variously transnational, accented, diasporic, or hybrid cinema, "we still parse the world by nations," in the felicitous words of Dudley Andrew.[14] Apposite as that reminder may be, France funds filmmakers from all over the world, including the United States, compiling a stunning record of films produced by non-French directors. France almost certainly invests more in work by non-French filmmakers than any other country in the world, including some by the most celebrated contemporary filmmakers.[15] That certain idea of cinema cannot be sustained exclusively in the greenhouses of festivals but must be nourished in local soil, by national film industries that conform not to "essentialist" theoretical constructs but to a definition like the one proffered by Irish film scholar John Hill: "The 'national' cinema, which is properly 'national,' must be capable of registering the lived complexities of 'national' life, be sensitive to the realities of difference (of nation, region, ethnicity, class, gender and sexual orientation) and alert to the fluidity, as well as assumed fixity, of social and cultural identities. It must also recognize the increasingly hybrid and relational character of cultural identities both within the 'nation' and between nations."[16]

EXCEPTION TAKEN

1

INTERNATIONAL DOMINATION
BY THE U.S. FILM INDUSTRY

I n the one hundred years since World War I, the U.S. film industry has grown into the world's largest. It often draws more spectators to its films in foreign markets than films produced by the national film industries in those countries. In the second half of the twentieth century, various countries took measures to protect their national film industries, but they did so without coordination with other countries. Before the spread of television, the cinema had no rival as a mass entertainment medium, and many national cinemas produced waves of internationally renowned films during the 1950s and 1960s.

During the 1950s, theatrical attendance reached unprecedented heights in most countries, then fell spectacularly, with Hollywood taking the first and fastest plunge. Hollywood lost almost three-fourths of its audience in theaters between 1950 and 1970; some of the largest European film industries saw audiences decline by almost 90 percent (see figures 1.1a–1.1f).

Historians have identified multiple factors behind this worldwide decline, including the rise of television, the expansion of alternative leisure activities, and the introduction of VHS and DVD.[1] Nonetheless, theatrical exhibition remains the crucial first window for the cinema industry, even if downstream windows now supply the bulk of revenues.[2] After hitting bottom in the early 1970s, Hollywood recovered later in the decade and pressed its advantage internationally, leading to its massive domination of most national markets. Following the conclusion of the General Agreement

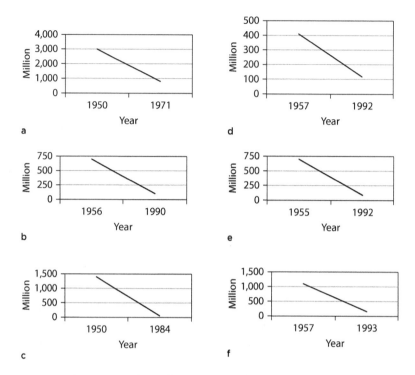

FIGURE 1.1a Cinema attendance, from post–World War II high to low in the United States (total loss was 73%)

FIGURE 1.1b Cinema attendance, from post–World War II high to low in Germany (total loss was 84%)

FIGURE 1.1c Cinema attendance, from post–World War II high to low in the United Kingdom (total loss was 96%)

FIGURE 1.1d Cinema attendance, from post–World War II high to low in France (total loss was 72%)

FIGURE 1.1e Cinema attendance, from post–World War II high to low in Italy (total loss was 88%)

FIGURE 1.1f Cinema attendance, from post–World War II high to low in Japan (total loss was 86%)

on Tariffs and Trade (GATT) negotiations in 1993, many countries, led by France, managed to arrest that dominance and demonstrate that submission to U.S. hegemony was not inevitable. Even as parochial discussion in the United States prefers to stigmatize government involvement, France has shown that in the increasingly globalized and digital world, national industries can survive if—and probably *only* if—the state intervenes judiciously to support both commercial success and artistic ambition. In many ways, globalization has been driven by an ideology of free trade, dismantling barriers to trade erected by individual countries. In earlier years, countries might object to pressures to open their markets, but free trade agreements in the most recent era of globalization locked countries into commitments to lower trade restrictions. Consequently, resistance has required building counterhegemonic alliances, for globalization seeks to weaken the power of states, especially alone, to control the more harmful consequences of free trade fundamentalism.

Before we look more closely at forms and sites of resistance to Hollywood hegemony, contextualizing the contours of the film industry internationally provides a needed perspective. A small number of developed countries account for most of the production, attendance, revenue, and screens across the world. It is often claimed that India has the largest film industry in the world. In certain ways, that claim is accurate but also misleading. India does produce more films than any other country, and its films draw many more spectators in theaters than any other country, as figure 1.2 indicates. Indian cinema also dominates its domestic market, capturing over 90 percent of all theatrical attendance.[3] However, in other significant ways, Indian cinema pales in relation to that of the United States. In absolute terms, Indian cinema earns less than 15 percent of U.S. domestic movie revenues, even with a population four times as large and twice as many spectators. The average Indian films costs about $500,000,

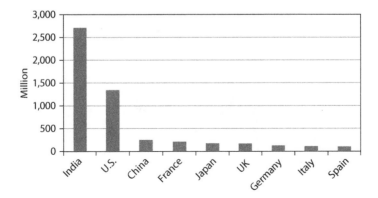

FIGURE 1.2 Theatrical attendance in selected countries, 2010

compared to an average of $60 million in the United States. More detailed comparisons are difficult to make because of the absence of available figures for Indian cinema, but it is safe to say that promotion costs in India are a small fraction of what is spent on U.S. films. Once one begins to factor in the enormous size of India's population, the figures reveal a popular but financially modest industry compared to other countries with much smaller populations. India has over 1.3 billion people and ten thousand movie screens; with less than a quarter of India's population, the United States has almost forty thousand screens. France, with only 62 million people, has 5,500 screens, and annual theatrical revenue of the French film industry exceeds India's box office. With population factored in, India's per capita box office revenue ranks below that of all other major national film industries (see figures 1.3–1.4).

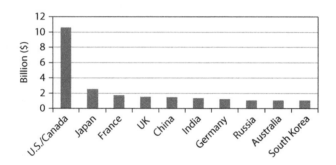

FIGURE 1.3 Domestic box office receipts in U.S. dollars, 2010

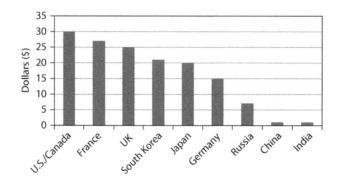

FIGURE 1.4 Per capita box office revenues in U.S. dollars, 2010

The comparison becomes even more dramatic beyond the borders of the two countries. Plausible anecdotal evidence suggests that Indian cinema is popular in other countries, but those countries are generally poor, with small markets and film industries. Despite the critical interest in Indian cinema in more developed countries, Indian cinema barely registers in the domestic box office of the developed world.[4] Even in a country like Great Britain with a considerable population of people with Indian backgrounds, and where some observers find a sizeable audience for Indian films, the market share for such films is probably no more than 1 percent.[5] Indian films do attract diasporic Indian spectators, but those films rarely compete with non-Indian films in the developed world. In addition, the Hindi-speaking cinema known throughout the world as Bollywood represents less than 20 percent of polyglot India's annual production, so most Indian national production goes virtually unseen outside its borders by nondiasporic audiences.[6]

The People's Republic of China is another special case. Also with a population of more than a billion people, annual theatrical attendance reaches 400–600 million, or one-fifth of India's total. Figures are also elusive for the PRC's cinema industry, but revenues appear to have exploded in recent years from $455 million (2007) to $3.5 billion (2013), leaping past India ($1.6 billion).[7] While estimates of the number of theatrical screens in China vary wildly, some sources indicate that the number of "modern" screens rose from 6,256 (only slightly more than France) in 2010 to 18,195 in 2013, still less than half the number in the United States. It is difficult to ascertain the export numbers for Chinese cinema, and the brief emergence of Hong Kong cinema as a phenomenal industrial success, producing hundreds of films popular throughout Southeast Asia, complicates the story, to say nothing of the film festival embrace of Taiwanese cinema in recent years. That particular constellation of three Chinas has led scholars to speak of Chinese *cinemas*, since the films and filmmakers increasingly cross the political borders.[8] And political considerations play a critical role in the PRC cinema, for the government strictly controls the number of non-Chinese (and Chinese) films permitted to be shown in theaters. Thus, China allows only a small number of foreign films into the country each year, primarily U.S. films.

In the context of this book, the Indian and Chinese cinemas each represent anomalies. Both of their cinema industries maintain large domestic market shares of the theatrical audience. Without (or with few) import restrictions, Indian cinema consistently draws over 90 percent of the annual attendance. With so few foreign films allowed to enter the country, China's domestic market share also remains high, but that situation appears to be changing, as China has raised the number of films it imports, and since the domestic audience has been given the choice of watching more foreign films, the Chinese film industry's domestic market share has begun to decline, dipping below 50 percent in 2012.[9] Together, then, the two countries with the largest populations in the world produce a large number of films, seen by billions of spectators, with only modest box office revenues compared to the rest of the world. But the reach of their cinemas beyond their borders is limited to their regional neighbors or diasporic communities.

In most other countries, including *all* the wealthiest developed countries, the U.S. cinema draws a staggering percentage of domestic viewers, and domestic market share is arguably the best single measure of the health of a national film industry.[10] Setting aside for the moment technical questions regarding the nationality of films, and excluding the special cases of India and China, U.S. films garner 70–80 percent of the world theatrical cinema box office.[11] However, the market shares for domestic industries have improved in many countries over the past two decades, suggesting that cinema industries may still be viable in other countries and perhaps even more significantly, that the medium of cinema, as a theatrical phenomenon, has a future, defying the many prognostications of its death in recent years. But given the massive Hollywood presence on screens in so many countries, the nature of that future remains unclear.

In 1995, a famous *Variety* headline appeared to be true: "Earth to H'wood: You Win!"[12] At the time, the Hollywood market share in the most developed countries, with the largest national film industries and the most remunerative foreign markets, stood at roughly 70 percent; the *Variety* article reported that Hollywood films took in 90 percent of world cumulative box office revenues of $8.34 billion (see figure 1.5).

For many years, however, voices have expressed concern about this domination, often under the rubric of "cultural imperialism." According to these critics, cultural products like movies have potentially negative effects on foreign audiences, for they spread ideological influence that both crowds out home-grown cultural expressions and imposes uniformity in the cultural sphere, which can thrive only through diversity.[13] This critique has also spawned responses that question the implicit—and

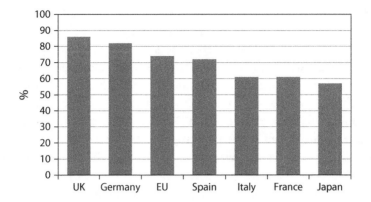

FIGURE 1.5 Percentage of U.S. market shares, 1994

condescending—claim that foreign audiences are incapable of deciphering the ideological influence and developing their own creative works that are not mere reproductions of the hegemonic Yanqui culture.

These kinds of tensions and contradictions fuel reductive accounts describing some kind of deeply rooted French hostility to the United States, sometimes described as pathological.[14] Cultural commentators in both countries pluck evidence from any number of domains, whether literature, the art world, or cinema. In 2007, a U.S. writer based in France wrote an article for *Time* with the Proustian title "In Search of Lost Time."[15] For the European edition, *Time* designed a cover with a photograph of Marcel Marceau, complete with beret, and splashed a new title across the cover, no doubt in search of French readers: "The Death of French Culture," followed quickly by a book with the same title. The author, Donald Morrison, inventoried the alleged contemporary irrelevance of French culture. According to him, few people outside France read French books, museums showed little interest in French artists, and French cinema had produced no filmmakers of international renown since Truffaut and Godard in the 1960s. Though writing as a self-described Francophile (living in "a country I rather like"), Morrison examined the traditional arts and found no prominent contemporary French artists in any area, with the lone exception of architecture. Unsurprisingly, angry reactions poured forth in the French press.[16]

Morrison's book, published the following year, included comments from Antoine Compagnon, a professor of French literature at the Collège de France and Columbia University, which had appeared in *Le Monde*. Compagnon offered an informed and balanced assessment of Morrison's autopsy, pointing out that Morrison was only repeating what the French already were well aware of in terms of the decline of French culture on the international stage, observing matter of factly that "seen from the US, after existentialism and structuralism, after Malraux, Sartre, and Camus, or Barthes, Foucault, and Derrida, the articles from France no longer inspire the intellectual avant-garde."[17] Nor did Compagnon share the anxiety many French writers expressed. With the loss of its colonies and its decline as a world power, it stood to reason that France would no longer occupy its former cultural prominence internationally either: "the influence of French culture abroad is now consistent with the geopolitical heft of France in the world, and with its foreign trade."[18]

Morrison had dismissed "French films today [as] . . . amiable, low-budget trifles for the domestic market," a market where half the audience prefers to pay for U.S. films at the box office, though he found encouraging several recent French films that enjoyed some renown beyond the borders. Compagnon took little solace in Morrison's embrace of these popular successes, such as those he happened to see on airplanes (as they belong to "the type of films Air France shows to its captive passengers"): *Amélie Poulain* (Jeunet), Luc Besson's *Taxi* films, *L'auberge espagnol* (Klapisch). Among the reasons behind the decline of French culture, Morrison pointed to the state subsidy system. Aside from finding state support disproportionately large in comparison with other countries, Morrison cited French critics who believed that subsidies ensure mediocrity, or "trifles." While Morrison, perhaps understandably, displayed some basic ignorance about the admittedly complex French system of cultural support for cinema, he referred to a book by Frédéric Martel about U.S. cultural production as evidence for the subsidy assertion.[19] In a thick volume based on research and interviews, Martel had described the extensive web of philanthropic funding for the arts in the United States. Morrison cited Martel's admiring observation that "if the Culture Ministry is nowhere to be found [in the United States], cultural life is everywhere."[20] It is true, as Morrison said, that Martel did marvel at the efficacy of arts funding in the United States. However, what Martel found surprising was that private sources provided such largesse, not a government ministry.

In fact, Morrison failed to note that Martel actually argued at the end of the book that France should take the information he had compiled about private funding and use that information *in defense* of French government funding in the recurrent trade battles with the United States over culture. Martel wrote in his preface that he wanted to try to understand better how U.S. arts funding worked, as foreigners had little grasp of its functioning. Martel was impressed with American cultural vibrancy, but he also maintained that despite the apparent lack of state funding, the government—governments, actually, for he looked at federal, state, and local funding—at all levels had established elaborate tax mechanisms for cultural organizations, which then took advantage of those breaks to distribute funds to artists and cultural institutions.[21] Funding could be traced to these fiscal inducements, nonprofit tax deductions for the moneyed classes, which were, in fact, subsidies lavished by the state on the arts. In France, and Europe more generally, the equivalent of philanthropic funding often came directly from government entities (even if free trade ideologues regularly inflate the size of what they often inaccurately call subsidies).[22] But contrary to Morrison's characterization, Martel actually concludes his book with a call to use his research into U.S. arts funding to buttress the French position *in favor of the cultural exception.* Referring to a "certain American hypocrisy," Martel points out that

> all these direct and indirect funding sources constitute public aids to culture. . . . Instead of trying to eliminate the public subsidies to culture by Europeans, in the interest of the liberalization of markets under globalization, the Americans should begin by acknowledging that they subsidize their culture as much as the Europeans. In legally dissimulating their colossal indirect subsidies, the implicit quotas which favor their citizens and the numberless regulations which exist in the cultural sector, the Americans believed they could make people forget that they also have erected a real "cultural exception." All these types of financing described in this book can then be used to expose the American pretensions in calling for the liberalization of culture in the international negotiations.[23]

These tensions over cultural policy in an era of accelerated globalization are the subject of this book.

Assessing the health of a film industry entails identifying weaknesses and stresses. In the case of Hollywood, there is only one possible weakness: declining profits. All thinking in Hollywood goes into improving the bottom line. When television took off in the 1950s and 1960s, contrary to popular myth, Hollywood found ways of working with its perceived competitor.[24] When VCRs and videotape appeared, some studio heads fought the new technology, taking Sony to court for copyright infringement.[25] But others recognized that videotape, like television before it, could actually be a new source of income to replace the disappearing theatrical audience.[26] Industrial histories of Hollywood, often forced to work with the meager statistics available to the public, look at gross box office numbers, sizes of production and advertising budgets, and the changes in leadership and ownership of the studios, but they say little about state funding. Douglas Gomery has written that he begins his research with an investigation of studio ownership patterns.[27] He concluded his 2005 book, *The Hollywood Studio System*, by claiming that the "key to success remains the same: a skilled leader," the visionaries who successfully navigated the future.[28] He cites as one example Lew Wasserman, once head of Universal, who understood the potential of the blockbuster strategy and built Universal's success around it. But Wasserman failed to anticipate the potential riches of videotape, which ended his tenure at Universal. Steve Ross, Gomery's other example, purchased Warner Bros. as another holding in his sprawling empire, but he recognized before others that there was more upside in the strategy of "tight diversification,"[29] so he sold off the nonmedia holdings and diversified into horizontal acquisitions of complementary media companies, culminating in the mega-merger of Time and Warner in 1989 and the ill-fated gamble of AOL–Time Warner in 2000.[30]

A small number of critics on the left, describing their approach as critical political economy, find fault with this focus on the owners. In her account of the political economy of Hollywood, Janet Wasko has tried to revive the ethical dimension of political economy, which was dropped when political economy became simply economics in U.S. academia.[31] For Wasko, scholars should not stop at simple description but should bring a normative perspective to their work. They should not limit their investigations to how Hollywood has worked but should ask how Hollywood *should* work. Toby Miller, perhaps the most outspoken critic of a classical economics approach, has repeatedly insisted that the real key to understanding Hollywood's long-term success is government support for the industry, which scholars refuse to probe or even acknowledge: "Contrary to the conventional view, which sees Hollywood's success resting on the free-market efficiency and narrative transparency [of the films], we argue that its commanding position has been held for nearly a century thanks to various forms of aid and protection from the state, across all levels of governance."[32]

Thomas Guback, also writing as a critical political economist, tried to document U.S. support for Hollywood in the postwar period, but the period covered by his major work ended in the late 1960s, before the generous tax breaks granted by the government during the tumultuous 1970s.[33] At the beginning of the 1970s, Hollywood was reeling from the long-term effects of television competition and the conjunctural crisis of overproduction. Then the federal government approved tax breaks for investment in the film industry, which eased the industry through its crisis. That recovery further strengthened its position as it steadily rebuilt its international dominance after 1980. Ultimately the breaks led to so many abuses that the programs largely ended in 1976, when Hollywood had already started its recovery.[34] Others, including Miller, have touched on the question, but documentation remains scarce.[35] Many writers have noted the ability of Hollywood studios to practice cartelistic activities abroad that U.S. anti-trust laws do not allow domestically. The colorful, longtime Hollywood lobbyist Jack Valenti openly admitted that one such anticompetitive provision, passed in 1918, was an indispensable aid in prying open protectionist foreign markets: "Without [the 1918 Webb-Pomerene Act] the American film industry would be an invalid . . . [as it] is peculiarly vulnerable to unfavourable action by foreign governments and by foreign private interests, by industry cartels, and by an avalanche of non-tariff barriers that are both endless and ingenious . . . [Webb-Pomerene has enabled the Motion Picture Association of America] to counter these restrictions . . . and preserve the freedom of the American film industry to compete fairly in the world entertainment marketplace."[36]

This book takes a political economy approach for reasons similar to, but also different from, those suggested by Wasko. Critical political economy of the media normally seeks to expose the structures hidden behind the concentration of power in the hands of a small number of companies that benefit from government policies that receive little public scrutiny. Despite its complexity, the French support system for cinema is far more accessible for examination. The following chapters look into its many moving parts, but more to explicate the system's inherent tensions than to uncover its nefarious machinations. But the book will try to follow Wasko's injunction that "analysis must also include an understanding of the interaction between the industry and the State."[37]

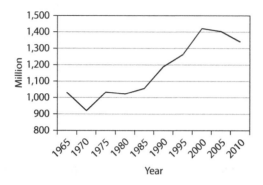

FIGURE 1.6 Cinema attendance in the United States, 1965–2010

Before considering the reasons behind the international success of the U.S. film industry in recent decades, it bears recalling that Hollywood confronted economic woes similar to those experienced by other national film industries in the post–World War II period, but it overcame those difficulties sooner. That early recovery strengthened its position as it steadily rebuilt its international dominance after 1980. As figure 1.6 illustrates, cinema attendance picked up in the mid-1970s and rose steadily through 2000. Most historians attribute the turnaround to the strategy of blockbusters inaugurated with the release of *Jaws* in 1975.[38] While the plunge in theatrical attendance caused by television affected all countries, the chronology of television adoption varied from country to country.[39] Widespread television adoption occurred first in the United States, so Hollywood weathered the drop in theater attendance first. By the 1970s it was able to reassert itself domestically and abroad at a time when other countries were continuing or entering steep declines (see figures 1.1a–1.1f). Similarly, after videotape was introduced in the late 1970s, Hollywood realized, after initial hesitation, that the new technology would boost revenues. Thus, by the 1980s, a reborn Hollywood saw its domestic revenues rise and pushed its advantage in foreign markets to phenomenal success.

What explains the success of Hollywood on foreign screens? Many critics, scholars and cultural commentators have tried to answer the question.[40] Tyler Cowen, an economist who often writes for the popular press, synthesized many of the conventional arguments in "Why Hollywood Rules the World, and Should We Care?"[41] He begins with an excellent hypothesis. If Hollywood's domination, contrary to the claim of critics, does not actually reduce diversity as it fills world theaters, then "we" should not worry about illusory harms imputed to globalization. The large and wealthy domestic U.S. market alone churns out more revenue than any other market, 50 percent more even than the combined markets of the EU5 countries (France, Germany, Great Britain, Italy, and Spain), so the U.S. film industry can afford to produce expensive films and market them with unmatched promotional budgets. More people speak English as a second language than any other language, so Hollywood can press that linguistic advantage abroad, for it reduces the "cultural discount" that cultural goods encounter when they cross borders. Available figures support those quantitative observations.[42]

However, once Cowen ventures into the qualitative terrain, his argument degenerates into circularity. According to Cowen, spectators prefer films with larger budgets, and films with larger budgets are actually better films. Better in what way? Better because more people want to watch them: "more expensive movies are better movies, at least in the eyes of the audience, if not always in more objective aesthetic terms." Once he acknowledges that these films may not actually be better in "more objective aesthetic terms," whatever that minor reservation might mean (how can aesthetic terms be objective?), he undermines the pretensions to the superior "quality" of the expensive films. He then goes on to say that "the American values of heroism, individualism, and romantic self-fulfillment are well suited for the large screen and for global audiences," though he fails to explain why those values are American. Cowen also repeats the familiar legend that Hollywood films must first satisfy the large polyglot domestic audience, used apparently to show the universal—not "American"—appeal of U.S. films: "Hollywood's universality has, in part, *become* a central part of American national culture. Commercial forces have led America to adopt 'that which can be sold' as part of its national culture."[43] On the one hand, then, purportedly "American values" appeal to world audiences, but at the same time those same values are also apparently "universal," proven by the size of the world audience for Hollywood production. A French scholar has offered another view: "It's not because American cinema is 'universal' that it is present everywhere in the world; but it is because it is present everywhere in the world that American cinema is universal."[44]

Such is the received boosterism recycled by a prominent U.S. social scientist seeking to explain the international dominance of U.S. cinema.[45]

More expensive films are better because they attract more spectators, even if they are not better in "aesthetic terms." American values, at once "American" and "universal," happen to be values that audiences prefer. If that fundamentally circular argument fails to explain anything, Cowen also reassures us about why "we" should not care about Hollywood dominance. He notes that domestic and foreign writers and artists have excoriated the toxic influence of U.S. "cultural imperialism" for sucking the oxygen out of local or national artistic production, force-feeding Hollywood uniformity on captive audiences and reducing creative diversity. Cowen is pleased to report, however, that on the contrary, Hollywood actually fosters world diversity. Domestically, scaled-back studios can produce only so many blockbusters, so the large balance of releases are a variety of "microbudget," independent productions. Abroad, countries cannot compete with blockbusters, but they should not despair. Following the sacrosanct economic law of comparative advantage, their strength, Cowen asserts with no argument whatsoever, let alone evidence, lies in producing art films, for "the natural European advantage is in making art-house films, not blockbuster or special-effects spectaculars." According to him, "the dirty little secret of today's cinematic world" is that "Hollywood's asymmetric economic strength . . . in fact supports aesthetic diversity." While Cowen writes as a champion of free market orthodoxy—he chose Joseph Schumpeter's famous doxa of free market capitalism for the title of his book—he recognizes that culture may be a special case that merits state interest. For better or worse, "Once the dynamic of Hollywood export superiority is in place, most European productions, as we know them, cannot survive without governmental assistance." But "in the long run," European cinemas should be weaned from the public trough, "induced to make a more commercially appealing product."[46]

The convolutions of Cowen's account reflect the inherent difficulty in sorting out the strands of film's dual status as art and industry. The U.S. film industry has always been built on the pursuit of commercial success. And the traditional narrative of U.S. cinema is set as a long battle between the aesthetic indifference of studio executives (Louis B. Mayer, Harry Cohn . . .) and the frustrated aesthetic ambition of valiant artists (Erich von Stroheim, Josef von Sternberg, Orson Welles, Nicholas Ray . . .). As is well known, a group of French critics (many of whom later turned filmmaker) during the 1950s excavated the alchemy of art and industry of Hollywood. Developing a critical practice known as "auteurism," they showed how certain artists, with strong, personal, "authorial" visions managed to fight past the commercial constraints of the factory system in Hollywood to produce a body of work that deserved to be called art. These cinephile critics dared to claim this popular form of entertainment as art. Earlier writers, of course, had discerned the art behind the industry, but the French critics aggressively and polemically offered a hierarchized taxonomy filled with florid panegyrics to their favored auteurs, a hyperbole most taste arbiters in the United States found hard to apply to the weekly product they viewed more soberly as good, or bad, entertainment.

One such earlier writer was the famous and dashing French novelist, art critic, aviator, freedom fighter, filmmaker, and first French minister of culture, André Malraux. At the end of an essay devoted to artistic aspects of film, Malraux concluded with a sentence that has served as an axiomatic koan for French writers ever since: "On the other hand, the cinema is also an industry."[47] Since the end of World War II, France has tried to design policy to attend to, if not submit to, the industrial requisites of cinema. Faced with the perceived invasion of U.S. cinema after the war, France negotiated an early agreement to guarantee a minimum time for screening of French films in theaters. An early law imposed a tax on theater tickets to help finance the industry.[48] Several years later, in 1953, the national cinema office offered grants to filmmakers according to their "quality."[49] And one of Malraux's first acts as minister of culture in 1959 was to institutionalize those quality grants in what is surely the most famous government (however modest financially) support mechanism in the world, the *avance sur recettes*, a cornerstone of French cinema that continues to this day.

France's efforts to balance both the art and industry of film production have undergirded state cinema policy since the end of World War II. Those efforts assumed greater urgency in the 1980s, in response to the travails of the film industry. With an activist minister of culture, Jack Lang, in a Socialist government, France began to devise measures to strengthen the industrial base of cinema and at the same time satisfy many noneconomic criteria, including the access to theaters in rural areas and support of quality filmmaking. As even supporters of French policy have pointed out, pursuit of these two goals can result in policies rife with contradiction.[50] The economic health of the industry may require concentration of integrated firms to take advantage of economies of scale, but artistic accomplishment often depends on independent sectors of production, distribution, and exhibition, which the market may not sustain without government aid. The government, then, encourages concentration, a strategy of "national champions," at the same time that it protects the smaller fish from the depredations of the market.[51] In a 2006 brochure celebrating forty-five years of the *avances sur recettes*, Minister of Culture Catherine Colonna traced its policies to the tensions integral to the "visionary intelligence" of Malraux: "Favor innovation and creative audacity, ensure the renewal of talent, correct the influence of the laws of the market on cinematic creation, ensure the diversity of genres."[52]

Critics often find fault with French policies to "correct the influence of the laws of the market on cinematic creation." Like Morrison and many others, Cowen indicted European cinema's dependence on state subsidies, a litany intoned by countless propagandists for neoliberalism and globalization. For Cowen, France, as the most outspoken supporter of state intervention in the film (or more generally, the audiovisual) industry, or even the culture industries as a whole, incarnates the etiology of European cinema's failure to climb aboard the neoliberal bandwagon: "The problems of European cinema are, in large part, the problems of French cinema." But it is precisely the difference between the French cinema industry and all other European film industries that concerns us in these pages. As we will see, the French cinema outperforms all other European cinemas on any quantitative scale. France invests more money, in more films, for more spectators, on more theatrical screens. In addition, France pours more money into European co-productions than any other European country and supports more non-French filmmakers than any other country. Furthermore, though the debate often hinges on technical definitions of terms, and contrary to the claims of ideologically blinkered critics, France has arguably fulfilled its commitment to art and industry without large state subsidies. The more pertinent question is, what is the French cinema industry doing right, and can the system behind that success be applied or adapted elsewhere?

2

THE LANG YEARS

By 1980, European film industries had experienced staggering attendance declines from the high point of the 1950s (see figure 2.1). The figures varied, but even in France, which resisted best, attendance in 1980 was less than half of its peak postwar number of 411 million. Great Britain lost 90 percent of its 1.4 billion spectators in 1950. Market shares for national films fell below 50 percent in all countries. France and Italy still held on to more than 40 percent of the market, but Germany, Great Britain, and Spain managed only 10–20 percent. The United States had also seen its domestic audience fall by 75 percent, but by the 1980s, Hollywood had rebounded and was commanding near-majority market shares in most European countries, again with the exception of France and Italy, though those countries would soon follow the trend. With the election of the Socialist government under François Mitterrand in 1981, and in particular with the appointment of Jack Lang as minister of culture, France began to intervene massively in the film industry to ensure its survival, a campaign that continues to this day.

Before 1980, France already had a support system for the film industry. In 1948, France, through the Centre national de la cinématographie (CNC) instituted a fund known as the Temporary Aid for the Film Industry.[1] A *taxe spéciale additionelle* (TSA) on all tickets sold in theaters went into a special account, the *Compte de soutien*, which would be made available to production and exhibition sectors of the industry. Film producers would

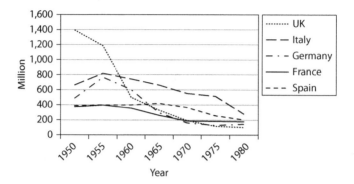

FIGURE 2.1 Cinema attendance in EU5 countries, 1950–1980

receive money for their next film based on the success of their previous film at the box office.[2] If a film drew 500,000 spectators, a percentage (varying year to year from 10 to 14 percent) of the price of those tickets would generate earnings for the Compte de soutien, and exhibitors and producers could "withdraw" francs from "their" account. As the tax gathered funds from within the industry and the revenues did not go into the general tax fund of the government, the money stayed within the industry, so to speak, and was therefore referred to as "forced saving." Because the money did not come out of general tax revenues, the money disbursed could not properly be called a subsidy.[3] Most of the aid distributed was called "automatic" because the amount was directly proportional to the box office receipts of a theater or film, thereby not subject to bureaucratic decisions about its artistic merits.[4] The temporary aid law was renewed in 1953, and the CNC also awarded funds to projects, known as *primes de qualité*, based on their "quality," an assessment made by the head of the CNC following recommendations from a commission. Initially, the funds were limited to short films but were expanded to feature films in May 1955.[5]

These measures taken immediately after the war were part of an effort by the government to rebuild the French film industry. As Laurent Creton chronicles, the Vichy government had actually tried to place the industry on a firm financial footing following the rancorous and inconclusive debates over film policy in the 1930s. Thus, the Comité d'organisation de l'industrie cinématographique (COIC), formed under Vichy, gave way to the CNC, created in 1946.[6] At the same time, France was negotiating with the United States over postwar aid, and part of those discussions involved talks about film exhibition in France. Those talks resulted in the once-notorious Blum-Byrnes agreement, which stipulated minimum screen quotas of four *French* films every thirteen weeks.[7] The apparent French failure to secure better terms provoked massive public protests by prominent French film figures, including Jacques Becker, Jean Gremillon, Louis Daquin, Simone Signoret, and Jean Marais.[8] Scholars recently have concluded that the agreement actually helped French cinema by sheltering it from even greater U.S. penetration and provided needed breathing space for the French film industry to recover.[9] But while the Blum-Byrnes affair turned into a historical footnote, the controversy almost certainly was the impetus for the inclusion of an exemption for screen quotas in the only clause (Article IV) of the 1947 General Agreement on Trade and Tariffs (GATT) that even touched on cultural matters, a tiny protectionist sliver in the aggressively free trade foundation of GATT, a sliver that would assume extraordinary prominence when the screen was the television screen during the final GATT negotiations in 1993 (see chapter 4).

AVANCE SUR RECETTES

As is well known, young critics at *Cahiers du cinéma* attacked the French production system during the 1950s, tarring it with the mocking label of "the tradition of quality." Some of these young writers and cinephiles, including François Truffaut, Jacques Rivette, and Jean-Luc Godard, were not disinterested observers and eventually made their own films as part of the French New Wave, though their harsh judgment of the elder generation probably deserves to be more nuanced.[10] Partially to respond to these charges, the first head of the newly created Ministry of Culture, André Malraux, appointed by de Gaulle after his return to power in 1958 as president of the newly formed Fifth Republic, transferred the CNC from the Ministry of Industry to the Ministry of Culture and announced the creation of a new funding law, passed on June 16, 1959, which included the famous avance sur recettes.[11]

This measure effectively formalized the more ad hoc nature of the primes de qualité, which would still award funding from the newly named Compte de soutien (support account) to applicants whose projects were deemed artistically worthy. Following the institutionalization of the primes de qualité with the avances sur recettes, a CNC commission would consider proposals and distribute funding, then, on the basis of quality.[12] Initially, the avances were awarded only after completion of the film; after 1962, producers could submit scenarios in a competition. Winners would receive modest funding for their films. It was called an advance against receipts, for the producer was to reimburse the support account out of receipts once the film was released. The presumed artistic ambition of the films meant that few of them succeeded at the box office, so often they were not repaid.[13] Because funding decisions depended on the artistic judgments of the commission members, and thus were not automatic, this aid was called a "selective aid" (like the earlier primes de qualité).[14]

However, both the automatic aid and the new selective aid drew from the same Compte de soutien, filled largely by box office receipts. Because the avances sur recettes were awarded on the putative quality of the submissions, of the completed film or screenplay, this instrument was meant to balance, however disproportionately, artistic value with the original automatic aid rewarding commercial success.[15] Thus, like the primes de qualité of the 1950s, the advances facilitated bringing new talent into the industry and, however coincidentally, began just as the New Wave was ushering in a new generation of filmmakers, even if the avance sur recettes continued to fund the directors of the *tradition de qualité*.[16] At the same time, out of the Compte de soutien, roughly 70 percent of the fund took the form of automatic aid, and for films receiving the avance, the aid averaged only 11 percent of the budget.[17]

While the avance sur recettes, still distributed today, has become the best known emblem of the French support system, its chronological association with the output of the New Wave should not overshadow other forms of support. The avance represented the institutionalization of the primes de qualité, so the avance itself did not begin the recognition of the criterion of quality in the award of funding. From its start, the CNC also devoted funds to building and refurbishing theaters, reconstructing the exhibition sector. As with production, exhibition received automatic aid after the war. Thus, just as automatic aid flowed to producers and filmmakers to finance their films, aid also went to theaters. The digressive rates of automatic aid reduced the percentage of the TSA granted to theaters as weekly receipts passed various thresholds, an attempt to direct resources to smaller theaters in less populated areas, which reflected a continuing concern to promote cinema access throughout the country.[18] Apprehensive about the

European Economic Community's proscription of "state aids" in the 1957 Treaty of Rome, the law of 1959 did not contain any support funds for theaters and even called for the progressive phasing out of automatic aid to production.[19] But after the steep decline in attendance during the 1960s, automatic aid for theaters was restored in 1967.[20]

However innovative the New Wave may have been, most of its films, like most films everywhere, did little business at the box office, so it hardly rebuilt the French audience. The first films of Chabrol, Truffaut, and Godard, all made before the avances sur recettes, were box office successes; most of their next films failed commercially.[21] During the 1960s, French theaters lost half of their spectators. Then, after a period of relative stability during the 1970s, attendance resumed its steady postwar decline, just as Jack Lang was beginning his first tenure as minister of culture in 1981 (see figure 2.2).

The previous administration of the Ministry of Culture, under President Valéry Giscard d'Estaing, summarized its accomplishments between 1974 and 1981 in a pamphlet titled "Une politique française du cinéma." In his introduction, Giscard d'Estaing noted that "the number of film spectators in the world is currently showing considerable growth," a claim clearly not true of France or the other European countries over the decade of the 1970s, as the charts demonstrate. By 1980, attendance dropped by 38 percent (from 1,453 to 897 million) in the EU5 (France, Germany, Italy, Spain, and the United Kingdom) (see figure 2.3). The amount available in the avances sur recettes tripled between 1974 and 1980, from 10 to 30 million francs, while the Compte de soutien grew from 153 to 342 million francs.[22] The government also invested in cinema exhibition, creating almost 1,400 new theaters and more than doubling the number of multiscreen theaters from

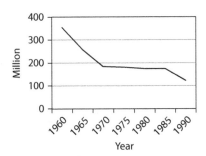

FIGURE 2.2 Cinema attendance in France, 1960–1990

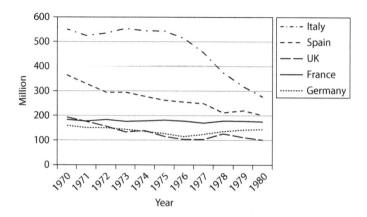

FIGURE 2.3 Cinema attendance in EU5 countries, 1970–1980

263 (749 screens) to 609 (1,942 screens). The report indicated support for smaller theaters, especially in rural areas. The industry also gained new resources from a reduction in the value-added tax from 17.6 percent to 7 percent, worth about 200 million francs at the time. Nevertheless, these increases were relatively modest in scope and size in comparison with the initiatives of the 1980s.

Like any governmental office, the Ministry of Culture releases progress reports, but titling its report as a "French cinema policy" indicates the government's active role in the film industry, a responsibility that is part of a broader strategy of a *politique culturelle*, or cultural policy, pursued by the Ministry of Culture. This topic receives considerable discussion in France, probably more so than in any other country, and these debates would be increasingly important in France, Europe, and internationally in the 1980s and beyond. The tensions and polemics to come are not evident in the 1981 report but would increase in prominence as regional and international agreements began to impinge on the autonomy of countries to develop their own cultural policies.

LANG I (1981–1986)

After he was named the new minister of culture, Jack Lang solicited a report on the film industry from Jean-Denis Bredin. The Bredin report, released in 1981, acknowledges the dangers of concentration tendencies in the industry, both horizontal and vertical integration, but it recommends against restricting that tendency.[23] In the section headed "Vertical Integration," the report first rejects parallels to the vertical integration in Hollywood during the 1930s and 1940s that led to the "consent decrees," beginning with the Paramount decree of 1948. After various abortive attempts in the United States to examine the issue beginning in the late 1930s, the courts found that the integration of production, distribution, and exhibition—all controlled by the Hollywood majors—did indeed restrict competition. In particular, the studio ownership of first-run theaters gave them unfair advantages in bidding for films. Studios were able to engage in monopolistic practices like block booking and blind selling, and independent theaters were forced to accede to the dictates of the studios.

The Bredin report describes the differences between a highly concentrated U.S. film industry and a more artisanal French film industry. First, the complaint in France was the power of the theater circuits, for they were the only ones with sufficient funds to force their decisions on distributors, reversing the Hollywood practice. Second, the integration of exhibition and distribution had a long history in France, an alliance dating to what Bredin called *les belles années* of (French) cinema. "What is new is the accelerated disappearance of independent distributors now incapable of supporting the increase in their commercial risk." As for the vertical integration itself, the report identifies two potential concerns—one artistic, one commercial. The report does not consider that the power of large theater circuits is necessarily harmful to artistic production, for "it is not clear that the elimination of the integrated groups [exhibition-distribution] would solve the problems of the independents lacking resources. . . . No one can fail to recall that auteur cinema is sometimes better served by the most enlightened circuits than by certain independent distributors."[24]

Moving on, the report recognizes the threat that vertical integration could restrict competition, but for similar reasons it recommends no changes. Because exhibitor-distributors have the resources to invest in films, breaking them up would risk what "the Mission views as a fundamental principle: any rule that might prevent a film from being made is a bad rule." The report recommends what has always been predominant in French policy: support production, above all. "It seems preferable to hope that the financial policy proposed elsewhere will stimulate independent production and distribution, currently so precarious."[25]

In another part of the report, "Liberation of the Screens," Bredin does call for separating two large Parisian-based circuits (Gaumont and Pathé) that had joined forces in an alliance known in France as a GIE.[26] Bredin found that the union in itself was not necessarily harmful, but it did restrict competition to the extent that the decisions for exhibiting films were not taken on a film-by-film basis: "There is never a question about preventing a film from being shown on a particular screen. The rule here is crystal clear. It is a question rather that it may be shown in a theater formerly not available to it, when in fact that theater would be better suited to it." This discussion takes place in the part of the report labeled "Antitrust Policy," but it concerns horizontal integration of exhibitors. But even with this decision, Bredin does not take a rigid stance. "The idea of an application pure and simple of the regulations against mergers should be thus more about persuasion than legal action."[27] Thus, even while calling for the break-up of the GIE, the report advocates not taking a strict position opposing horizontal integration.

In a sense, Bredin wants to have it both ways. The recommendations resist moving aggressively to inhibit both vertical and horizontal integration, two forms of concentration. At the same time, the report aims to encourage independent distributors and exhibitors by directing more financial resources to them. Curiously, given the historic failure in France to mount large production companies on the model of Hollywood studios, albeit on a smaller scale, the report opens with a strong defense of the system of a large number of small companies: "French cinema must retain its artisanal character."[28]

Following the submission of the report, Lang proposed a panoply of measures over the next four years. He sought to increase the Ministry of Culture budget to 1 percent of the total government budget, double its previous allotment. At the beginning of April 1982, six months after the release of the Bredin report, Lang held a press conference outlining his sixteen-point plan for the cinema. The printed materials released for the news conference identified five themes bearing on the long-term development of French cinema:

1. Weakening of French cinema abroad.
2. French cinema does not attract a popular public.
3. Excessive economic concentration risks asphyxiating the opportunities for creation and renovation.

4. Cinema's economic and financial structures remain fragile.
5. Relations between cinema and new techniques of audiovisual communication have yet to be established.

The document concludes the diagnosis by stressing the risk of the "development of a double film sector." On the one hand, the state would support the health of a modern cinema with broad commercial appeal accompanied by massive advertising; on the other hand, there still existed a marginal cinema of cinephiles watching increasingly esoteric films. Lang viewed that as an unacceptable dichotomy. "We must reject this duality that I believe is harmful to all of cinema, which is why the meaning of the reform I am proposing is completely different."[29]

With the exception of the seven years from 1960 to 1967, the government consistently provided funding for the refurbishment of theaters. Multiplexes (with eight or more screens) came late to France, compared to many other countries, but France opened its first cinema with multiple screens (three) in 1967, Les 3 Luxembourg (in Paris), which still functions today. Once state aid to exhibition was restored after 1967, France rebuilt the theater infrastructure, funding both renovation and new theater construction. By 1985, 75 percent of all French screens were new.[30] That same year, 63 percent of all screens were housed in multiscreen theaters.[31]

The automatic aid to theaters disproportionately benefited the theater chains, for they were able to pool their TSA proceeds into one account. Over the course of a year, the circuits would have accumulated enough combined returns to finance new construction. Individual, independent theaters had only their own revenues as the base for the TSA account, so they would have to wait a longer period of time before renovating.[32] The financial advantages accruing to the circuits fomented greater concentration in exhibition, giving the theater chains more power over the distribution of films, for they had greater leverage with distributors in obtaining copies and in convincing distributors not to make the films available to the independent theaters.

The legislature approved a new law on cinema in July 1982, followed as is customary in France by a series of *décrets* implementing the general provisions of the law. One of the first measures was a new fund specifically directed to film production, the Institut de financement du cinéma et des industries culturelles (IFCIC). U.S. studios had developed relationships with large banks over many years, but the relatively modest financial size of French production companies made establishing such collaborations more difficult in France. The government, then, basing its plan to some extent on financial support facilitated by the state for small and medium enterprises (*petites et moyennes entreprises*, or PMEs, with fewer than five hundred employees), would guarantee part of these specially designed loans, often finishing funds, available to producers at reduced interest rates. The partial responsibility of the state would reduce the risk to producers and the banks joining the initiative, but producers would also be risking some of their investments.[33]

For the first time, the Ministry of Culture would increase substantially its financial commitment to the avance sur recettes. The avance depended primarily on the TSA for its funding, collected in the support account, but now the government doubled the amount devoted to the avance with contributions from its own budget. The plan also created a second *collège* (or commission) to make decisions on the applications for the avance. The new *collège* would consider first-time filmmakers; the other would decide on all other applications.

Lang proposed a series of steps to preserve theaters in underpopulated zones. The Agency for the Regional Development of Cinema (l'Agence pour le développement régional du cinéma, ADRC) was formed in 1983 to improve the availability of films to theaters in rural areas. In collaboration with the Ministry of Culture and distributors, the ADRC would make additional copies of popular, often big-budget, films for theaters in towns with fewer than twenty thousand inhabitants, and even to agglomerations with fewer than five thousand people. The 1982 law also had provided for a mediator to hear complaints from theater owners unable to obtain popular films from distributors. In practice, many agreements between distributors and theaters were verbal ones, not easily documented.[34] The mediator could examine complaints more effectively than a legal proceeding, and might direct a distributor to make a copy available, but was also empowered (and funded) to authorize that additional prints be struck for theater owners deemed to have legitimate complaints.[35] The state would seek to aid the functioning of many theaters—comprising as many as a thousand screens, more than one-fifth of the national total—that were in danger of closing. With the crisis of shrinking attendance during the 1980s, and so many theaters unable to remain afloat, the government encouraged municipalities to assume responsibility for the theaters in a variety of ways, which would also preserve the density of theater coverage.

The Bredin report observed that 1,800 theaters in towns with fewer than twenty thousand people had closed, though 1,600 new theaters had opened in larger population centers with commercial shopping areas. The report proposed new ways of keeping those theaters in operation by encouraging and aiding municipalities to assume some of the responsibility for the theaters. Often this would take the form of promoting discussions between municipal governments and local theater owners to reach some mutual agreement to fold the theaters into the cultural activity of localities.[36] And if one way of rebuilding the theater audience was through the formation of cinephiles, the state would formalize earlier experiments of teaching film appreciation to children at all levels, from elementary school through high school.[37]

The law also directed selective aid to theaters. Just as the avance sur recettes was meant to both reward proven artistic merit and promote new talent, selective aid to theaters sought to preserve art cinemas in France, a designation officially recognized in France as *cinémas d'art et essai*, theaters with a commitment to ambitious (noncommercial) programming complemented by pedagogical initiatives of visits by filmmakers, debates with critics, printed notes handed out to viewers, ciné clubs, special screenings for children, and so on. Art cinemas even had their own subcategories, with a sliding scale of reward depending on the level of cinephilic promotion (see chapter 7).

To mark his first three years of activity, Lang's Ministry of Culture released an elaborate brochure in 1984, "The Cultural Policy, 1981–1984." The document included separate pamphlets for different arts (books, music and dance, theater, etc.). The summary for cinema and audiovisual began with the claim that "the crisis of cinema has been overcome." The ministry had certainly increased the funds for the film industry, and the short-term results compared favorably with 1980–1981. Attendance, receipts, and investment rose, and market share remained stable around 50 percent, though production declined. But however successful the initial reforms may have been, the crisis returned and the triumphalist rhetoric subsided.

Given the historical reticence of banks to invest in the high-risk enterprise of filmmaking, in 1985 Lang established another government-backed entity known as the Sociétés pour le financement de cinéma (SOFICAs) to attract private investors in cinema. Special banks were authorized to offer significant tax advantages to wealthy individuals and businesses, defraying as much as 25 percent of the tax obligations for individuals and up to 50 percent for businesses. The banks would guarantee a certain minimum return on investment if private investors would agree to deposit their capital for a minimum of five years. While the SOFICAs were designed to attract private capital, their tax advantages would benefit disproportionately investors in the highest tax brackets, and an early assessment noted the small number of investors who actually participated.[38]

Other countries had already experimented with tax shelters, so the French could learn from those experiences in implementing the SOFICAs. As noted in chapter 1, U.S. tax shelters for cinema investment during the 1970s had led to such glaring abuse that they were discontinued. One French account described how such funds had been misused: the projection of an Indian film once in an empty theater, the production of pornographic films, the financing of big-budget tourist films with no commercial return.[39] In the second half of the 1970s, German cinema investment funds had been diverted to finance U.S. films. To avoid abuses, SOFICA money had to be invested in special holding companies, not in individual films; the companies would decide which films to invest in. The design of the SOFICAs, however, brought in only modest funds, effectively plugging some of the hole left by the withdrawal of distributor financing to the industry, but various constraints restricted their appeal as investment opportunities, especially for small investors.[40]

TELEVISION

The SOFICAs and the IFCIC did bring new investment to the industry, some 10 percent of all production funding, but a growing resource was about to be tapped: television. When Mitterrand was elected, French television was still entirely state-owned, with only three national stations, none of which broadcast twenty-four hours a day. In the United States, of course, following the model of radio, television was almost entirely private from its beginnings, with weak oversight from the Federal Communications Commission (FCC), created with the Communications Act of 1934. The act called for serving the public interest, but the FCC placed few restrictions on private operators, and actual public stations operated at public expense with a low percentage of the television audience.

As in many other countries, France financed television through a user fee, or license, known as the *redevance*, supplemented by limited permissible advertising.[41]

Mitterrand had made reform of the electronic media one of his campaign pledges.[42] After first allowing the operation of private radio stations, in 1982 Mitterrand announced the formation of a new television station, to show reruns and cultural programs, and the new station would require no cost to the state.[43] Evidently, the station would be some form of pay television. Behind the scenes, Mitterrand named one of his political cronies, André Rousselet, to run the station. Rousselet, Mitterrand's former chief of staff, had left to become head of the government-owned publicity agency Havas, and he learned that researchers at French Television had already begun plans for a new station, to be modeled on the pay (cable) station HBO in the United States.[44] Typical of French dirigiste practice, Mitterrand held no public bidding for the franchise and did not even demand direct financial compensation for this authorization. During 1983 and 1984, Rousselet tried to find investors.

But the state did impose certain restrictions or obligations (known as *cahiers des charges*) on the new station. Because Canal+ was to be a private pay-television station, one of Europe's first, it would generate income far above the revenues gained by the limited publicity allowed on the public stations, and it would be broadcast over the air, avoiding the enormous cost of a cable infrastructure. This first private station signed a charter stipulating its obligations.[45] Canal+ agreed to invest fully 25 percent of its revenue in the cinema. As cinema and sports were to constitute the biggest attractions of the new station, it was logical that Canal+ would take a financial interest in supporting the film industry. After start-up difficulties put the new station's viability in doubt, Canal+ convinced the authorities to reduce the 25 percent figure to 20 percent; of that 20 percent, Canal+ would devote 9 percent to French films and an additional 3 percent to European films. Conforming to what is now known as the "chronology of media," Canal+ was allowed to show films only one year after their release in theaters; other stations had to wait three years (unless they were co-producers). In addition, while government television stations could show only 192 films per year, Canal+ could broadcast up to 320 films.

The time delays for permissions to show films after their theatrical release assumed greater importance as the number of subsequent "windows" increased with the technological advances of videotape, DVD, satellite, and the Internet. Before television, the earning life of a film corresponded more or less to the length of its time in theaters, and some films remained in theaters for years.[46] Once television began showing films, the film industry naturally wanted long delays before television screenings in order to maximize theatrical returns. For similar reasons, the state regulated the times that films could be shown on television, proscribing times when most people went to theaters, such as Saturday night and Wednesday afternoons when schools did not have classes. While the measures clearly favored the film industry in the competition with television, state-owned television traditionally paid low fees for television screening rights, so the arrangement with Canal+ was not necessarily an unfair exchange between the two media.

COHABITATION

Once France broke the state monopoly with the creation of Canal+, the government embarked on additional television privatization. Early in 1985, only two months after Canal+ began broadcasting, Mitterrand stunned Rousselet with his decision to create two more private stations. After the Socialists lost the legislative elections in 1986, the cohabitation government under Jacques Chirac extended the privatization initiatives introduced by Mitterrand but also maintained and even strengthened the commitment to French cinema. The Chirac government took the unprecedented step of selling off public station TF1, the largest French station at the time, with a market share over 40 percent. Intense public debate had accompanied the creation of the two private stations announced by Mitterrand in 1985, originally named La Cinq and T.V. 6, which began operating in 1987 with small market shares. (La Cinq would fail in 1992.) Also, based on the established principle that television channels, as beneficiaries of cinema, should take some financial responsibility for the films they were showing, a 1986 law required all stations to pay a tax of 4.5 percent (raised to 5.5 percent in 1987) on their income. That tax, like the tax on theater tickets, went directly into the Compte de soutien. While some of these regulations were not new, the sums involved were significantly higher than those paid by stations before the creation of Canal+.[47] The contributions of television to the support account jumped from

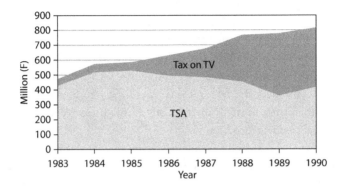

FIGURE 2.4 Main sources of contributions to the Compte de soutien support account in francs, 1983–1990

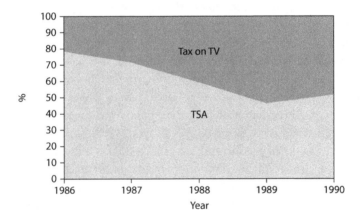

FIGURE 2.5 Percentage of contributions to the Compte de soutien from main sources, 1986–1990

10 percent to almost 50 percent, overtaking the receipts from the TSA in 1989 (see figures 2.4–2.5).[48]

At the same time, the government applied investment requirements to all television stations. Canal+ had already agreed in its *cahiers des charges* to invest 20 percent of its revenues in cinema, which meant prepurchase agreements for films to be shown on Canal+. By 1990, Canal+ was investing in 86 out of a total of 107 French films, or 80 percent.[49] All other stations had to invest 3 percent of their income in cinema, either through prepurchases or participation in co-production. Co-production investment would entitle stations to a reduction in the time delay after release of the film in theaters from three years to two years. The investment percent was applied to all revenues of the stations, derived primarily from the license fee (*redevance*) for public stations and advertising for all stations. Combined, the five stations broadcast free over the air contributed a similar amount to production but more or less evenly split between prepurchases and co-productions.

Beginning in 1986, all television stations had to abide by broadcast quotas stipulated in another law. Canal+ had already agreed to quotas of 60 percent for European cinema, and 50 percent for French cinema. The new law imposed those numbers on all stations. At the time, cinema drew the largest audiences to television. Films represented thirty-nine of the fifty most popular programs on television in 1986.[50] The controversial theatrical screen quotas contained in the 1946 Blum-Byrnes agreement had lapsed many years earlier, so the new battleground over quotas was television, a topic explored in subsequent chapters. In the rapidly changing audiovisual environment of the 1980s in France, stations could afford to pay for cinema, the most popular program content, but original programming for television, subject to the same quotas, posed a more difficult challenge, for production of fiction programs was far more costly than licensing foreign series, especially U.S. programs selling at prices far below the cost of national productions for a much smaller audience.

To gauge the total contributions of television to cinema, then, entails tracking two forms of investment. The tax on television fed directly into the support account, previously funded largely by the TSA, the tax levied on box office receipts, directly proportional to the performance of films in theaters. Unscrambled over-the-air stations also had to fulfill separate investment obligations of 3 percent after 1986. By 1990, the combination of those contributions approximated 45 percent of all French investments in cinema (see figure 2.6).[51] Essentially, then, with attendance once again falling during the 1980s, when theaters lost another sixty million annual viewers, or 40 percent of the cinema audience, France sought to replace the money draining out of the Compte de soutien with revenues taken from television. The desertion of the audience was a European-wide phenomenon, and despite the size of the falloff during the decade, France did resist better than its European counterparts Germany, Italy, Spain, and Great Britain (see figure 2.7).

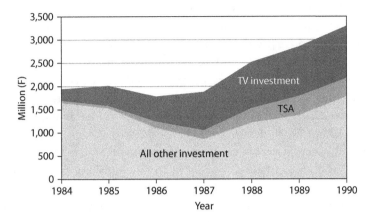

FIGURE 2.6 French investment in cinema in francs, 1984–1990

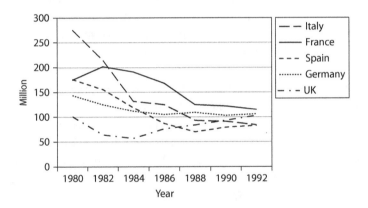

FIGURE 2.7 Cinema attendance in EU5 countries, 1980–1992

France had intervened in support of the film industry for many years before Lang became minister of culture, but Lang came to office determined to revamp the relations between the state and the culture industries, not just cinema. He succeeded in doubling the budget for the Ministry of Culture, apparently largely because of his personal relationship with Mitterrand. As a lawyer who had worked as cultural director for various theater organizations, Lang brought executive experience to the job. He understood funding issues in the cultural realm and wanted to craft new ways of balancing cultural and industrial demands. Until the appointment of Chirac as prime minister in 1986, Lang presided over and directed the most concerted French efforts to arrest and reverse the long-term decline in French cinema. The central conundrum, which remains just as pertinent in the twenty-first century, is how to foster creativity without ignoring box office performance. In principle, the selective aid of the avance sur recettes is designed to promote new talent, support films that take artistic risks, and nurture filmmakers who have already distinguished themselves artistically. Automatic aid exists to reward films that have found popular success and enable their producers to continue making films. Problems arise when the avance fails to deliver creativity, and when the box office results siphon funds away from more creative projects or even seep into the criteria for grants to creative work.

Jean-Denis Bredin's 1981 report on the film industry had paved the way for Lang's reforms. The new minister of culture, François Léotard, who had come in with the Chirac government in 1986, commissioned his own report in November 1987. By the end of the decade, the film industry had suffered new decline, hence the dire opening line of Léotard's charge to Jean-François Court: "The current crisis of cinema that reflects the fall in attendance in theaters affects more directly the theater owners." Yet again French cinema was in crisis. Léotard asked Court to examine immediate measures to arrest the decline but also to look beyond the present moment at "future perspectives." Two months later, in February 1988, Court completed his report, "French Cinema Faced with Its Future," which informed readers that "French cinema is at a crossroads."[52] The most pressing challenge, according to Court, was bringing spectators back to the theaters. Interestingly, Court warned against seeing television as the scapegoat for the film industry's problems. He showed how quickly television had asserted itself as the biggest investor in cinema. While television contributed only 10 percent of film investment in 1985, by 1987 it was investing more than 33 percent, and Court called Canal+ the "largest film exhibitor in France." Contrary to the experience in the United States, where sources of financing were more diversified among theaters (40 percent), video (30 percent), and television (less than 30 percent), the weight of television financing in France "runs the risk of a certain 'dictatorship' of television." And in a key observation, which would be echoed in future reports, there is a risk of "passing from a logic of investment to a logic of prefinancing."[53] That is, films could now be financed in advance with funds from television, from a SOFICA, from state aids (automatic and selective). In such a situation, there is no longer any risk to producers' capital; producers are simply putting together a financial package of others' money, a development that could encourage their indifference to the performance of the film in theaters.

Court recognized the attraction of big-budget films for spectators, especially young viewers, but warned against a dangerous Malthusianism that a focus on blockbusters might engender. If the total investment available for film is relatively constant, then favoring production of more expensive films will necessarily reduce the funds available for other productions, which would constrict the diversity of supply. As the size of a film's budget is no guarantee of theatrical success, disproportionate concentration of investment in expensive films would risk bankrupting the entire system. Moreover, since Léotard had passed a law requiring a 50 percent quota of French films on French television, the industry must be capable of supplying that demand with real films, and not, as Court warned, turn into a production mill of telefilms.

Court then pursued this line of thinking with the hypothesis that striking the right balance requires a commitment to modest films. Citing Godard's barb that "there is no longer any average to average," Court interpreted it to mean that there is a problem with average productions, modest in budget, modest in artistic ambition. "The real core of the French industry, aside from 15 'big films' and 20–30 auteur films, are the 50–80 average productions, comedies, crime films, etc., aspiring not to the exceptional, but to healthy entertainment."[54] Pointing out that distinguishing average films from what could turn out to be only telefilms, Court confessed that he had no solution. Rather, he said that the professionals of the industry must resolve the question among themselves, for the state could not.

The report offered five "avenues of reflection." First, the state should facilitate the development of "powerful groups" capable of mustering their own funding independent of television, taking advantage of the possibility of wider exportation of French film, on the model of U.S. companies like Gulf and Western-Paramount.[55] Of course the danger of this avenue was one of concentration and the oligopolistic practices that concentration abets. Second, again looking to the United States as a model, France should encourage successful independent producers, like George Lucas, Steven Spielberg, and Francis Ford Coppola. Third, France should allow videotape to expand; it was virtually nonexistent in France at the time, but it already had overtaken theatrical revenue in the United States.[56] Fourth, Court addressed the role of the SOFICAs. In the space of only three years since their establishment, the SOFICAs had turned into guarantees of high-interest returns on investments that already offer tax advantages. The SOFICAs avoided risk by directing their investments into rights for the films made by the large companies. This arrangement diverted SOFICA investment from independent producers but also gave the big producers rights to the negatives, which were often effectively guaranteed by the quotas requiring television to purchase those films. Finally, the report recommends rethinking the Compte de soutien, both the automatic and selective aids. The automatic aid had a sliding scale of reward, with less automatic aid awarded as attendance increased. Court viewed this as a penalty for success, whereas the state should have been doing all in its power to reward theatrical success. If the automatic aid should provide more return for successful films, the selective aid, such as the avance sur recettes, should be more supportive of films of real "creation and research."[57]

The Court report, then, provided an overview of the state of French cinema after half a decade of momentous changes. Despite Lang's reforms, attendance had continued to plunge, but exclusively at the expense of French films. The industry, thanks to the new funding sources Lang put together, maintained a relatively steady output of films (average of 146 from 1982 to 1987).[58] Court noted, hopefully, that attendance in the United States and Great Britain had actually risen in those years, as had the number of screens and multiplexes, suggesting that declining attendance was not irreversible. Nor was there a direct correlation between U.S. blockbusters, with attendant promotion, and theatrical success. Looking at studies of the audience, Court found that two-thirds of the audience went to the theater five to six times per year, with a small but significant cinephile population (10–15 percent of annual audience) going several times per month. He also devoted considerable attention to exhibition. Despite two decades of theater renovation, the exhibition sector in France had not yet developed multiplexes, with their additional amenities of banked seating and sumptuous concession spaces; nor did the theaters offer subscription cards. By the end of the next decade, French theaters would develop those options and would see a marked increase in attendance in response.

LANG II (1988–1992)

With the Socialists' return to power in 1988, Lang resumed his position as minister of culture, and quickly announced a new agenda for cinema. In many ways, the Lang plan laid out a program similar to the one recommended in Court's report. For a press conference by Lang on February 7, 1989, only a year after Court's report, the Ministry of Culture distributed an "Action Plan in Support of Cinema." The first plank described a reorientation of the avances sur recettes, which would now concentrate on French films, or co-productions, but only those shot in French: "Faced with a crisis that affects the identity of French cinema, the commission of the avances sur recettes must set its goal as the search for and affirmation of a new, ambitious cinema capable of taking its place at the highest level of international production." At the same time, the government would continue its commitment to accomplished filmmakers from other countries who were unable to complete projects in their native countries: "France has always, in cinema as in other forms of expression, enriched its cultural tradition by an openness to foreign artists for them to address, confront, question a perception or sensibility too strictly national."[59]

Other measures also conformed to those outlined by Court. In particular, to facilitate the production of more big-budget films, "targeting a very large audience which could contribute to turning around the decline in attendance," the government would revise the design of the IFCIC to enable it to raise risk funds for investment in these films. Court had noted that the IFCIC was actually avoiding risk, resulting in the purchase of rights for downstream exhibition of less ambitious films. In his plan, Lang wanted the IFCIC not simply to ease credit for conventional films but also to have the government ensure credit for big films that would accept the conditions of risk associated with release in theaters, not the sale of rights reliably anticipated with purchase by television. As an additional incentive to reward success in theaters, the automatic aid would no longer be awarded on a digressively sliding scale of compensation based on the number of box office admissions. In the past, the most successful films received proportionately less money from the automatic aid as the number of spectators exceeded several thresholds. Now, all films would receive 120 percent of the amount generated by the TSA on all theater tickets sold.[60]

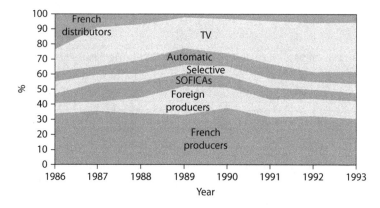

FIGURE 2.8 Percentage of sources of investment in French cinema, 1986–1993

As theatrical receipts continued to plunge, reducing the exhibition sector's proportion of the Compte de soutien, another key contributor to funding for production began to withdraw its support, though it never figured in the funding of the Compte de soutien. In the past, distributors would advance money for production based on anticipated receipts in theaters. Distributors could count on a certain percentage of theatrical revenues, so they would pledge funds to producers, following a long tradition. As those revenues ebbed with the fall in attendance, distributors had fewer resources available for investment in production (see figure 2.8).

Furthermore, the nature of the audience decline had a disproportionate impact on distributors. Theater owners depended on the total size of the audience. Spectators paid the same price, more or less, for all films. French distributors, however, distributed French films. Theaters, then and now, were French-owned, but the exhibitors had no reason to care about the nationality of the films shown in their theaters. If the U.S. films fared better at the box office, so much the better for them. Independent French distributors, by contrast, operating without partnerships with U.S. distributors, suffered directly from the flight of spectators from French films, which translated into driving down the amount they could make available for production (see figure 2.9).

The diminution of distributor revenues also affected the amounts they could spend on publicity, thereby aggravating the downward spiral for the performance of French films at the box office. U.S. films enjoyed several

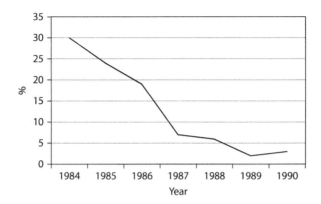

FIGURE 2.9 Role of distribution in financing French film (percentage of total), 1984–1990

advantages over French films in terms of publicity. First, U.S. distributors could draw on publicity materials already developed in their films' domestic market. Second, before the current practice of simultaneous international releases, U.S. films arrived in France already having earned reputations at home. Third, France did not allow advertising of films on television, probably the most effective means of promotion in the United States. French distributors relied on posters and newspaper advertising. In fact, this prohibition on television advertising resulted from a decision to protect newspapers from the loss of income they would face if film advertising moved to television.

The decline in attendance in France certainly reduced the amount of money in the Compte de soutien (even as television money injected some additional funds), but what may have been more alarming was that most of the decline could be attributed to the loss of spectators for *French* films. The total attendance went from 202 million in 1982 to 121 million in 1989, but figures for U.S. films climbed from 61 to 67 million while French figures slipped from 108 to 41 million. France began the decade with a domestic share of 48 percent, the United States with 37 percent. By the end of the decade, French market share stood at 34 percent, and the U.S. figure was 57 percent (see figures 2.10–2.11).

Yet this troubling development led to one arresting, if ultimately logical, positive outcome for French cinema production. The share of the Compte de soutien derived from theaters did not depend on the nationality of

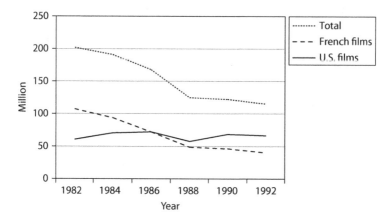

FIGURE 2.10 Cinema attendance in France for French and U.S. films, 1982–1992

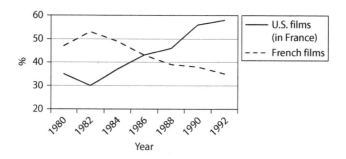

FIGURE 2.11 Market share for U.S. and French films in France, 1980–1992

the films screened; the same percentage applied to every ticket sold. However, the Compte de soutien was available only to French or European producers. Thus, the coefficient applied to the automatic aid went up as French market share went down. That is, French producers would receive proportionately more for the performance of their films the higher the market share won by U.S. films in France. The combination, then, of the rise of U.S. market share and the increased contributions from television resulted in French cinema being financed by its two rivals, U.S. cinema and television.[61]

Effectively, U.S. films shown in France subsidize French production. Because the theater tax is paid on all films regardless of nationality and goes directly into the Compte de soutien, and only French and European producers have access to that support mechanism, those producers all receive a percentage of that tax back according the success of their films in theaters. U.S. producers are therefore paying a tax yet receive no direct return. Hence, U.S. films released in France contribute to the support for French production. As one writer observed, "Without the United States and their sources of direct or indirect financing, there would already be no French cinema."[62]

This aspect of the French support system raises questions about what critics refer to as "protectionism." Many countries practice some form of protectionism for domestic industries, whether tariffs for foreign goods entering the country, raising the cost of those products relative to domestically produced goods, or outright subsidies. One of the goals of the neoliberalism ushered in under U.S. president Ronald Reagan and British prime minister Margaret Thatcher was the elimination of both trade barriers and "protectionist" subsidies. Such measures restrict the free functioning of the market, which, according to the theory of comparative advantage, will reward efficiency and maximize the best use of resources; prices also will fall once they are no longer propped up artificially by trade barriers. This argument is central to the theory of classical economics seeking to find the best use of limited resources. At the same time, classical economics also recognizes that the public interest may not always be best served by purely economic considerations. Profit supplies the motive for capitalist activity, but public goods, such as education and health care, are not best served by profit motives. Thus, "protectionism" is a normative term, and states will inevitably disagree over how broadly it should be applied, and to what industries.

Tariffs, one traditional means of protecting national industries, restrict trade among nations. Direct governmental subsidies within a country could also be seen as restricting trade by helping industries that might fail on their own in a "free" market. Normally, subsidies would come from general tax revenues, paid by the entire population. The government could then take some of those revenues to distribute to domestic industries, for instance an emerging or "infant industry" that faces large start-up costs before it can stand on its own. Governments might subsidize research in alternative energy sources today in order to reduce the dependence on oil long-term. A government could employ its own scientists to work on the problem, but typically it will direct the public investment into private firms in the interest of efficiency.

Was the Compte de soutien a recipient of subsidies? This question will assume greater relevance in the discussion of GATT and the WTO in chapter 4, but the French maintain that it does not receive significant subsidies, for most of the resources of the Compte de soutien do not flow out of general tax revenues.[63] The general population, that is, does not pay into the Compte de soutien. Instead, theatergoers pay what could be called a user's tax, which is funneled into the support account. The money then goes directly back into the industry. The French refer to it as "forced saving" within the industry. The film industry, in a sense, views the Compte de soutien as "its" money. People who don't buy tickets are not contributing to the fund, so they are not "subsidizing" the cinema industry.

The same argument could be extended to the new requirements imposed on television stations. Before the reforms of the 1980s, television revenues came from two basic sources: the *redevance*, paid by all television owners, and advertising, tightly regulated by the government. If cinema spectators were the users of films shown in theaters, television viewers and advertisers were the "users" of television. At the time, films were by far the most popular programs shown on television. Thus, like theater owners, television companies were being asked to pay a "tax" on their revenues to be channeled back to cinema (and to television, with the formation of the Compte de soutien financier de l'industrie cinématographique et de l'industrie des programmes audiovisuels [COSIP] in 1986). The investment percentage imposed on Canal+ was considerably higher than the requirement for the other stations because Canal+, a private company granted a franchise to broadcast with no license fee, was authorized to show many more films than the other stations, and it received certain advantages over those other stations, such as the right to show films only one year after their theatrical release. Subsidies are criticized for throwing good money at bad industries, rewarding inefficiency. Television was a still emerging and increasingly thriving industry in the 1980s, so the user's tax paid by television stations, arguably not a subsidy at all, certainly did not cosset inefficiency.[64]

Quotas are another area often accused of restraining free trade. Quotas can be applied to imports, setting limits to the amount of a product allowed to enter the country. The Blum-Byrnes agreement specified minimum quotas for the screening of French films in French theaters (but the agreement placed "no restriction of any sort on American imports").[65]

The 1986 French law established quotas for the broadcast of French films on French television. Discussions of free trade involve relations between nations, and free trade may conflict with national interest. If the flood of foreign goods at lower prices drives up the importing country's unemployment rate, the nation might, and often does, place a designated national interest like unemployment above principled adherence to free trade. Quotas may inhibit free trade according to classical economic theory, but they do not necessarily harm national interests. Again, a theoretical economic efficiency may not trump national interest, which properly becomes a political discussion.

Another fundamental tension characterized Jack Lang's efforts to strengthen the cultural industries, one that would increasingly affect other European countries in varying ways. With the privatization of television, that industry grew enormously from the 1980s on. Cinema, at least in its traditional guise as a theatrical phenomenon, was shrinking, evidenced by the dramatic decline in theatrical attendance, and by a more muted decline in production, from 557 to 415 releases (25 percent) during the 1980s for the EU5 countries). Lang's reforms sent more of television's resources into the film industry. So even as attendance in theaters was falling, more films were now being shown on television, and they remained the most popular programs. Thus, institutional symbiosis increased between the two traditional rivals. Lang sought to shore up the film industry's financial stability by carving out part of television's income for the film industry. At the same time, he wanted to address one of the perennial weaknesses of the film industry, its artisanal production sector (which Bredin had vigorously defended). That meant countenancing greater concentration in the hope of building stronger industrial producers, capable of competing in the international market.

Through the 1980s, what the French call the "French audiovisual landscape" (*paysage audiovisuel français*) was undergoing massive transformations. The coinage of that term reflects the nature of these changes. Cinema and television operated in separate regulatory domains before the 1980s. Cinema was a private industry, financed by private funding; television was entirely state owned and operated. As theater attendance fell, the state assumed a greater role in the film industry, seeking to identify new funding sources. The IFCIC and the SOFICAs provided some relief, but with the breakup of the state monopoly and the privatization of television, the medium took on a larger role in financing cinema. That role would only grow in future years. As the key state-administered funding source for cinema was the Compte de soutien, when television was forced to raise its contributions to the support account, the institutional link between the two tightened. In recognition of this new configuration, in 1986 the Compte de soutien became the Compte de soutien de l'industrie des programmes audiovisuels (COSIP), now indicating that the account served both cinema and television, with the CNC administering separate cinema and television sections. In French, a certain ambiguity still surrounds the term "audiovisual," for it normally refers to television alone, as in "audiovisual programming," which means television programming, but the adoption of "audiovisual landscape" was intended to encapsulate both cinema and television.

Of Lang's policies to support and prime cultural industries, his efforts in film may be most prominent. But the film industry had its own tensions and competing interests. French exhibitors did not necessarily object to screening Hollywood films, for the tickets sold had no nationality. And theaters in France, unlike the case of other countries, were French-owned, so their revenues went to French companies. Producers saw audiences deserting French film, so they suffered financially from the drop in attendance. With large distributors aligned with exhibitors, and with Hollywood majors in output deals (rights to distribute Hollywood films in France and other European countries), the former simply reduced their financing for French cinema. Lang walked a fine line trying to balance these competing interests. But despite the Bredin report's call to defend artisanal production, and the separation of the film circuit GIE into Pathé and Gaumont, Lang's policies were designed to strengthen the industrial base of cinema. Many of the major lobbies could agree with that goal, which would redirect state support toward greater sensitivity to market preferences.

These efforts to salvage the film industry occurred as television was gaining strength with privatization. The relaxation of restrictions on television advertising and the creation of new stations drew new financing to television, as industrial giants began to invest in television, leading to greater concentration in the audiovisual sector. The Compte de soutien was increasingly fed by television money, as distributors withdrew from financing and falling film attendance in theaters drove down film's contributions to the fund. As in the United States, companies began to discover the upside potential of buying up film rights. Theatrical revenues were falling, but receipts from subsequent runs on video and television were growing. In 1990, the Compagnie générale des eaux (CGE) and the Lyonnaise des eaux, two venerable water companies with distribution infrastructures already in place, began purchasing rights with an eye toward exploiting them with the anticipated rise of cable in France. CGE bought shares in various cable companies, as well as in the French film company UGC; it also became the principal financial backer of the major theater circuit UGC. As *Le Monde*'s film reporter wrote in his history of French cinema since the New Wave, "In a general manner, the impulsion given by the most prescient of the [film] professionals since the end of the 1970s, then with the powerful impetus of Lang making the state an essential and constant partner of every important action, unleashed a movement which took on a momentum of its own."[66]

Over the course of the decade, a Socialist government and a Conservative government had intervened in unprecedented ways to reverse the decline of French cinema. The Socialists had actually broken the state monopoly of television with the formation of Canal+ and the creation of two new private stations. The Chirac government pushed transformation of television further with the privatization of the largest French public station, TF1. With all stations required to devote almost 10 percent of their rising income to film,[67] and new government instruments (IFCIC, SOFICAs) generating new funding sources, French cinema was able to maintain its level of investment. Attendance fell dramatically for French films, and theaters closed, but the governments also encouraged theater renovation, even in the least populated areas, so the exhibition sector avoided collapse. France lost 10 percent of its screens in the second half of the decade, but it ended the 1980s with the same number of screens in 1990 (4,518) as in 1980 (4,540), still more than more populous Germany (3,754) and far more than the United Kingdom (1,602).[68] In short, despite the rapid expansion of television and videotape as alternative viewing venues, the French government, with the crucial assistance of the well-established CNC evidenced a consistent commitment to the cinema, both a commercial cinema and an art cinema, however difficult it was to achieve a viable balance in practice.

Finally, the Lang plan of 1989 had special sections, for the first time, on some recent European initiatives that France had sponsored to develop filmmaking on a regional level. The Court report, in a discussion of the importance of raising export sales for French films, commented that "the only real European film was U.S. film," for only U.S. film enjoyed wide popularity in all markets of Europe. Throughout the 1980s, in fact, Lang had lobbied European partners indefatigably as France tried to influence the European Economic Community's strategy for drafting a policy on European television, the topic of the next chapter.

3

EUROPEAN FILM POLICY AND
TELEVISION WITHOUT FRONTIERS

While France intervened more actively in its audiovisual sector than other European countries during the 1980s, changes in the audiovisual landscape affected all of those countries' film and television industries. In the 1970s, the other major European film industries suffered more severe deterioration than was experienced in France (see figures 3.1–3.4). Attendance and domestic market share plunged in Italy, Spain, and Great Britain, while the French industry showed comparative stability. France was the only country where film production actually increased, and attendance and market share were almost unchanged. Nonetheless, France was the catalyst during the 1980s and beyond in drawing attention to the gravity of the problem and calling on the other countries to address it, yet another demonstration of the importance accorded film in the French national patrimony. At the same time, on a parallel track, Europe was moving, however slowly, toward increasing forms of unification, which would ultimately lead to the formation of the European Union in 1992. Largely behind the public leadership of Jack Lang, France pushed to shape the new European policies on film and television.

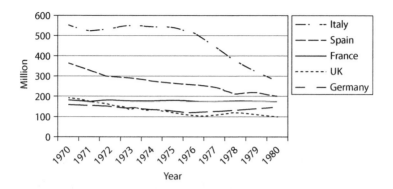

FIGURE 3.1 Cinema attendance in EU5 countries, 1970–1980

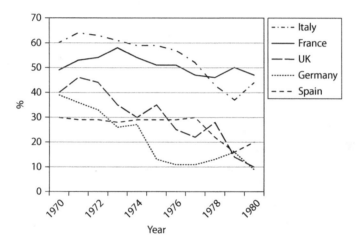

FIGURE 3.2 Domestic market share for national cinema in EU5 countries, 1970–1980

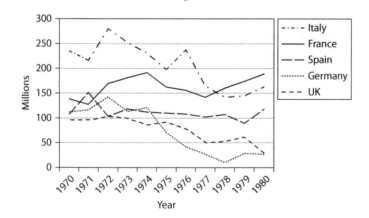

FIGURE 3.3 Number of feature films produced in EU5 countries, 1970–1980

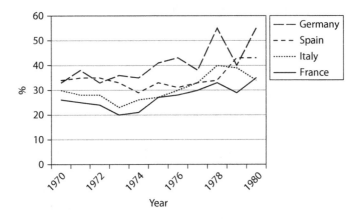

FIGURE 3.4 U.S. market share in European film markets, 1970–1980

EARLY EEC FILM POLICY

As the name suggests, the European Economic Community (EEC), created by the Treaty of Rome in 1957, had no cultural remit, and there was
little coordinated European-wide activity that related to the film industry.
Occasional studies examined national film industries in a comparative
perspective but, as a rule, outside the official orbit of the EEC. Because
the treaty mentioned neither culture nor cinema, decisions regarding the
applicability of the treaty to cinema depended on legal, and ultimately
political considerations. As the treaty was a liberal document,[1] committed to reducing trade barriers among the original six countries—Luxembourg, the Netherlands, France, West Germany, Italy, and Belgium—the
potentially relevant provisions to cinema were those prohibiting state
aids, especially Article 92, which began as follows: "Save as otherwise
provided in this Treaty, any aid granted by a Member State or through
State resources in any form whatsoever which distorts or threatens to distort competition by favouring certain undertakings or the production of
certain goods shall, in so far as it affects trade between Member States, be
incompatible with the common market."

One study from 1965 illustrates the tentativeness of discussions regarding the treaty's relevance for European film industries. Claude Degand, a
researcher at the CNC, examined the individual industries and the treaty's
implications for the future of cinema. At that time, the EEC had passed

two directives on cinema, both attempting to facilitate movement of films among the member countries. The first directive tried to ease the rules governing the circulation of films in the European common market, in particular the designation of the nationality of films. The directive shifted the attribution from the nationalities of the "authors" of the film to the structure of the financing, a more stable legal footing.

The second directive eliminated import quotas and limits on dubbed films, but it also took aim at the state aids. Article 4 proposed "eliminating aids accorded by member states which distort conditions of establishment." Such aids could be seen to provide an advantage to national films or firms. For countries having quotas on the minimum number of national films to be screened, quotas would have to accept films from other member states as applicable to the quota, and the countries could raise the quota requirements so long as they did not restrict the number of imports allowed from other member states. Degand did not comment on the quota question. Because attendance in 1965 had already started to fall, and theaters were closing, he identified taxes on theaters and films as the most pressing concerns: "It is clear that for the theater owners whose situation is precarious and who subsist with difficulty dependent on auxiliary receipts, such as candy and advertising during intermission, significant tax relief would constitute the necessary oxygen balloon which should enable them to adapt and survive."[2] Degand did not foresee any immediate threat to the systems of aid at a time when the film industries were in crisis because of falling attendance. Quoting the Permanent Inventory of Aids catalogued by the European Commission (EC), Degand explained that film and other industries, such as shipping, were "important industries undergoing structural difficulties" and would benefit from specific aid systems. Because the aids were harmful to intracommunity competition, the EC would have to find solutions. "The future will say if the solutions in question will consist in a community system of financing or in a harmonization of national regimes [of aid]," he concluded.[3] For the most part, Degand pursued his analysis in economic terms. The EEC might want to tolerate aid systems that carry some industries through a rough patch and transient crisis, but, he observed almost parenthetically, other considerations also might apply. Thus, aids could be justified by "the random nature of film production, the unprofitability which accompanies it, in the taxes which reduce the box office receipts; but there is also the fact that Cinema is one of the principal carriers of culture, and that a

State is unable to ignore the medium thanks to which it exports its *way of life* throughout the world."[4]

Another early study of the European cinema, from 1967, concentrated almost exclusively on aids to the cinema industry.[5] Catherine Sieklucka examined in detail the various aids allocated to cinema in each EEC country (with the exception of the tiny Luxembourg). She outlined how the different regimes of state support failed to justify any special exemption from the proscription in Article 92 of state aids, whether in the form of direct subsidies, fiscal support from taxes, or parafiscal measures regulating transfers of receipts not fed into general tax revenues. Writing several years after the appearance of the directives, Sieklucka noted that there had been no follow-up, but she identified a potential problem, which would indeed return years later as a major concern of the EEC: "the question of an eventual contradiction between the spirit of the Treaty, and more specifically Article 92, and the aids as they crop up in comparative law."[6]

Given the cultural arguments mounted later in defense of state aids for cinema, Sieklucka, like Degand, surprisingly devoted little space to claims that cinema should be exempt because it falls under the category of culture and is thereby not subject to the authority of the treaty:

> The dispositions of the Treaty, in articles 92 and following, are formal, and the analysis we have presented tends to prove it: the financial aids set aside for the film industry in certain countries of the Common Market exempt them, and no exemption is possible without the recognition of the specificity of this industry by a decision of the Council of Ministers of the CEE. . . . In other words, until such intervention of such a decision, if it is taken one day, the financial aids offered by the countries are prohibited, even though their existence is motivated by a protection against the American competition.[7]

As we will see in chapter 4, "recognition of the specificity of this industry" became the key sticking point in the dispute over the General Agreement on Trades and Tariffs in 1993. Already in 1967, Sieklucka alluded to "film professionals," or what might be called the film lobby, who fear that "the day that the subsidies are eliminated, the French, Italian and German cinemas will be irremediably damaged," and Sieklucka concurred in that fear.[8] She added that it was unlikely that the EEC would take such an action, given the loss of jobs it would cause, as well as the loss of "one of the most useful instruments of international propaganda." Echoing a well-known sentiment of policy makers in the United States, she referred to a French scholar's observation that "the cinema follows American diplomacy, as once the missionaries followed the conquerors."[9] She ended her inquiry with a call for harmonization of cinema policies within the Common Market, which would also include carefully designed policies to promote a European cinema program, drawing on funds raised at the European, not national, level. The report ends with a remarkable foreshadowing of how this question of state aids would play out twenty-five years later in the GATT battle: "Only the Community [EEC] could present to GATT a common front sufficiently large and solid to resist the attacks which will not be absent from the gigantic United States."[10]

This early assessment did not speak of "European film" but of a rationalization at the level of the EEC of laws and financing, which would effectively "harmonize" separate and at times "incoherent" systems of support operating in the individual member countries. Most of the EEC countries did have support systems for their cinema industries, but those industries were in clear decline. Weakening those support systems only would have obstructed a possible recovery. The expansion of television played a role in that decline, but countries were still making critically acclaimed films and were probably not ready to withdraw state support from the most popular mass medium. Television, still developing, could not yet compete with cinema in terms of cultural status or economic significance. Furthermore, the EEC was still a recent regional experiment. Great Britain had refused to join, as did Spain under Franco. (The two countries joined the EEC in 1973 and 1986.) All countries shared concerns about a loss of sovereignty on more consequential economic issues, such as agriculture, so the idea of fighting over aids to cinema, despite their apparent incompatibility with the treaty, did not advance beyond the early directives.

Ten years later, in 1978, the Council of Europe, which forms one part of the "variable architecture" of the EEC, held a conference on "Cinema and the State." With more than two hundred representatives from all over Europe, the discussions at that event presumably offer a full range of thinking about the future of cinema in relation to the evolving plans of the EEC. Curiously, speakers devoted little attention to the question of the future of state aids. Perhaps the legal concerns Degand and Sieklucka pointed out over the incompatibility of state aids with the treaty had receded, if not disappeared. No doubt the declining fortunes of the European film industries formed the backdrop for the discussions, as the keynote speaker highlighted by introducing his remarks with the observation that "cinema is in crisis."[11]

Much of the discussion revolved around the relationship between film and television. At the time, television was still almost exclusively state-owned throughout Europe, so some speakers saw television as the preserve of the public interest. Thus, if some participants expressed concern for the low prices paid to show films on television, Nicholas Garnham, from Great Britain, formulated the question in terms of which industry should be subsidized by the state for its defense of the public interest. Because television was a public industry, Garnham argued, the state had an obligation to protect its scarce resources for quality programming; forcing stations to pay higher prices for the screening of films would necessarily reduce the funds available for television programming: "One can affirm in general that the audiovisual production in television is a more authentic expression of national culture than cinema production. One may regret it, but that's the way it is."[12] Actually, Garnham was not trying to score polemical points about the relations between film and television. From his perspective, forcing television to supplement the dwindling revenues of film meant moving public money into private hands: "the public sector will support the losses [of cinema] and the private sector will pocket the profits. Public funds will be transferred from a public service controlled by the state to a private sector."[13] Garnham acknowledged that he was speaking from an English context, where film did not occupy as prestigious a position as it did in France, for example. But given the vastly larger audience that watched television, was that medium not the true guardian of national culture? To the extent that film also transmitted national culture, it was the subset of art films that were relevant, those that tended to be recipients of selective aid, preselected as it were for their cultural—as opposed to commercial—ambition. As Claude Degand put it, "I wonder whether we should reserve the word 'aid' for those [aids] which are rather selective and which, being selective, are more cultural, while the aids now called 'automatic' would be called 'financial support,' of financial structures accompanying the economy of film."[14] Degand was citing the distinction in France between support given "automatically" to films according to their success at the box office and those films granted aid "selectively" on the basis of the quality promised by their scripts before production.

In "observations" included in the published record of the proceedings, the Belgian professor Jean-Claude Batz was the only person to take on directly the problem of the Treaty of Rome's prohibition of state aids. Such aids, he claimed, though practiced by most of the EEC countries, distorted cinema markets and were part of the difficulty in responding to cinema's crisis. "On the economic side, [state] aid is a failure, for it has never succeeded in establishing the financial autonomy of the European national cinemas."[15] Batz may have been right in asserting that state aids alone would not help European film industries achieve solvency, but many feared that those film industries would disappear without state aids. Paolo Bafile, Italy's former minister of tourism and spectacles, called for learning from the success of the U.S. industry and forming European integrated studios, which would be able to engage in blind bidding and block booking and thereby compete with the Hollywood on its own terms. "Here is, you say, a neo-capitalist type of thinking. So be it! Without fearing words, let us ask only if the program is useful and if it is do-able."[16] A number of speakers did support the idea of harmonizing support systems across Europe, including EEC financing, but there were equally emphatic rejections of producing "European films."

GESTATION OF A NEW POLICY

It would seem, then, that the question of state aids had made little progress in the EEC bureaucracy during the 1970s. The proscription of state aids in the Treaty of Rome continued to hover, for "Europe [was] still only in its 'economic' phase, making no place in its construction for more 'political' considerations like culture."[17] That phase came to a close in the 1980s. The European film industry continued to deteriorate dramatically, as the wave of neoliberalism promoted by the Thatcher and Reagan governments in Great Britain and the United States gathered strength. Of course the sea change that privatized television throughout Europe was arguably even more fundamental to the film industry's future. Whatever the combination of causes, the question of government support for cinema and television began to draw EEC attention, with critics of all state aids on one side and defenders of national prerogatives on the other.

Of the more than two hundred participants at the 1978 Council of Europe conference, the list in the printed proceedings does not indicate any ministers of culture. In fact, there were few ministers of culture in Europe at the time. That situation would change over the course of the next decade in response to several factors. Perhaps most significantly, the privatization of television and various technological developments started to elicit the attention of the European Commission. The economic weight of television increased as European countries opened their airwaves to advertising and the number of channels exploded. New delivery systems, including cable, pay television, and satellite put ever greater pressure on European authorities to develop policies to regulate the cross-border transmissions.

France took the lead in fostering European discussion of responses to these developments. France had established a Ministry of Culture in 1959, when de Gaulle named André Malraux as the first minister of culture.[18] Under Malraux's guidance, the ministry sought to formulate what the French call a *politique culturelle*. English does not have an equivalent translation for *politique*. It is probably best understood as "policy" but with a slight thrust not unrelated to "political."[19] In principle, a new ministry should have some sort of policy, and Malraux came to the office with a long and celebrated history as an artist himself, both a writer and filmmaker.[20] Malraux was most concerned with the dissemination of high culture, making it accessible to all. The July 24, 1959, decree defined the Ministry of Culture's mission as "rendering the great works of humanity . . . accessible to the largest possible number of French people, to assure the most vast audience for our cultural patrimony, and to favor the creation of works of art and the spirit that enrich it."[21] One of his innovations was the *maisons de la culture*, local cultural centers that would popularize high art. However, despite the official installation of the selective film support system known as the avances sur recettes in 1959, Malraux's *politique culturelle* did not really have a significant impact on cinema, with the notorious exception of the Langlois affair in 1968. Even the *maisons de la culture* initiative lost momentum after the departure of Malraux in 1969.[22]

Jack Lang shifted the idea of Malraux's *politique culturelle* from the centrality of access to culture to the promotion of culture, especially creative production, under the new *politique* of *action culturelle*, not simply appreciation. Film, of course, arguably the most paradigmatic example of artistic production at the crossroads and art and industry, would fall more centrally in the purview of this new *politique* than it had previously. Lang pumped new funds and energy into the Ministry of Culture (see chapter 2), but he also worked to develop European ties with other countries, to build a more united front to face the pressures exerted by the EEC, in particular the European Commission, the executive body of the EEC. Lang held informal meetings with cultural homologues across Europe in an attempt for forge common EEC policies on film and television. For example, Lang attended a meeting in Venice of ministers of culture in June 1982.[23] In July, he met with representatives from other countries and claimed, "If we don't take the means of organizing ourselves, we risk being submerged by the multinational groups."[24] At the same time, he voiced a refrain that would become familiar, encouraging other countries not to "accept the decisions of the European Commission in the name of an excessively narrow application of the Treaty of Rome . . . that questions the aid mechanisms of each country," and to refuse "in the name of Europe that they destroy Europe."[25] Just prior to that meeting, Lang had invited French and West German professionals and directors to discuss official collaboration, following the completion of a co-production agreement between the two countries at the end of 1981. The joint statement from the gathering contained a commitment to "affirm the national identities of European countries."[26] In the fall of 1982, Lang attended a meeting in Naples with other EEC cultural officials. News reports suggested that the meeting was a failure, for after all the speechmaking, it "gave birth to a mouse." One journalist opined that such efforts should "warn Lang and his friends of the vertigo of meetings, symposia, or other institutes that just produce bureaucracy."[27]

Of course Lang's most famous, or notorious, intervention was his Mexico City speech at the UNESCO world conference on cultural policies in July 1982. In the speech, he called for "a real crusade against—let's call things by their real name—this financial and cultural imperialism." Although he did not name the United States, the U.S. delegation walked out in protest. But the uproar following that rhetorical grenade actually overshadowed a more radical shift in cultural policy contained in the same speech, when Lang averred that "economy and culture [are] the same battle."[28] Even Lang's Socialist supporters were taken aback by this assertion, for the left traditionally insisted on the difference between cultural production and the commercial production of goods.[29] Following the critique associated with the Frankfurt School, the left viewed the commodification of culture with alarm. The very expression "cultural industries" implied that cultural production was already commodified. Lang, however, understood that industries like film and television, the audiovisual sector, could not survive without carefully crafted economic policies that could withstand legal and, more significantly, political challenges as part of the increasing unification of Europe. In retrospect, Lang's Mexico City speech, viewed by many as a provocation, seemed less an attack on the United States than an effort to extend his plea to countries beyond Europe to address the increasingly pressing question of culture. One U.S. writer found it to be a reasonable and respectful position statement.[30]

Lang, then, complemented his domestic campaign to secure support for cultural production with constant efforts to cultivate allies among France's European partners. He organized conferences and meetings with cultural officials in other countries, trying to rally them to defend and support countries' prerogatives to preserve their cultural industries, all under threat by encroaching U.S. cultural production.[31] The subsequent history of the EEC's disputes over audiovisual policies illustrates the volatility of the political terrain. France led the camp resisting the application of liberal precepts to cultural production, occupying what is often known as the dirigiste position. Dirigistes argued that states must intervene in the affairs of ailing industries; at the EEC level, dirigistes wanted to preserve their governments' autonomy to develop their own policies, often correcting what were viewed as the negative results of an unregulated free market. Liberals, or ultra-liberals as some would have it, placed their faith in the unfettered functioning of the market. The film industry, like any other in a capitalist economy, must find ways to succeed in the marketplace. If U.S. cinema was displacing national production on theatrical and television screens, national film industries must figure out on their own how to win back audiences. Great Britain under Thatcher was the standard bearer of liberalism among the major film-producing countries. Other countries oscillated between these two poles as the wheels of the EEC bureaucracy turned.

Perhaps in response to the media brouhaha that followed the UNESCO speech, Lang organized a sumptuous event in Paris the next year. In February 1983, Lang invited "a dazzling array of novelists, movie stars, directors and intellectuals," including a broad contingent of U.S. artists and writers, to a conference to discuss "creation and development."[32]

The proceedings took place at the Sorbonne, and the news coverage in both the United States and France had a difficult time taking it entirely seriously, as the U.S. participants wondered what it was all about, evidently unaccustomed to a government so concerned about culture. While Susan Sontag evidently felt quite at home—"In our country, we don't have a minister of culture and, if we did, we wouldn't have someone like Jack Lang. We'd have Clint Eastwood"—others sounded pleasantly bemused. For Sidney Lumet, "It may be hot air, but it's hot air I care about, not hot air I don't care about."[33] Kate Millett remarked, "I'm just flabbergasted that the government gives a damn about what intellectuals think."[34] More partisan observers in both countries derided the whole enterprise. One writer for the *Wall Street Journal* recommended, "Instead of worrying about *Dallas*, Jack Lang should spend his time wondering why France is a nullity in contemporary, active world culture."[35]

In addition to these occasional international forays, Lang continued his lobbying program among the European countries. In November 1983, the Greek minister of culture Melina Mercouri, in collaboration with Lang, held an informal meeting of ministers of culture in Athens, described as the first such meeting since the passage of the Treaty of Rome.[36] Speakers brought out figures to demonstrate the mushrooming audiovisual demand. While countries were producing 1,000 to 4,000 hours of television programming at the time, demand would leap to 250,000 hours of fiction programming in ten years. Lang tried to impress on the other ministers the urgency of planning for this future, recognizing these cultural developments also as economic challenges demanding economic policies: "Why is it that what is legitimate [to discuss] with material goods becomes illegitimate with immaterial [cultural] goods?"[37]

Shortly before the release of the European Commission's *Green Paper on the Establishment of the Common Market for Broadcasting, Especially by Satellite and Cable* in June, the ministers of culture of the ten EEC countries met for the first time formally. Prior to that meeting, Lang had met with the president of the EC, Luxembourg's Gaston Thorn, seeking to explain the position of France, no doubt wanting to prepare him for the upcoming event in Brussels, though his tone was not conciliatory: "The Commission is interested in creators only to cause them misery in seeking ceaselessly to question the autonomy and rules of protection used by member countries; this would make Europe, in the name of Europe, lose what is most precious. . . . It's about choosing between two logics:

either we do everything to remain creators and conserve our identities, or we transform ourselves little by little into a simple market of consumers under the pretext that we have not known how to create a European cultural space."[38] Thorn warned Lang to "beware of protectionist temptations. If you want free access to universal culture, culture is not a bar of soap or pigs."[39] At the meeting France, Greece, and Italy fell on the side for EEC intervention, with Denmark, Great Britain, and (to a lesser degree) West Germany opposed. While this first formal meeting did not lead to any agreement, Thorn did say, if somewhat cryptically, "All this is little, but it is a lot."[40] On the other hand, the British minister of the arts, Lord Gowry, took the customary British neoliberal position: "Don't protect, go out and compete."[41] Several months later, in November, Lang arranged yet another meeting, with thirty filmmakers in Paris, which released a statement supporting the commitment to preserve national cinemas, as opposed to the more diaphanous term "European cinema": "We think that European film should remain one of national inspiration, even as it has the right to take advantage of the entire European space as a market."[42]

In short, Lang's strategy to strengthen the French film industry was two-pronged. In France, Lang introduced an unprecedented series of reforms that directed money flows into the film industry during a time of radical change in the audiovisual landscape, marked especially by the privatization of television and the decline of film. While the Mexico City speech drew headlines for invoking cultural imperialism, the title of the talk, "Economy and Culture: Same Struggle," actually identified a more dramatic theme. Rather than protecting a cultural preserve free of mercenary taint, Lang argued for facing the economic challenges threatening cultural production. Instead of fearing the transformation of cinema into the Frankfurt School's commodified culture industry, he acknowledged the inextricability of art and money, designing a cultural policy that would balance these two realms, formerly considered antithetical. The production of film art required substantial investment. With the drop in attendance, a long-term structural problem affecting film industries throughout the world, not a cyclical anomaly, theaters and distributors were no longer taking in enough revenues to finance production. The market was not going to correct the imbalance, for the rise of U.S. market share in European theaters threatened to marginalize European film industries; the state had to step in.

At the same time, Lang fought to convince the European partners to resist the neoliberal pressures being applied by the EEC, and more specifically the European Commission. As his first tenure as minister of culture was coming to a close, Lang reflected on his accomplishments. In an interview from early 1986, he acknowledged that film and television were his most important priorities. After ticking off one by one his reforms, he concluded that "the entire thrust of my activity for four years has been to reconcile art and money. It is for me a great success to have rehabilitated what we call today in a sense no longer pejorative, 'the culture industries.' "[43] The degree to which Lang succeeded in changing the attitude of the European partners and the EEC may be difficult to measure, but in 1986, the EC declared 1988 the "European Cinema and Television Year" in order "to stress the importance [the Commission] attaches to the audiovisual industry and to give further encouragement to a sector which presents a challenge to Europe as a whole, not only to defend its identity but also to seize new opportunities of affirming that identity."[44]

All of Lang's organizing activity took place just before the EEC crafted the Directive on Television Without Frontiers (TWF) and the Council of Europe developed the Convention on Transfrontier Television. For the first time, the European Community was trying to fashion a supranational audiovisual policy. Lang had already staked out France's position, and France strongly advocated a prominent role for the state in designing audiovisual policy.[45] Even though the Socialists lost the legislative elections in 1986, and President Mitterrand had to govern through a "cohabitation" with the right, the new minister of culture, François Léotard, largely, if not entirely, followed the path blazed by Lang. While the French did not manage to impose their position on the final versions of the two documents, both passed in 1989, French lobbying efforts formed the crucial backdrop to the final GATT battle in 1993, when France was able to convince its European partners not to cede the audiovisual future to the United States.

The rise of television as a major focus of discussion pushed the earlier questions about state aids to cinema into the background. The two major French government studies at both ends of the 1980s (examined in chapter 1) do not even mention the EEC threat to the vastly expanded French support system. The Bredin report from late 1981 makes several recommendations about the aid mechanisms, including an idea to create a private station devoted primarily to film, which should be required to contribute financially to the film industry, specifically through the Compte de sou-tien. Bredin even suggested greater state contribution to the Compte de soutien, which might take the form of a "true subsidy,"[46] a term far more likely to attract the interest of the EEC than "aid," which at least reflects some rhetorical effort to deflect charges that the government is subsidizing an industry. Not until the conclusion does the report refer to European policy, and only to say that "the establishment of a European cinema policy" is one of several questions not treated in the report. Court's 1988 study, coming after the creation of Canal+ and the privat-ization of TF1, recommends significant changes in the organization of the support system but never raises the question of the compatibility of any of the aids with either EEC rules or the Treaty of Rome.[47] Court does look to co-production with European partners as an essential way to deal with rising film budgets and recognizes the problems posed by the diffi-culty of determining the nationality of films, but the study does not view "Europe" as an obstacle or adversary.

Lang, however, clearly was aware of the pressures mounting in the European bureaucracy to develop some audiovisual policy. Only shortly after his appointment as minister of culture, a dispute over the pricing of books in France spilled out into European jurisprudence. In response to the practice by several large French retailers of selling all books below the recommended retail price, Lang successfully proposed a law in 1981 declaring a single price for books, prohibiting any discounts more than 5 percent. One large retailer, FNAC, responded ultimately by contesting the law in the European Court of Justice (ECJ), claiming that the French law violated the Treaty of Rome's protections for free competition. The European Court of Justice sided with the French government, holding that other member countries regulated their own book pricing, and the law did not violate provisions of the treaty. However, the court did not retain the French argument, articulated by Lang during the Senate debate on the proposed law, that "the book was not a product like other products." Only months into his term, Lang laid out, in that claim, the core of what would become the cultural exception: "The book is not a product like other products; it is a creation of the mind, one of the most noble creations of the mind and the imaginary and which, as such, cannot be subjected, without a specific protection, to the law of the market alone."[48] Lang took the position that creative works cannot be left to the whims, and perhaps depredations, of the market. The state must exercise its responsibility to protect those works, and the EEC has no jurisdiction to interfere in member state prerogatives in defending creative work. The ECJ ruled on more narrow terms, leaving this broader claim an open question: "The Court has not upheld the argument presented by the French government which maintained that the legislation in question had as its goal to protect the book as a cultural medium against the negative effects that would ensue for diversity and the cultural level of publishing from a savage competition on retail prices on the one hand, and on maintaining the existence of a network of specialized bookstores faced with the competition of other distribution channels on the other hand."[49] In an interview some years later, Lang recalled the tensions attending that decision, a key backdrop to the long subsequent process led by France to hammer out the Directive on Television Without Frontiers and the European Convention on Transfrontier Television, where the same legal issues were played out in relation to the audiovisual sector.[50]

A film case came up shortly afterward concerning the release history of a big-budget production, *Le Marginal*, with Jean-Paul Belmondo. The film opened in October 1983, just as the market for videocassettes was forming. France had already fixed the chronology of media, stipulating that the video release had to wait one year after the theatrical premiere. The reasoning was clear enough: protection of revenues earned in theaters. After the VHS copy was released on January 15, 1984, fewer than three months after its theatrical opening, theaters sued and the cassettes were seized.[51] Belmondo countersued for restriction of free trade. The French courts refused to hear the case, so Belmondo sought relief at the European Court of Justice. A decision in favor of Belmondo would have disrupted the whole French system of the chronology of media and, more significantly, signaled the denial of the right of individual countries to set their own audiovisual policies. The court ultimately supported the French position, and more importantly, specifically recognized that culture is not a good like other goods and that images belonged to the sphere of culture, which was not covered by the Treaty of Rome. France's right to determine its own audiovisual policies prevailed in this instance, but the case illustrated the potential juridical disputes that could threaten the regulations formulated in individual countries.

Commentators differ on what prompted pressures to develop European audiovisual policies, but the release of a three-hundred-plus-page green paper by the European Commission in the middle of 1984 firmly placed the issue on the agenda.[52] Both a study document and a set of recommendations, it approached the issues at length, including Technical Aspects, Cultural and Social Aspects, Economic Aspects, Legal Aspects, and Freedom to Provide Services. Richard Collins characterized its bureaucratic beginning as a proposal representing the position of the "ultra-liberals" in the General Directorate (DG) III (Internal Market and Industrial Policy).[53] Various DGs would contribute to EC documents, and Collins describes the process of the TWF directive as a battle between dirigistes and ultra-liberals.[54] More tendentiously, Jean-François Polo quotes one French professional's view that the members of DG III were "Ayatollahs of the market."[55] Attempting to determine the status of cultural activity in relation to the Treaty of Rome, the paper's authors argued, "Contrary to what is widely imagined, the EEC Treaty applies not only to economic activities but as a rule also to all activities carried out for remuneration, regardless of whether they take place in the economic, social, cultural (including in particular information, creative or artistic activities and entertainment) sporting or any other sphere."[56] This capacious view of the Treaty of Rome effectively treated cultural production as an economic activity once remuneration was involved, which would cover any product or service that had a price attached to it, whether a music recording, a seat at a play, or a movie theater ticket. Written in collaboration with large advertising interests, the green paper included limits to advertising on television considerably above current rates, setting a cap of 20 percent, when most rates at the time did not exceed 15 percent.[57]

THE TELEVISION WITHOUT FRONTIERS DIRECTIVE

The policy pendulum swung in the opposite direction with the release of a twenty-page draft directive only two years later, in 1986.[58] Apparently, the dirigistes in DG X (Culture, Information, Communication), outflanked by the ultra-liberals of DG III in the development of the green paper, had managed to take charge in writing the draft directive. Unlike the green paper, which mentioned quotas only once as a measure to be avoided, the draft directive included a specific article (Article 2) requiring minimum quotas for "broadcasts of Community works":

> 1. Member States shall ensure that internal broadcasters of television reserve at least 30% of their programming time not consisting of news, sporting events and game shows, advertising or teletext services for broadcasts of Community works within the meaning of Article 4, of which in the case of initial transmissions at least one third shall be reserved for first broadcasts in the Community.
>
> 2. This percentage shall be progressively increased to reach at least 60% after the expiry of three years from the date specified in Article 22.[59]

As might be expected in these first attempts to articulate a European policy on broadcasting, the language was open to a wide difference of interpretation. There was no definition of what constituted a European work or any indication of when such works would have to be shown; a country might decide to screen European films late at night to meet the quota but fill prime time with imported fare. Nor did the draft directive indicate whether co-productions qualified as European.

In fact, quotas could cut two ways. To fill the quota, a country would have to either produce local programming or seek works from other European countries, an obvious benefit to producers. At the same time, television companies, whether state-owned or not, would have to spend considerably more to finance national production, so purchasing U.S. productions at lower cost made more financial sense for them. Quota proponents feared this latter threat, for U.S. television programs could always compete with European production at a lower cost to European television, a practice that many characterized as "dumping," a proscribed trade practice because prices were set below the cost of the products in their initial market.[60] If the prices in the first market were based on covering the real costs of production, lowering the cost elsewhere would automatically confer an unfair advantage on the seller, thereby harming national industries, which would be selling their productions at prices reflecting their real initial costs.

But quotas introduced a more knotty legal problem. Requiring a minimum percentage of European works on television screens (*not* theater screens) would normally be considered a clear restraint of trade, thus contrary to the liberal precepts of the Treaty of Rome. Quotas violate the national treatment and most favored nation principles of international free trade, for by definition they discriminate against some countries, in this case, non-European countries, which clearly meant the United States, as its programs or films were the only ones threatening to compete with European works. Articles and speeches regularly identified U.S. productions as the principal danger.[61] Disagreement over quotas continued to roil the waters. Great Britain, a staunch opponent of quotas, supported by West Germany and others, submitted an alternative proposal, a convention on transfrontier broadcasting, to the Council of Europe late in 1986 to head off the draft directive.[62]

In addition to the provision on quotas, the draft directive also specified time delays between the theatrical release of films and their subsequent programming on television. These requirements followed the chronology of media rules already in place in France. Fortunately for the French, the European Court of Justice had already ruled in the case of *Le Marginal*, upholding the requirement of a delay of one year between theatrical release and video release. The directive set the delay at three years for television screening, the same period mandated in the 1986 French law for most stations. Television stations in France must negotiate a *cahiers des charges*, or set of obligations with the state agency with authority over television.[63]

This system reflects a traditional tension found in the exhibition sector. Once the Hollywood studio system consolidated its vertical integration during the 1920s, release patterns were carefully designed to exploit the oligopolistic power conferred by vertical integration. At a time when theatrical exhibition was the only revenue window for films, the major studios instituted practices known as run, clearance, and zoning. Run referred to the order of release to theaters: first-run theaters, second-run theaters, and so forth. Clearance was the time delay between each run. Zoning established the geographical placement of theaters according to their run, normally calibrated to maximize the potential receipts of a given area. Latter run theaters would be those in smaller, less wealthy areas.

One U.S. scholar, Mae Huettig, demonstrated in the 1940s how these practices concentrated theater receipts in the first-run and affiliated theaters, and why. Vertical integration entails ownership of all industrial factors, from production through distribution to sale. In the U.S. film industry at the time, the studios owned the major production facilities, distributed the films through studio-owned distributors, and showed the films in studio-owned or affiliated theaters. Huettig showed that the studios actually owned relatively few theaters, but they were predominantly first-run theaters.[64] Because the studios controlled the run, clearance, and zoning, they were able to set high prices at their first-run theaters and then enforce long delays in clearance. Most of the subsequent run theaters were independently owned and had little bargaining power in negotiating with the studio-owned distributors, leading to the abuses of power detailed in the antitrust suits: block booking, blind bidding, price-setting, and so on. So even though they owned only less than 20 percent of all theaters, studios earned almost 50 percent of all theatrical receipts, a direct result of the distortion of competition consequent to the studio control over run, clearance, and zoning.[65] While these terms were well known in the industry, it was not until the Justice Department sued the studios for antitrust violations in 1938 that the restraint-of-trade implications became clear. Once the studios were forced to share some of their financial data, other scholars were able to demonstrate how the system squeezed oligopolistic profits for the majors.[66]

The chronology of media developed in the 1980s reproduced the dynamics of the run-clearance-zoning tensions. Theater owners, now the first-run exhibition, seek a long clearance between theatrical release and subsequent releases. Those later runs are now DVD as second run and television as third run. Early run operators want long clearances; later run operators press for shorter clearances. During the studio system, the majors could dictate the terms of trade by virtue of their oligopolistic power. The court's consent decrees forced the studios to divest their ownership of theaters, ostensibly restoring some power to the theaters, though with mixed results, as theatrical attendance fell steadily in the years following the consent decrees.[67] Once again, this time at the European level, regulatory authorities intervened in these industrial affairs to try to balance competing interests.

The "clearance" of three years stipulated in the Directive on Television Without Frontiers evidently favored theater owners, arguably the most powerful sector of the European film industry. Thus, one can fairly conclude that the final form of the directive conformed to the preferences of the powerful film lobby, which makes sense, in that film was a mature industry whereas European television, still largely state-owned, was yet to experience the accelerated growth unleashed by privatization during the 1980s. The multiple organizations of the film lobby were the prime private movers outside the EEC and the Council of Europe as the two documents worked their way through the debate and approval process.

The appointment of the conservative Jacques Chirac as prime minister in 1986 accelerated television privatization in France. In the same year, the government privatized the largest public station, TF1, which had a market share of 40 percent.[68] This move was followed quickly by the attempt to form a new station, La Cinq. When one of the new private stations failed, Italy's Silvio Berlusconi emerged as a prospective new owner. Troubled by this development, a Communist senator from the working-class Paris suburb of Aubervilliers and an active expert on audiovisual matters, put together a new organization in 1987: the États généraux de la culture, formed in reaction to the "monetarization of culture."[69] The movement held a series of meetings, building to a November 17, 1987, event that drew six thousand people and three hundred artists, and produced a "Declaration of Cultural Rights," which announced that "a people which abandons its imaginary to financial speculation condemns itself to precarious lilberty."[70]

Following comments from the European Parliament, the EC revised the draft directive in April 1988. While the broad outlines of the directive remained intact, significant changes in details indicated a strengthening of dirigiste preferences. On the crucial provision on quotas, the EC removed the reference to an initial minimum of 30 percent: "Member States shall ensure that television broadcasters and cable operators retransmitting television broadcasts reserve at least 60 percent of their programming time not consisting of news, sporting events, game shows, advertising or teletext services for Community works of which at least one-third shall be reserved for first broadcasts in the Community. This percentage shall be achieved gradually on the basis of appropriate criteria within a period of three years from the date specified in Article 22."[71] Another change reduced the original generous space allotted to advertising from 20 percent of broadcast time, to 18 percent per hour. And one new introductory paragraph elaborated on the attempts to encourage European production: "Whereas in addition to this Directive other Community measures to promote the international competitiveness of European cinema and television production are needed, in view of the strength of the non-European media industry, not only in order to achieve the economic objectives of the Community but also to counteract any loss of linguistic and cultural identity."[72] By referring to "the strength of the non-European media industry," the draft implicitly acknowledged that the EC was responding to the threat of the U.S. audiovisual industry.[73]

With backing from the head of DG X, film professionals, led by the French, had succeeded in having 1988 declared "The Year of Cinema and Television" by the Council of Europe.[74] In September 1988, artists and producers met in Delphi to discuss the theme of the "Role and Importance of the Cinema Work." The gathering adopted an "Audiovisual Charter," noting "the cultural crisis caused by the threat of American hegemony." They implored the EC to do everything possible to resist "the invasion of the logic of commerce." Six thousand members of the Federation of European Filmmakers signed the charter.[75] Nevertheless, the French accepted a "Stockholm compromise" for the Convention on Transfrontier Television in November, ceding on mandatory quotas.[76]

Differences continued to delay agreement on the TWF directive. On February 26, 1989, the Council of Ministers of the Internal Market was unable to reach consensus, and put off debate until March 13, following a request from the EEC to hold off on final approval. On March 15, the Council of Ministers adopted a text with the same language on quotas as the convention, specifying that television stations require "a majority proportion of their broadcast time" for European works, dropping the earlier specified 60 percent figure, provoking outrage among professionals. On April 3, 1989, after the passage of the convention but before approval of the directive, five hundred "personalities from the artistic and cultural world," including Robert Bresson, Jean-Luc Godard, Joris Ivens, Claude Lanzmann, Claude Lelouch, Louis Malle, Claude Moulet, Luc Moulet, Jean Rouch, and Bertrand Tavernier signed an open letter to the president of the republic urging that France uphold its support for the 60 percent quotas for European works on television, "without which it would abdicate again and would be renouncing definitively all cultural ambition for Europe."[77]

On May 23, 1989, members of the États généraux, allied with another new group, the Action Committee for the Europe of Film and Television, boarded a train—"a train named culture"—to Strasbourg to demonstrate at the European Parliament on the eve of its vote, the last step in the approval process of the Directive on Television Without Frontiers, in favor of restoring obligatory quotas.[78] Though film was barely mentioned in the final version of the documents, the film lobby had managed with the quotas to secure real, if limited, gains in its growing competition with commercial television. The next day, May 24, a letter from U.S. trade representative Carla Hills to the head of the European Parliament was made public. In the letter, sent the previous week, Hills warned against including quotas in the directive, decrying them as contrary to free trade and potentially damaging to relations between the United States and the EEC. Hills went so far as to threaten recourse to GATT litigation under Article 301, which could lead to retaliatory measures by the United States.[79] While the parliament recommended strengthening the quota requirement, among other revisions, the head of the General Affairs Committee, Jean Dondelinger, rejected the idea, claiming that too many countries were opposed to quotas and a revised document did not have the needed votes.[80]

The directive still lacked final approval. According to one source, the French, with Jacques Delors as president of the European Commission (since 1985), requested a postponement of the vote by parliament until the beginning of October, hoping that the European Assises, scheduled for the end of September in Paris, would provide an opportunity to calm the waters.[81] The Assises européennes de l'audiovisuel, then, proved to be the last round in the long bout leading to the approval of the final version of the directive. Once again the energy of the French, especially the representatives of the French film industry, was behind this first European meeting, sponsored jointly by the European Commission and the French Ministry of Foreign Affairs. In the event, the Assises did not weigh in polemically on the two European documents. In his address on the first day, Mitterrand referred to the danger posed by U.S. imports, but not to attack those products, only to emphasize the importance of raising European production. At a time when the applicable treaty did not speak of culture, Mitterrand observed, "It is . . . through the audiovisual that we can approach today the problem of European cultural identity. Here is the starting point for our consideration."[82] For Mitterrand, culture represented "the very cement" of European construction.[83] Other speakers presented reports on various working groups, sketching out the European audiovisual terrain, occasionally referring to the convention and the directive. In fact, it was the resolutely mild-mannered EC president Jacques Delors who delivered the most defiant words during the proceedings:

> Culture is not a piece of merchandise like others. . . . We cannot treat culture as we treat Frigidaires or even cars. Laissez-faire, the market, they are not sufficient. Thus, one can say without hypocrisy: no protectionism and no laissez-faire.
>
> To our American friends, who just several days before these Assises have brought action through GATT . . . against four countries that have adhered to the Convention of the Council of Europe, I would like to pose simply one question: Do we have the right to exist? Have we the right to perpetuate our traditions, our patrimony, our languages?[84]

The following day, the Council of Ministers passed the TWF directive, still with quotas but now diluted by unenforceable conditions:

> 1. Member States shall ensure *where practicable and by appropriate means*, that broadcasters reserve for European works, within the meaning of Article 6, a majority proportion of their transmission time, excluding the time appointed to news, sports events, games, advertising and teletext services. This proportion, having regard to the broadcaster's informational, educational, cultural and entertainment responsibilities to its viewing public, should be achieved progressively, on the basis of suitable criteria.
>
> 2. Where the proportion laid down in paragraph 1 cannot be attained, it must not be lower than the average for 1988 in the Member State concerned.[85]

Following the detailed account by Collins of European audiovisual policy during the 1980s, the various documents included contrasting conceptual differences. The Treaty of Rome stated that "closer unity" was one of its goals, and the EC, with support from the dirigistes, included that idea as one of its premises. But while unity itself might be difficult to define, some countries feared that a commitment to unity in the audiovisual sphere might lead to dominance by the largest linguistic group in the EEC, the Anglophones. Hence, according to Collins, France and others shifted the emphasis to the arguably oxymoronic "unity in diversity," with a new tilt toward diversity, which would protect the industries of the other linguistic communities.[86] Collins concludes that the two documents did little to advance a European audiovisual policy, thanks to irreconcilable policy differences among the various member states.[87] The quota issues reflect a basic ambivalence. The liberals had prevented mandatory quotas, even adding a signing opinion averring that the clause had political meaning but no juridical meaning.[88] The dirigistes ensured that the quotas were retained even though watered down by the qualification "where practicable and by appropriate means."

In addition, the debates inevitably raised questions about culture, for the arguments were often couched in terms of "European culture." But as was well known, the Treaty of Rome, an economic document, did not mention the word "culture," dealing exclusively with economic questions regulating the flow of goods. The insertion of culture, especially the notion of "European culture," into official EEC discussions stood in marked contrast to the repudiation of "European film" in various fora just a few years earlier. In his keynote address at the "Cinema and State" symposium at Strasbourg in 1978, sponsored by the Council of Europe, Joop Voogd had rejected emphatically such a possibility: "As I see it, it is only with a European policy that we can rebuild our national cinemas in the face of U.S. competition. But I want everyone to understand clearly: it's a question of reinforcing the organization of cinema in Europe by respecting national cultural identities. But *we must exclude categorically any idea of a European film.* A cinema policy at the European level can be effective only if there exists an effective policy in each of the countries concerned."[89] At an International Symposium on Culture in Venice in 1982, Lang called for cooperation between the film and television industries to hold off the U.S. invasion and to affirm the identities of each of the countries, though he also referred to *European identity.*[90] Collins cited Jean Cluzel's assertion that "in the cultural domain, Europe is a delusion."[91]

However volatile the veering of positions on a European policy may have been during these years, there should be little cause for surprise. After years of inaction, it is perfectly understandable that divergent interests, first within the individual member countries and then within the often warring General Directorates (especially DG III and DG X) of the EC, would seek to impose their positions. If the redoubtable bureaucracy of the EEC failed to reach effective consensus during the 1980s, the parties at least succeeded in making their positions known, as the cascade of documents from that decade attests. By decade's end, the European Communities, both the EEC and the Council of Europe, had agreed on two compromise documents, reflecting a broad and at times contradictory range of views on the way forward. The 1992 Treaty on European Union (the Maastricht Treaty) forging a tighter Europe was on the horizon, following passage of the Single European Act in 1986. That act, with little practical import of its own, announced the imminence of an expanded Europe, which the Maastricht Treaty formalized with the establishment of the European Union seven years later. Despite the unresolved tensions over audiovisual policy and many other issues that still separated member countries, those discussions actually provided an essential preparation for a far more consequential battle, when Europe would have to negotiate with one voice in the historic GATT confrontation in 1993.

4

GATT

The decade of debates that led to the passage of the Convention on Transfrontier Television and the Directive on Television Without Frontiers provides the backdrop to the even more consequential drama that attended the completion of the General Agreement on Trade and Tariffs (GATT) negotiations at the end of 1993. During that decade, Europe went through unprecedented political, economic, and technological changes. The Single European Act in 1986 prefigured the transformation of the EEC into the European Union (EU) in 1992. Neoliberalism came to Europe as the state receded in favor of deregulation. State-owned monopolies of television ended in all countries, and private investment poured into the audiovisual industry for the first time. Movie theater attendance plummeted, and videotape, followed by DVDs, became the most popular window for cinema viewing.

Faced with these rapid changes, the European countries tried to adapt their national audiovisual policies, just as the European Commission and the Council of Europe were asserting their voices in the same matters. Those institutions sought to remove trade barriers between countries, and satellite television forced the institutions to confront the challenges of such technologies leaping ahead of appropriate legislation. For the first time, countries had to worry about the compatibility of their national support systems for cinema with the newly energized regulatory centers under the concentrated scrutiny of the EEC.

Given the differences among countries, the decisions and agreements worked out at the supranational level were necessarily compromises. Some countries opposed quotas for audiovisual works, others mandated them in national directives. France required 60 percent quotas of European works on television, 40 percent for French works. Great Britain wanted no quotas. In the end, the Directive on Television Without Frontiers set quotas of "a majority of all works," or 50 percent, with the toothless condition "whenever practicable," effectively removing any recourse to enforcement. The Council of Europe established Eurimages to support European production but voted funds for it that many considered inadequate.

Nonetheless, the compromises had required extensive discussion of the relevant issues. France typically spearheaded the dirigiste initiatives, pressuring other countries to support its positions, mobilizing the cinema professionals—actors, directors, producers—to organize and demonstrate their unity behind these measures, including quotas and state aids. If the French positions did not necessarily prevail, they placed both their technical and principled concerns on the table, drawing others to the discussions. As all countries had cinema and television industries, all had an interest in the policies being debated. While only three countries began the decade with ministers of culture, most countries had created Ministries of Culture by 1990.

The countries may have differed in their approaches, but most faced the same set of problems plaguing their film industries. By the early 1990s,

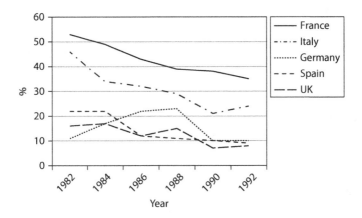

FIGURE 4.1 National film industries' domestic market shares in EU5 countries, 1982–1992

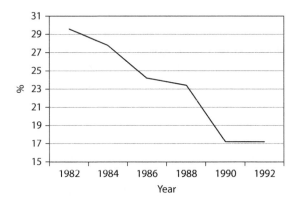

FIGURE 4.2 Overall market share for national film industries across EU5 countries, 1982–1992

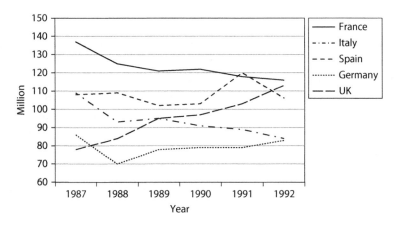

FIGURE 4.3 Cinema attendance in EU5 countries, 1987–1992

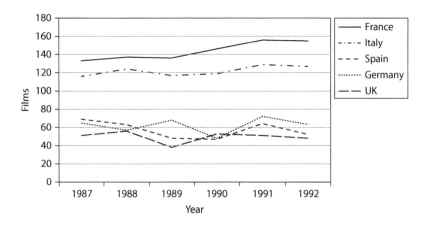

FIGURE 4.4 Number of feature films produced in EU5 countries, 1987–1992

production had inched up slightly, attendance had declined, the cost of films had risen, exports were down, and, above all, all countries had suffered a loss of market share to the same competitor: the United States (see figures 4.1–4.4). France may have spoken loudest in defense of its film industry during the 1980s, and taken the most aggressive measures to support it, with quotas, fiscal policies, state aids, banking policy, and more, but no country wanted to see its film industry simply disappear. Whatever the differences, then, that had surfaced during the 1980s, the full airing of disagreements during those years actually benefited Europe in the next major battle, over GATT, which played out on the international level, this time with one well-defined antagonist: the United States.

BACKGROUND

After World War II, the Allies opened discussions to liberalize international trade. Developed countries wanted to reduce tensions that might arise between nations over trade disputes. Those talks resulted in the passage of the General Agreement on Trade and Tariffs, in 1947. This first agreement articulated basic rules of a world trading system, which would be refined periodically in a series of multiyear "rounds" of negotiations. The three fundamental principles inscribed in GATT were all based on nondiscrimination. The GATT agreements dealt with goods only, operating under several well-defined principles of international trade. The consistent thrust of GATT was to remove barriers to trade through the application of three fundamental principles: most favored nation (MFN) status, national treatment (NT), and market access. According to the MFN principle, countries could not offer preferential trade privileges to one nation and not to others. The United States could not reduce import duties for Chinese goods if it did not offer the same advantage to all other countries. NT meant that counties could not grant advantages to their national industries that were not also available to foreign industries. Subsidies for U.S. car manufacturers could not be provided if they were not also provided to foreign industries. Market access meant that countries agreed to increase access to domestic markets over time and would not reduce access below current limits. In all three cases, the object was to prohibit discrimination among countries in international trade.

These principles rest on the classical economic premise of comparative advantage.[1] According to that concept, different countries have different economic strengths and resources. The most efficient use of resources would entail each country concentrating on its strengths, for export prices for goods would be lowest from countries that could produce those goods most efficiently. Conversely, countries would not waste resources producing goods that were more costly on the international market. If all countries designed their production policies according to this principle, net international production efficiency would be maximized and waste of resources would be minimized. Subsidies to domestic industries distort international trade, for subsidies reduce the cost of production and allow export at lower prices, below real cost, than unaided production would permit. U.S. agricultural subsidies enable domestic producers to export at prices below their real cost, for example. Such subsidies only waste domestic resources that should be devoted to industries capable of selling goods at real costs that are competitive in the international market.[2]

One classical exception to this reasoning is the example of the "infant industry." If the cost of extracting and producing fossil fuels rises as the natural resource becomes more scarce—and the external diseconomies of pollution also increase, which should be included in the cost to society—alternate fuel sources might result in a net cost saving for the country. In that case, high startup costs for alternative fuels might be covered by government subsidies until the new industry can reach maturity and reverse the cost pressures on fuel production. In this case, subsidies would represent a country's investment in a new industry in the hopes that costs would fall once more efficient production of fuel could be established. In his research for the European Parliament, Jacques Barzanti used exactly this argument to justify government support for national film and television industries when he spoke of television as an "emergent industry."[3]

In the real world, of course, economics inevitably must contend with political considerations. Subsidies may prop up inefficient industries, but they will also reduce unemployment. In economic terms, subsidies abet inefficiency, for companies are being paid to produce inefficiently. Efficiency would be served by directing workers to more efficient industries, thereby reducing the net costs of all goods. Countries face all kinds of special cases in favor of inefficiency. Most countries would prefer to produce their own military goods for reasons of national security. No country wants to be dependent on foreign suppliers for national defense.

The same considerations might apply to other goods deemed vital to national security, such as energy. Articles XX and XXI in GATT explicitly recognize such exceptions, the latter granted to protect "security interests."[4]

One services industry, and one services industry only, received special attention in GATT.[5] Article IV conferred a special status on the film industry. While GATT generally did not countenance quotas, this article permitted minimum screen quotas for "cinematograph films."[6] France was one of the countries that insisted on the inclusion of Article IV, an early indication of the importance France attached to cinema.[7] Though this provision was written into GATT at a time when the European film industries were still recovering from the war, all subsequent rounds left this clause intact, and it remains in force.[8]

The debate over the Television Without Frontiers directive had revolved around a similar quota to be applied to television screens, not film theater screens. By the late 1980s, however, far more people watched films on the small screen, a disproportion that only increased with the spread of videotape.[9] While television barely existed in most countries during the years leading up to the 1947 GATT agreement, for somewhat technical reasons none of the subsequent GATT rounds added television to the agreement.[10] In 1986, however, a new set of GATT negotiations began in Uruguay. The Uruguay Round was fundamentally different from and more ambitious than all previous rounds. The GATT regime was scheduled to end with the conclusion of the Uruguay Round, ushering in the new World Trade Organization. And the Uruguay talks would for the first time reach an agreement on trade in services, the General Agreement on Trade in Services (GATS). If there had been persistent ambiguity about the status of film and television in earlier GATT agreements, in principle the audiovisual industry would have to be covered in some way by the new combination of GATT and GATS.

The U.S. protest and threat over TWF in 1989 accurately foreshadowed the outline of the future disagreement over quotas in the 1993 GATT talks, though it is unclear how seriously the United States took the directive at the time. U.S. negotiator Carla Hills had warned that the commercial harm would be "disastrous" for Hollywood, but the EEC ignored U.S. threats.[11] Though it is true that the audiovisual sector, reputed to be the second largest exporting industry in the United States, was small in relation to industries like agriculture, health care, and telecommunications, the real weight of the audiovisual sector resided in its link to culture and, perhaps more controversially, national identity.

Culture may be a notoriously difficult concept to define, but many countries view national cultural production as expressions of national identity. Some countries, especially countries with rich film traditions, which would encompass all the major European countries, did not want to see their film industries interred under the weight of U.S. imports. For whatever reasons, France appeared to care more deeply about the health of its film industry, and constructed the most elaborate support system for its film industry. Even in the industry's darkest hours, which came between the beginning of the debate on the TWF directive in 1986 and the conclusion of the GATT agreement in 1993, the French film industry out-performed all other European film industries. The European Commission president Jacques Delors's exasperated question on the eve of the passage of the TWF directive—"Have we the right to exist?"—conveys some of the urgency attached to the defense of culture.

The discourse of national identity can also elicit racist practices of exclusion. France, like other countries, has a colonialist history, a domination of other countries and cultures carried out under the banner of a *mission civilatrice*, not only imposing by force French power but also imputing some unitary meaning to a French culture. With decolonialization after World War II, and correlative demographic changes in many European countries, France was faced with the challenge of integrating former colonial subjects into metropolitan France, which led to racist backlash by groups and political parties defending exclusionary constructions of French identity. Does a defense of these anachronistic and chauvinist notions of French culture undergird modern pleas for a defense of "French culture" in international trades disputes? No doubt such dangers always lurk in invocations of cultural identity, and France cannot claim either absolution or immunity, nor for that matter can other former colonial powers, but, no doubt for better and worse, France for many years, certainly since the French Enlightenment and the French Revolution in the eighteenth century, has tried to lay claim to represent universal values.[12] Those hubristic aspirations may ring hollow today, but the French film industry can evidence demonstrable support for, and from, filmmakers from many cultures, to a degree far more extensive than any other country. As France has mounted a cultural defense of cinema, many foreign filmmakers, whether financed by France or not, have joined French campaigns in favor of film, not just French film. Whatever merit there may be to charges of paternalism in the funding of foreign filmmakers, at least those filmmakers were able to direct films, and many of them threw their support behind French efforts to carve out a productive space for filmmaking outside of Hollywood.[13]

URUGUAY ROUND

The last round of GATT talks convened in 1986, in Montevideo, and was known as the Uruguay Round. Negotiations were to conclude with an agreement not only on goods but also, for the first time, on the rapidly growing area of services, and the United States made known its interest in extending the reach of GATT to include film and television, known more commonly in Europe as the audiovisual sector. Whether cinema was a good or service had remained unclear during the previous rounds, and television had been able to dodge the reach of GATT partially because the European Court of Justice had determined in the 1974 Sacchi case that it was a service.[14] With the addition of GATS, both goods and services would be covered by the agreements, which would all be folded into the new World Trade Organization in 1995.[15]

The contretemps over TWF effectively served as a prelude to the even more contentious GATT/GATS set-to, and France would again play a seminal role. Though the TWF negotiations took place exclusively within the EEC, the U.S. audiovisual industry loomed as the obvious, if nonparticipant, antagonist, for U.S. films were steadily gathering increased market shares throughout Europe and U.S. programming threatened to make similar inroads in the newly privatized and increasingly lucrative television market. While the United States did not take part in the TWF deliberations, the U.S. trade representative, as noted, expressed displeasure over the final directive, even with the watered-down wording ("where practicable") that rendered the quotas voluntary.[16] And the major Hollywood companies certainly weighed in. Jack Valenti, reputed to be the highest paid lobbyist in the United States, represented the Motion Picture Association of America (MPAA), the trade association of the major Hollywood studios. The irrepressible and garrulous Valenti was a relentless promoter of Hollywood's interests and an ardent believer in capitalism and free trade, as his own uncharacteristically subdued remarks on the day of the passage of the TWF directive made clear: "The European Community

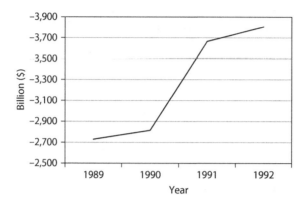

FIGURE 4.5 EU audiovisual deficit with United States in U.S. dollars, 1989–1992

today, in my judgment, took a step backward in time. They said no to competition and viewers' choice, and yes to trade barriers."[17]

The audiovisual trade deficit between the United States and the EEC countries climbed steadily after the TWF directive was passed in 1989, so in fact the damage harmed Europe, not the United States (see figure 4.5). The long GATT talks proceeded in the years leading up to 1993, but the cinema dispute did not break out until 1993.[18] Following his election in 1992, President Bill Clinton asked Congress for "fast-track authority" to conclude the negotiations, which set a firm deadline of December 15, 1993, for completion of the Uruguay Round. And he appointed a new U.S. trade representative, Mickey Kantor, who had close ties to Hollywood, as did the Democratic Party.

The 1992 Maastricht treaty, which formed the European Union out of the European Economic Community, had broached the question of culture for the first time in the history of the EEC. The cross-border reach of satellite television and other factors accelerated the need to formulate language that would clarify the role and status of culture in the new EU. If the term "culture" did not figure in official EEC documents before 1992, culture was clearly implicated in the debates around the TWF and the Convention on Transfrontier Television. Neither the compromise on the TWF directive nor the new culture clauses included in the Maastricht treaty resolved the many tensions that had surfaced during the 1980s, but at least there was now official language that the

European Commission and the member countries could begin to interpret and implement. In a sense, then, culture hovered as an undefined term in the discourse attending European unification during the 1980s, so its eventual appearance in the Maastricht Treaty in 1992 had been preceded by ample discussion, and served as the legal reference point for European jurisprudence after 1992.

In contrast, the question of culture had not occupied any role in previous GATT rounds, all committed to reducing trade barriers to goods to raise world efficiency according to the concept of comparative advantage. Culture, of course, cannot be evaluated exclusively in terms of efficiency. Many argue that cultural production itself is a positive externality for society, even if its production may be inefficient. In the context of GATT, the value of cultural production might be acknowledged, but why should culture have any particular national provenance? Nevertheless, many countries defended the importance of cultural production as an essential aspect of national identity. In the TWF debates, various commentators had insisted that culture was deeply implicated in national identity and that imported culture threatened those national identities. Conscious of the corollary dangers of an exclusionary definition of national identity, many of those same speakers, including President Mitterrand, were quick to advocate for a diversity of cultures, open to multiple influences, domestic and foreign. Tensions arise when countries see their autonomy to set their own policies as under siege, and that is what happened in the final stages of the 1993 GATT agreement.

While the EEC debates over television during the 1980s helped the EU as it approached the GATT negotiations, the United States had had its own preliminary discussion, in a confrontation with Canada over cultural policies. During efforts to work out a bilateral trade agreement in the late 1980s, Canada had objected to the application of strict free trade principles to cultural production in a proposed free trade agreement. The United States ultimately agreed to an article excluding the audiovisual sector from the Canada–United States Free Trade Agreement (CUSFTA) in December 1988, but the article also specified that either party reserved the right under GATT's dispute settlement provision to take retaliatory measures to compensate for claimed incurred losses.[19] The CUSFTA offered one precedent: simple exclusion of the cultural sector. But the United States had contested that exclusion, and the stakes were far lower than with GATT. In addition, the exclusion clause included the right of either party to seek damages for losses caused by discriminatory domestic policies, thereby building in a mechanism for challenging exclusion. The United States already dominated the culture industries of Canada, and their market, though an affluent one, held only about thirty million people, but that massive commercial advantage did not prevent the United States from bringing legal action against Canada.[20] With four hundred million people in the largest foreign audiovisual market for Hollywood, Europe was a far more lucrative target, and the United States had already signaled that it would not accept such a solution in GATT.

In the GATT talks, the EU adopted a similar position to that of Canada, now known as the "cultural exception." The precise origin, if not the meaning, of the term remains murky, but the closing remarks of Jacques Delors at the Assises européennes de l'audiovisuel in 1989 (see chapter 3) convey the essence of its meaning: "Culture is not a piece of merchandise like any other and must not be treated as such."[21] Delors did not use the expression "cultural exception," and the phrase does not appear in *Le Monde* until March 1993.[22] In the intervening years, however, there was considerable institutional activity circulating around the future of the audiovisual sector. European countries still had to ratify the TWF directive, which was not scheduled to take effect until January 1, 1993. The Single European Act had been passed in 1986, as prelude to the drafting of the Maastricht Treaty. Canadian press coverage of CUSFTA did use the expression "cultural exception" on rare occasions in 1991, years after the agreement, but only when the phrase was adopted as a rhetorical position in trade discussions in 1993 did it acquire its defiant resonance.

In a sense, then, though the United States had expressed its dissatisfaction with the inclusion of quotas in TWF and the Convention on Transfrontier Television, the audiovisual question remained in the background before 1993, even if the outlines of the later disagreement were easy enough to anticipate.[23] The United States wanted to see significant progress on trade liberalization following the fundamental principles of GATT since the first agreement of 1947: most favored nation status, national treatment, and market access. It viewed any protectionist measures for the audiovisual sector to be antithetical to the regime of GATT and argued for their elimination.

Despite the internal divisions among European countries over such protections, the EEC and the Council on Europe had succeeded in passing the first two documents regulating the audiovisual sector, though the language of the final versions reflected those divisions, especially the dilution of the television quotas. However, the documents established only minimum guidelines for quotas and lacked any enforcement mechanism, unlike GATT, which contained a formal dispute procedure. As part of its efforts to include compulsory quotas in the TWF directive, France had instituted in 1986 a quota requirement for television broadcasts within France, which was perfectly legitimate under EEC law, but under the final directive (and convention), other countries were under no constraint to adhere to the minimal recommendations of a majority of European works.[24] In the words of one commentator, a partisan in favor of protecting European audiovisual space, "This interpenetration of logics of liberalization, conforming to the basic principles of Community construction, and the logics that it is not pejorative to call protectionist, explains the largely equivocal nature of the dispositions ultimately included in the text of the Directive."[25]

Only a year before the Uruguay Round was scheduled to conclude, Europe, in its new guise as the European Union, had included culture in its legal apparatus. It is true that the Maastricht Treaty had no jurisprudential precedent to indicate the practical import of this innovation, but the United States still had to contend with that changed status of culture in the GATT negotiations. The EU would have one voice in the GATT talks, but the union also functioned with a "subsidiarity principle," which prescribed that the EU could not impose rules when member states were capable of addressing issues at the national level.[26] In other words, member states were free to develop their own policies unless problems required resolution at the EU level. The final version of the directive, allowing individual countries to develop their own positions on quotas, bears witness to the strength of subsidiarity.

The differences that had caused strains during the EEC's consideration of the transformations in the media environment did not evaporate with the formation of the EU in 1992. Once again, the countries had to arrive at a European audiovisual position. The head GATT negotiator for the EU was the Sir Leon Brittan, vice president of the European Commission, a British proponent of free market principles whose views were at odds with those of the French president of the EC, Jacques Delors. Though Great Britain and Germany, and some of the smaller countries like Luxembourg, opposed the confrontational stance of France, in the GATT negotiations they all shared a common antagonist, the United States, as even the European Commission's liberal green paper on broadcasting from 1984 acknowledged, and the documents produced during those debates return time and again to that theme. During the 1980s, countries and interest groups were trying to steer the EC toward their preferred outcomes, when the EC had its own vying seats of power (in the disparate DGs), so there was arguably less common ground on which they could agree. GATT may have covered over one hundred countries, but the United States, Europe, and Japan were the power players. And as Japan took a position similar to that of the United States on the audiovisual front, Europe would be the only formidable adversary to the United States during the Uruguay Round.[27]

While Europe's television industry experienced momentous changes during the 1980s, the U.S. entertainment industry was also evolving rapidly. As with the introduction of television, the sales of VCRs and the marketing of films on videotape revolutionized Hollywood. In the span of one decade, at the beginning of which two studios (Universal and Disney) had taken Japanese hardware companies to court over copyright infringement, videotape revenue overtook theatrical revenue. Even before the resolution of the case, which ruled against Universal and Disney, other studios quickly embraced videotape. The Hollywood majors depended far more on distribution income than on theatrical proceeds, and production facilities were often rented out to independent film companies and to television companies, which had been barred in 1970 from owning their own studios. At the same time, the Reagan administration's policy of deregulation allowed major studios to purchase theaters again, enabling the return of vertical integration, which the Paramount decrees had prohibited in 1948. Yet the once grand Hollywood majors no longer dominated the entertainment industry.

Vast conglomerates, pursuing horizontal synergy, shed many peripheral holdings to concentrate on what one scholar aptly labeled "tight diversification."[28] In the 1960s, conglomerates like Gulf and Western and Kinney Industries had taken over Hollywood studios, to some extent grabbing them to take advantage of the sudden appreciation of the value of their large film libraries, newly valuable for screening on television. As attendance fell in the 1960s and the old films gathering dust in storage vaults suddenly acquired new value, studios became ripe for takeover by the large conglomerates with holdings unrelated to film, and in which the studios were often minority revenue sources.

Scholars differ on determining when this "New Hollywood" actually took shape,[29] but most agree that the strategy of blockbusters introduced in the 1970s was the next innovation that changed the economic profile of the industry.[30] The divestiture of theaters following the Paramount decision effectively dismantled the monopoly system of run-clearance-zoning that had given the studios their financial power (see chapter 3), eventually leading to large theatrical release for films like *Jaws* and *Star Wars*. Studios parlayed the theatrical success of blockbusters with merchandising tie-ins, creating profit machines built on expanding ancillary markets. New windows of videotape and cable television opened up, turning theatrical release into the crucial first window, even if theaters functioned as loss leaders.[31] Theatrical release, accompanied by massive advertising, especially television advertising, would announce the new product, but the ancillary streams would return the real profit. Even though few blockbusters might achieve success, those few more than compensated for the flood of other releases. Thus, the five most successful films in 2005, for example, brought in more revenue than the other 345 films produced in the United States combined.[32]

Ancillary markets—the new windows or the new "runs"—often resided in related entertainment media, such as music and publishing. Hence the corporate transition into "tight diversification" through horizontal integration of those industries. The new, much-touted synergy would reduce costs of rights for music and press advertising. This trend of the 1980s culminated in the formation of Time Warner in 1989, with combined assets of $14 billion. The advantages of horizontal integration led the conglomerates to unload unrelated businesses to concentrate on the "core" business: entertainment. Parent company names changed to reflect this transformation.

With videotape reaching saturation at that time in the United States, and the DVD bonanza not yet taking off, these new companies recognized that foreign markets promised to be the most attractive area for expansion. Though reliable figures appear to be sketchy, foreign revenues accounted for a rising percentage of entertainment sales, and whatever the exact numbers, Hollywood already claimed to be the second-most-successful U.S. exporter, after the aeronautics industry.[33] The combined revenue of foreign film and television exports, for example, stood at $4 billion in 1993, offset minimally by imports of only $346 million, leaving a surplus of over $3.7 billion, with a fivefold increase for film since 1985.[34]

Comparing profit curves, Hollywood could anticipate faster revenue growth from those foreign markets than from the domestic one. And while Japan represented the largest foreign national market, its attendance reached only 126 million in 1992, compared to 558 million in the EU.[35] Hence the importance of prying open Europe's market doors before the conclusion of GATT. By the early 1990s, then, Hollywood had refined its business and industrial strategies, boosting its domestic revenues considerably, and viewed Europe as the most lucrative foreign market for expansion.

Voices from the United States stressed both economic and ideological reasons in their arguments against "protectionism." For the United States, quotas and subsidies were archaic fetters in the new world order of trade liberalization, one of the central virtues of globalization, whence Valenti's plaint that Europe was taking a step backward when it passed the TWF directive. National restrictions only hindered the expansion of trade, rewarding inefficiency. Favoring national companies or discriminating in favor of selected trade partners reduced the net benefits for the world's citizens, the latter more properly seen as customers or clients whose collective interests would best be served by more U.S. films. Capitalism had triumphed in the economic and political aberration known as the Cold War, and capitalism prospered from competition and free trade.

Europe, however, could survey the swath cut by U.S. entertainment products in their domestic markets and understandably questioned the motives behind the U.S. claims. The enormous and growing U.S. trade surplus with Europe easily gave the lie to the commercial advantages likely to accrue to European countries by opening up the markets of their culture industries to even more U.S. products. For the film industry, the Europeans saw their domestic market share of theatrical revenue drop from 30 percent to 16 percent in the decade before the Uruguay Round (1982–1992), while the U.S. share in the top five European markets (France, Germany, Italy, Spain, Great Britain) rose from 70 percent to 83 percent (see figure 4.6). With delayed videotape penetration in Europe, U.S. domination was even greater, and it promised to increase as videotape reached maturity; DVD technology was likely to follow a similar pattern (as in fact it did during the 1990s).

Ideological arguments were murkier territory. Delors had asked in 1989 whether Europeans had the right to their own identities. As far back as 1978, Joop Voogd had expressed the widely shared view that European film as such did not exist, for European films could be only films that bore national identities.

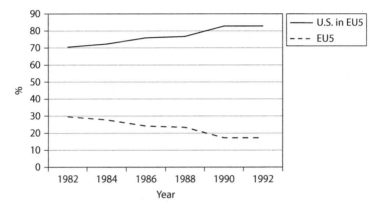

FIGURE 4.6 Market share of US and EU5 films in EU5 countries, 1982–1992

Other commentators during the 1980s observed wryly that the only real European films were U.S. films, for only U.S. films succeeded in crossing borders in Europe. None of the European national film industries succeeded in exporting its films to other European countries. France led its European partners in exports, but the French average market share in other countries was roughly 5 percent, far behind the U.S. share. According to one source, the market share of European national films in nonnational European markets was 7 percent in 1992. Thus, as the U.S. market share in Europe went from 35 percent in 1965 to 79 percent in 1995, European films lost their export market in Europe.[36]

One recurrent complaint among Europeans was the difficulty of producing films with sufficiently large budgets to compete with U.S. films, whose average budgets were ten times larger than European films. Co-productions were thought to offer one way of combating that differential. France had a long history of bilateral co-productions with other countries and pressed during the 1980s for European support for multilateral co-productions.[37] Co-productions offer various advantages, including release in more than one national market and access to the state support mechanisms in the co-producing countries. In 1987 the EEC took its first hesitant steps toward European co-productions when it approved the first MEDIA program.[38] The Council of Europe pursued a similar initiative with Eurimages. But the funding was inadequate to have any significant market impact, and some of their productions were submitted to withering criticism as Europuddings, a derisive term referring to the risible ratatouille of stars and locations trying to pass as "European" films. Nevertheless, co-production has remained popular for European films, with perhaps 25 percent of releases as co-productions as of 2007, and many of those have achieved critical success.[39] The Europuddings may have attracted considerable funding, but most co-productions have budgets similar to those of 100 percent national films, even if they appear to be somewhat more successful in other markets, for they are more likely to be shown at least in the co-producing countries (though that is not always the case, or may be true for only one screening to satisfy the co-production contract). The financial role of programs like Eurimages remains minimal compared to the total funding of European cinema,[40] so in that sense, it's not clear that supra-European programs have changed the nature of European filmmaking in a structural way.[41] Furthermore, despite a variety of funding sources, most co-productions remain fundamentally national.[42]

But those efforts were still nascent at the end of the 1980s, and most countries focused on national—not supranational—identity. Germany shied away from such questions of national identity, given its (still recent) Nazi past, and state cultural support there passed through the regional governments known as Länder. France, of course, took an active interest in French culture. The absence of any reference to culture in the Treaty of Rome reflected the economic emphasis of the early moves toward European unity, but the pressures of globalization during the 1980s pushed culture onto Europe's agenda. The Uruguay Round of GATT aimed to include services in the final agreement, and the privatization of television in Europe forced consideration of cultural questions throughout the EEC deliberations on the directive (and the convention) at the same time. The synchrony of the Single European Act and the beginning of the Uruguay Round in 1986 foreshadowed the inclusion of culture in the 1992 Maastricht treaty and the 1993 GATT agreement.

ENDGAME: THE CULTURAL EXCEPTION

For the most part, the GATT negotiations took place behind closed doors, but in 1993, hostilities erupted in the French press. MPAA head Jack Valenti gave an interview to *Le Monde* in March in Los Angeles implicitly criticizing the European position, saying, "It is our future which is at risk. If we are prevented from trading freely abroad, we are going to suffer. In the same fashion, if the American market is closed, the foreign businessmen will suffer also. Regarding film and television, the American market is completely open. We ask only that each country allow its citizens to see, read or listen to what they want."[43] Valenti claimed that exports of U.S. television shows had fallen, partially because of the quotas specified in the TWF directive, though in fact the U.S. audiovisual surplus had increased to $3.7 billion in 1992, up more than 50 percent from $2.3 billion in 1987. Even more provocatively, Valenti asserted, "The U.S. will not sign an agreement which makes culture an area of exception."[44]

Two weeks later, *Le Monde* published a "dossier" of responses. Taking issue with Valenti's assertion that spectators watched U.S. television programs because they preferred them, Jack Lang explained that "television stations show the programs not because the spectators ask for them, as M. Valenti appears to believe, but because the broadcasters believe they can make money by buying cheaply on the international market a product already amortized [in the U.S. domestic market]."[45] Although Delors had sketched out in 1989 the basic rationale of the objection to treating cultural production like the production of other goods, this was the moment the term "cultural exception" became the key phrase in the public debate. In his contribution, Dominique Wallon, head of the French CNC, accused the United States of "dumping" cheap television programming, a practice considered an unfair practice in international trade, and also contested Valenti's claim that spectators simply preferred U.S. programs.[46] The state had a responsibility to intervene under such circumstances, for as the airwaves "are a scarce public resource, it is normal that the government take an interest in preserving the minimum cultural pluralism that the Directive's 'majority proportion of European works' clause represents." Wallon added, apparently using the term *exception culturelle* for the first time as a negotiating position, that the "cultural exception demanded by the [European] Community (and not only France) in the GATT negotiations consists only in recognizing that the trade in cultural works, which have such a profound influence on the identity of each people, cannot be reduced to trade in goods. The free trade agreement concluded recently between the U.S. and Canada explicitly recognizes this cultural exception."[47]

CUSFTA did exclude audiovisual products, but unlike the final GATT agreement, the exclusion was written explicitly into the CUSFTA accord.

Wallon implied that the EU/EEC had staked out its position in the talks and would be pursuing that stance in the ongoing negotiations. However, the diluted compromise of the directive and convention had not resolved the disagreements among the European nations or the divisions within the EU bureaucracy. And the lack of transparency in the functioning of the EU only exacerbated the problem, for outsiders could not know how the EU was actually handling the knot of complex trade issues, in which the audiovisual sector carried miniscule economic weight. Even twenty years later, no one knows exactly how the agreement was arrived at.

Given this opacity, and perhaps because of film's declining revenue relative to television, the film community waged an increasingly public campaign to defend its interests, and politicians consistently expressed their support. While there was extensive commentary on the GATT audiovisual affair after the final agreement was reached, the arguments that surfaced during the negotiations tended to be more pragmatic than theoretical in the tense final months before the signing.[48] The U.S. claim was the simplest one. It wanted the agreement to prohibit any protectionist measures in European countries. Representing Europe, the EC emitted mixed signals. If the real reason for the U.S. objection to an exception for the audiovisual industries was a financial one, as opposed to a principled stand against a violation of GATT, it was hard to sustain. As one of the principal European negotiators observed shortly after the conclusion of GATT, "The decline of the European audiovisual sector and the success of the U.S. sector are the background for the EU–U.S. battle in the Uruguay Round."[49]

The Europeans considered three different positions. As Wallon suggested in Le Monde, the EU could just insist on a clause excluding the audiovisual industry from the final agreement, as in CUSFTA. Though Wallon described that option as the "cultural exception," a more accurate term would be "cultural exclusion," for one annex of CUSFTA explicitly stated, "Cultural industries are exempt from the provisions of this Agreement."[50] A second alternative would bring the audiovisual industry into GATT under certain conditions, known as the "cultural specificity" option. At a meeting in Mons in early October 1993, the Council of Culture Ministers listed six conditions for this strategy:

1. Exemption from the most favored nation clause.
2. Preserving public aids and subsidies.

3. Maintaining the right to regulate technology and modes of transmission.
4. Preserving the right to aid the audiovisual sector.
5. Refusal to commit to additional trade liberalization of the sector.
6. Maintaining commitment to the TWF directive.[51]

This proposal, which might also be called "cultural inclusion" to better render its relation to GATT, entailed an agreement to have the audiovisual sector come under the new GATT regime but only under those specified conditions. For one supporter of the cultural exception, this attempt to specify conditions in the text of GATT was based on a "dangerous casuistry."[52] At a time of rapid changes in audiovisual media, the danger was that any practices not specified in those six points would be covered by the general principles of GATT, and clever lawyers and policy wonks would be able to hack away at any conditions. As late as October 5, after approval by the Council of Ministers, this approach was the official European position, abruptly reversing the earlier commitment of the European Commission to the cultural exception.[53]

A third, more complicated option, was to include no reference to culture at all. In that case, the "cultural exception" would refer to an action not taken, which is probably the most accurate way of describing it, and in fact this is what transpired, an outcome often described as "an agreement to disagree." What complicates such a description, however, is that the Uruguay Round intended to cover a much larger economic array than all goods, the domain of GATT. The complementary agreement on services, GATS, was to apply to all services. While the EEC, and then the EU, had consistently claimed that television, deemed a service in the 1974 Sacchi ruling, was not subject to GATT, the EU could not argue that television was not a service, for then television would dangle unmoored and unprotected, neither a good nor a service. In the end, television, or more precisely "audiovisual services," did fall under the purview of GATS, but as will be seen in chapter 6, the EU was able to choose to make no official "commitments" in the relevant GATS schedules of services.

As the official GATT talks proceeded, for the most part with limited press coverage, there were conflicting reports on the votes of the European Parliament and Council of Ministers. Meanwhile, politicians and film professionals lobbied in the press. French president François Mitterrand dramatically announced in Gdansk, Poland, on September 21, 1993 that "France, and I hope all Europe will defend the clause of the cultural exception in the international negotiation. . . . What is at issue is the cultural identity of our nations, the right of each people to its own culture, the liberty to create and to choose our images. A society which abandons to others its means of representation, that is, the means of representing itself to itself, is an enslaved society."[54] A week later, more than four thousand artists, filmmakers, and producers appealed to European leaders to defend the cultural exception, and dozens of them traveled to Brussels to meet with EC officials Delors and Brittan.[55]

The almost simultaneous release of two big budget films, one French (*Germinal*) and one U.S. (*Jurassic Park*) provided the occasion for U.S. filmmakers to weigh in. Directors Martin Scorsese and Steven Spielberg, while (no doubt) sincerely expressing their appreciation for European cinema, took a principled stand in favor of freedom for all filmmakers, which meant the freedom to show their works unimpeded by the threat of quotas. "I am both puzzled and saddened by views publicly offered by some of my fellow cinema artists in Europe whose work I admire but [with] whose support of quotas and restrictions I must reluctantly beg to differ," Spielberg stated. "Filmmakers cannot exist without freedom. . . . Filmmakers can find no comfort when their film is barred, or restricted, or otherwise frustrated when they try to take work to the global public." Scorsese released a similar statement: "Whenever I hear of quotas and restrictions that would affect the free circulation of a filmmaker's work outside of his or her own country, I become alarmed."[56] These Hollywood directors agreed with Valenti that European spectators should have the right to choose what films they wanted to see. Yet their comments coincide with the release of *Jurassic Park* on 550 screens, while *Germinal* debuted on 450.[57] With U.S. films dominating screens throughout Europe, and few cinema quotas in Europe, their well-meaning remarks got swept up in the ideological battle taking place around GATT.[58]

Apparently, the French film community felt betrayed by the ministers' decision to seek the option of "cultural specificity" over "cultural exception." The best contemporary account of the tensions can be found in the proceedings of the third annual Rencontres de Beaune, a conference of film professionals held at Beaune, near Dijon, at the end of October. Sponsored by the ARP, the most prestigious French organization of filmmakers, the conference brought together the most established filmmakers and producers, and high officials and politicians often attended as well.

The topic of the 1993 meeting, appropriately enough, was "Europe–United States," and the first session was called "GATS Negotiations in the Field of Audiovisual."

ARP, later called "a bastion of the cultural exception" by *Liberation*,[59] had invited figures directly involved in the negotiations, as well as the current minister of culture, Jacques Toubon. David Hartridge, British Director of the Permanent Secretariat of the GATT, spoke first. Hartridge identified the three options as exclusion, exception, and specificity and explained that the "EEC will seek to introduce a clause of cultural 'specificity,' which would reserve a special regime for the audiovisual sector," though he also admitted that he did not know what such a clause would contain.[60] The secretary-general of ARP, Pascal Rogard, moderating the discussion, commented that he had not heard of this development (though the "Six Points" of the cultural specificity strategy developed at Mons had been reported in the press earlier in the month). Rogard then recognized Karl Falkenberg, section head of DG I (External Economic Relations) of the EC, the DG known as a free trade proponent within the EC. Falkenberg acknowledged that Leon Brittan, the lead negotiator, had referred to the idea of "specificity" instead of "exception" on occasion, but the EC had not taken a position on the question yet, so it remained on the agenda. Hartridge responded that the EC might propose that cultural production be added to Article 14, which allowed for exceptions to the GATT provisions for questions of morality, public order, and so on. Though he did not know what the EC would ultimately decide, he doubted that the final agreement would harm the European audiovisual industry: "I would be very surprised . . . if at the end of the negotiations the position of the European industry would be seriously compromised. I said that I would bet my house on it. If you knew my house, you might think that I am risking little. But it's the only one I have!"[61]

Jean-François Boittin, undersecretary of foreign economic relations in the French Ministry of Economy and Finance, immediately took issue with Hartridge's reassurances. He insisted that the threat posed by the general GATT negotiations was clear: progressive liberalization that "lays out precisely the fate of quotas and subsidies, etc. That is, systematically, their dismantlement." The French ambassador monitoring the development of the GATT negotiations for France, Bernard Miyet,

did not pull punches in his pronouncement on the introduction of specificity, describing

> this electro-shock provoked by the Commission, when, without any
> warning, it broached the term specificity. Without any previous discus-
> sion, without knowing what it would cover, without juridical definition.
> Still today, we wonder about the very content of the concept. I believe
> that there is, simply, a tactical concern, which would not come from a real
> analysis of the needs of the member states and the defense of the interests
> of the sector. I think that for the Commission, regarding past practices
> which were done in secrecy, with no transparence, no contact with the
> professionals, we have to make sure that the same spirit of discussion,
> the same symbiosis exists in the Commission between the competent
> DGs, between the Commission and the members states, and between the
> Commission and the professionals, so that we are not in a situation where
> several bureaucrats negotiate, outside of any contact with the reality of
> the sector.[62]

A member of the European Parliament, Leon Schwartzenberg, recounted
his history of the term "exception":

> What to do, given that [films, books, paintings, and records] are artistic
> works, and one could say, exceptional goods? So exceptional that they
> have required that we use the term exception to refer to them. It was
> difficult to mobilize the European Parliament because the French mem-
> bers were, virtually, the only [ones] to be concerned by the problem.
> We did, nonetheless, succeed in voting, on July 14, 1993, a resolution
> demanding total respect for all the prerogatives belonging until now
> to the Europeans, using the term specificity, which have been obtained
> by a compromise with a large political organization. At the request of
> the French government, I have to say, we anticipated a new resolution
> which . . . replaced the first. On September 30, we used the term ex-
> ception. Which raises a semantic debate, for the term exception can
> have two definitions. Either the maximal definition, that is to say, ex-
> clusion. The goods are so "exceptional" that they must be withdrawn
> from GATT and will not be discussed in the framework of GATT. The
> majority of French people understand, today, the term exception in
> the sense of exclusion. And then, there is the minimal definition, used

by Sir Leon Brittan and by the European members who voted for the first resolution in which it was equivalent to the term specificity. These goods are exceptional enough to deserve a special treatment, a specific treatment. This is the fundamental question.[63]

Jacques Toubon, minister of culture and Francophony, had the last word:

Our fight, if we consider it in the dialectic of identity and universality, is not limited to identity[;] it is for universality. If one considers the alternative of closing and opening, our fight is not for closing, it is for opening. Identity and universality: from this point of view I'd like to say one little thing, in looking over quickly a list of what the French system of cinema means, for the filmmaker. Not for the French alone, but for all filmmakers. If there was not a French system and the system of European co-production, there would have been no Manuel de Oliveira, Souleymane Cissé, Youssef Chahine, James Ivory, Arturo Ripstein, Farid Boughedir, Michelangelo Antonioni, Fernando Solanas, Sembène Ousmane, Idrissa Ouedraogo, Emir Kusturica, Pereira dos Santos, Théo Angelopoulos, Aki Kaurismaki, Andrej Wajda, Satyajit Ray, Krzysztof Kieslowski, Pavel Lounguine, Lucian Pintilie, and I'm leaving out better and worse. . . . Our battle is not at all an identity battle. It defends the cause of French cinema, of European cinema, and of world cinema.[64]

Toubon, too, saw the exception in terms of Article 14, in which the audio-visual sector would be exempted from the rules of GATT, just like the other exemptions already found in the Article 14: national security, public order, safety, health, and private life.[65]

Clearly, even at this late date, six weeks before the conclusion of seven years of negotiations, there was no unified position. The exception, which appeared least likely to be the ultimate choice, would take the form found in CUSFTA. According to Toubon's formulation, the "thesis of exception" would be placed within the agreement, in Article 14, explicitly shielded legally from challenge within GATT. A second option, which actually was not discussed as such, was to reach no agreement. Finally, the "specificity" option would delineate the areas protected from the free trade rules of GATT, though challenges to the specifics could be heard in the future by appeals panels.[66]

What ultimately prevailed, even if it did not conform to the "cultural exception" (or, perhaps more properly, the "cultural exclusion") included in the CUSFTA, was to pass over the issue in silence. The audiovisual sector would not be included in the final document at all. However, without any specific language in the agreement, either to specify the exceptions to the GATS principles or to explicitly exclude it, the sector's status remained undefined, rendering the de facto exclusion entirely provisional, vulnerable in the future to new liberalizing pressures. Nonetheless, as Jean-Pierre Jeancolas later wrote, France "won the battle of GATT, not the war. Yet it was more than a battle. It asserted, even in inchoate form, the principle that culture was different from other goods. Those cultural goods still have not been folded into international agreements."[67]

For any number of reasons, the EU did not develop a clear rationale for the cultural exception in those last months. With deep fault lines separating the views of the member countries, and with time running out before the December 15 deadline for conclusion of the talks, the EU could not reach a consensus position. Only after negotiations concluded was there time to develop arguments around the issue. Jack Valenti actually backed off the issue after 1993, proclaiming to French film professionals at Beaune the following year what an admirer he was of French culture and, somewhat implausibly, that the U.S. had no objection to French support of its film industry. As we will see in chapter 7, while the cultural exception persisted as a fundamental reference to the need for special treatment in international trade, the phrase was formally replaced by "cultural diversity" at the end of the decade.

However tenuous its legal status, the cultural exception marked the first time that the cultural industries formally confronted the pressures of globalization in an international legal arena.[68] The cultural exception represented not only a legal challenge in international law but also a cry of resistance to U.S. cultural hegemony. Despite intense U.S. pressure, Europe, led by France, refused to accept the threat of the death of its audiovisual production. The cultural exception may not have been the most impregnable defense of its cultural industries, but it galvanized opposition at the time and raised issues that persist today. Even after an international consensus did form around cultural diversity, the cultural exception continues to be invoked when a more militant and activist stance is called for.

5

FROM CANAL+ TO CANAL−

The rapid rise of Canal+ was perhaps the single most dramatic change in the French media landscape since 1980. However oxymoronically, the Socialist government created Canal+ as the first private television company, and the station soon emerged as the largest investor in French cinema. Modeled on HBO in the United States, Canal+ established its brand broadcasting recent film and sports.[1] In the second half of the 1990s, however, the successful Canal+ found itself swept up in the whirlpool of media concentration. With the creation of Vivendi Universal, Canal+ was briefly seated at the table with the Hollywood majors—in Hollywood. These changes sent shock waves through the French film industry, and beyond, revealing potential dangers to the very existence of French film, which had grown dependent on one private company. Questions about globalization crystalized for the French film industry—and France—when Jean-Marie Messier, head of Vivendi and self-acknowledged "Master of the World," took it upon himself to announce the death of the French cultural exception in New York in December 2001. With these massive transformations in the status of French cinema's principal benefactor, what would the future of French cinema look like?

THE FIRST PRIVATE STATION

The gestation history of Canal+ remains murky, obscured by political machinations behind the scene. According to one version, President François Mitterrand wanted to liberalize the state-owned electronic media, long criticized for their political obeisance to the government. After authorizing private radio stations, he announced the creation of a fourth television station, the first private one, which would not receive state funding. Apparently, Mitterrand had no clear idea of how the new station would function. A number of ministers, including Jack Lang (Culture) and Georges Fillioud (Communication) advocated a public service mission, concentrating on education and culture.[2]

But the debate over the direction of the future station took place behind closed doors, and the political infighting led to a more commercial orientation proposed by Mitterrand's close political ally André Rousselet. Rousselet had been Mitterrand's chief of staff when the new president took office in 1981. After stepping down from that post in July 1982, he headed the state-owned Havas Publishing. Havas, founded in 1853 as a government firm, was a venerable and prestigious French company. Several years earlier, a team of young developers working for state television had visited California and studied the business model of HBO in hopes of introducing a similar system in France. They tried to convince Rousselet to back their plan for the new television station. Rather than offer some modified variant on French public broadcasting, they designed an elaborate business plan built on movies and sports. Minister of Communication Fillioud signed a *cahiers des charges* with Havas for the new station late in 1983.[3]

Rousselet needed to ensure a supply of programming that would differentiate the station from the familiar fare of the state-owned stations. As the model was HBO, which specialized in recent movies, Rousselet had to strike a deal with the French film industry. Given the corporatist nature of the film industry, reinforced during years of state support, Rousselet had to face well-organized and well-established film lobbies. Jack Lang, obviously a strong promoter of film as minister of culture, had already negotiated new, more remunerative, arrangements with those lobbies. Rousselet initiated talks with the largest and most powerful lobby, the Bureau de liaison des industries cinématographiques (BLIC) in March 1984. At the time, theater attendance had not yet begun its plunge, so panic had not set in for the film industry, and the wary film professionals did not feel pressure to complete a deal with Rousselet. Many observers mocked the folly of the new station, certain it would not be viable economically. While such derision turned out to be unfounded, nobody could predict the future of the first subscription television. The deal they settled on set the number of films that could be shown each year (320; other stations could show only 192), the number of screenings per month (6), and the crucial permission to screen the films only one year after their theatrical release (the public stations had to wait three years, two years if the station co-produced the film). Canal+ agreed that 60 percent of the films it showed would be European, and 50 percent would be French, another boon to the industry, though this domestic quota requirement would prove knotty in the Television Without Frontiers debates later in the decade.[4]

In addition to securing supply, the business plan required finding investors, for Mitterrand had announced that the state would not supply any funding. Despite widespread skepticism in the business community, Rousselet managed to secure commitments from a small number of investors. The tightly regulated and wholly state-owned television stations had funds more or less limited to collection of the *redevance* (a license fee paid by television owners) and tightly regulated advertising, and (as explained in chapter 2) they paid minimal fees to the film industry for the television rights. To protect the attendance of films in theaters, the television regulatory agency (Haute autorité de l'audiovisuel), in addition to the three-year delay, proscribed the broadcast of films on Wednesday afternoons and Saturday evenings to avoid competition with films in theaters during those times of high volume attendance. Broadcasting licensees also had to negotiate a *cahiers des charges* in exchange for the right to broadcast, as Havas had done on December 6, 1983.

Canal+ began broadcasting on November 4, 1984. One newspaper declared it "already a failure" on that first day, but the station had almost reached its target of 200,000 subscribers by that time.[5] Despite some technical glitches, the station slowly built its subscriber base.[6] It faced a major challenge when Mitterrand stunned even his minister of communication by announcing in a television interview on January 16, 1985, that there would be eighty-five new television stations.[7] Rousselet was apoplectic at the idea of new, private competitors and used the announcement as leverage to renegotiate the 25 percent of income figure Canal+ had pledged to invest in cinema, whittling it down to 20 percent, where it remains today.[8] Mitterrand's announcement chilled the atmosphere for new subscribers, stanching cash flow, but Rousselet succeeded in obtaining a loan of 100 million francs from the government. Canal+ weathered these storms, and by 1990 the number of subscribers was above three million, providing most of the revenue of 5.4 billion francs. With investment in cinema pegged to that income, Canal+ was soon contributing over 500 million francs to French cinema production, more than all the other private and public stations combined (see figures 5.1–5.4).

Canal+ honored its commitment to invest 9 percent of its income in French cinema, so as it prospered, Canal+ poured ever more money into the film industry. To reach its (minimum) threshold of a 20 percent

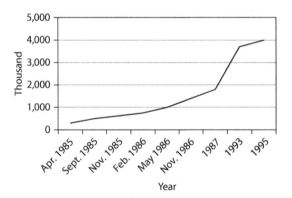

FIGURE 5.1 Canal+ subscribers, 1985–1995

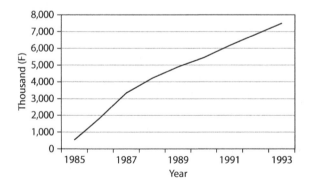

FIGURE 5.2 Canal+ revenues in francs, 1985–1995

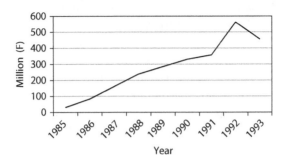

FIGURE 5.3 Canal+ investments in French cinema in francs, 1985–1993

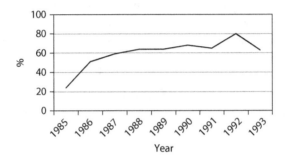

FIGURE 5.4 Percentage of French films invested in by Canal+, 1985–1993

investment in cinema, Canal+ added 3 percent backing for non-French European filmmakers, and with the remaining 8 percent, the station purchased rights to U.S. films, establishing releasing agreements with Hollywood studios.

French television stations also formed their own production subsidiaries. The rules proscribed owning more than 49.9 percent of any production facility, in order to protect producers from direct control over their operations, but the television stations developed special relationships with certain companies. Subject to the same restrictions, Canal+ formed StudioCanal in 1990, under the direction of René Bonnell. A lifelong cinephile, in 1978 Bonnell had earned a doctorate at the most prominent cinema program in France (Université de Paris III, Sorbonne Nouvelle), with Jack Lang on his doctoral committee, and worked at Gaumont before joining Canal+ in 1983 to direct cinema operations there. In 1990, Bonnell recommended forming a production company in the orbit of Canal+;

StudioCanal was established under his direction the same year.[9] Canal+ did not want to keep buying broadcast rights without also having access to revenue from distribution elsewhere, including France. By owning parts of those productions, the station could benefit from screenings of films in theaters and subsequent windows beyond the French broadcast. StudioCanal would invest in co-productions, acquiring parts of the films, which would then qualify them for revenue from future releases in theaters and television screenings by other stations. As Bonnell argued in an interview published in *Le Monde*: "This situation is completely absurd. The Canal Plus money would be much more useful if it served, in part, to finance the development and writing of ambitious films capable of defending Francophone expression and European culture through export throughout the world."[10]

Once established, StudioCanal invested not only in French and European films but also entered into a co-production agreement with the successful independent Carolco Studio in Hollywood to ensure supply of U.S. films and reduce the cost of their acquisition. This relationship initially proved beneficial with the production of some big-budget successes (*Terminator 2*, *Basic Instinct*), but subsequent failures forced Carolco into bankruptcy in 1995, leaving Canal+ with hundreds of millions of francs in losses. Yet the station was so successful in France that it was able to remain profitable even with those losses. Similarly, distribution arrangements with various U.S. studios, including Warner Bros. (Bel Air) and Sony, provided Canal+ with rights to release U.S. films in the European market.

Canal+ offered popular options of more movies and sports to French viewers. Because it broadcast over the air, Canal+ had the option of sending out an unscrambled signal (up to four and one-half hours daily) that all viewers could receive, whether subscribers or not, and the regulations allowed the station to sell advertising during those unscrambled transmissions. But more important than the advertising income was the popularity of those shows.[11] They were satirical shows lampooning public figures, especially political figures not normally subjected to ridicule on state-owned television. These inventive, irreverent programs attracted many viewers and established the reputation of Canal+ as fresh, creative, modern television, offering a true alternative to state television, one that was overdue in France, and represented the future of television.[12] Less remarked upon in the histories of Canal+ was its inclusion of pornographic films (once a month), never available previously on television.

While the fare turned out to be attractive to audiences, Canal+ benefited enormously from its monopoly of pay television in France for over
ten years. Its profits soared, even as it met all of its obligations to French
cinema. Canal+ continued to grow, building its subscriber base from
1.5 million in 1986 to 3.8 million in 1992.[13] Over five years, its revenue
grew tenfold, from 545 million to 5.445 billion francs, and its investment
in cinema went up by the same proportion. Over the same period, the
percentage of French films invested in by Canal+ went from 24 percent to
68 percent. Both of those figures would continue to rise through the rest
of the decade of the 1990s.

EXPANSION

With its rapid success in France, Canal+ pursued European ambitions.
Flush with cash, Canal+ invested in similar operations in Belgium (1989),
Spain (1990), and Germany (1991) with Bertelsmann. Though it also
tried to gain a foothold in Great Britain, Rupert Murdoch's BskyB was
already in place there, and its initial overtures did not pan out. Despite
its losses in Hollywood, Canal+ was still a highly profitable business,
with a strong subscriber base in France, benefiting from its monopoly
position in pay television. Strategically, then, Canal+ sought to extend its
dominance of pay television in Europe, while shoring up its supply line
with the United States.

In 1984, Canal+ had raised its start-up capital from three primary
investors. Rousselet, given the state's approval to strike out in the new
uncharted territory of private television, initially had difficulty attracting capital, as many potential investors questioned the viability of the
new station. Rousselet had no experience in the world of film and television, and many in the financial world deprecated his business experience
as head of a taxi company in Paris. His political experience and backing, however, served him in good stead, for he succeeded in attracting
investments from partially state-owned companies. As head of Havas,
Rousselet could draw directly on its funds, but he needed far more than
Havas could provide. Rousselet first obtained a commitment from a bank,
Société Générale, that had put together a group of banks for a 20 percent stake.[14] He found less substantial support from other companies.

One company, the one-hundred-and-thirty-year-old Compagnie Générale des Eaux (CGE), after a disappointing first offer, agreed to purchase a 15 percent share. According to several accounts, the head of CGE, Guy Dejouany, had faced a hostile takeover bid in 1983, when Rousselet was Mitterrand's chief of staff. Rousselet convinced Mitterrand to block the action, and Rousselet could call in that chit.[15] By the end of December 1983, Rousselet had gathered the needed backing.[16] Rousselet did have to draw on his political connections to overcome a slow start, when Canal+ succeeded in the easing of some obligations and obtaining the 100 million franc loan from the government, but after that early setback, Canal+ took off.[17] The stock price soared from €42 in 1987 to €198 at the end of 1993, an almost 500 percent appreciation for stockholders. With subscriptions pouring in by the day, Canal+ set up a counter for new subscribers in its building, reaching 2,300 per day, or one every 15 seconds. Rousselet chose not to distribute the profits in salaries or to lower the subscription fee, preferring to use the profits for expansion in foreign markets. To solidify its position as a sports broadcaster, in 1991 it purchased a stake in the bankrupt soccer team Paris St. Germain (PSG).[18]

By 1994, Canal+ was the leading pay-television company in Europe, with some 3.7 million subscribers in France, plus another 2.2 million abroad.[19] Rousselet had steered Canal+ through many obstacles, financial and political, and he had done so with a single-mindedness and an independence that he guarded carefully. He had confidence, vision, and an ability to hire talented collaborators, whose contributions he was able to maximize, and because of his sense of timing that Canal+ would triumph if given the opportunity, he made many of those hires rich. They, in turn, were devoted to him, for he allowed them the freedom to develop their creativity. In recognition of his leadership of Canal+, he received an Emmy award in December 1993, as the best media manager in the world that year.

Of course, Canal+ had benefited from having a monopoly on pay television in France since its inception. The government had granted its license without any bidding, and aside from the programming restrictions, Canal+ effectively exploited the absence of competition to amass profits. Furthermore, the station was not subjected to any public service obligations.[20] A French economist analyzed the benefits of its monopoly status in 1993 and determined that its revenues exceeded its costs by a factor of two; French subscribers to Canal+ paid 6.5 times the price of HBO subscribers in the United States.[21]

Yet not everyone who had contributed financially to this success appreciated Rousselet's independence. One of the first investors, Guy Dejouany, director of CGE, resented Rousselet's power and outsized profits at Canal+. Dejouany had put up 15 percent of the start-up capital for the station, but he was not satisfied simply to be the second largest stockholder. Canal+, at the crest of its success, was awash in money, the most remunerative of the companies CGE had an interest in. Dejouany hatched a plot with other large stockholders to take control of the station and ensure a voice in its future direction. Under anti-concentration legislation, prior to 1993, no group could hold more than a 25 percent stake in Canal+. However, with the conservative Édouard Balladur now prime minister, the new Carignon law raised that ceiling to 49 percent. Dejouany orchestrated a deal to have Havas (the largest stockholder with 24 percent) and CGE (20 percent), with a smaller participation from the Société Générale bank (4.8 percent), assume effective control of Canal+.

To bring off this coup, Dejouany entrusted the operation to a young, ambitious banker from Lazard Frères. Jean-Marie Messier had worked under Balladur in the Ministry of Finance on privatizations in the 1980s and then moved on to Lazard Frères, where he had a meteoric rise. Born in 1956, he was still in his thirties. Messier was particularly canny in networking in the upper reaches of French finance, and he had a flair—if not a mania—for communications. Exploiting his contacts at Lazard, Messier designed the strategy to convince Société Générale and Havas to seize power at Canal+. Rousselet, despite his own business acumen, perhaps slightly overconfident, did not pick up on indirect hints of the coup. Dejouany phoned Rousselet the day before the Canal+ board meeting in February 1994 to alert him to the plan, leaving Rousselet no time to prepare a counter-strategy. At the meeting the following day, Rousselet walked out in a fury. He resigned the following week.

Several days later, Rousselet published an article in *Le Monde* with the curious title of "Edouard m'a tuer."[22] The headline was inspired by a scandalous recent crime story in the south of France, but unpacking the meaning of the title and the import of the article reveals some of the deep structure of the imbrication of politics and business in France, and ultimately, provides a glimpse of how globalization would buffet the French film industry.[23] Evidently, Rousselet saw Prime Minister Edouard Balladur as the intellectual author of the plot. With elections approaching, Rousselet believed that Canal+, seen as a political maneuver of the Socialist

Mitterrand, was to be pulled back into the embrace of the government, reflecting the widely shared suspicion in France that political machinations lay behind business deals in the upper reaches of French industry. The engineer of this particular gambit was the head of the CGE, highly dependent on local governments throughout the country for its concessions in municipal services (water, waste, etc.). CGE may have feared that the irreverence of Canal+ would tar its image with a left taint and concluded that Rousselet's fabled independence had to be reined in. Whatever the merits of those fears, the station's satirical unscrambled shows, the real mark of its difference in the audiovisual world, did consistently attack Balladur during the election campaign, as if exacting revenge for the downfall of their patron. During the same electoral period, the shows on Canal+ treated Chirac, the only likely rival to Balladur, with deference. And Chirac carried the elections, leading one commentator to opine that Balladur might well have responded to Rousselet's attack with "André m'a tuer."[24]

Apparently, Balladur was so displeased with the turn of events that he assigned an assistant in the Finance Ministry, Nicolas Sarkozy, to salve the situation. At the end of 1983, Canal+ had been granted the franchise to broadcast for twelve years. In 1994, that franchise was coming up for renewal. Some government representatives had approached Rousselet about some concessions they would like to see in the new license conditions for Canal+. Rousselet had flatly refused any such political meddling, but he knew the company would have to confront potentially difficult negotiations, given the station's public success. Following the coup, Sarkozy essentially released Canal+ from any of the scheduled new conditions, presumably with the blessing of Balladur. Canal+ would not have to contribute to the growth of cable; it could retain its reduced value-added tax and keep its advertising revenue from unscrambled transmissions; and it would not be asked to raise its support for French cinema (already high relative to all other stations). Canal+ received the new license with no new obligations, the "posthumous victory of André Rousselet."[25]

Guy Dejouany may have been the instigator of the takeover of Canal+ and may not even have sought the removal of his old friend Rousselet per se, but the skill and stealth with which Messier constructed the raid on Canal+ convinced the seventy-three-year-old Dejouany that he had found a worthy successor. Dejouany had been watching Messier for several years, and he had given him assignments as early as 1989.[26] If Dejouany had engineered the first sortie against the independence of Canal+, Messier's war of position would eventually ensnare Canal+ in his dream of transforming CGE from a prosaic if lucrative water company into a communications giant, chasing a chimera of convergence. The consequences would reverberate throughout the French film industry and beyond.

Jean-Marie Messier was one of France's best and brightest. After schooling at the prestigious École nationale d'administration (ENA),[27] Messier landed the job in the Balladur government overseeing privatizations, which included the transformation of the largest state television station, TF1, into a private company. His tenure in government had placed him in the Balladur orbit, lubricating his rapid ascent in the world of finance. When Dejouany installed him as his heir apparent at CGE in November 1994, seven months after the fall of Rousselet, many were dismayed. Aside from his youth, Messier had never managed a company. Critics questioned the wisdom of placing a still-unknown banker at the head of the vast CGE, with thousands of affiliates scattered all over France. But Dejouany, like many others, was seduced by the charm and putative brilliance of this man of vision and handed over the reins to Messier in 1996.[28]

From the start, Messier demonstrated little interest in running businesses. His passion was acquisitions and growth.[29] As the director of CGE, part of the newly formed alliance with Havas and Société Générale, Messier was in a position to direct the fortunes of Canal+. Rousselet had been correct to warn his successor, Pierre Lescure, about the threat to Canal+'s independence.[30] Rousselet had battled in the trenches to fend off a series of attacks in its earliest days. He had convinced Mitterrand that Canal+ would in fact become successful, and Rousselet's faith and managerial skills had led Canal+ to phenomenal success.

Canal+ was about to face its first serious setbacks since the start-up pains. Its subscriber list would level off in France, and while the company had subscribers abroad, most of those foreign joint ventures had not turned any profit (with the modest exception of Belgium). StudioCanal had lost millions of francs in the ill-fated venture with Carolco in Hollywood. So while Canal+ remained profitable, its foreign initiatives were eating into the profits, and the markets it had entered—pay television and satellite delivery—were maturing, attracting large media interests, ratcheting up the competition.

Dejouany did not view the media as a strategic interest. What attracted him to Canal+ was its success, its positive cash flow, hence the appeal of exercising control over it. Messier, however, had grander visions. Merely running a water company, even one as large and wealthy as CGE, would hardly satisfy his ambition, and it would certainly not slake his thirst for media attention. He set his sights on constructing the world's second-largest media company, which would eventually materialize for a short but blazing moment as Vivendi Universal.

Messier was still only one of the three major shareholders of Canal+, with Havas and the bank consortium. When Rousselet resigned as head of Canal+ he counseled Pierre Lescure, his second in command, to succeed him. Working under the protective leadership of Rousselet, Lescure had helped pilot Canal+ to its unprecedented success, but his strengths lay in attracting a dynamic, creative team, not running a large enterprise with thousands of employees spread across Europe.[31] Though Lescure had witnessed the financial manipulation that effectively forced Rousselet's resignation, he probably did not adequately take the measure of Messier as the mastermind behind the scenes of Rousselet's fate. As the founder of the station, Rousselet saw immediately that he had lost his corporate independence, only one year after he had accepted an Emmy as Best Media Manager of the year. Unwilling to continue with his power compromised, Rousselet had chosen to resign, but he counseled Lescure to succeed him, warning him that his freedom of maneuver would be limited. Though Havas director Pierre Dauzier had a replacement for Rousselet in mind, Messier convinced the board to retain Lescure, who then managed Canal+ through the transition.[32]

Like Rousselet, Lescure viewed Europe as a strategic growth area for Canal+.[33] It had purchased a minority (37.5 percent) share in the German station Premiere in 1991, and Lescure tried to work out a deal with Bertelsmann for a controlling share in Premiere, for Germany was the most lucrative potential market in Europe. That deal fell through when Bertelsmann signed with Kirch, marginalizing Canal+ in Germany. To replace that German market, Lescure proposed a merger with NetHold, holder of satellite franchises with 2.7 million new European subscribers, including the Benelux countries (Belgium, Netherlands, Luxembourg), Scandinavia, and 45 percent of the Telepiù satellite company in Italy (700,000 subscribers), in exchange for granting Johann Rupert, the South African billionaire head of NetHold, a 15 percent share in Canal+.[34] However, Telepiù was losing money, and would continue to bleed Canal+ for years to come—critics described piracy (of decoders) as a national sport in Italy.[35] Nonetheless, Messier approved Lescure's proposal, and Canal+

bought NetHold for €7.2 billion, a price analysts viewed as overvalued.[36] In his memoir, former Canal+ executive and media expert René Bonnell called the Telepiù deal the "kiss of death" for Canal+.[37]

At the same time, Canal+ was about to lose its monopoly hold on the French pay television market. While undeveloped cable television posed little threat to Canal+ in France, satellite was another matter.[38] Canal+ launched its own satellite, CanalSat, in 1992, offering a variety of European programming, but CanalSat broadcast an analog signal as digital was already on the horizon, so the station had to launch another, digital, satellite in 1996. Competitors soon sought to pare away its competitive advantage with their own satellite services. In 1996, the largest private French station, TF1 (privatized in 1986), with some 40 percent of the broadcast market, entered into a partnership with new private station M6 and French public television (Fr2, France3) to form Télévision Par Satellite (TPS) to compete with Canal+.[39] TPS started slowly, with its own (much lower) obligations to invest 3 percent of its revenue in French cinema, but it began just as Canal+ was reaching the end of its period of constant growth in France. Canal+, with four million subscribers, was having increasing difficulty in signing up new customers, as the subscription curve leveled off and the cost of new subscribers mounted.[40]

TPS could not offer the same level of quality programming developed over the previous decade by Canal+, but it did seek sports contracts for European football coverage, and a bidding war broke out, threatening to deplete the cash reserves of Canal+, which had enjoyed exclusive contracts in the past. While Canal+ had previously signed a football contract for €122 million, the competition with TPS forced it to submit a bid of €260 million, far larger than its investment of €140 million in French cinema. To make matters worse, in its first years TPS took Canal+ to court for abuse of dominant position, and the courts ruled consistently against Canal+, fining the station €1.5 million in 1998.[41]

VIVENDI UNIVERSAL

Having made the strategic determination that communications would be the core of his global expansion, Messier had begun a campaign to build a communications empire, vertically and horizontally integrated. The pact of CGE and Havas to hold 49 percent of Canal+ did not give Messier control of Canal+, but he did hold veto power over strategic decisions, so Lescure often discussed plans with Messier, who did not intervene in the creative side of Canal+. In 1998, Messier consolidated his grip on Canal+ by maneuvering to swallow its parent company, Havas, the publishing and advertising giant. To proclaim the change of focus, Messier unveiled a new name for his growing enterprise: Vivendi.[42] The newly named company started selling off its former core businesses for cash as Messier trolled for new ones, and Canal+ found itself under a new corporate umbrella. That same year, the Group Canal+ posted its first loss.[43] The French station Canal+ remained profitable, even if its subscriber growth had slowed and greater resources had to be devoted to retaining subscribers, but the losses of the foreign operations continued to mount, driving the larger company into the red. In 1998, Telepiù lost €133 million, and €171 million in 1999. Even though Canal+ turned a profit of €120 million in 1999, Group Canal+ lost €136 million.

Late in 1999, Messier learned through Lescure that Edgar Bronfman Jr., scion of the family that had built Seagram into the largest spirits company in the world, was interested in selling Universal Studios. Bronfman had been granted operational leadership of Seagram in 1995, so he was still a young executive testing the waters of corporate wheeling and dealing, under the watchful eyes of his father (Edgar Sr.) and uncle (Charles), founders of the company in 1929. In one of his first major deals as head of Seagram, Bronfman acquired MCA in 1995 for $5.7 billion. Besides its library of recorded music, MCA owned Universal Studios, a major fallen on hard times after its purchase by Matsushita in 1991.[44] At the end of 1998, Seagram added the British-based Polygram company, for $10.4 billion.[45] Polygram had devised a successful business plan of decentralized music labels, and Seagram suddenly held the rights to Universal Music, the largest collection of recorded music in the world. The company's film division, Polygram Filmed Entertainment, had tried to apply the same strategy to film, but after early success, it suffered large losses when it tried to produce its own large-budget films.

At the end of 1999, with the Internet bubble in full expansion, Time Warner merged with AOL to form the largest media empire in the world, a deal valued at $60 billion. Though Messier had already identified communications as the strategic future of Vivendi, the AOL–Time Warner megadeal spurred him to pursue discussions with Bronfman.

Negotiations continued through the spring of 2000, culminating in the announcement in June of Vivendi's purchase of Seagram for $32–35 billion to form Vivendi Universal (VU), which would be the second-largest media company in the world. The merger brought together the music and film content of Universal and the Vivendi delivery systems of telephony, Internet, and television, with 80 million subscribers across Europe (see figures 5.5–5.6).[46]

The French film industry demanded to know the status of its great patron, Canal+, in the new configuration. Not everyone agreed with the Canal+ executive's reassurance in June that "what's good for Canal+ is good for cinema."[47] In particular, who would own Canal+, and would it even remain a French company? As noted above, the Carignon law that raised the bar of investor control from 25 to 49 percent enabled CGE to take control of Canal+. But was VU still a French company?

The merger required approval of various authorities in the United States, Canada, the European Commission, and France. After green lights from the first three, the only remaining obstacle was approval by

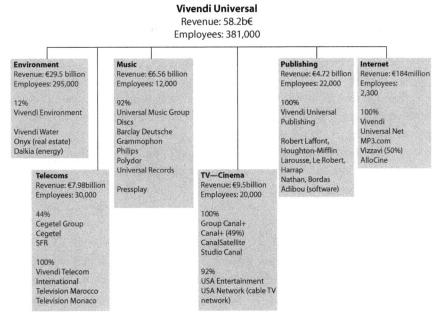

FIGURE 5.5 Main business divisions for Vivendi Universal, 2000

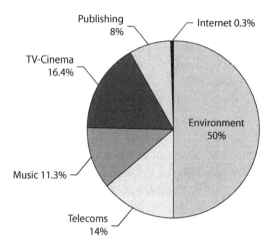

FIGURE 5.6 Percentage of assets for Vivendi Universal, 2002

the French audiovisual authority, the Conseil supérieur de l'audiovisuel (CSA). The CSA had given an initial approval in July, but new questions arose in the fall. Press reports indicated that Lescure and his colleagues were worried about the independence of Canal+ within the new structure and had fought with Messier over the demand for guarantees that VU would not interfere in the decision making at Canal+. The CSA returned to the case in the fall. It would have to determine whether the deal conformed to French law, in particular the rules limiting ownership of any over-the-air station to 49 percent and the restriction of any non-French ownership to 20 percent.

The head of the CSA, Hervé Bourges, apparently sought the counsel of André Rousselet, who once again jumped into the act with an article in *Le Monde*, "Canal+, suite ou fin?" (Canal+, to be continued or finished?), expressing concern for the future of the station he had founded.[48] He hoped that his protégé Pierre Lescure would refuse to buckle to Messier, for the deal ultimately revolved around the acquiescence of Lescure and Canal+, the real cash cow on the French side. This time Lescure himself responded, writing to *Le Monde* the following day, titling his response "Canal, plus et mieux" (Canal, more and better). Lescure defended the merger, lecturing his predecessor and mentor that visionary leadership required growth, and Canal+ would be part of this expansion. In an unkind cut to Rousselet, Lescure began, "The age of adulthood, according to the psychoanalysts, is when one pardons one's parents. Since you left it, Canal+ has become an adult, my dear André Rousselet. The proof. It pardons you. It pardons you for no longer knowing it. And for understanding it so little."[49]

The following week, representatives of the film industry joined the fray. With "spectacular" unanimity, more than eighty filmmakers submitted a petition to the CSA, conveying their worries that failure to obtain adequate guarantees for the independence of Canal+, "its editorial autonomy, the independence of its income and investments, the control over subscription lists, the continuity of its current policy as well as its obligation to cinema . . . would present a death threat to French cinema and serve as an example to desert national and European production."[50] Messier eventually agreed to carving out some autonomy for Canal+ by creating a new Group Canal+, controlled fully by VU, and a separate entity Canal+, the station, limiting VU's ownership share of the latter to 49 percent, conforming to the Carignon law. The CSA granted its approval at the end of November.[51]

The next year, however, revealed the precarity of the enterprise, politically and then financially. On December 17, 2001, Messier completed a deal to purchase USA Networks from Barry Diller for $10.4 billion and a part (10 percent) of John Malone's U.S. satellite company, EchoStar, for $1.5 billion.[52] While Pierre Lescure had been named to head the Vivendi film operations at the fusion of Vivendi-Seagram-Canal+, now the fulcrum of power shifted to Hollywood, where Diller would lead the newly resurgent Universal Film. Lescure would be effectively demoted to the more modest role directing Canal+. Now VU would have new conduits (cable, satellite) in the United States for its content, realizing Messier's goal of forming a real major able to compete in the U.S. market and abroad through its European branches of Canal+.

DEATH OF THE CULTURAL EXCEPTION

Many in France had hailed the creation of VU as a French triumph of capitalist acumen, but Messier committed a monumental political error just before Christmas in 2001. Responding to the large press contingent after the announcement of the new purchases at the St. Regis Hotel in New York, Messier announced, "The French cultural exception is dead." As discussed in the previous chapter, the expression *exception culturelle* had first come to prominence during the tense months leading up to the final GATT battle, when France led the fight to have audiovisual products and services excluded from the new world trade agreement. The entire French political spectrum had supported this concept—indeed, some commentators remarked that the most surprising aspect of the battle was the unanimity of French politicians to support the cultural exception, as did French filmmakers—and the system of support had not been tampered with by successive governments. So Messier's claim was received as a bombshell in France, where it reinforced fears that Messier was selling out France in his new partnership with Seagram Universal.[53]

In the press conference, Messier adroitly proposed that VU was committed to the concept of "cultural diversity." In this he was not alone, for French and other policy makers were already replacing the "cultural exception" with "cultural diversity" in their discourse (see chapter 7). Messier's formulation was in itself probably not so incendiary or noxious, but he was perhaps the last person who should have said it, to say nothing of the fact that he said it in New York, in English, where he had purchased a palatial residence for VU on Fifth Avenue for $18 million. Moreover, exacerbating the fears pulsing through the film industry, Lescure told *Le Monde* at the same time that the system of support for French cinema had to be revisited.[54] Other executives at Canal+ began to hint that the channel would have to renegotiate—which is to say reduce—its financial obligations to the film industry, citing competition.[55]

Whether Messier's rhetorical overreach was cause or symptom, the whole edifice of VU—constructed so carefully, if perhaps incoherently, over the five years since Messier had assumed leadership of CGE—began to unravel quickly.[56] The CSA returned to the VU case, looking carefully at the rule restricting ownership by non-French companies to 20 percent. But when that rule was first passed as part of the major new audiovisual law in 1986, identifying ownership shares was simple. Fifteen years later, the company now traded stock, and nobody could identify the stock's nationality with sufficient accuracy to enforce the rule; the CSA turned the question over to the Council of State, which concluded that even the efforts of specialized accounting firms could not determine the nationality of the "floating stock."[57]

Meanwhile, business observers were already losing confidence in Messier's grand plans when VU announced a loss of €13.6 billion in March 2002, the largest loss ever by a French company, which Messier shrugged off by saying that the VU situation was "better than good."[58] The supreme self-confidence and conman's charm eventually failed him once the real numbers began to spill out in the press. The trade paper *Écran Total* reported in April that Canal+ had lost fifty thousand subscribers in 2001.[59] The value of its stock plunged from a high of €150 in 2000 to €14 in July 2002.[60] Panic was setting in at Canal+, with the dismissal or resignation of executives. On April 16, Messier fired Lescure, ending the eighteen-year tenure of one of the original architects of the phenomenal success of Canal+. The falling stock and the flight of confidence plunged Vivendi further into debt, and Messier fought desperately to convince the board that his strategy was sound so long as they stayed the course. With the leadership in disarray and the market hammering the stock, the previously supine board of directors grew restive and dismissed Messier on July 3, 2002, ending his Promethean dreams in disgrace (see figures 5.7–5.8).

While a series of factors sealed Messier's fall—the technology bubble, intemperate expansion, and unmanageable debt all played a part—one theory is that his increasingly grandiose ambitions to transform Vivendi into a world media power, shedding its French identity, provoked traditional French capital to cut him down to size.[61] After all, when he asked, in the subtitle to his autobiography, "Must we fear the new economy?," he was implicitly attacking the French capitalist establishment for their parochial national purview.[62] According to press reports, one of the leaders of the old guard, Claude Bébéar, engineered Messier's removal and then named his interim successor, Jean Fourtou, who pursued a strategy of selling off assets to reduce the debt and raise cash but preserving Canal+ as a French company.[63]

END OF AN ERA

Rather than interpret this tawdry corporate implosion as a reflection of Canal+'s role in potentially gutting the French film industry, it is probably more fruitful to understand it as the end of an era at Canal+ and in French

FIGURE 5.7 Messier on the street: "I accept any job as Master of the World." Cartoon by Luz, from *Charlie Hebdo*, July 3, 2002

television. Essentially, the privatization of French television in the 1980s and 1990s turned out to be fabulously lucrative, and Canal+ reaped the enormous benefits of a monopoly position in pay television over its first fifteen years. But Canal+ had already reached the end of that growth by the time of the Universal merger. The subscriber base had stagnated at 4.5 million and it cost increasing amounts of money to retain them. The super *branché* (hip) shows that had captured and captivated audiences—*Nulle part ailleurs, Les guignols de l'info*—had lost their freshness and irreverence. Canal+ had nothing new to draw in new subscribers and had lost its luster as the cool new guy in the audiovisual landscape. Further, more competition eventually caught up with Canal+. The TPS satellite system

FIGURE 5.8 Soon at ANPE (National Employment Office): "Boss. There's a weirdo at the window who's looking for a job as Master of the World at €1 million a month . . . not including bonuses . . ." "Messier?!" From *Canard enchainé*, July 3, 2002. Copyright © Lefred-Thouron–Le Canard enchaîné—tous droits réservés

offered an alternative pay television, and TF1 engaged in bidding wars for the rights to football. In short, Canal+ no longer enjoyed the super-profits of its effective monopoly position in pay television.

Shortly after the restructuring of VU, Canal+ returned to its traditional vocation. During the first two years of VU under Messier, the film industry tried to discern shifts in the strategy of Canal+ toward the Hollywood pole, away from French cinema. Some analysts noted that Canal+ was investing in fewer French films, with more money directed to more expensive films, a possible signal that it was abandoning its support of smaller films, which were the guarantors of diversity.[64] Yet that dip turned out to be short-lived, as the station continued to finance most French films, investing as much as all other television stations combined (see figures 5.9–5.11).

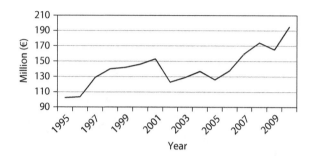

FIGURE 5.9 Canal+ prepurchases of French films in euros, 1995–2010

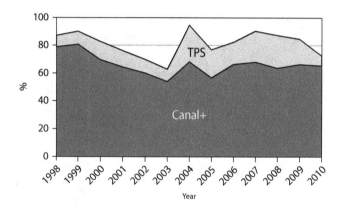

FIGURE 5.10 Percentage of French films invested in by Canal+ and TPS, 1998–2010

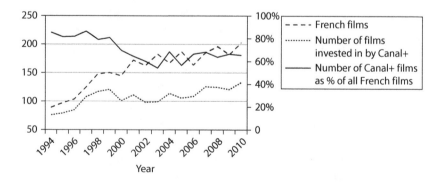

FIGURE 5.11 Canal+ investments in French films, 1994–2010

Lasting barely two years, the episode of Vivendi Universal under Messier, which had received considerable backing from the French government, dramatized the disproportionate dependence of French cinema on a single financier, Canal+. As the state had introduced only a series of minor measures during the 1990s, and cinema's fortunes revived, with steady growth in attendance, buoyed by the success of multiplexes, and production, now irrigated—some say flooded—by television money, the time had come to begin the first comprehensive examinations of the state of the film industry since the reforms of the Lang years.

6

BILAN(S)

The conclusion of the General Agreement on Tariffs and Trade negotiations roughly coincided with the end of the slide of the French film industry. French filmmaking revived more or less steadily, though unevenly, after 1993. While various factors combined to effect this turnaround, probably the single most significant was the rise in attendance, fostered by the first multiplexes in France. With growing television money pouring into the film industry, more films were made and many new filmmakers appeared. Despite mounting globalization pressures, embodied in the formation of the World Trade Organization in 1995, European countries, again led by France, maintained reticence about endorsing the unfettered globalization promoted by the United States. As privatized television prospered, new Cassandras warned of the dangers of cinema's dependence on television money. New technologies transformed the audiovisual landscape, abetting increased concentration of the media, while the multiplication of audiovisual platforms blurred the boundaries separating them. Within Europe, integration proceeded at a slower pace, tamping the tensions that had attended the passage of the Directive on Television Without Frontiers. The 1990s ended with the formation of Vivendi Universal, the first European media superpower. By acquiring its own Hollywood studio, Vivendi tested its maturity on a grand scale. But the maneuver had proved an overreaching exercise in hubris brought on by the twin lures of vertical integration and the marriage of content and delivery systems taking place in the hothouse atmosphere of the Internet bubble. Because of the extent of government involvement in the resuscitation of the film industry through resources and administrative directives, government agencies and experts undertook studies—no fewer than fourteen between 2000 and 2003—to diagnose the industry and assess the efficacy of the regulations (see box 6.1).

BOX 6.1:
Reports Discussed in This Chapter

1992

Cluzel, Jean-Paul, and Guillaume Cerutti. "Mission de réflexion et de propositions sur le cinéma français." Rapport no. 92–372. Paris: Inspection générale des finances, December.

1998

Cluzel, Jean. "L'efficacité des aides publiques en faveur du cinéma français." Rapport no. 1107 (National Assembly) / Rapport no. 11 (Senate). Paris: National Assembly and Senate, October.

2000

Delon, Francis. "Les multiplexes: Rapport au ministre de la culture et de la communication." Paris: Ministry of Culture, January.
    Goudineau, Daniel. "La distribution des films en salle: Rapport à Mme la ministre de la culture et de la communication." Paris: Ministry of Culture, May.

2002

Fansten, Michel. "Le cinéma français face à l'évolution technologique et à la transformation des marchés." Paris: Réalisations et recherches audiovisuelles, November. Included in Gaillard and Loridant report (2003).

2003

Cluzel, Jean. *Propos impertinents sur le cinéma français*. Paris: Presses universitaires de France.

BOX 6.1 CONTINUED

"Les modes de financement du film français sont-ils adaptés aux perspectives d'évolution de ses différents marchés?" Paris: Département d'études stratégiques sur l'audiovisuel et le cinéma (DESAC), January.

Leclerc, Jean-Pierre. "Réflexions sur le dispositif français de soutien à la production cinématographique: Rapport établi à la demande du ministre de la culture et de la communication." Paris: Ministry of Culture, January.

Gaillard, Yves, and Paul Loridant. "Revoir la règle du jeu: Mieux évaluer l'efficacité des aides publiques au cinéma: Rapport d'information fait au nom de la Commission des finances, du contrôle budgétaire et des comptes économiques de la Nation sur les aides publiques au cinéma en France." Rapport d'information no. 276 (2002–2003). Paris: Senate, May.

Thiollière, Michel, and Jack Ralite. "Exploitation cinématographique: Le spectacle est-il encore dans la salle?" Rapport d'information no. 308 (2002–2003). Paris: Commission des affaires culturelles, Senate, May.

2004

"Cinéma français et État: Un modèle en question." *Quaderni* 54 (Spring): 65–131.

Following the flurry of reforms pushed through by minister of culture Jack Lang in the 1980s, the government proposed only relatively minor changes to domestic production through the 1990s.[1] The government wanted to assess the results of the reforms and evaluate their effectiveness. Aside from the semiautonomous CNC, which regularly conducted its own studies, the Ministry of Culture and both branches of Parliament (the Senate and National Assembly) ordered multiple investigations, partially to monitor how the money diverted to the film industry was being handled. Strictly speaking, the monies were not government funds per se, but the money flows were following the paths charted by government actions. For example, the laws requiring television stations to deposit a percentage of their income into the Compte de soutien for film and television,[2] did not always direct the money into general tax revenues, and for that reason it was not considered government money. Nonetheless, since the government did impose the obligations, it had an interest in tracking the itinerary of those transfers.[3]

MINISTRY OF CULTURE REPORTS

In June 1992, Jack Lang, then in his second term as minister of culture, requested a report from the inspector general of finance, Jean-Paul Cluzel. Cluzel submitted his report, titled "Mission de réflexion et de propositions sur le cinéma français," in December 1992, only months before the GATT dispute broke out.[4] In the introduction, Cluzel began with the perennial observation that French cinema was undergoing "an unprecedented crisis." He noted the drop in attendance for French film by two-thirds, while attendance for U.S. films had actually increased by over 13 percent between 1982 and 1991 (from 61 to 69 million; see figure 1.10 in chapter 1). A similar, if less pronounced trend, could be found for films shown on television. By the early 1990s, U.S. productions had replaced French ones as the most popular films screened on television.[5] Cluzel concluded that television had not caused the decline in theatrical attendance. Rather, French films had lost their appeal to audiences.

Production, however, had remained relatively steady. Television money effectively had replaced falling theatrical revenues. The Lang reforms included the tax on television income sent to the Compte de soutien, and the requirement to either prepurchase broadcast rights to films or invest directly in film production. The new arrangement meant that film producers no longer looked to theater audiences to earn back the cost of the films, but relied on television to cover production costs even before a film was released. Concurring with Jean-François Court's observation from 1988 (see chapter 2), Cluzel described the new financing environment as "promoting a logic of pre-financing at the expense of a logic of amortization."[6] That is, with the fall in attendance, producers received a sharply reduced return on their investment from theatrical runs. Instead, they depended increasingly on advances mandated by the legal obligations placed on television, since these advances were now guaranteed before production. Once entirely dependent on theatrical receipts for earning back their investments, producers now had less incentive to maximize performance at the box office.[7] With the fall in attendance and the shrinking of theatrical receipts for investment—and given that the decline in attendance had affected French films, not U.S. films—producers no longer felt the same urgency to seek theatrical success, hence the new "logic of pre-financing." Cluzel offered a detailed sketch of both the conjunctural and structural problems facing French cinema and catalogued many of the challenges that have persisted ever since; reports from the next decade in many ways subscribed to the same analysis laid out by Cluzel. He also included a series of proposals to address the problems.

Regarding attendance, Cluzel first considered the state of exhibition. He found that France enjoyed the best geographical distribution of theaters in Europe. He surveyed the number of theaters in population centers with more than 100,000 inhabitants, as well as the coverage of areas with fewer than 20,000 people. This concern reflected one of the values attached to exhibition: that people all over the country should have access to the cinema. While the distribution of theaters was important for access, Cluzel also pointed out that those agglomerations of less than 20,000 still represented 15 percent of all theater admissions, so there was an economic rationale to complement the public interest concern.

Renovating theaters, however, would not necessarily increase admissions to French films, since large audiences continued to attend U.S. films. Here arose the more vexing question about the quality of French films. Cluzel broke down the production profile into three categories: big-budget, middle-budget, and small-budget films. He identified more expensive projects as the only ones that could compete with the U.S. films, which regularly benefited from budgets five times as large as the largest French productions. State funding should go to them: "French cinema needs ambitious films, with spectacular subjects, with budgets necessarily large, to compete with American productions in France and abroad. The state cannot, in our view, avoid an interest in these big films. It must, if necessary, participate in their financing, or at least allow them to be financed in optimal conditions."[8]

Cluzel concluded his overview with a clear call on the film industry to take responsibility for responding to the (latest) crisis:

> [We] underline how much the future of French cinema is more than ever in the hands of the professionals. The mechanism of support established by the state is reaching its limits, both in terms of the extreme

complexity of its mechanisms and the financial commitment that can be devoted to it.

The renewal of French cinema must take place above all with a recognition by cinema people of the desires of the public and the importance of theatrical success.[9]

Cluzel's proposals concentrated on revitalizing all aspects of French film. "The first series of proposals, which concerns all stages of the cinema industry (production, distribution, exhibition, export, release on other media) aims . . . at restoring to the judgment of the public, positive or negative, the role that it has increasingly lost." Most of his suggestions were relatively technical, adjusting the mechanisms already established, or refined, under Lang. With production, for example, he called for shifting some of the funds going to the Compte de soutien from television to film.[10] That diversion would raise the percentage of *aide automatique* returned to producers from 120 percent to 140 percent.[11] Because the number of films produced had not declined as much as the attendance for French films, there were few recommendations for raising production levels.

Distribution, too, displayed a troubling trend. Traditionally, before the privatization of television, distributors provided minimum guarantees up front to producers, based on expectations about theatrical performance. Theater owners had their own agreements on rentals for the films, and those rental fees would go first to the distributors to compensate them for the costs of distribution, including promotion expenses and the minimum guarantees already advanced to producers. As theater receipts for French films declined, distributor income fell, leading to the disappearance of fully one-third of all distributors.[12] While distributors contributed on average as much as 30 percent of all production investment during the 1980s, that number had dropped to 4 percent in 1991. The one sector that had the greatest interest in and responsibility for the theatrical success of French films was withdrawing from the financing of films, aggravating "the disconnection between the films produced and the expectations of the public."[13]

Turning to the relations of film and television, Cluzel walked a fine line between encouraging television to take a greater interest in the theatrical careers of the films it had invested in and acknowledging the potential threat that television posed to the creative autonomy of producers (and by implication, writers and directors).[14] Current rules required television to devote at least 50 percent of their investments in film to pre-purchases, in order to limit their direct role in co-production. The report, focused on its paramount goal of incentivizing theatrical success, observed that the rules actively discouraged television from sharing in the risk-taking of (co-)production. Film producers objected strenuously to additional television participation in production, Cluzel noted, precisely because producers would then have to give up some of their claim on theatrical receipts and rights in downstream windows, exactly the objection Bonnell raised when explaining the rationale behind the creation of StudioCanal (see chapter 5).[15]

Even more important for the producers were the claimed "risks of aligning film production with prime-time criteria." Producers contended that television interference in creative production would inevitably dilute the quality of French films by imposing its own value criteria, which correspond to the lowest-common denominator values essential for prime-time success. This kind of reasoning reflected the deep aesthetic biases of film producers, and the film community in general, which tend to disparage the artistic qualities of commercial television. Unfortunately, Cluzel did little to reassure producers when he cited the box office success of films co-produced by television, which have "no reason to blush in comparison with films produced by the large groups or independents." He had earlier claimed that "it is clear that the public will be won back by the quality of the films more than by the quality of the theaters," though the success of multiplexes later in the decade would disprove that assumption.[16] In fact, the report's occasional references to quality had a pro forma character. By equating box office success with artistic success here, he was responding to an aesthetic argument voiced by film producers, who of course had their own reasons for wanting to denigrate television standards of value.

A long section on the state of the exhibition sector followed. The report affirmed several key principles. First, the role of the state should be to "verify that there are sufficient theaters to ensure an appropriate coverage of the territory," repeating the earlier emphasis on the importance of reasonable access to theaters throughout the country. Second, the state should ensure the existence of a "significant representation" of art cinemas.[17] A brief review of the evolution of exhibition during the 1980s demonstrated that concentration in this sector had increased, despite earlier efforts to break up some of the consolidation.[18] But the hopes that new agreements would allow independent theaters greater access to films controlled by the large circuits had failed. Nonetheless, once again betraying a bias in favor of dominant players, the report judged that "vertical integration of the large groups must be preserved. . . . The vertical integration of the large groups . . . is indispensable to optimize a production policy [favoring large-budget productions], even if this is contrary to the credo of cultural pluralism and free competition."[19]

In this extended discussion of exhibition, Cluzel anticipated future developments in the sector with remarkable accuracy. First, with theaters closing in the large cities, new theaters with multiple screens would be constructed on the outskirts of towns in an attempt to draw back audiences. In the smaller towns, single theaters would adapt. The large circuits would maintain their theaters in these areas, and the most "dynamic" and "original" art cinemas would survive. Finally, the smallest municipalities would continue to intervene to save their theaters. The report made no recommendations to accelerate or retard those tendencies, but in fact, the decade did see the first appearance and rapid growth of multiplexes, the emergence of an innovative art cinema circuit coupled with a strengthening of art cinemas generally, and an increasing number of theaters in smaller population centers taken over or managed by the municipal authorities.

One issue received only minimal mention in the report. Despite French efforts to design and promote initiatives at the European level of Europe, MEDIA within the EEC and Eurimages through the Council of Europe (see chapter 4), the report referred to the European question only peripherally. The official obligations of Canal+ stipulated that it must devote 3 percent of its income to European films. The report proposed imposing a similar rule on the other broadcast channels. Thus, while those channels already had to invest 3 percent of their income in film, a certain percentage (0.5 percent) of that might be reserved for "a corridor" of European films. The brief but trenchant final section was called "And Europe?" It recounted how active France had been in supporting European cinema, participating in fully one-third of all European co-productions. Similarly, France had been the "motor" driving MEDIA and Eurimages. Such a commitment "favors French cinema itself by favoring the emergence of a European alternative to the massive supply of American films, and facilitates French producers of large budget films finding an indispensable complement for financing with our neighbors." At the end of the report, Cluzel comments on a debate taking place within the EU film community. Some unnamed commentators, which presumably would have included French producers like Luc Besson, supported production of big-budget films in English capable of competing with U.S. films on their own terms. Others took an opposite stance, "recognizing that the best argument for selling European films rests on their national specificity, and that an attempt to fuse the national cinema languages would lead only to their elimination."[20]

The Cluzel report contained mainly small adjustments to Jack Lang's major reforms of the 1980s. Though parts had indeed contracted since the release of the Bredin report in 1982, the French film industry still compared favorably to its European counterparts. Production was continuing at a level higher than that of other countries in Europe, as television money more than replenished the revenue lost in the Compte de soutien from the drop in attendance. Trying to balance industrial concerns with artistic ones, Cluzel insisted on the importance of big-budget French productions, even as he encouraged backing independent production in various ways, such as allowing more art films to be shown on television and requiring television to set aside a minimum percentage of the cinema investments for independent films. This concern presupposed that innovation and artistic invention were more likely to come from independent production, the artistic conscience as it were of government film policy, and future agreements would formalize that policy. With ever-increasing television investment flowing into production, and contributions from distribution shrinking, theaters were identified as the key sector to respond to the crisis in attendance. As the report pointedly endorsed vertical integration, the large theater circuits would have to be the locus of the recovery. And, in fact, that is what occurred.

The next Ministry of Culture reports did not appear until 2000. Besides the GATT battle, that eight-year span witnessed the continuing success and European expansion of Canal+, the creation of the European Union and other trade skirmishes, and an initiative led by the large circuits that transformed French exhibition. The multiplex phenomenon took off in France and is often credited with the rise in attendance, for both French and U.S. films, with attendance at French films doubling between 1994 and 2004, while the number for U.S. films rose by only 22 percent.

Unlike movie theaters in many other countries, French theaters were owned and operated by French companies. U.S. companies, then, did not control direct access to the theaters, though the output deals with French distributors assured U.S. companies of wide releases of their films, and vertical integration facilitated that access, for the large integrated distributors handled the most successful films. Even the plummeting cinema attendance between 1982 and 1992 was only for French films, so it was not clear that audiences were no longer interested in seeing films in theaters, even if television and video undoubtedly cut into the national theater attendance figures. Thus, theater owners, particularly but not exclusively the major circuits, were in a position to renovate their theaters. This was also when the industry constructed the country's first multiplexes. Not only were the new theaters successful, but attendance in general rebounded, from a low of 115 million in the year of the Cluzel report (1992) to 166 million in 2000.

The multiplex phenomenon reached France late. The U.S. company AMC had introduced multiple screens in Kansas City in 1966.[21] It constructed the theaters in or near commercial centers located outside of city centers, more easily accessible by car and able to attract suburban populations. AMC and others built even larger theaters, known as megaplexes, during the 1980s, and the trend has continued ever since, reaching as many as thirty screens at the AMC Ontario Mills, California, in 1996. Despite the large investments required for construction, the boom continued because it brought results, with attendance curves rising in direct proportion to the creation of megaplexes. In the United States, attendance grew by 15 percent between 1990 and 1998.

Various U.S. companies extended multiplex construction to Europe in the mid-1980s, beginning in Great Britain. Established ties between the film industries in Great Britain and the United States, as well as the vertiginous fall in attendance in Great Britain since the 1940s (during which period British cinemas lost 90 percent of their audience) with corresponding shuttering of theaters, facilitated multiplex construction in that country. Other countries followed suit, including Belgium in 1987, then Germany and Spain, eventually reaching all European countries, with the numbers varying widely from country to country.[22]

Initially, France resisted the trend. French theaters had undergone a wave of renovation during the 1970s, with the construction of complexes with several screens per establishment, and France maintained a larger and better distributed web of theaters than elsewhere in Europe. Following the revival of attendance in countries with multiplexes,[23] and the loss of eight hundred theaters in France between 1987 and 1992,[24] the first multiplexes opened in 1993 in Toulon and outside Paris (Thiais), each with twelve screens.

Multiplex construction accelerated through the rest of the decade. At the end of 1994, there were only four multiplexes in France. The next five years saw the opening of sixty-one new multiplexes, representing some 14 percent of the screens in 1999, and 27 percent of all attendance. Virtually all commentators attribute the rise of 43 percent in national attendance and the market share for French films (29 percent to 33 percent) to the construction of the multiplexes. In 2000, multiplexes accounted for 20 percent of screens and 35 percent of admissions.[25]

As the number of multiplex screens doubled, so did the annual attendance at multiplexes (see figures 6.1–6.4). This trend would continue after

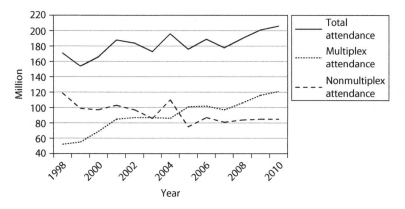

FIGURE 6.1 Attendance at multiplex and nonmultiplex theaters in France, 1989–2010

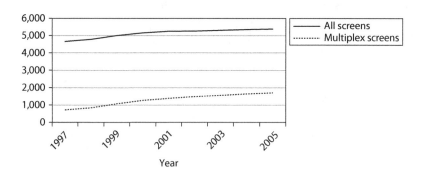

FIGURE 6.2 Number of screens in France and in multiplexes, 1997–2005

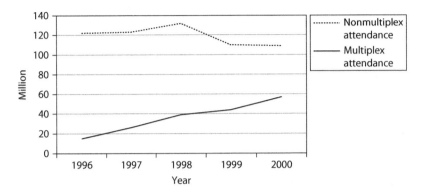

FIGURE 6.3 Attendance at multiplex and nonmultiplex theaters in France, 1996–2000

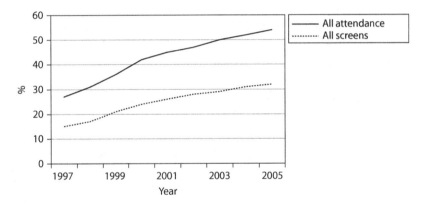

FIGURE 6.4 Multiplexes' share of French exhibition sector, 1997–2005

the Delon report on multiplexes (2000), aggravating problems that were still too early to assess in 2000. However, the Delon report did identify certain issues that related less to the film industry than to urban policy.[26] The scale of multiplex construction, mobilizing large infrastructure investments, threatened to disrupt not only the traditional commercial role of smaller, older theaters but also the balance of commercial interests in the urban areas where multiplexes took root. The large number of spectators were also consumers, not just of films. Placed within, or adjacent to, shopping centers or malls, multiplexes drew customers to those establishments, which meant that those customers were less likely to patronize older shopping areas. Because multiplexes needed a large clientele to survive, they often purchased land on the periphery of urban areas in the hope of attracting both city dwellers and residents of the surrounding suburbs. Commercial businesses in the city centers, then, saw the multiplexes as a threat, one that local authorities would be sensitive to.

France quickly sought to regulate multiplex development. Because the phenomenon was new, regulations had to be revised repeatedly during the 1990s. Catherine Trautmann, the minister of culture, commissioned a report on the difficulties engendered by the multiplexes in October 1999, assigning Francis Delon a broad area to review: "The evaluation that I am asking you to undertake should have as a goal . . . to measure the likely effects of the new situation created by these implantations [multiplexes] with regard to several criteria: the planning of the territory and urban policy; conditions of competition; the level of concentration of the sector and the condition of the exhibition and programming of films, in particular of European films and films distributed by independent distributors."[27]

France first tried to place multiplexes under the existing authority (1973) governing commercial equipment at the department level, but when that proved inadequate, the government passed new laws in 1996, 1998, and 1999. Most of Delon's report was devoted to an assessment of the success of those laws in dealing with the phenomenon of multiplexes, paying relatively little attention to Trautmann's other questions. It turned out that most multiplexes had been built before the latest laws had had a chance to be applied; Delon noted that "of the 65 multiplexes operating on December 31, 1999, only 14 passed through the authorization process."[28] Nonetheless, enough commentary on the procedure had been heard for Delon to address the criticisms in a structural way. Because the basis of the regulations was the 1973 law on territorial planning, local committees were assigned responsibility for granting permits for multiplex construction. The discussion was fairly technical, analyzing the composition of the local committees, revealing that cultural representatives were normally not consulted and that local theater owners were rarely called to testify about the possible impact of multiplex competition. Similarly, spectators played no role in the decision making, thereby excluding the potential clientele.[29] Because permits were assigned to a planning commission, commercial considerations tended to take priority for them, effectively marginalizing cultural questions.

The demonstrated success of the multiplexes would continue in the next century, but the changes they effected in the film landscape had occurred at the initiative of the big players. The industry itself finally had embarked on modernizing and had reversed the most troubling trend in French cinema, the downward spiral of attendance. Though still somewhat modest and uneven, the effect on French and European market share was positive. Setting aside 1998 as an anomalous year because of the phenomenal international success of *Titanic*, French films attracted a larger domestic audience during the late 1990s after the low point of 28.3 percent in 1994.

While the letter from the minister of culture setting out the charge to Delon was brief, Trautmann was clearly concerned about the relatively unregulated growth and especially the growing weight of multiplexes in the film industry. She observed that the first authorization law was then three years old, and it was time for an evaluation. "It seems to me in effect that the current authorization procedure—planned initially for commercial equipment in general—does not always take into account the issues specific to the film industry, which relate essentially to its cultural dimension."[30] This allusion to a possible tension between commercial and cultural imperatives condensed the far more elaborate concerns found in a letter Trautmann sent to the local officials responsible for granting approval to multiplex applications. In that communication, Trautmann, all the while speaking within the context of the legal language contained in the regulations, emphasized the importance of consulting with local theater owners and operators:

> To contribute to an improvement in the treatment of the applications, it will help if the advisers of the DRAC [Direction régionale des affaires culturelles] ensure that the relevant theater owners can contribute information necessary for the assessment of the applications. The decision is your responsibility, but a minimum of information from the operators naturally can enrich your deliberations. To this end, it seems indispensable that the heads of cultural affairs can hold interviews with operators who request them, allowing them to gather the information necessary for applying expertise to the regional plan.[31]

The Delon report made some recommendations for ensuring greater participation of the film industry in the planning and approval of multiplexes, specifically inclusion of local independent theaters and spectators, but beyond the particulars of Delon's analysis, the study reflected a certain anxiety about the degree to which the regulations were failing to control effectively the growth of multiplex expansion. The overall conclusion was that the multiplexes were welcome, but the local commissions might not be exercising adequate vigilance about the cultural development. In other words, multiplexes had boosted attendance figures, but at what cultural cost? Was preference being given to multiplexes on the urban periphery, sucking business and creative energy from the center? Was the magnetic pull of the multiplex reducing attendance at smaller local theaters? Was multiplex programming diluting the diversity of film exhibition? Had the bump in attendance favored U.S. films, justifying those critics who dubbed multiplexes "aircraft carriers of U.S. cinema?"[32] Because it appeared when multiplex growth was still in full expansion, the report offered only tentative answers to these questions. That growth would taper off only several years later, by which time the number of multiplex screens had tripled (from 576 in 1998 to 1,734 in 2007) and the potential dangers could be assessed more concretely.[33]

The Goudineau report, focused on distribution and released later in 2000, also eschewed any radical recommendations. Daniel Goudineau found a clear concentration in distribution, with the top three distributors capturing 50 percent of the receipts for French films, though distributing only some 10 percent of those films.[34] Yet he counseled against any structural changes. With so many small or even tiny firms releasing the large majority of French films, Goudineau wrote, tampering with the tight tissue of all these small firms would disrupt the distribution sector. Thus, none of the twenty-four recommendations found in the report addressed problems of concentration in the distribution sector.[35] Instead, the report suggested relatively timid changes, including further study of some key questions, such as the reasons given for ending a film's run and the length of time individual films had to find their audiences. The proposed measures promised modest ways of squeezing out slightly more revenue for the distributors, such as excluding television co-producers from the Compte de soutien, rewarding distributors for releasing films in traditionally fallow periods such as the summer, and providing bonuses for those concentrating on French films. Goudineau repeated one well-known weakness of distribution in France, namely the prohibition of film advertising on television, which many commentators claim is the single most important form of film promotion. In the United States, television advertising often accounts for 50 percent of all promotion expenses; in France, the biggest publicity expense is on posters, which represents more than 50 percent of what are obviously promotion budgets of incomparably smaller size.

A 2003 report by Jean-Pierre Leclerc also recognized concentration tendencies, but his conclusions focused on finding additional funding resources for production.[36] Writing before the turmoil of Canal+ had subsided, he noted two structural worries: the future of the financial contributions of Canal+ and the uncertainty surrounding the position of the European Commission on the French financing mechanism, which he saw as "difficult not to see as a system of aid."[37] Of the thirty-three recommendations in the report, only one concerned concentration, calling simply for discussion with the appropriate authorities about the law of competition. Others proposed administrative changes, such as reforming the *commission d'agrément* or establishing an *observatoire de la production cinématographique*. The financial reforms included a new tax on DVD purchases, expanding television's contributions in various ways (such as including foundation income in the calculation of their receipts), pursuing export efforts, encouraging the commitment of regions, and introducing various fiscal changes.[38] Leclerc also repeated Goudineau's suggestion to bar television from automatic aid drawn from Compte de soutien receipts; the 3.2 percent tax rate on television stations should be real, not discounted by back-door loopholes.[39] For each recommendation, Leclerc listed the amount it would cost the government and the expected return to film investment. Like the 2002 CNC report on financing,[40] the Leclerc report proposed applying the tax on DVDs to retail instead of wholesale sales. Shifting the DVD tax to retail sales would generate €5–7 million per year, costing the government nothing.

Leclerc also proposed increasing the tax benefits available for film investment to attract more private investors. Among his many reforms of the state support system in the 1980s, Jack Lang had established a tax shelter mechanism known as SOFICAs. The SOFICAs, partially backed by state guarantees, were essentially investment groups seeking funds exclusively for the production of French films for which investors received tax benefits. When introduced in 1985, the SOFICAs contributed roughly 10 percent of all investment in French film. However, over time, despite measures imposed in 1996 to reverse this trend, the SOFICA percentage of total investment fell to 3 percent. The innovation was designed specifically to support independent production, but the minimum percentage of SOFICA investment to be devoted to independents was only 35 percent. Because independent production entailed a higher risk, most of the money went into large-budget films with lower risk, and independent producers balked at some of the conditions imposed by the SOFICAs. Leclerc proposed raising the minimum to be invested in independent production to 65 percent. Other technical adjustments would involve tying the investments more to real risk, rather than having a higher return guaranteed by the government even if films were not released or performed poorly at the box office. According to Leclerc, raising the state support of SOFICAS by €55 million would return €80 million newly available for production, of which €58 million would be earmarked for independent productions.

While most of the reports addressed the search for greater production funding, the biggest challenge, and the recurrent theme of all of these documents, appeared to be preserving or promoting diversity at all levels of the industry, even as concentration tendencies continued apace. The quantitative translation of diversity took the form of precise percentages to be applied to independent film professionals, whether in production, distribution, or exhibition. As the costs of big-budget films, produced normally by large integrated companies (referred to as *groupes* in France), had tended to rise, taking a proportionately larger share of the investment pie, the film industry negotiated a "diversity clause" with Canal+.[41] First adopted in 2000, it required 45 percent of the company's investments to be in productions below a threshold of €5.4 million. Beginning in 2003, this rule also applied to other cable and satellite stations. Multiplexes, owned for the most part by the *groupes*, tended to fill their screens with the expensive films, so one proposal would require them to keep independent films on their screens for at least two weeks. Such rules could take several forms. The state, through its film arm, the CNC, could develop procedures and then insist on adherence to them. The changes in the *agrément* rules in 1998 fell in this category. But the government often preferred to avoid official intervention, not wanting to draw the attention of the European Commission, which carefully monitored state actions that could be considered restraints of free trade among EU member states. One alternative was to encourage the main actors, such as the television stations and various professional organizations in the case of the "diversity clause" of Canal+, to reach voluntary agreements.

Most discussions shrank from taking on aesthetic questions directly. The diaphanous term "diversity" normally performed this task. In a general sense, diversity referred to a maintaining a variety of participants, at any point in the film *filière* (industry).[42] A diversity of films meant a variety of small-, medium-, and large-budget films, quantitative terms, not qualitative ones. While individual big-budget productions are not necessarily the most likely to be remunerative, they have less trouble attracting financing, so diversity agreements call for minimum percentages to be devoted to lower-budget films, as noted above. Diversity in exhibition involved supporting small-theater owners who did not have the financial resources to invest in multiplex construction, so the CNC installed measures to aid small theater renovation. Similar steps were taken with distributors; Goudineau, for example, recommended rewarding distributors that distribute first films (French or foreign), poorly distributed or short films, and so forth.

Inevitably, as the state tried to "correct" unwelcome results of the market, certain unanticipated effects occurred. Several studies have identified a bipolar distribution of film budgets: a relatively small number of expensive films and a large number of low-budget films, leaving a relative void in the mid-budget films that are thought on balance more likely to have successful careers. But the diversity clause specifically limited its backing of just such films, and there was no provision to index the €5.4 million figure to inflation. Solution? Leclerc suggested raising the figure to €7.5 million, illustrating how the endless tweaking could develop its own momentum.[43]

The proposed revision in the funding of the Compte de soutien offered another apparent conundrum. The Compte de soutien, filled by the tax on theater receipts and television revenues (essentially advertising and subscriptions), funneled funds back to the industry. Most of the *aide automatique* was returned to French producers, but with a coefficient that varied according to the market share of French films.[44] The tax applied to all films shown in France, including U.S. films, but only French (and European) producers could draw on it; thus, U.S. films, like all films, paid a tax that went directly to French and European production. However, while the amount of the Compte de soutien was indifferent to the market shares of French and U.S. films, a larger market share for U.S. films raised the coefficient. Conversely, if French films managed a larger market share, the coefficient would decline, with producers sharing (as it were) smaller contributions from U.S. films to the Compte de soutien, yielding less money available for reinvestment to each producer. In short, one of the principal sources of *new* production money (for future productions) got smaller as French films whittled away market share from Hollywood fare, penalizing French producers. In fact, there is no paradox here. The automatic aid was designed to reward box office success. If French films in a given year draw a high market share, then French cinema has achieved a certain success, and on the macro level should need less government support.

These reports identified problems in virtually every sector of the industry. Producers were churning out more films than ever before, but there was still not enough money for production. Distribution grew increasingly concentrated, particularly in companies handling U.S. films, and provided less and less financing, with French films bearing the brunt of this disinterest of distributors in the performance of many French films in theaters. Exhibitors had even less financial interest in French films, for their receipts were independent of the nationality of the films, and their preference among French productions supported films financed by the *groupes*, exacerbating concentration.

For the most part, then, these reports recommended measures designed to coax out more money from the system, a system in 2000 already disbursing some thirty forms of aid and roundly criticized for its opacity and complexity.[45] But they refrained from rethinking fundamental principles, specifically the relations between film and its current benefactor, television, and the threats to diversity posed by accelerating concentration aggravated by international capital ententes. Leclerc concluded his report with the observation that the problems with investment financing flowed from the *distribution* of resources more than from the global amount. This reticence in the face of profound changes probably reflected the corporatist nature of the whole support mechanism.[46] The CNC, from its inception, had worked closely with professionals in the cinema industry, and often sought to clear its recommendations with industry figures, who are normally the principal interlocutors during the work of the various studies. As most commentators agree, the system has functioned well over many years, and the privatization of television has unquestionably pulled French cinema back from the brink of collapse, a success unmatched by any other European film industry.

PARLIAMENTARY REPORTS

The reports commissioned by the Ministry of Culture and Communication examined very specific, and traditional, aspects of the film industry: exhibition (Delon), distribution (Goudineau), and production (Leclerc). There is overlap of course among the reports—a discussion of exhibition can hardly avoid mentioning distributors, for example—but their principal purview is limited to their particular sectors. Consequently, while not simply echoes of film lobbying groups, the reports acknowledge that they are not looking at the industry as a whole. Parliament also conducted its own reports, and these tended to be more independent of the industry, though not necessarily less informed; in addition, these reports often either commissioned their own technical consultants or relied on more independent sources.[47]

In 1998, the Senate completed its own report, titled "The Effectiveness of Public Support for Cinema." Senator Jean Cluzel, who had closely followed audiovisual developments (especially television) for many years, submitted the report, written by the Bureau d'information et de prévisions économiques (BIPE) and Stratorg International, a company specializing in such research. This long and data-rich study surveyed the entire industry with a particular emphasis on assessing the role of public aids to cinema. With the looming formation of the European Union in 1993, the CNC had already begun to make some minor technical adjustments to conform to EU rules, such as the criteria to qualify for state support. But a CNC report in 1996 showed that the generous conditions for co-production in France risked bleeding the French support system, as EU partners took advantage of the French system without appropriate reciprocity. In response, France introduced a new scale to define cultural criteria (use of French language, employment of French technicians, and so on) for the disbursement of French aids.[48]

Looking at a wide variety of state aids, the report concluded that the "objective was fulfilled, but at a heavy cost." The objective was "maintaining a national cinema and encouraging cultural diversity."[49] The cost included a finding from Court's report ten years earlier (and the 1992 Cluzel study) that French cinema had evolved "from a logic of amortization to a logic of pre-financing," leading Jean Cluzel to conclude that the support system "disconnects the companies from the constraints of the market, that is, from the tastes of the public [in theaters],"[50] for producers by then supplied only 25 percent of production financing, compared to 40 percent ten years earlier. The report did note, significantly, that public aid amounted to only 15 percent of total investment in French film production, lower than in any of the other leading European film industries, with the exception of the United Kingdom (12 percent). That analysis implied that direct government intervention was relatively limited, an important clarification in relation to the concerns of the European Commission. BIPE called state support "less a system of direct subsidy . . . than a mechanism of regulation, redistribution, and investment obligations imposed on television."[51] BIPE did question the value of the tax shelter SOFICAs, which attracted only wealthy taxpayers and financed only four or five films annually. And the report included no recommendations, even though it did underline the "risk of a financial crisis in the medium-term future," warning specifically of the possible stagnation of television financing. That medium-term crisis arrived with the Vivendi Universal debacle several years later.[52]

By the time of the Vivendi Universal collapse in 2002, still other parliamentary studies had identified serious structural problems, unlike most of the other studies that had categorized problems as conjunctural. In a 2003 Senate Rapport d'information, Senators Yann Gaillard and Paul Loridant differentiated their investigation by noting that it looked at the whole industry, not simply individual parts.[53] Though completed only months after the Leclerc report for the Ministry of Culture, the preface concluded with the assertion that "the whole list of 'resources' developed by M. Jean-Marie Leclerc . . . will not adequately confront the anticipated crisis." Michel Fansten, in yet another report, completed for the group Réalisations et recherches audiovisuelles and published as an annex to the Gaillard and Loridant report, emphasized two observations: "the analysis is more pessimistic; the measures that it proposes are more radical."[54] At the same time, a report by the Départment d'études stratégiques sur l'audiovisuel et le cinéma (DESAC), an audiovisual think tank, saw a shift in the "tectonic plates" of the French film industry.[55] With Messier's roller-coaster piloting of Vivendi Universal and the fate of Canal+ still unclear, for the first time since the privatization of French television in the mid-1980s, the viability of the French model was on the table for discussion.

Gaillard and Loridant commented extensively on both the Fansten study and the Leclerc report. Writing as representatives of the Commission de finances, they tried to follow the money the state spent on film. Thus, they called for increased transparency in the support system and better monitoring of the various aids; they also recommended eliminating the tax on television from the automatic aid (though retaining it in the selective aid), for those funds belonged to television. Apparently because films had lost their preeminent popularity, the authors rejected the original argument that television benefits from its screening of films. In addition, they repeatedly expressed concern over the aggressive free market thrust of the European Commission; since the completion of the report, the EC's trade commission has repeatedly extended its approval of France's film support policies.[56] However, Gaillard and Loridant also cautioned against any abrupt changes in the system, recognizing, even insisting, that such changes would threaten its stability:

> The spirit in which [we] approach this "recasting" is not one of scrapping the old system, which if it were done too quickly and was perceived as radical would only destabilize an already fragile system; on the contrary, [we] propose instead the idea *of a progressive process of adaptation*, emphasizing the need for continuity with the existing system, for it is essential to *guarantee to the profession*, independently of an eventual change in the system, *the continuity* without which all reform of the whole would fail.[57]

While this statement may have been appropriate tactically to avoid incurring the wrath of the cinema industry, the authors also questioned whether the government had effectively abdicated its responsibility to set policy by contenting itself with being a *simple spectateur engagé*, a clear acknowledgment and tacit criticism of the corporatist nature of the relations between the CNC and the film industry.[58]

In contrast, and perhaps because it was commissioned as an independent report to accompany the work of Gaillard and Loridant, the Fansten report does not edulcorate the pessimism of its analysis. And its title indicates an even broader context than the cinema industry: "Le cinéma français face à l'évolution technologique et à la transformation des marchés."[59] Thus, on the first page, unlike the previous studies, this report announces that despite the apparent signs of cinema's good health, "All the ingredients taken together suggest that [the cinema] will face, relatively soon, a major crisis." Fansten stressed that the "primary factor of fragility relates to the weight of television in the financing of cinema" and, perhaps most significantly, with an eye on the fallout from the VU debacle, that television's role in the resuscitation of French cinema had ended. While the Leclerc report concentrated on identifying new funding sources, Fansten warned against restricting reforms to that solution: "The questions of financing are in effect only indicative of growing problems that French cinema is going to have to confront."[60]

Fansten devoted explicit attention to the problems posed by globalization. His analysis, though supported by detailed figures, presents a broader picture of the central tensions faced by the industry (including the inflation of promotion costs for big-budget films and the accompanying rise in the number of release prints). The threat posed by concentration surfaces throughout the discussion. Fansten invoked the economic theory of William Baumol to explain these tendencies.[61] As the costs of production rise, an industry can find productivity savings and/or enlarge the size of the market to cover those expenses. But if, as in the case of cinema, those options are not available, the competition for revenue drives escalating marketing costs, a process Fansten refers to as "la survalorisation des enjeux de concurrence" (intensification of competition).[62] Those costs drive out the weakest economic actors, resulting in greater concentration. In cinema, the search for revenue entails larger budgets of the films and higher promotion costs, with ever-increasing numbers of copies released in theaters controlled by a smaller number of operators holding a large market share.[63]

While Fansten knew that this process was not a new one, what was new was the role of the large communication groups. As noted above, various reports refer back to the Bredin study from 1981 (discussed in chapter 1) when addressing concentration, in particular vertical integration. At that time, Bredin recommended against government intervention aimed at discouraging vertical integration. Unlike some of the other writers, who appear to concur with Bredin's position,[64] Fansten contended that there were three essential differences between the situation in 1981 and that of 2002. First, the process of vertical integration had assumed an international dimension, in which a financial logic (of mergers and acquisition) had replaced an industrial one (efficiency of production, building markets, etc.). Second, the cinema industry, in particular film production, constituted only one aspect (and the least profitable one) of the activities of integrated groups.

The risk was that the companies' cinema activities could be sacrificed to retain only those business sectors considered more strategic for the future. Third, the regulatory machinery of the CNC and the Conseil supérieur de l'audiovisuel (CSA) were no longer adequate to track and control transformations occurring outside the cinema and television industries. The highly publicized saga of Canal+ within VU clearly underwrote Fansten's analysis. He concluded that serious discussions should begin between the government office responsible for regulating competition and the various professional organizations. These discussions would also require theoretical work on the rationales undergirding eventual corrective measures in order to coordinate them with the European Commission, which Fansten viewed as a bastion of free trade ideology (see chapter 7).[65]

OTHER VOICES

These concerns over the viability of the film support system alarmed figures outside the industry. Jean Cluzel, author of the 1998 parliamentary report, perhaps smarting from the industry's continuing resistance to change, despite his earlier recommendations, published in a 2003 book a splenetic attack on the corporatism of the cinema industry.[66] What Cluzel regarded as the complete disconnect between film production and the market drove his polemic. While some writers described film production as necessarily a casino, where commercial success could never be predicted, Cluzel called the Compte de soutien a *"casino à la française,* where the players never lose." French cinema was a "cinema under transfusion," and those working in the industry, "under hypnosis," addicted to the largesse of state aid. So resistant was the industry to change that reform "would require a veritable revolution in *mentalités.*"[67] For Cluzel, who fervently argued for the defense of French culture, change needed to entail dropping the red flag of the *exception culturelle,* linking aid to market expectations as in Canada and Denmark, working in concert with European partners, and, above all, breaking the power of the French cinema lobby.

Cluzel claimed that the French rooster proudly serving as the logo of Pathé for a century had been replaced by an ostrich. French cinema insisted on burying its autarchic head in the national sand, wanting "to see nothing, understand nothing, and ignore everything." Meanwhile, globalization required tapping into the internationalization of markets. Luc Besson had demonstrated that France could export films internationally, even if Besson made some of his films in English. Cluzel's 1998 report had also decried the disconnection between the financing of films and their performance in theaters, but the book five years later considered that as the overarching weakness of French cinema, a weakness he documented at length. Yet the failure of French films at the box office was in no way unique. Comparisons with other film industries, including the U.S. industry, show that most films everywhere fail at the box office, with theatrical receipts clustering around fewer and fewer big-budget films. Furthermore, as many of his fellow rapporteurs made clear, the French support system was based largely on directing the funding from theaters and television according to box office success and did not represent selective aid that does rely on subjective decisions by the commissions that Cluzel found so objectionable.

A dossier titled "French Cinema and the State: A Model in Question" appeared the following year.[68] Daniel Sauvaget, one of the contributors, wrote that the system was on the verge of "collapse."[69] Joëlle Farchy and Laurent Creton, who published two synoptic looks at the French film industry at the same time, used less apocalyptic language, but both suggested that the system had to make some structural changes if it was to adapt to rapidly changing circumstances.[70]

In a related article, Creton, trying like Fansten to assimilate lessons from the Vivendi/Canal+ meltdown, traced vast changes in the nature of media companies, in which film played a less and less significant role. As he assessed it, the image industry was going through its second big transformation. With the privatization of television in the mid-1980s, and especially following the fabulous growth of Canal+, film on television had lost its independent luster for audiences and had instead worked out a modus vivendi with the world of television and video. The new dependence of film on television financing "explains the structural ambivalence of the relation between these two poles: a cocktail more or less spiced with confrontation and cooperation."[71] Both television *and* film had to find new places in the new world of the communication empires, with their proliferation of screening windows and cross-industry markets. In these empires film in theaters functioned now as a first "window" (in the stream of receipts), one of the least remunerative, followed, according to the "chronology" of media, by video (cassettes and DVD), television (pay-per-view, pay TV, broadcast TV, thematic TV on cable and satellite), and the Internet. Because the theater box office window was financially modest (about 15 percent of total industry receipts), film had to fight to retain its "aura" while moving through the downstream windows, of which television had become only the third in the journey (or occasionally the first).[72]

Paradoxically, given Walter Benjamin's embrace of film as the destroyer of art's "aura," Laurent Creton considered that French films were in the process of losing their "aura" as films.[73] Others referred to the phenomenon as the "banalization" of French films by virtue of their constant exposure on television, a practice aggravated by the tendency to show the same films over and over again.[74] Thus, films on television had come to be seen as moments of nostalgia, for young and old alike, especially in prime time. While Benjamin welcomed cinema as a new art form that would remove the cultlike aura from art, thereby democratizing it, French cinema had suffered from the very loss of aura that distinguished it from the commercial products of television. Indeed, one of the reasons France prohibited film advertising on television had been the concern that it would turn cinema into just another commercial product.[75]

In this new communications generation, Creton and Farchy both noted that media megaliths (AOL–Time Warner, Vivendi Universal, Bertelsmann, etc.) now held so many companies that they could simply jettison weak profit performers. And their global reach relieved management from local—in this case national—responsibilities. Creton, who has also written a detailed and indispensable history of the French support system since its inception under Vichy,[76] took the long view that the system has adapted in the past and will have to be able to adapt once again to preserve French cinema. Preservation would have to encompass diversity, that ubiquitous if always elusive term permeating virtually every diagnostic. Farchy, in her contribution to the dossier, after careful examination of the battle over the language of diversity—the pliant slide from "cultural exception" to "cultural diversity" and on to "pluralism"—reached a similar conclusion, though she stressed the centrality of political will in a strategy for cinema's survival.

The Ministry of Culture reports identified new funding sources, even as they encouraged preserving the obligations of television. Nevertheless, the declining appeal of film on television and television's power over the films it invests in are likely to continue. Consequently, television's demands will become more pressing. If television continues to accept its financial obligations, it will seek more television-friendly films. Alternatively, or perhaps concurrently, television will exert its influence to reduce its financial obligations. So far, the new funding sources promise only limited infusions of production money. In any event, Gaillard and Loridant view the total production pot of money to be virtually a zero sum: there is only so much potential funding available. Increasing one window's obligations will only replace shrinking receipts elsewhere in the *filière*.[77]

The concentration challenge remains a long-term problem, as all writers recognize, but a solution, if one exists, eludes them. Fearing the power of the U.S. majors, the authorities appear willing to countenance concentration nationally, even to encourage it. At the same time, virtually every report proposes measures to ensure diversity. Diversity has come to represent art in the tension between art and industry throughout the film *filière*, supporting small theaters in exhibition, small distributors, and low-budget production. Thus, as concentration puts ever-greater pressure on independent actors, the studies seek ways of propping up those independent sectors through placing new obligations on the large firms or groups. In a 2000 study for the CNC, Farchy and Kopp called this approach "largely contradictory."[78] While it is tempting to attribute some of this bind to the pro-market bias of the European Commission, and that is no doubt a factor, it is also true that the 1981 Bredin report rejected fighting vertical integration in a fashion similar to the "consent decrees" in the United States after World War II.

The Leclerc report posed one key question that virtually all such studies have sought to answer: which changes are conjunctural and which permanent? In principle, conjunctural challenges are tractable, and government policy can attempt to influence them. The basic tension between art and industry will always apply, though the particular constellation of variables inevitably evolves. If the weight of television took on increasing importance after it was privatized, television had already affected the fortunes of cinema. A dossier of excerpts from trade publications, the "Economic Situation of French Cinema," from 1980, can provide some perspective on the changes in the film industry over two decades.[79] Two critics already had enumerated some of those developments at the end of the 1970s, when television was still entirely state-owned.[80] As state enterprises, television "exercised a certain pressure on auteurs and filmmakers, prohibiting films with subjects deemed dangerous." Repertory cinemas had virtually disappeared under the pressures of theaters seeking first-run films. With the number of movie copies exploding, the time in theaters was reduced to several weeks. "The sale to television appeared thus practically as a godsend, even if the [purchase] prices remain relatively low." If the time-frame was premature, Pierre Billard predicted accurately the future relations of film and television: "Little by little, a new perspective is dawning, which would constitute a radical reversal of alliances. From enemy, television can become partner, an ally. We are not there yet. This will be the problem of the 1980s."[81]

With the multiplication of theaters, especially the generation of cramped *multi-salles* in France, before the development of the more sumptuous modern multiplexes, the projection conditions deteriorated, with "screens getting smaller and smaller . . . we understand easily that people prefer to stay home to see a film in more comfortable conditions with an image quality barely inferior to what they can see in theaters." Multiplexes introduced in the 1990s improved the projection conditions, but they programmed the most popular films, including so-called commercial art films, drying up supply for repertory or art theaters. As for concentration, one writer cited a statement from the Association de défense du cinéma and de ses spectateurs, an activist spectator group that traced the deterioration of exhibition to the efforts "to create the maximum profit for the trusts that monopolize all the sectors of cinema."[82]

Setting aside the increasing complexity of the system, the French state's strategy has two prongs. On the one hand, the authorities tacitly accede to vertical integration in the chimerical hope that French majors will grow sufficiently to compete with the Hollywood majors in France.[83] Some even express hopes for building European film structures built on collapsing assets of the national film industries. On the other hand, the diversity requirements proliferate to compensate for the market failure of the bulk of French production. Farchy accepts that quality can emerge only from sufficient quantity, arguing that there is no need to worry over producing too many films,[84] but other writers are less sanguine about it. Furthermore, the anxiety that clouded the GATT negotiations has shifted from the national trade battle with the United States to a constant worry about the articulation and acceptance of French media policies within the neoliberal regulatory structure of the European Union, a factor cited in the formulation of many of the reforms. Finally, as the communication companies continue to consolidate, horizontally and vertically, and especially across traditional industry boundaries, national borders begin to fade away and escape the regulatory apparatus.

The French support system is built on elaborate national definitions in order to identify, track, and capture currency flows. Housed within the Ministry of Culture and Communication and charged with implementing government policy, the CNC directs the proliferating mix of aids distributed in all directions. The temporal convergence of CNC reports, parliamentary studies, academic analyses, and independent examinations in the years of VU's tumultuous rise and fall reflected deep anxieties over the efficacy and stability of the French support system. Everyone seems to agree on the basic outline of the problems, even if the urgency of the tone varies. The Ministry of Culture studies paint a worrying picture, though in a diminished key; parliamentary reports, perhaps freed from the interested pull of the industry and anxious about the hostility of the European Commission, yield more disturbing assessments; academics, in measured registers, speak about the need for fundamental reform; and private commentators are the most strident. The official confusion and even consternation over the status of Canal+ in the growing Vivendi empire forced all of the concerned parties to confront the possibility that the expansion of the global companies may render the pertinence and efficacy of the current cinema and television architecture obsolete, thereby shattering what had been for two decades the best model and hope for nurturing a national film industry in Europe. Despite the fears generated by the VU episode, Françoise Giroud's prediction that "Hollywood will swallow Messier"[85] did not take long to be confirmed, though foreign companies' failure to occupy the Hollywood majors' inner circle has many antecedents. While the continuing hegemonic pressures of the United States did not subside, France increasingly had to contend with the more proximate neoliberal gaze of the European Commission, which the official reports constantly alluded to. In response, France sought shelter in a new rhetorical and political strategy: cultural diversity.

7

FROM CULTURAL EXCEPTION
TO CULTURAL DIVERSITY

The public buffeting of Canal+ in the early years of the new century followed other developments roiling the audiovisual world. Boundaries between television and film were eroding, and the accrued power of television aggravated anxieties in the French film industry. Massive media conglomerates prowled for new acquisitions across national frontiers, and countries scrambled to adjust their film industries to conform to new regional and international regulations. France had pushed back against the neoliberals in the European Commission during the long debate over the Directive on Television Without Frontiers in the 1980s and then fought off the United States in the GATT confrontation in the early 1990s. While those battles were significant, the war continued. The European Commission soon set its sights on the French system of aid to film, and the World Trade Organization regularly placed audiovisual practices on its agenda of trade liberalization in trade negotiations. Thus, while France led the dirigiste charge in the earlier encounters, it was constantly looking over its shoulder at the threats looming from supranational organizations. Seeking to develop a less defensive policy, France, often working closely with Canada, increasingly promoted "cultural diversity" as a goal of national policy to justify its support system for cinema and fend off the neoliberal pressures of the officials steering the EU and the WTO.

REGIONAL POLICY CHANGE: MAASTRICHT

The inclusion of culture in the 1992 Treaty on European Union (the Maastricht Treaty) established a new legal environment for cultural policies in Europe. The Treaty of Rome (1957), successor to the European Coal and Steel Community, was an economic document, reflected in the name given to the organization it created: the European Economic Community. The Treaty of Rome came with the appropriate provisions of liberal orientation, including rules to promote competition and increased trade, encouraging free markets and reduced state intervention. Member nations of the EEC pursued those policies internally and negotiated trade arrangements with non-EEC countries as a single entity. The treaty in principle did apply to trade in goods, and film would later be considered a good, based on the terms of GATT, whose Article IV allowed screen quotas for "cinematographic films." As television barely existed at that time, in 1947, there was no legal precedent governing the treatment of television. In the Sacchi case of 1974, the European Court of Justice ruled that television was a service and thus fell outside the purview of the GATT agreement, which applied only to trade in goods, though the boundary between goods and services still remains blurry.[1]

The Treaty of Rome contained no provisions for culture. The Maastricht Treaty, however, included a new article and several clauses on culture, providing the EU a more stable authority to intervene in the affairs of film and television. However, while these clauses referred to the rights and responsibilities of member countries to support culture, they were pitched at a general level and did not address key questions; those would have to be clarified later by EU legal interpretations.

Thus, there was a basic tension between the liberal precepts of the Rome treaty and the ill-defined protections for culture in Maastricht. One central axis, for example, concerned the injunction against state aid, which risked distorting free competition, and member country support systems for cultural production. While there had been one earlier skirmish over state aid to culture,[2] the next salvo came from the European Commission in the late 1990s over state aids to cinema. The Maastricht Treaty contained the same prohibition on state aids to industries as the Rome treaty had: "1. Save as otherwise provided in the Treaties, any aid granted by a Member State or through State resources in any form

whatsoever which distorts or threatens to distort competition by favouring certain undertakings or the production of certain goods shall, in so
far as it affects trade between Member States, be incompatible with the
internal market."[3] The principle being applied was the preservation of
competition, an economic foundation for the original and later treaties.
Exceptions considered "compatible with the common market" were listed
in the following paragraphs, allowing for states to provide support for
distressed populations or areas suffering from abnormal conditions such
as high unemployment or natural disasters, though even those dispensations would be granted only for a limited time. In the same article, the
Maastricht Treaty introduced a new exception, and the only one granted
to an industry: "(d) aid to promote culture and heritage conservation
where such aid does not affect trading conditions and competition in the
Union to an extent that is contrary to the common interest." This new
allowance conformed to the new article on culture, which encouraged the
EU to "contribute to the flowering of the cultures of the Member States,
while respecting their national and regional diversity and at the same time
bringing the common cultural heritage to the fore," and also for the first
time allowed that the activities of the European "Community shall take
cultural aspects into account in its action under other provisions of the
Treaties."[4] But these clauses were extremely general and obviously subject to a broad range of interpretation. The European Commission would
have to test the applicability of the language of the new treaty in practice.

The EC ruled in 1998 that French aids to cinema were acceptable. In
its decision, the EC laid out four criteria to be satisfied in order to receive
approval:

1. The aid is directed to a cultural product. Each Member State must
ensure that the content of the aided production is cultural according to
verifiable national criteria (in compliance with the application of the subsidiarity principle).

2. The producer must be free to spend at least 20% of the film budget
in other Member States without suffering any reduction in the aid provided for under the scheme. In other words, the Commission accepted as
an eligibility criteria territorialisation in terms of expenditure of up to
80% of the production budget of an aided film or TV work.

3. Aid intensity must in principle be limited to 50% of the production
budget with a view to stimulating normal commercial initiatives inherent

in a market economy and avoiding a bidding contest between Member States. Difficult and low budget films are excluded from this limit. The Commission considers that, under the subsidiarity principle, it is up to each Member State to establish a definition of difficult and low budget film according to national parameters.

4. Aid supplements for specific filmmaking activities (e.g. post-production) are not allowed in order to ensure that the aid has a neutral incentive effect and consequently that the protection/attraction of those specific activities in/to the Member State granting the aid is avoided.[5]

The first criterion permits member states to set their own "verifiable national criteria" for what constitutes cultural production, according to the subsidiarity principle. As defined in EU documents, the general principle of subsidiarity maintains that the EU can act only when questions cannot be resolved at the level of individual member countries, effectively proscribing EU action absent a demonstrated need for it.[6]

In paragraph 2, "territoriality" refers to requirements of where the aid must be spent. A state cannot demand that all such aid be spent on its own territory. The third rule stipulates that aid cannot cover more than 50 percent of the budget of a work, thereby requiring producers to raise at least half of the budget outside of state support. The same paragraph exempts low-budget films from this ceiling, implicitly acknowledging the difficulty that smaller films may encounter in finding financing. Countries are free once again to have broad discretion in determining what films may qualify as low-budget productions. The final rule prohibits singling out specific production activities for protection in a given state, since any such provision would confer a commercial advantage on that activity, thereby violating the principle of free competition.

The juxtaposition of the original treaty's article on state aid and the Maastricht Treaty's new article on culture frames a basic contradiction in the EU's policy toward cinema. Article 107 in the Treaty of Rome opens with the general statement on the incompatibility of state aids with the principle of free competition. The new provision for compatibility with "aid to promote culture" complicates the issue, for state aid to support culture—especially "cultural goods"—may by its nature conflict with Treaty of Rome's emphasis on free competition. In the 1998 decision, the EC's approach to assessing the compatibility of the French system concentrates almost exclusively on cultural works: "Although the production of films is considered in the present decision as a cultural activity, it is important to avoid subsidizing commercial productions which do not contribute to this notion of culture." On the one hand, state aid is prohibited; on the other, states can define "cultural products" as they deem appropriate. Thus, as one commentator noted in 2003, "given the fact that culture is, and most probably will remain, a matter of competence of the Member States [according to the principle of subsidiarity], it is tempting to conclude that the Commission, by checking the compatibility of national film funding systems with EU state aid rules, is exceeding the limits of its competence."[7]

Regarding television, a protocol in the 1997 Treaty of Amsterdam includes a specific provision for state-owned public broadcasting. The "Protocol on the System of Public Broadcasting in the Member States" stipulates:

> The provisions of the Treaty establishing the European Community shall be without prejudice to the competence of Member States to provide for the funding of public service broadcasting insofar as such funding is granted to broadcasting organisations for the fulfilment of the public service remit as conferred, defined and organised by each Member State, and insofar as such funding does not affect trading conditions and competition in the Community to an extent which would be contrary to the common interest, while the realisation of the remit of that public service shall be taken into account.

Here the new treaty exempts public service broadcasting from the reach of the European Community. Anticipating the changes in the media landscape to be effected by technological developments such as satellite television, both the EEC and the Council of Europe had reached a compromise agreement in 1989 on the Directive on Television Without Frontiers and the Convention on Cross-Border Television, the former representing the first audiovisual policy effort of the EEC. Once the Maastricht Treaty introduced articles on culture, including the term "audiovisual," television finally was integrated formally into the European treaty. This protocol, however, acknowledged that there was reason to distinguish between publicly owned television and private television. Public television performed with the remit of public service, to be determined by member states. Though it is not stated explicitly, presumably private television operates according to a purely commercial goal, fitting more seamlessly into the liberal orientation of all the treaties. Film, however, figured only indirectly, if significantly, in the European debates over how to fold television into advancing European integration. French efforts to include mandatory quotas in the TWF directive clearly were meant to enlist television to compensate for declining theatrical attendance. But film remained outside the legal orbit of the EEC.

On one rare occasion, in the case of the French film *Le Marginal*, the European Court of Justice (ECJ) had addressed the compatibility of film with European law (see chapter 3). When the filmmakers brought action in the ECJ, they were testing the jurisdiction of France to set national film policy. The court found in favor of the French law. Commenting ten years later on the possible significance of the more restrictive ruling, Jean-Michel Frodon wrote that the consequence could have been "huge": "If the European Court supported the complaint, it would bring film into [European] jurisprudence. It would thus end all hope of constructing a European system of regulation, but also any existing French system, not only for the video waiting period, but also on the delay for over-the-air television, for Canal Plus, and globally, of the whole French architecture, which would be thereby be declared incompatible with the EEC rules."[8]

In upholding the French law, the ECJ ruled that "in principle, the Treaty leaves it to the Member State to determine the need for such a system, the form of such a system and any temporal restrictions which ought to be laid down." As the treaty did not yet authorize competence in cultural matters, the court relied on the European Commission for advice in the case. In its decision, the court wrote, "The Commission maintains . . . that cultural aims may justify certain restrictions on the free movement of goods provided that those restrictions apply to national and imported products without distinction." Ultimately, the court did not find discrimination among member states, for the French law applied to both "domestically produced and imported cassettes alike."[9]

In this 1985 decision, the treaty referred to was the Treaty of Rome. As that treaty did not encompass culture, the court clearly deferred to the autonomy of member states to set their own film policy, even if it did so partially in relation to protecting what the decision referred to as the "profitability of cinematographic production." In any event, this judgment, and the paucity of cases relating to film in European jurisprudence, indicates that the EEC had trod lightly on national film industries.

That caution in interfering with national film policy began to change after the passage of the Maastricht Treaty, whose article 128 was specifically devoted to culture. As a further refinement, the Amsterdam Treaty of 1997 added one new short clause (in italics): "The Community shall take cultural aspects into account in its action under other provisions of this Treaty, *in particular in order to respect and to promote the diversity of its cultures.*"[10] This small change actually corresponded to a major shift in the orientation of strategies to resist intervention by supranational organizations—the EU and the WTO—in the formulation of national film policies.

INTERNATIONAL POLICY CHANGE: TOWARD A NEW STRATEGY

At about the same time, the tide began to turn in the international audiovisual standoff. After GATT, the next round of that struggle took place during the negotiations among the most developed countries in the Organization for Economic Cooperation and Development (OECD) for a multilateral agreement on investment (MAI). Conducted even more secretly than the final negotiations of the Uruguay Round, these talks received little coverage, and few details were released in the press. In 1997, Ralph Nader obtained an internal document and published it in *Public Citizen.*[11] The public learned that companies would now have the right to sue countries, further eroding the power of nations to control their own trade policies. The talks were scheduled to conclude in Paris in 1998, but in February 1998 a group of artists and filmmakers in France publicly protested both the process and the content of the proposed pact.[12]

Nongovernmental organizations throughout the world also registered their opposition to the MAI. The French government, alarmed at the terms, announced that a study group would assess the implications of the proposals. Prime Minister Lionel Jospin made known French reservations, and the study group completed and released the Lalumière report in September, recommending that France withdraw from negotiations based on the draft document.[13] In November, France summarily announced that it would not sign the agreement. Other countries followed suit, and the talks were called off definitively. Yet again, an international trade agreement encountered opposition initiated, joined, and widely publicized by the audiovisual industry, though this time the agreement was scuttled, with no chance of salvaging it.[14] This was also the year that French activist José Bové led a group of peasants in the dismantlement of a new McDonald's about to open in France, another highly publicized French expression of protest against the perceived dangers of globalization.

Over the next several years, the cultural exception ceded rhetorical ground to the emerging concept of "cultural diversity." The expression found its way into a series of new agreements, as in the Amsterdam Treaty's reference to "diversity of cultures." As discussed in chapter 4, the expression "cultural exception" had appeared on a somewhat ad hoc basis in response to Jack Valenti's March 1993 interview in *Le Monde*. Valenti had not said anything new about U.S. intentions in the GATT talks, but the French film professionals had been lobbying for years in the European context over these issues, if not over the phrase. Even if the French proposal for mandatory quotas on European television had not prevailed in the final compromise version of the TWF directive (1989), the film community had come together over the issue, demonstrating on many fronts—in the Estates General for Culture (1987), at the Assises de l'audiovisuel during the Year of European Film and Television (1988), in symposia and press conferences—essentially constructing the discursive foundation for what would be labeled several years later the cultural exception. And even more significantly, the film community managed to convince French political leaders of all parties to line up behind the defense of cultural interests as momentum built in the transition from the Single European Act in 1986 to the formation of the European Union in 1992.

The campaign for the cultural exception in a de facto sense did exclude culture from GATT, but that exclusion cut two ways. GATT did not explicitly acknowledge the exclusion of culture; it simply did not include culture in its provisions. But countries could not claim legal protection for their film policies if GATT did not recognize the exclusion. That recognition had been the aim of the cultural specificity clause floated briefly in the months leading up to the signing of GATT in December 1993, but the EU, with the backing of many film industry professionals, had rejected it. The less restrictive regime of GATS did not include audiovisual services unless countries specified which areas they wished to subscribe to.[15] Most countries with functioning film industries did not submit such applications. But GATS granted those waivers for only a maximum of ten years, even if France specified in its application that the exemption was claimed for an "unlimited" time, setting up the possibility of a renewed struggle over their future after ten years.[16] The victory of exclusion in GATS was therefore only provisional.

Canada initiated a new approach in 1998. It had confronted the United States ten years earlier during the bilateral Canada–United States Free Trade Agreement, a forerunner of both the NAFTA and GATT disagreements. Canada, suffering a far greater cultural trade deficit than France, argued strenuously for a special treatment for its film industry. The United States fought the request, agreeing to it only under the condition that it would reserve the right to retaliate in kind with trade sanctions equivalent to the damages sustained by the United States.[17] At the time, the United States enjoyed a large trade surplus with Canada, and Canadian films captured less than 5 percent of the Canadian film market.[18] In 1998, following the creation in 1997 of the Comité de vigilance against the MAI, the Canadian activist and minister of Canadian heritage Sheila Copps reached out to other countries seeking to retain authority over their national audiovisual practices. She called the new organization the International Network for Cultural Policy (INCP).

The adoption of "cultural diversity" as the new catchphrase in regional and international debates over the status of culture followed a similar path to that taken with the cultural exception. The basic outlines of the cultural exception argument took shape during the gestation period of the TWF directive. That expression became a standard shorthand for cultural autonomy only several years later in the months leading up to the conclusion of GATT in 1993. In both cases, the cultural exception did not achieve what its proponents sought. Defining the practical significance of the new clauses for culture in the Maastricht and Amsterdam treaties still awaited clarification in case law. The European Commission examination of French laws on state aid to cinema (1998) would be an early test case, amplified by the EC Communication on Cinema in 2001. But the cultural exception did not legally exclude culture from the WTO, and the audiovisual sector did fall within the orbit of GATS. Relatively few countries enrolled their audiovisual industries in GATS, however, so the nonsubscribing countries were acting properly, though the issue of the audiovisual industry consequently remained in a kind of institutional limbo, a definitional quandary aggravated by the persistent ambiguity of the boundary separating goods (GATT) and services (GATS).

The campaign for cultural diversity developed in this context as an attempt to build formal cultural protection into future trade agreements. The INCP brought together ministers of culture (or their equivalent) from interested nations.[19] At the first INCP meeting, held in Ottawa, June 28–30, 1998, Sheila Copps, using language immediately familiar from earlier disputes, declared that culture "is not a business like any other business. It is not just a product, and it is not a bargaining chip to be bartered away in exchange for some trade advantage. . . . We need to develop positive messages that at once promote identities and respect global cooperation. This ambition is just plain ordinary common sense. Let us work to reap benefits of trade and, at the same time, build respect for cultural diversity."[20]

According to legal scholar Serge Regourd, the European Council of Ministers signaled the shift from cultural exception to cultural diversity in its charge to the European Commission in October 1999, just prior to the November WTO negotiations in Seattle: "The Union will monitor, during the coming negotiations of the WTO, to guarantee, as in the Uruguay cycle, the possibility for the Community and its Member States to preserve and develop their ability to define and set in motion their cultural and audiovisual policies for the preservation of their cultural diversity."[21] The former concept of the cultural exception was considered by the European Commission, in the view of some commentators, to be "too defensive and protectionist, in favor of a more neutral notion, that of cultural diversity."[22] The Council of Europe released a declaration on cultural diversity on December 7, 2000.[23] The ministers of culture of the International Organisation of La Francophonie passed a similar declaration six months later, on June 15, 2001.[24]

The new phrase entered official French discourse in 1999. In August, President Chirac equated cultural diversity with "civilized globalization."[25] Two months later, Chirac announced, "France is leading the fight not for the cultural exception as it sees it but for cultural diversity in the world."[26] In the same year, Catherine Trautmann, the French minister of culture, attempted to explain the relationship between the cultural exception and cultural diversity. She underlined that "it is unprecedented that the Member States of the EU agree so clearly that the cultural exception remains the rule. We are incontestably better placed now than we were during the previous round [i.e., GATT]." After acknowledging that the cultural exception was a controversial term, she affirmed that "cultural diversity is not a substitute for [the cultural] exception. There is no semantic slippage dissimulating a hidden reality. . . . Very simply, these two notions are not placed on the same level. 'Cultural diversity' is about the goal to be pursued in negotiations. The 'cultural exception' is thus the means, in my view non-negotiable, to attain the goal of cultural diversity."[27]

Tensions over globalization more broadly conceived came to a head several weeks later in the street explosions that greeted the WTO negotiations in Seattle. Seattle represented the first concerted resistance to the neoliberal vision of globalization, as NGOs from throughout the world gathered to protest, bringing the battle over globalization to the streets. But the economically insignificant backwater of "culture" had contributed to this alter- or antiglobalization movement in previous years with many highly publicized and effective mobilizations, especially in France, first in the TWF debate, then the GATT set-to, followed by the quashing of the MAI. While the cultural exception had been the slogan used to deflect intense U.S. pressure during GATT, cultural diversity began to replace the cultural exception, and various activists and policy makers in Canada and France sought a phrase that would sound more positive. Instead of giving the appearance of defending national protectionist prerogatives as Luddite vestiges of economic parochialism, cultural diversity would argue for a world perspective on culture, one that would champion a form of labile cultural hybridity against the threats of cultural standardization represented by U.S. mass cultural production.

Advocates of cultural diversity tended to couch their arguments in terms of defending national identity. In practice, however, cultural diversity could also be understood as a defense of nationalism, with each nation constructing potentially regressive models of national identity. One U.S. legal scholar, Edwin Baker, proposed a different tack in an article published in 2000.[28] Picking up on one of the motivations behind the shift from the cultural exception to cultural diversity, Baker suggested linking the discourse of trade in culture to the tradition of human rights law. Applying a heterodox economic analysis, Baker rejected the free trade bias of most U.S. commentators and argued forcefully for "weak protectionism" to allow domestic media to survive.[29] Weak protectionism would permit subsidies and quotas, as opposed to "strong protectionism," which he argued would grant too powerful a role to the state in censoring or otherwise restricting imports. Baker gave close attention to "cultural diversity," for he was more concerned with how media strengthen democracy, and to expanding the public sphere.[30]

Baker also repudiated the notion of consumer sovereignty so central to the mantras of free trade champions.[31] Markets may offer consumers choices, but concentration in unfettered markets also restricts the range of possible choices. In this view, citizens need a stable cultural base in order to find their own individual cultural spaces. Local, domestic cultural production contributes to that base. Hollywood may attribute the appeal of U.S. films to audiences worldwide to the films' "universal" values, but Baker considered those values as essentially inflated investments in "action, violence, sex, and slick production qualities." According to him, most spectators would prefer domestic fare if it were available, but an unregulated market will effectively drive out domestically produced films, since few countries have anything approaching the enormous and wealthy domestic audience found in the United States. Because citizens are assumed to benefit more from domestic production, "trade rules that increase the likelihood of survival of those domestic products that would barely fail under a free trade regime could produce significant gains in social welfare."[32]

In other words, free trade thinking posits that the market will ensure efficiency and satisfy audience desires. Baker makes a "methodological plea . . . that those who invoke economic analysis should do so not merely from the perspective of the firm. Rather, they should recognize the normative concerns on which economics claims to be founded: people's welfare and preference satisfaction."[33] His argument for "weak protection" crystallizes around what he calls a "discourse" or "dialogic" conception of culture, as opposed to an "artifact" or "museum" conception. Cultural policy designed to preserve artifacts risks embalming culture, discouraging change, reinforcing traditional power relations. The discourse conception does not focus on content but on constant dialogue among members of a culture or cultures. Cultures, like languages, are always in flux. For Baker, cultures breathe and flourish when there is exchange between past and present, between old and new members, between domestic and foreign influences. But countries should privilege domestic discursive exchange, through which people articulate evolving formations of culture. "Weak protection" aims at securing national space for the nurture of that discourse:

> Rather than to preserve specific, backward-looking content, the relevant
> [weak] protectionist goal is to assure an adequate context for participation of members of the cultural community and to provide resources
> for the dialogic participants. Protection of culture in this context means

assuring that members of the cultural community have meaningful opportunities to be cultural "speakers." Culture as dialogue emphasizes both a past as context and a present as an arena for affirming, critiquing, and transforming identity.[34]

Though Baker's article tries to justify weak protection policy choices, he couches his discussion in a critique of classical economic theory and largely avoids the long roll call of multilateral agreements, with one exception. He shows that the same arguments in favor of free trade characterized the debate in the early 1980s over UNESCO's study of news media. That debate revolved around the controversial MacBride report on the New World Information and Communication Order (NWICO), which led to the U.S. withdrawal from UNESCO in 1985. The MacBride report, recognizing the power of large, well-funded, first-world media organizations, encouraged states to support indigenous news organizations to offer alternative sources for a better-informed citizenry. Developed countries claimed to worry that countries would take advantage of this power analysis to justify state propaganda, the very antithesis of what the report claimed as its intent: "[to advocate] the elimination of governmental interference and censorship, the decentralization of the mass media, high standards of professionalism for journalists, and a better balance in the contents and coverage of mass media reporting."[35] Baker suggests that one of the real reasons for the attacks on NWICO by the United States and others was the fear of applying antitrust laws to the commercial media. By replacing the cultural exception—associated with GATT, GATS, and the WTO—with cultural diversity, France, Canada, and other countries once again looked to UNESCO as a more effective forum for an alternative legal campaign for the defense of culture.

TOWARD AN ALTERNATIVE INTERNATIONAL INSTRUMENT: UNESCO

This momentum of forces eventually coalesced around an initiative to establish an alternative international legal framework for cultural diversity within UNESCO. UNESCO had declared the "World Decade for Cultural Development" in 1988, just as the EEC was completing its deliberations on the TWF directive, having already proclaimed 1988 as the Year of European Film and Television. At the end of that decade, in 1998, UNESCO held a conference in Stockholm and released a final declaration warning, "Globalization link[s] cultures ever more closely and enrich[es] the interaction between them, but [it] may also be detrimental to our creative diversity and to cultural pluralism."[36] The following year the federal government of Canada called for an international instrument to promote cultural diversity.

UNESCO passed the "Universal Declaration on Cultural Diversity" in November 2001. The document contained twelve articles, including one that maintained that "market forces alone cannot guarantee the preservation of cultural diversity." The declaration had no legal status, but an accompanying action plan called for "deepening the international debate on questions relating to cultural diversity . . . taking forward notably consideration of the opportunity of an international legal instrument on cultural diversity." Debate did continue in the following years in international venues, and UNESCO proposed a draft Convention on Cultural Diversity in 2003, setting the next two years for discussion of the draft leading up to a formal vote on a revised convention in 2005.[37] Many countries found points of tension in the draft text. A revised convention passed overwhelmingly in 2005, with 148 countries voting in favor, two against (United States, Israel), and four abstentions (Australia, Nicaragua, Honduras, Liberia). The headline in *Le Monde* referred to the convention as "A Manifesto for an Other Globalization."[38] The convention obtained the thirty votes needed for ratification by 2007, when the convention came into force, suggesting the depth of support among member countries.[39]

The convention, then, enjoyed the support of most countries, including all member countries of the EU, but critics have questioned its value. According to the Vienna Treaty of Treaties (1969), no international treaty can replace or abrogate earlier treaties. The WTO, officially formed on January 1, 1995, following the signing of the GATT and GATS agreements in Marrakesh in 1994, was recognized by most nations throughout the world. The WTO applied to virtually all trade. Whatever the still debated legal status of audiovisual goods between GATT and GATS, presumably they fell into the legal orbit of one or the other agreement, and both were subsumed under the WTO. If provisions in the UNESCO convention conflicted with the WTO treaty, the WTO, as the earlier document, would take precedence, and the UNESCO text explicitly stated that "nothing in this Convention shall be interpreted as modifying rights and obligations of the Parties under any other treaties to which they are parties." Furthermore, the convention contained no language requiring any action by signatory countries. Instead, it maintained that countries would be free to determine their own policies to achieve cultural diversity, with no mechanism for either assessing diversity or seeking legal recourse against measures that might be deemed harmful to cultural diversity. Echoing some of the new cultural clauses in the Maastricht and Amsterdam treaties governing the EU, the convention encouraged countries to promote cultural diversity. If challenged under the WTO, however, countries could not use the convention as a defense.

Some French writers expressed reservations about the shift to cultural diversity. Perhaps the near-unanimity of support for the convention provoked a certain wariness about its efficacy.[40] The cultural exception had grown out of a concrete political struggle over GATT with a clearly identified antagonist, and consequently it carried a militant charge deriving from a substantive political disagreement. Some government reports subsequently referred to the cultural exception as too defensive, apparently damaged from too many skirmishes fighting off the advance of neoliberalism. For example, in a report for the National Assembly, Deputy Roland Blum wrote that the "struggle for the cultural exception has been waged with a too defensive perspective [*optique*]. . . . Today a more offensive approach is needed, a more constructive one that takes account of the imperatives of competition as well as those of creation and diversity."[41] But Joëlle Farchy, after writing a book that did not answer the question posed in the title, *La fin de l'exception culturelle?*, developed her reflections on an answer in a subsequent article.[42] Farchy cited no less an authority than Jean-Marie Messier, using his remarks on cultural diversity to demonstrate the agility of the multinationals to coopt the expression: "Defending cultural diversity means allowing everyone to appreciate one's own culture and to open oneself to cultures of others. Cultural diversity is not the hermetic juxtaposition of more or less nationalist identity demands. It reflects the vitality of societies more and more mixed [*métisées*], with newly fashioned patrimonies, with multiply rooted creations."[43] Linking these remarks from April to Messier's announcement of the death of the cultural exception at the end of 2001, Farchy noted how adroitly Messier, and multinational firms more generally, had rebranded product diversity as cultural diversity, the former an obvious business necessity with markets opening in so many varied global cultural bazaars. In the interests of profits, all companies serving a globalized marketplace would have to design a variegated product line superficially customized to cater to the sovereign consumer.[44]

If cultural diversity could be so easily and rhetorically retrofitted as a sales strategy, it might not be the most effective weapon in the new digital age. While Farchy emphasized the danger of the temptation to withdraw into a narrow, nativist nationalism—as had Messier—she also noted that film production still takes place in national contexts, with plural local identities, requiring national policies that can be designed and adapted only with political commitment, precisely the element that the installation of cultural diversity risks leaving behind.[45] One partisan legal scholar, after noting that the final version of the convention contained no reference to quotas or preserving national prerogatives over the recipients of state aids, offered the following sobering verdict: "Despite the satisfaction, if not triumphalism, heralded by spokespeople of the relevant sectors, not only does this eagerly anticipated 'juridical instrument' resolve none of the problems that the emergence of the cultural exception had brought forward, but it ends up totally diluting the objective."[46]

Perhaps the most trenchant critic of the convention, though an ardent supporter of cultural diversity, is Christophe Germann, a Swiss lawyer and expert on international law. For many reasons, Germann views the document as inadequate to its stated goal of encouraging policies that will contribute to cultural diversity. He has proposed instead a "radical paradigm shift" as a solution to realizing that end.[47] Germann persuasively demonstrates how the convention cannot challenge the ruling principles codified by the WTO, specifically the three liberalizing pillars already undergirding the original GATT agreement of 1947: national treatment, most favored nation, and market access. Relatively few countries had made such commitments since the passage of the WTO, so most still preserved the right to design their own cultural policies. However, the United States has strong-armed countries into liberalizing their cultural policies through a series of bilateral agreements, despite the passage and ratification of the UNESCO convention.[48]

The case of South Korea illustrates this process. Though the Republic of Korea had passed a screen quota law in 1966, it was not enforced, and U.S. films dominated the South Korean market. As the political situation moved toward democracy in the late 1980s, the government liberalized its economy, relaxing many regulations. During that time, filmmakers lobbied the government to support the film industry and resist the pressure of the United States to eliminate the screen quota law. The Republic of Korea passed new legislation requiring quotas for the projection of national films in all movie theaters for 146 days every year. Prior to the new law, South Korean cinema managed a domestic market share of only 16 percent; within ten years, the South Korean market share had risen to 55 percent (2005), or even 64 percent (2006).[49] In bilateral trade talks in 2005, the United States demanded a revision in the quota law. South Korea cut the quota in half; by 2008, the domestic market share had fallen to 42 percent while the U.S. market share rose to 49 percent, up from 39 percent in 2005.[50]

Germann and others view this strategy of the United States as a consequence of one of the exceptions "won" in the GATS agreement. The EU had pushed to allow countries to conclude bilateral agreements with other countries to promote cultural exchange in the interest of diversity. However, bilateral agreements normally favor the more economically powerful partner, thereby perpetuating unequal power relations between the countries, leading to a likely reduction in cultural diversity. These bilateral arrangements bypass the putatively more equitable rules of the multilateral treaties, abetting policies built around cultural nationalism. As many writers have pointed out, especially champions of transnational films, cultural nationalism actually threatens to reduce cultural diversity. Despite the widespread support for cultural diversity, the latter phrase lacks rigor. Typically, most countries interested in promoting cultural diversity find their domestic screens filled with U.S. films. Even in Europe, which still has functioning national film industries, U.S. films garner 60–80 percent of theatrical attendance; in most of the rest of the world, especially the developing countries, that number is even higher. Countries that seek to increase the diversity of their own films provide support for filmmaking in a variety of ways that constitute cultural policy, such as often costly subsidies or quotas. Such policies as a rule are designed to raise domestic production and national market share in their home markets. Those policy tools may boost domestic production, and perhaps domestic market share, but does a market essentially made up of two production sources, the U.S. (foreign) and national, contribute to greater diversity?

Germann believes that raising national production will not necessarily improve diversity, for he wants to define diversity in a broader way. If spectators in most countries have a range of choice effectively circumscribed by U.S. and national films, they will have little exposure to films from other countries. Thus, Germann examines the market share of films from other countries. According to this scheme, defined by nationality, the U.S. market is one of the least diverse in the world, for U.S. cinema captures 95 percent of the domestic audience. He calls this situation one of "cultural uniformity." Because South Korea had succeeded in raising its national market share to over 50 percent, with the "oligopoly of the U.S. majors" taking 40+ percent, leaving only 1–7 percent for content from third cultural origins, he labels that distribution "cultural duality." The EU countries, led by France, have low (if varying from 10–40 percent) domestic market shares, with some 70 percent on average taken by U.S. films, but there is still some minimum exposure of films not only from other EU countries but also from the rest of the world, a situation of "quasi cultural diversity."[51] As the figures for the EU5 countries indicate, national and U.S. films draw more than 85 percent of admissions, so quasi cultural identity means that non-U.S. foreign films draw no more than about 15 percent in the most diverse case (Italy), and no more than 2 percent from outside Europe, though the supply of—as opposed to the attendance at—films is almost certainly more diverse; in France, for example, non-U.S., EU4 films represented 12 percent of all new releases and non-U.S./non-EU4 foreign films about 15 percent in 2011.[52] Admissions, however, lagged behind the supply of films screened (see figure 7.1a–e).[53]

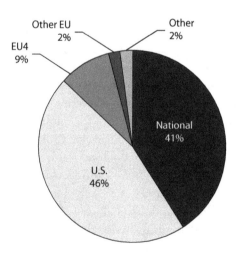

FIGURE 7.1a Film market shares for France, 2012

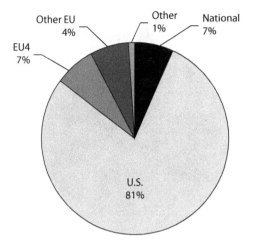

FIGURE 7.1b Film market shares for Germany, 2012

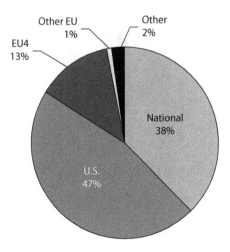

FIGURE 7.1c Film market shares for Italy, 2012

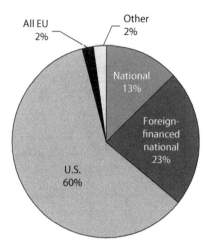

FIGURE 7.1d Film market shares for United Kingdom, 2012

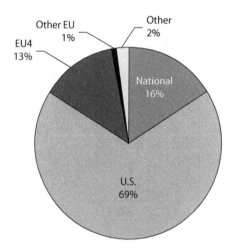

FIGURE 7.1e Film market shares for Spain, 2012

Germann's taxonomy begs certain questions. Germann feared that the autonomy granted to individual countries in UNESCO's convention would lead to cultural nationalism, yet his schema rests on relative representations of market shares from individual nations. As many have noted, especially recent promoters of a "transnational" approach intended to dilute what they deride as the archaic (and chauvinist) pull of nationalism, increasing numbers of countries must rely on co-productions to engage in filmmaking at all. Co-production is not a recent phenomenon. As Anne Jäckel has pointed out, co-productions have been common in Europe for many years, led in the post–World War II era by agreements between France and Italy.[54] Similarly, one might observe that there is considerable diversity within some countries' national production, especially in countries like the United States and France, whose industries release many types of films. Nonetheless, given the domination of U.S. cinema in most markets, it is reasonable to offer a first clarification of cultural diversity around different national cinemas, even if the market share of cinemas "other" than U.S. and national cinema may be only 10 percent in order to qualify as "quasi cultural diversity." At least Germann's schema does try to put flesh on the vagueness of cultural diversity.

Much of the discussion of film in the context of GATT, the WTO, and the UNESCO convention is necessarily rather technical and takes place in specialist venues. In the United States, the most extensive studies have appeared in law journals, where authors parse the legal language and for the most part view dirigiste, especially French, measures as protectionist, intentionally obstructing the inevitable triumph of free trade thinking.[55] But these critics of disguising bald self-interest behind the façade of the cultural exception insistently ignore the demonstrable reality of ever-widening trade deficits in favor of the U.S. audiovisual sector, which grew in the years after GATT from $4.3 billion in 1994 to $8.1 billion in 2000. While Baker wanted to increase cultural diversity as a tool to strengthen democracy with more local "dialogue," he also identified avoiding antitrust scrutiny of giant media multinationals as the unspoken motive behind U.S. withdrawal from UNESCO. Yet that is exactly the problem with many legal arguments indicting French efforts to deflect the rigid application of international trade rules to audiovisual exchange. As Fansten wrote about the strict observance of Queensbury Rules between a super-bantamweight and a superheavyweight, willful indifference to inequity will simply reproduce initial disparities.

BEYOND UNESCO

Picking up on some of Baker's ideas, Germann has advocated a much more aggressive and direct intervention in the struggle between free trade and culture. Like many others, in particular the Canadian scholar Ivan Bernier, Germann sees little hope in the UNESCO convention, for it has no injunctive language on enforcement.[56] Nor is there any language obliging countries to support cultural production; that language was proposed and rejected during the deliberations over the final draft.[57] The convention encouraged policies leading to cultural diversity but demanded no actions by governments and has no dispute-resolution provisions. Like Baker, Germann does not accept Hollywood's argument that the popularity of U.S. films reflects audience preferences worldwide. Unlike Baker, Germann does not attack the profit-seeking motive of the large media firms, nor does he call for the use of a different set of values built around social welfare or human rights demands. Instead, Germann wants to rely on an alternative, but arguably just as fundamental, economic principle subtending the free trade regime of GATT and the WTO. While Germann identifies himself as an advocate of cultural diversity, he also writes as an experienced international lawyer and builds his argument around the failure of international agreements to actually safeguard competition. He stakes out a position concerned with outcomes, not unlike rationales for affirmative action to achieve diversity in the United States.[58] As is well known in the United States, on an unequal playing field, nondiscrimination will not lead to equitable outcomes. He asks how underrepresented cultural expressions find space for exposure.

Germann begins with the fundamental dominance of U.S. cinema in most national cinema markets. He rejects as self-serving U.S. melting-pot arguments that a polyglot audience in the United States demands films whose domestic appeal translates into international box office success, satisfying shared audience tastes cross-culturally. For Germann, the real significant characteristic of U.S. cinema from a market perspective is not the enormous size of the production budgets but the massive investments in promotion and advertising. It may be true that no advertising campaign can force people to watch a particular film, but saturation of national exhibition space with wide release, heavy marketing expenditures, and financial partnerships with local distributors and exhibitors will at the very least restrict the range of choices offered to spectators.

Consequently, such a playing field cannot be level: "If no other choice is provided to the audience in the marketplace, the audience is obliged to consume the cultural goods and services supplied by the Hollywood oligopoly. One does not know, however, whether this supply would also meet the demand in a context where unbiased cultural diversity would prevail; that is, where films from a variety of cultural origins would enjoy equivalent marketing investments and a distribution on a level playing field."[59]

Germann does not accept the premise that U.S. films draw large audiences because of their competitive success at telling universal stories. He also sees no evidence to support Baker's assertion that audiences prefer films with more local content, however reasonable the claim may sound. Germann believes that U.S. films are decidedly local, or domestic in Baker's terminology. Their international success derives from their ability to impose themselves in foreign markets in the guise of universality: "the particularity of the dominant is their ability to pass off their particular way of being as universal."[60] Germann's analysis, and his ambitious proposal for a new international cultural regime, are based on a careful legal examination of precedent in case law of the WTO, the EU, and U.S. jurisprudence: "As a cultural diversity advocate (and not just an international trade lawyer) I dare to state the heretical opinion that the refusal of the U.S. and their fellow countries to adhere to the UNESCO Convention should actually be considered as an opportunity for the cause of cultural diversity."[61]

According to Germann, both the WTO and the EU effectively grant too much autonomy to individual countries to set cultural policy. GATS allows countries to escape the fundamental principles of national treatment and most favored nation. As noted, national treatment is not a default requirement in GATS (positive-list approach), and countries must specify what audiovisual areas they wish to place under most favored nation rules, if any.[62] The EU countries have even broader freedom to set their own cultural policies under the principle of subsidiarity.

Paradoxically, Germann views these refuges for national production as exacerbating the problem of the lack of cultural diversity. Without multilateral agreements enforcing obligations to promote cultural diversity, countries can construct policies that protect "cultural nationalism," policies that will not necessarily encourage true cultural diversity.[63] Like the many critics of nationalism, Germann sees pursuit of raising domestic market shares as an inadequate measure of cultural diversity. If cultural diversity is to foment creativity, it should seek representation from multiple cultures, not just a flattened home national culture capable of some minimal competition with U.S. cinema. Successful polices will raise the representation of many other cultures. Most countries have diverse cultural expression within their own borders, but those cultural practices normally share many characteristics of the nation-state and will display more similarities among themselves than they will with foreign cultures, hence Germann's description of U.S. cinema as cultural uniformity ("mono-cultural"), with a domestic market share of 95 percent. Two French scholars referred to such measures as taking on "the allure of a Maginot line faced with globalization, with technological advances which bring new economic conditions of distribution and the economic weight of [large] communication groups. Because the needs of identity no longer coincide with state frontiers, the defense of cultural identities does not mean only the defense of national policies."[64]

The UNESCO convention, then, can be read as a well-intended intervention in the debate over international trade in cultural goods, but its bias in favor of nations only reinforces current disparities in cultural diversity.[65] In his book, Germann lays out in detail his proposal for new international cultural instruments that would occupy a coequal status to the WTO and other international trade agreements, especially TRIPS (Trade-Related Aspects of Intellectual Property). He labels those instruments "Cultural Treatment" and "Most Favored Culture." Germann takes the long view regarding their potential efficacy. The GATT regime lasted almost fifty years and never managed to incorporate services like television, yet the successive rounds of negotiations did benefit world trade. The final Uruguay Round attempted to integrate cultural production but ultimately accepted a weak promissory note to allow a waiting period of ten years to work out the details, and most countries have refused to liberalize their cultural markets. The UNESCO convention, passed and ratified during that time, represents an effort to define an alternative approach. The convention, however, lacks legal force, though the rapid and broad support for ratification reflects widespread dissatisfaction with the liberalizing pressures of the WTO in the cultural sector. In the absence of a binding international agreement, countries with strong cultural industries have pursued the back-door recourse to bilateral agreements, in which the strong can impose their will on the weak.

Despite the wealth of substantive critical discussion of international cultural disparities, perennially conducted in the shadow of U.S. hegemony, few writers have proffered robust programs for reform. Germann is one of the few who has, especially in the extended discussion found in his untranslated book. While his arguments may be unfamiliar to Anglo-American writers, he emphasizes the real equity potential of the economic foundations of trade agreements, not dissimilar to the free-market-based Anglo-American perspective, so it is worth examining Germann's proposals in some detail. While political considerations almost certainly trump legal argument, and French efforts in this domain are perhaps the best illustration of that cultural realpolitik, Germann's careful attention to the goals of free trade thinking provides a sense of the complexity of the issues. Legal acumen may not tip the power scales, but it is undoubtedly a necessary component of a successful trade strategy.

Germann claims that the WTO actually does not contain supple rules on preservation or protection of competition, so he examines the jurisprudence of the more developed EU rules on competition. In order to determine the presence of competition, there must be a way of identifying "like products," which in turn requires determination of the "relevant market" in order to identify the relation between price and value among products.[66] In the relevant market, prices must provide a way of measuring value; prices that do not reflect value are symptoms of a lack of competition. As part of their argument that films are not like other products, Europeans regularly observe that the industry produces nothing but prototypes: each film is different. Therefore, it is impossible to predict the value of films before they reach viewers, and quantitative analysts consistently emphasize this signal characteristic of films.

In order to test for the presence of competition, economists look first for the "relevant market." For Germann, while there are three "initial markets" for any movie, the relevant market for the film industry is the exchange between distributors and exhibitors. The first market is the one where producers offer films to distributors, who buy rights to sell the films to exhibitors. In the second market, distributors face exhibitors as buyers, but exhibitors are unable to ascertain the relation of price to value, regardless of the budgets of the films on offer. In the third market, exhibitors sell films to spectators, but they show blockbusters for the same price as small independent films, so an invariant price cannot possibly be pegged to value. However, Hollywood enjoys a special advantage in this market beyond the production budget, which may be no more likely to draw spectators than inexpensive films. The U.S. majors devote massive resources to prints and advertising, conferring on their films an unfair competitive advantage. For Germann, then, the second initial market, the exchange between distributors and exhibitors, defines the relevant market, and like products in that market are those that mobilize like advertising budgets. Thus, promotion expenses tilt the retail playing field, for large advertising budgets accompanying Hollywood films create information deficits for less heavily promoted films, distorting competition.[67]

Here Germann's analysis draws on Arthur De Vany's concept of "information cascade."[68] According to De Vany, some spectators base their moviegoing decisions on purely quantitative information corresponding to early box office returns (attendance and revenues, which vary with release strategies, most especially the number of screens a new release plays on). That "lemming-like behavior" is characterized as a *noninformative* information cascade, for there is no subjective or quality factor in the purchase decision, only the number of tickets previously sold. Subsequent sharing of information by spectators, complemented by reviews, triggers an *informative* information cascade, which can either extend or limit the length and remuneration of a run.[69] At that point, word of mouth begins to establish the value of the film (in Hollywood vernacular, the movie "acquires legs").

Though De Vany's empirical research showed that both noninformative and informative cascades play roles in run lengths, Germann concentrates on the noninformative cascade, for that factor can be measured by the size of the promotion budget in order to identify "like products" needed for measuring degree of competition. Thus, based on like promotion budgets, Germann calls *Minority Report* and *Spider-Man* like products and *Goodbye Lenin* and *All About My Mother* like products. Once the informative cascade effect kicks in during the first run in theaters, adjustments to correct promotion budget disparities are no longer needed; the financial performance during the theatrical run will have supplied comparable information that the secondary markets of television, DVD, and Internet can use to determine appropriate pricing offers that correspond to value.[70]

If the relevant market in fact distinguishes between groups of like products according to their promotion budgets, competition can be improved by reducing the differences between those expenses. With that goal, Germann invokes the "essential facilities" doctrine in U.S. law. Early in the twentieth century, the U.S. Supreme Court ruled that railroad companies could not deny access to other carriers when those carriers were unable to construct alternatives. Concentration in the railroad industry allowed the most powerful companies to control those facilities, with their market power enabling them to restrict competition, a practice deemed by the court to represent "anticompetitive animus."[71] The court devised a remedy that required companies to open access to essential facilities under tight restrictions. Adapting that reasoning, Germann concludes that the dominant U.S. motion picture firms, the oligopoly of majors, must share access to their finely tuned distribution networks to level the playing field of new releases.

To buttress his argument, Germann wants to build in sanctions from the international agreement on intellectual property, TRIPS, also part of the new WTO regime. TRIPS covers creative rights. For Germann, the "refusal of the majors to invest in the promotion of films from culturally varied origins is not justified by a respective demand of spectators, but results from a systematic cultural discrimination, which is motivated by ethnocentric considerations and which is put in place thanks to the dominant collective position that the oligopoly of majors holds in most of the cinema markets of the world."[72]

Germann identifies two WTO cases as precedents. In 2000, Ecuador lodged a complaint against the EU for failure to honor its commitments to NT and MFN in the trade arrangement for the importation of bananas. Rather than interrupt its export of bananas, Ecuador proposed suspending payment for certain intellectual property rights to extract compensation, a right recognized under the WTO and approved by an arbitration ruling in the Ecuador case.[73] Thus, if a country can prove violations under GATT and GATS, it can apply sanctions under TRIPS to a different industry when no efficient alternative is available in the industry where the discrimination is alleged. "If the mechanism of sanctions based on protection of intellectual property right is shown to be effective to enforce the prohibition of economic discrimination in the banana industry domain, it should, with even greater justification, be applicable in the area of cultural goods and services to contribute to cultural diversity."[74]

Similarly, based on WTO case law, recourse to sanctions on intellectual property should be permissible in the event of majors failing to share access to promotion expenses. The WTO allows certain exceptions to NT and MFN principles when countries develop policies to protect the national interest in defined sectors, such as public health and national defense. South Africa argued that it would not pay the exorbitant prices charged by the big pharmaceutical companies for AIDS medications. The ownership of patents concentrated in these large companies gave them a dominant market position that they could abuse by controlling the prices, an option they had because of inadequate competition. Furthermore, those companies had originally secured those patents with considerable support from government investment in research and development, such that the patents should not belong exclusively to the companies. But above all, Germann wants to install a criterion above a purely economic one, and also to outline a workable system of remedies to reduce discrimination. "It would be contrary to the public interest to spend public funds to protect the intellectual property of an oligopoly if it is shown that it systematically practices cultural discrimination at the planetary level by abusing its dominant position on different national markets."[75]

The "cultural exception" represented a French-led effort by the EU to write in a broad exemption of cultural goods and services from the economic imperatives of the emergent WTO, creating a protected space for trade in cultural goods, one not subject to an exclusively economic logic. The novelty of Germann's approach lies in his acceptance of that economic rationale for cultural trade, which he identifies as a proscription of economic discrimination. NT prohibits special privileges for domestic companies, and MFN precludes favored treatment for individual countries, both principles of nondiscrimination. Germann makes a crucial link between nondiscrimination and free competition. Economic competition in the relevant market cannot be free when powerful companies organized in oligopolies—specifically the major Hollywood studios—discriminate against competitors. Excessive market power, exercised by monopolies and oligopolies, distorts free competition, which antitrust legislation is designed to preserve. The U.S. Department of Justice applied this argument when it sued the majors for antitrust violations, and the Supreme Court found affirmatively that they had accumulated sufficient market power to discriminate against potential competitors.[76]

Germann objects to the GATT, EU, and WTO bias in favor of nations. Wealthy nations can simply turn around and bring their economic weight to bear on the less wealthy countries, subverting the multilateralism putatively characterizing those agreements. However, the WTO accords do not include rules on competition, leaving that area to the discretion of states.

His introduction of the concepts of "cultural treatment" and "most favored culture" seeks to inscribe nondiscrimination against cultural production based on cultural—not national – origin. The assumption is that the enormous market shares the Hollywood majors earn throughout the world do not reflect the preferences of spectators but result from the saturation of national markets through spending on prints and advertising, which local (national) distribution companies cannot come close to matching. If cultural diversity is truly a goal of countries, and the commitment of most countries to the UNESCO convention suggests that it is, then national policies should be constructed to realize the desirable outcome of cultural diversity. According to the Hollywood litany, whether intoned by longtime MPAA president Jack Valenti, U.S. trade representative Bonnie Richardson, or academic professor Tyler Cowen, audiences must be free to choose their own film consumption, rid of the "protectionist" policies of quotas and subsidies. This logic reads recent history, driven by accelerated globalization, as proving that given that "free" choice, audiences will flock to U.S. films. The originality of Germann's argument lies in contesting that logic on its own economic terms. It is patently obvious that no country, or company, can hope to compete with the advertising budgets devoted to major Hollywood releases. Real consumer choice can take place only with a more equitable distribution of promotion resources, which only new competition rules can effect.

Germann displays great care in wading through the legal swamp surrounding culture in multilateral trade agreements. He is firm in his insistence that one country's industry is dominating world cinema, yet he refuses to attribute that success to the intrinsic "quality" of U.S. cinema. The goal of more diverse outcomes propels the analysis. Against the customary obeisance paid to the ability of Hollywood to satisfy tastes throughout the world (with the asymmetrical exceptions of India, where audiences actually prefer their national cinema, and China, which has built a great wall blocking most foreign cinema), Germann identifies the distributor-exhibitor negotiation as the key relevant market. Even Baker, who stressed the importance of national cultural production as part of the essential fabric of any aspiring democracy, grants U.S. cinema a special talent for universalizing its storytelling, a comparative advantage no other country can compete with in most of the world. According to Baker, citizens of democracies may actually prefer national films, but the size of their domestic markets does not allow them to assemble sufficient resources to meet U.S. cinema on its own budgetary terms (though, as Germann points out, Baker adduces no evidence to support these unsatisfied national preferences). Instead Baker regards the lack of national films as harming public welfare by impoverishing the discourse essential to democracy.

The literature on the questions of the cultural exception and cultural diversity, especially in the United States, must treat the minutiae of the applicable rules, regulations, laws, and jurisprudence. Free trade advocates want all countries to commit their legal systems to the fundamental liberalizing principles of GATT, GATS, and the WTO: market access, most favored nation, and national treatment. For their advocates, those principles will raise all boats, for they will increase efficiency and reduce discrimination. While often accepting the economic logic of the liberals, opponents argue that the principles lead to concentration in markets, with large multinational firms abusing their dominant positions, crowding out competitors. Germann does not call for an entirely different regime for trade in cultural production. In fact, he wants to adapt "the juridical instruments used for the promotion of international trade to the ends of promoting in an effective and lasting manner cultural exchanges at the international level [for] . . . the immaterial well-being of peoples and individuals."[77]

Neither the WTO nor the EU nor UNESCO has solved the riddle of cultural exchanges. To a large extent, the wealthy EU countries have guarded their autonomy to set national cultural policies. The UNESCO Convention on Cultural Diversity may not have resulted in a new cultural trade regime, but it did succeed in demonstrating the broad international consensus on the importance of cultural diversity as a desired goal. Measures to achieve that goal have proven more elusive, and the speed of technological change in the audiovisual industry may discourage the crafting of new rules since they can risk immediate obsolescence. Even after hundreds of pages of meticulous legal, economic, and political analysis, Germann cannot avoid a conclusion that reverts to support for an undefined "creation": "In an ideal world, the artistic and artisanal genius of creation as well as the demand of consumers should supersede the grip of marketing and state protection." Thus, instead of national origin forming the foundation of international cultural trade, the rule of "cultural treatment" would not prohibit discrimination by national origin but would instead "accord to cultural expressions . . . of every other cultural origin, in relation to all measures bearing on the promotion of cultural goods and services, a treatment no less favorable than that which it accords to its own like cultural expressions."[78] Such formulations have the considerable virtue of removing the national bias in the legal language, even if the category of "every other cultural origin" leaves enormous scope for interpretation. Furthermore, Germann's proposal acknowledges the downside of state interventions as costly and unsustainable long-term policies, as well as discriminatory toward countries unable to afford them in the first place.

In the years after the inconclusive standoff of the GATT negotiations on cultural exchange, the United States backed off slightly from its aggressive stance on some issues in favor of taking the contest to the digital battlefield. Article IV of GATT, allowing screen quotas, survived the talks and remained in the WTO rules, and quotas could not be introduced by countries that had not authorized them previously. Subsidies were prohibited in principle, but exceptions that fell in the category of "actionable" were permissible under certain conditions; countries could claim a need to invest in research and development, for example, or assert the needs of public health services. Furthermore, countries could challenge subsidies as anticompetitive only if they could prove damage to their national industries, a test the U.S. film industry would be hard pressed to substantiate given their international market dominance. But for the United States, the explosion of digital services obviated the arguably justifiable need in an earlier era of informational scarcity to guarantee some minimal level of national content on television. The sprawl of stations constituted a qualitatively new "marketplace," with consumer choice no longer subject to hardware limitations. The United States, then, set its sights on the future, relenting on the predigital demands of the GATT era.[79]

Most other countries balked at this new gambit. As seen above, most countries abjured commitments to liberalization of their audiovisual spaces under GATS, and ten years later only the United States and Israel voted against the UNESCO Convention on Cultural Diversity. Other developed countries, especially those in the expanded EU, took the lead in contesting U.S. pressures to eviscerate their national policies in order that they might retain their prerogatives to set their own cultural priorities. Despite the pressures brought to bear by the United States in bilateral trade agreements, and despite the reality that old and new international trade regimes favored the more developed countries, many countries now availed themselves of the exceptional legal space cleared by France and Canada as a fragile refuge to develop cultural autonomy. In the broadest formulation of cultural diversity, national identity would not be constructed on the model of a narrowly imagined "Fortress Europe," nor would it inevitably take place in the shadow of a hegemonic U.S. culture. National identities would evolve in response to changing demographics within their own borders and the hybrid influences of extraterritorial creation, as cultural diversity forged more fluid national—and democratic—identities.

8

WAS THE EXPERIENCE BENEFICIAL?

France has led, in European and global arenas, the struggle to protect national film industries against the most recent efforts of the U.S. film industry to reduce them to marginality, even in their home markets. In fact, the French film industry has been so successful at raising investment, production, and attendance that France found itself in an unfamiliar position in the new century. Ever since the end of World War II, French analysts have decried the "crisis" in French cinema. So constant has this chorus been that Daniel Toscan du Plantier, a successful French head of Gaumont during the 1980s, quipped that "French cinema has been in crisis since the eighteenth century."[1] Despite a downward plunge lasting into the 1990s, the industry appeared to be faring better in the new century, and lamentations have subsided to an unaccustomed murmur. *Télérama* even carried an article in 2009 titled "Why the [French] Cinema Has Never Been So Healthy."[2] Of course, not everyone concurs. Even as the overall health and stability of the industry have improved, familiar complaints persist. But while the CNC can generate ever more data to demonstrate the quantitative strides of the French film industry, have the elaborate and sustained state efforts borne artistic fruit, justifying those efforts? In supporting an industry, what has been the artistic result? The various studies examined in chapter 6 consistently employed the term "diversity" as the gauge of quality control, on the implicit assumption that diversity ensured artistic quality. Other assessors of the achievements of French cinema have tried to develop and apply more specific discriminations to take account of artistic qualities included in this quantitatively upbeat narrative.

Inevitably, as the government and CNC have responded to a range of threats, structural cracks either emerge or widen. In the 1980s, the government decided to impose certain rules on television to replace falling box office revenues for film. Once television became the largest investor in French cinema, some began to worry that television was using this financial power to assert its own criteria on filmmakers. In 2002, Jean-Michel Frodon, then a journalist at *Le Monde*, gathered filmmakers, academics, philosophers, and others in a think tank known as "L'Exception," to hold periodic group discussions, which would then be transcribed and edited into books. In the provocatively titled *Cinema Without Television*, Frodon excoriated television as the cookie cutter of French cinema.[3] As its financial place in the film industry expands, he said, television demands more flesh for their euros, what Frodon and others have dubbed "formatage." In the December 2005 issue of *Cahiers du cinéma*, he even identified what he called the "primal scene":

> The primal scene took place one day in May 1995. It took place on the scene of the Theater of the Champs-Elysées, during the 10th Festival of Paris. On that day the heads of French production and of all the television companies gathered, private and public, over-the-air or scrambled: Terzian, Toscan, Cleitman, Mougeotte, Tavernost, Lescure [all film and television executives] they were all there. "We need programs," [the television executives] said, "make us twice as many films." "If you pay, we'll make three times as many," [the film producers] replied. 'Let's start with two hundred . . ." After twenty years of paying, television has finally succeeded in imposing its logic.[4]

In February 2007, director Pascale Ferran, as part of her acceptance speech following the selection of her *Lady Chatterley* as the best French film of 2006 at the annual César Awards (French equivalent of Oscars), read a short presentation attacking "the system of financing" of films that separates the more and more expensive films from the extremely low-budget films. "This breakdown is recent in French film history," she charged.[5] Evoking a lineage of auteurs from "Renoir to François Truffaut, from Jacques Becker to Alain Resnais, [who] had the highest regard for spectators they spoke to and the greatest ambition for film art," she claimed that the "television stations were working very methodically to make [those types of films] disappear." She concluded with a call to arms: "Perhaps it is time to fight, equally methodically, to refound systems of solidarity under siege and restore the conditions of production and distribution of films which, showing the complexity of the world, ally artistic ambition with the pleasure of spectacle." An editorial the next day in *Le Monde* supported her charges, embedding them in its own melodramatic eco-language:

> The evil advances. It is attacking the biodiversity of French cinema and thus its future in the more or less long term. . . . The ecosystem of the French cinema for a half century allowed all films to coexist, and consequently the public to be able to appreciate them equally. It is today disintegrating under the baton blows of the law of the market. The address of Pascale Ferran to the politicians has no other goal than to sensitize them to this troubling evolution, and to remind them of a mission that for a long time has contributed to the [cinema's] cultural and artistic radiance in the world: ensure that all films can arise free and equal under the law.[6]

Ferran embarked on a study of the situation she had indicted with a diverse group of film professionals. With the support of the CNC, they began meeting, and in April 2008, this "Club des 13" issued a document called "Le milieu n'est plus un pont, mais une faille" (The middle is no longer a bridge, but a chasm).[7] While "Le milieu" suggests a focus on films "in the middle," with budgets of €4–7 million, in fact the report examines the state of the industry in many other aspects as well, with separate sections on the traditional categories used to describe the industry everywhere since at least the 1920s: production, distribution, and exhibition.[8] This was the starting gun for a new round of reports and books on the state of French cinema, now centered on "quality."

The report identified a number of problems all too familiar to anyone who has followed the discussions of the industry in the generalist press, such as *Le Monde* and *Libération* (or in specialist forums like *Écran Total*, *Le Film Français*, and *Cahiers du cinéma*). Does France produce too many films? Are too many films receiving the designation "art et essai"? Are multiplexes threatening the existence of art et essai theaters? Are the *cartes illimitées* (subscription cards for theaters) harming independent theaters? And echoing Frodon's attack, the report repeatedly described the baleful effects of television on the cinema.

Though the urgency of Ferran's plea might have suggested otherwise, these questions were not new. The stack of reports on these topics by the CNC, legislators, ministries, and many others over the previous eight years already stood very high. Indeed, much of the analysis can be found in the 2008 report by Jean-Pierre Leclerc and Anne Perot released in March, just a month earlier.[9] What is somewhat surprising in the Club des 13 report is the modesty of the proposals to solve the described ills of cinema. In particular, the report does not propose any radical changes in relation to that maleficent enabler, television.

The recommendations in "Le milieu" lay out a series of steps to add and redistribute money in the industry. Thus, in the Compte de soutien, they believed, a larger percentage should be devoted to the avance sur recettes, since the *aide automatique* favors large productions, while the avance sur recettes is understood to promote creativity. The *prix de reference* of the fidelity cards has not risen since it was first set, so that should be increased.[10] Instead of insisting on a minimum time in theaters for low-budget films, the split between distributor and exhibitor should be lowered to fifty-fifty for the first three weeks following the release, giving exhibitors more incentive to keep films in the theaters. *Producteurs délégués* currently have to sell rights to other windows in order to obtain funding for films, which means that they have no capital to use for the next film; the report proposes requiring that the *producteurs délégués* retain those rights.[11] Also, the report recommends that screenwriters should be given a higher percentage of the split with directors, to better value their work.

QUALITY TESTS

One theme motivating the Club des 13 report, the first of the ten "findings" listed in the opening pages, is the decline, "for some years," in quality of French cinema from one end of the spectrum to the other. Producers, the report claimed, no longer had the time to devote to their films amid their constant search for funding. Paradoxically, the increase in funding sources (regions, Eurimages) actually had made the financing of films more difficult, with producers putting all their effort into assembling the budget package.[12] Television, by contrast, could finance films using a small number of traditional sources (*aide automatique*, TV/DVD rights, SOFICAs) and keep all of the receipts, unlike the *producteur délégue* who must sign them away in the search for funding.

The report implored the CNC to make the needed adjustments. That is, the professionals looked to the state to resolve the industry's problems. The problems derived from the judgment that quantity may have been up—number of films made, attendance, domestic market share, number of screens—but the quality of French cinema was in decline. And indeed any commentator on the structure of the French film industry must eventually confront the question of quality. Is any national policy of support for cinema justified if the industry should manage to produce only mediocre or bad films, or perhaps worse, Hollywood clones?[13] Hollywood has always run as a commercial industry; with aesthetic value normally conferred only in later critical distinctions, producers have little reason to trumpet aesthetic quality, unless it can raise films' profiles and swell their earnings.

But if France was to continue to support its film industry, would a quantitative turnaround justify continuing state support? A certain auteur cinema continued to benefit from government support, but many of the rewarded auteurs had built their reputations decades earlier. Were new auteurs emerging, guaranteeing a renewal of the aesthetic distinction that clung to the coattails of renowned, still active, older directors? To be sure, historians had already written of post–New Wave directors, but aside from the ambivalent appreciation given to filmmakers associated with the so-called *cinéma du look* during the 1980s,[14] critics had not identified a cohort with the critical cachet once attached to the New Wave (whatever the inaccuracy of attributions of coherence to the New Wave).[15] Like critics and scholars all over the world, French commentators await developments that replicate a New Wave imaginary. As production slowly picked up in the 1990s, veteran observers began talking about a "young French cinema." Michel Marie, who has written copiously on the New Wave and Godard, edited a short compendium of fifty new directors in *Le jeune cinéma français* in 1998, followed only four years later by an expanded second edition by René Prédal, which ran to two hundred directors. Marie ended his short preface teasingly asking the reader (a quotation taken from the vendor of *Cahiers du cinéma* in *Breathless*) "Do you have something against the young?" Predal, by contrast, asserted that his thesis will be "a little like *a defense and illustration of the young French cinema of today*."[16]

While acknowledging the power of television and the changed financial conditions, Prédal wrote to celebrate the renewal specifically of the *art* of cinema:

> Certainly the young French cinema does not attract a large public, but the role of art has never been to fill the coffers of industry. Art creates at the front lines of (mass) culture. It pulls it higher, at least if one wants truly to help it instead of attacking its productions in the name of the (presumed) middlebrow taste of some spectator whose only (virtual) reality is that of the polling companies. The sociology of the media is a discipline that may be fascinating but has nothing to do with the aesthetic history of the cinema.[17]

Sociologists were unlikely to agree, and they had already weighed in on the effects of state support for the desired aesthetic outcomes of the French cinema. Arbiters of taste will argue about films, since they live on their disagreements on the artistic merits of films. The judgments of social scientists face even greater challenges when they try to evaluate the "quality" of contemporary French cinema. Rather than presume to apply their own aesthetic taste, the social science professionals have looked elsewhere for more a more "objective" yardstick. During the 1980s, when the EEC and the Council of Europe first turned their attention to the culture industries, the council chose France as the first country to examine. In 1988, the officially designated "European Year of Cinema," the council commissioned a French academic, Bernard Gournay, to conduct "the first attempt to evaluate the cultural policy [*politique culturelle*] of a European country in the framework of the Council of Europe." In the short preface, General Secretary Marcelino Oreja identified two objectives: "Collect information on the success and failures of the national policies in order to draw useful lessons for the other partner countries and . . . define a common ground facilitating ultimately the harmonization of these policies."[18] Gournay produced a long, detailed account of the cultural policy of France, especially since the formation of the Ministry of Culture in 1959, including passages on film during the 1980s, noting the irony of the Socialist government privatizing radio and television. He also claimed a certain continuity for the cultural policy with the change of government in 1986 (the first cohabitation). In addition, Gournay, "inspired by a method used for quality evaluation of work done by labs of scientific research," essayed a novel attempt to gauge the quality of French film production. "Did the selective aid for film production established by André Malraux reach the 'quality' objectives which had been assigned to it?"[19]

He asked the CNC for the names of "directors who were generally considered to have great talent." Of the 111 "good" directors whose names were supplied by the CNC, 101 had benefited from the avance sur recettes. Hence the first conclusion: "the large majority of the 'quality' directors had received, at some time, the avance sur recettes." Each of the 111 averaged about three avances; thirty-five had received the avance for their first feature films. Thus, the figures showed that "the avance had allowed, to a large degree, helping young talent, and not simply [rewarding] conventional practice." However crude the yardstick, Gournay at least developed some objective approach to the question of quality in order to assess the efficacy of the support mechanism, specifically the program created to promote quality.[20]

In the same year (as discussed in chapter 6), the Ministry of Culture conducted its own study of the film industry, "Le cinéma français face à son avenir."[21] While its author, Jean-François Court, referred at one point to the quality of French cinema as recognized at the major European festivals, he concentrated on the problem of raising the attendance for French films in theaters, especially for middle-level genre films: "French cinema needs great creators. But it has just as great—perhaps even greater today—need of great artisans, bringing their technical talent to the direction of good products, respecting the public without deprecating it, filling the theaters, attracting audiences on television." French cinema indeed had its auteurs, but the middle-level production did not depend on them:

> The auteur cinema is doing well, too well even. Without doubt there are not enough big films, but we know how to make them, and there is no reason that tomorrow they not be made. But what secures the foundation of the French industry, setting aside some fifteen "big films" and twenty or thirty auteur films, are the fifty to eighty middle productions, comedies, crime films, etc., seeking to offer not the exceptional but the healthy entertainment [sain divertissement], the good reason to go regularly to the cinema. The equivalent, if you like, of the good B films, which have done so well for the American cinema.[22]

And it was precisely this cinema that the automatic aid sought to support: "from the point of view of the State, this sector of middle production appears more linked to the automatic aid than the intervention of selective aid." In other words, Court makes a distinction between the highest quality of French cinema, the auteur cinema recognized for its quality with the prestigious festival prizes, and the middle production, providing year in and year out "healthy entertainment." In his words, "Everyone is not Jean-Luc Godard."[23] For Court, then, the health of French cinema rested above all on the quality of middle-level genre production, not unlike Ferran's "milieu," neither the French equivalent of the U.S. blockbuster nor the prestige work of certified auteurs.

Years later, French scholars Emmanuel Cocq, Alexis Dantec, and Florence Lévy-Hartmann picked up on Gournay's method of looking more closely at the results of the avances sur recettes for the same reason, but they used a different timeline, from the mid-1980s until the end of the century. During those years, production had more than doubled, so the avances sur recettes had played perhaps a smaller role in the global view. They also were writing after GATT, and the continuing drama and controversy over state support of film industries informed this research.[24] They found, for example, that extending the survey of festival prizes beyond Cannes (i.e., Berlin, Venice) showed a clear decrease in the percentage of French films recognized.

Other researchers, applying the same method, found that 90 percent of directors who had received awards at Cannes, Venice, or Berlin had also received three or more avances sur recettes, though fully 90 percent of them began their careers in the 1960s or 1970s, confirming Court's observation that the original French auteurs were faring perhaps too well, even while the majority of the first-time directors over the years had disappeared.[25] Nonetheless, Cocq, Dantec, and Lévy-Hartmann acknowledged that the avance sur recettes did finance new talent and the renewal of talent, concluding that many directors often began careers on the fringe of the "oligopolistic center" and then migrated toward films with wider release. The researchers thought that the automatic aid had been less successful since the mid-1980s, however. Lang's 1989 reforms, they believed, had contributed to increased concentration of top-budget releases, which nonetheless had failed to increase commensurate market share. Consequently, they supported the return of digressivity, which reduced the automatic aid if and when theater attendance reached specified thresholds.[26]

Thus, while some equated the health of the industry with recovering market share, they also emphasized the importance of diversity, which they found ill served by concentration.

More recently, Françoise Benhamou presented an "econometric analysis" of television investments in cinema that included a discussion of quality. She noted that economists have often used size of budget as a criterion of quality, on the assumption that larger budgets "permit more technical polish, [higher quality] photography, etc.," but she added that this approach automatically places blockbusters at the top of the quality ladder, which would simply correlate quality with size of investment. She argued instead for combining the *ex ante* decisions made by television investors and *ex post* judgments gleaned from the judgment of critics. She concluded that television quotas seemed to have little effect on the artistic value of films, and that the costs of monitoring and compliance with the quota regime outweighed their potential aesthetic benefits. Without the quota rules, "it is not clear that the financing and programming choices would be significantly different." Because she found that one of the public stations (TF2) had adopted a similar investment strategy to that of the largest free private station (TF1), she claimed that the distinction between investment choices of public and private stations was not pertinent. In her conclusion, however, Benhamou suggested tentatively that the source of a station's funding influences its investment decisions. The greater the reliance on advertising revenue, the more likely a station would seek to "satisfy the preferences of the average television viewer little inclined to consume films considered difficult."[27]

ART CINEMA AS ARTISTIC CONSCIENCE

As it happens, for many years the French government had developed an elaborate system for supporting just such "difficult" films beyond the venerable but modest largesse of the avance sur recettes. Audiences in big U.S. cities can watch art films at informally designated art cinema theaters, but France, characteristically, has professional art-cinema organizations to defend and promote their interests, and the CNC officially recognizes and funds both art films and art cinema theaters. Private film societies flourished in France from the 1920s until the end of the 1970s.[28] As the state began to intervene more systematically in the industry after World War II, a group of five art cinemas formed the Association française du cinéma art et essai (AFCAE) in 1955.[29] In 1962, the CNC officially included the AFCAE, with forty-nine theaters, in the state support system. The CNC established four categories, or "labels," of art cinemas, according to the theaters' level of commitment to art cinema and the size of the population in the area of the theater.[30] A commission screening films every week would determine which films qualified as art cinema, and the designation of art cinema would entitle theaters to CNC grants. One criterion, then, for official designation as an "art cinema" theater was the percentage of art films screened. Effectively, this criterion was a form of automatic aid, as it was generated automatically based on the annual box office receipts, exactly like other forms of automatic aid, but specifically targeting the category of art film. Other criteria referred to the number of visits by filmmakers to the theater, the number of debates among critics, distribution of pedagogic materials, publicity outreach, and so forth, all leading to selective aid determined by the CNC. Many of these theaters were small operations, but in the 1950s, as attendance reached its high point of 400 million spectators in 1957, these theaters could survive. Furthermore, theaters in smaller population centers had more lenient criteria in order to qualify for the designation. While theaters in Paris must program art films at least 70 percent of the time, the smallest population areas must reach a minimum of 25 percent (with a congeries of additional conditions that get factored in).

Before the reform of 2002, art theaters represented roughly 25 percent of all screens in France. When the CNC changed the relevant designation from screens to theaters in 2002, the art et essai percentage of national exhibition jumped in one year from 25 percent to almost 50 percent. The goals of the art et essai theaters have remained the same since their inception, preserving a space for screening of films with less commercial potential, including repertory, patrimony, and foreign films. Changes in the exhibition sector naturally affected art et essai theaters as well. Art et essai theaters pioneered the introduction of multiscreen exhibition, as theaters redesigned their spaces to squeeze more screens into the same single theater formerly housing only one screen.[31] France already had 659 multiscreen theaters in 1980, holding 30 percent of all screens; by 1990, with attendance dropping by 30 percent during the 1980s, there were almost a thousand fewer theaters but virtually the same number of screens.

The multiplication of screens took far less space than the addition of any new seats: there were 30 percent fewer seats in the country. In other words, even before the arrival of multiplexes in France in 1993, 70 percent of all French theaters had more than one screen, which explains how France was able to maintain a relatively constant number of screens even as the annual attendance was cut in half.

When multiplexes first appeared, with all their modern conveniences (parking, concession stands, indoor waiting areas, cafés), many feared that they would sound the death knell of art cinemas.[32] And then there were the so-called fidelity cards introduced by the large theater chains in 2000, allowing unlimited entries for a monthly subscription fee. But the initial fears may have been unfounded. Art cinemas received considerable funding from the CNC to modernize their facilities during these years, and they more or less held their own against the multiplexes, even though multiplexes do compete with the high-profile, wide-release art films (*Amélie*, *Kill Bill*). The CNC has certainly monitored the multiplex phenomenon, beginning with the Delon report (see chapter 6), but it has not arrived at any definitive judgments.[33]

One organization, the Agence pour le développement régional du cinéma (ADRC), created by Lang in 1983, whose mission is "to help maintain a diverse group of theaters throughout France, seeking in particular a better access to a variety of films [for the theaters],"[34] does have some relevant, if still limited, information on the effect of multiplexes. A study done for the ADRC in 2004 noted that the national fall in attendance affected the art cinemas least, followed very closely by the multiplexes. But the "generalist theaters," that is, the ones that show commercial fare similar to the multiplexes, suffered a significantly higher loss, almost four times the figures for the other two categories. It would be premature to conclude that multiplexes in fact harm most the generalist theaters, but that study did suggest that including these generalist theaters in subsequent analyses may offer a better perspective on the effect of multiplexes on the exhibition sector.[35]

The CNC released four linked reports on art cinema in October 2006.[36] It also commissioned a study of the conditions of film releases in theaters. The first set of reports on art cinema are relatively descriptive, full of statistics on art cinemas throughout the country, with the dizzying array of parameters typical of CNC studies: number of art films shown in art cinemas in different-sized population centers; number of theaters run by local governments; number of screenings held for schoolchildren; number of spectators for art films broken down by age, region, gender, occupation, and so on.

The year 2006 saw Jean-Pierre Leclerc's return to the premier ranks of report writers. The report on the conditions of release of films was policy driven.[37] With so many changes in the film industry over the previous ten years, the CNC wanted some guidance on how to proceed and chose a veteran student of French cinema to provide it. Leclerc's 2003 report (see chapter 6) had examined production resources. His 2006 effort was a compact report of some 100 pages (the art cinema reports ran to hundreds of pages) that concluded with a set of possible policy options. Typically of the CNC's corporatist approach and identity, Leclerc tried to speak with representatives in the industry, across a wide spectrum, including the views of independent professionals.[38] The most likely proposals would impose minimum time requirements on all releases of films in independent theaters in order to slow the rotation of films, to allow them more time to find an audience, and exclude distributors controlled by television from automatic aid to distribution. This exclusion reflects one of the recurrent themes in recent debates, the move by television into distribution, as the stations funneled more money and promotion resources into their own films.

Leclerc leaned toward self-regulation for his policy suggestions, knowing that it offered the path of least governmental resistance in these neoliberal times. What is conspicuous in his report, as in virtually all such policy-oriented reports on the cinema, whether issued by the CNC or government studies, is the resistance to restrictions on vertical integration. These studies consistently raise the question of vertical integration and finish by endorsing the argument presented in the 1981 Bredin report. As discussed above in chapter 2, Jean-Denis Bredin essentially accepted vertical integration, maintaining that horizontal integration was the greater danger. For twenty-five years that conclusion became one template for official commentary on the French industry, which routinely accepted and sometimes explicitly approved vertical integration in the hope of creating a true industrial base, a matter that became even more pressing as the European Union was taking shape. The doomed spectacle of Vivendi Universal under Jean-Marie Messier might be considered the nightmarish realization of that hope.

Setting aside the immediate question of the number of releases and copies, what may be most interesting about the recent developments is the meaning of the idea of art cinema. Does it still exist, and if so, what does it mean now? More than other countries, France considers film to be part of a citizen's general education. There are national curricula built around film screenings, for elementary, middle, and high schools, reaching millions of students. The state intervenes massively in support of cinema, politicians across the spectrum express their support, France lobbies the European Union constantly in favor of the cinema, as both industry and art. But with fully 70 percent of French production now classified as art cinema, does art cinema still represent the creative energies and aesthetic accomplishment that it once did?

As one might expect, filmmakers and theater owners, in their efforts to defend art cinema, have expressed their concerns about this question. As far back as 1991, some art cinema owners, dissatisfied with the conservative politics of the AFCAE, formed the Groupement national des cinémas de recherche (GNCR). A former president of the GNCR, Geneviève Troussier, lamented in *Cahiers du cinéma* in 2006, "We are first defending the economy of cinema, not the artworks. We have to separate the notion of art film from the problem of the survival of the exhibition sector."[39] Her organization, though also one representing art theater owners, spoke for the owners most committed to art cinema, for art cinemas also have their own administrative breakdown. The word *recherche* in GNCR refers to those theaters that show the most risky, experimental films, attracting small audiences but working creatively to promote such works. In his 1990 study of art cinema, the former editor of *Cahiers du cinéma* Serge Toubiana called such theaters the "art cinemas of art cinemas."[40]

In 2004, the Association du cinéma indépendant pour sa diffusion (ACID, Association of Independent Cinema for its Distribution), an activist group founded in 1992, released a manifesto, "Libérons les écrans" (Liberate the Screens), published in *Le Monde*, *Libération*, *Cahiers du cinéma*, and elsewhere, calling for limiting any release to 10 percent of all screens: "Let us free the screens from this logic of consumption. Films are not just another form of merchandise."[41] This language, of course, recalls precisely the rhetoric of the cultural exception surrounding the GATT battle of 1993, though this time directed not at the U.S. cinema but at French multiplexes and the national theater circuits and distributors. As formulated, this demand turned out to be a bad solution to a real problem, for so uniform a practice would deprive smaller theaters in less populated areas of the very films that ACID was eager to defend, promote, and distribute (and ACID, with the Société des réalisateurs de film, did revise that demand in a later work document).[42]

Virtually all of the critics of these developments look to the CNC to "correct" these developments. The public ADRC describes its mission as correcting the damage caused by the market.[43] Frodon called for the CNC to shift the balance between automatic and selective aid to favor selective aid, a way of restoring fiscal meaning to the term "art cinema."[44] Even ACID, arguably the most militant of the chorus of critics, saw the CNC as the needed arbiter.[45] Consistent with the traditionally strong role of the state in France, the state is the entity expected to correct the excesses of the market. What is striking about the latest round of the crisis is that unlike the late 1980s and early 1990s, when the cinema was in real peril, confirmed by the alarming statistics of plummeting production, attendance, and market share, one encounters the same discourse over art cinema now as then, suggesting that these particular problems are serious structural ones, not simply conjunctural.

But when Toubiana warned in his 1990 report of the competition of the multiscreen theater with the art cinemas, it was before the arrival of multiplexes in France. Now consumption rules. Has the love of cinema migrated from the eye, from scopophilia, to the mouth, now not only figuratively as an object of visual consumption but also literally as a bauble thrown in with the popcorn, or as the question might be posed in French rhetoric, from cinephilia to cinephagy, the latter a term the French resort to with some frequency.[46] A writer in the sober *Le Nouvel Économiste* in 2004 called the multiplexes "cathedrals of cinephagy,"[47] where the most remunerative products are the comestibles, a situation with which North American audiences are all too familiar.[48] In the book on television put together by Frodon, the head of the cinema division at the CNC itself, François Hurard, characterized French television as "very cinephage,"[49] even if the waning of the appetite for television in the digital age has raised fears of the closing of the television funding spigot.

RAISING DEMAND: TEACHING CINEPHILIA

Any number of critics have tried to emphasize the need to recover a sense of aesthetic mission in cinema. Amid the official lip service granted to diversity, with policy documents proudly measuring it in terms of quantity—figures of films produced, audience size, number of screens, global investment in cinema—commentators have been seeing the downside to this success. Specifically, they call for constructing—and not necessarily retrieving—a new relationship to the films, one that will not succumb to what Antoine de Baecque, in his 2003 book *Cinephilia*, saw as the only remnant of classical cinephilia after its death in 1968: nostalgia and melancholy. This new relationship would look forward, perhaps cutting the lifeline that television was forced to throw it, one that has now turned into a noose.[50]

Cinema viewing has changed in two fundamental and measurable ways since the end of World War II. First, attendance at theaters has shrunk by billions of spectators in all developed countries. Second, videotape and then DVDs, supplemented by growing Internet viewing, have become the dominant venues for watching films. As with television, the Hollywood majors first resisted the successive revolutions in spectatorship. Despite the early chicken-little-ism, Hollywood soon learned to harness the new technologies and now enjoys greater revenues from those income streams than from theatrical revenue, a trend that emerged in most countries with the penetration of video and then DVD. Nonetheless, according to Anglophone scholars like Douglas Gomery and Thomas Schatz, or Laurent Creton in France, theatrical attendance is still the most important single factor in the ultimate revenue for films. In that sense, the marginality of theaters should not be exaggerated. Theaters remain the most important outlet, if no longer the most remunerative, the crucial first window where product branding takes place. Once established by wide release and massive promotion, on television especially, films can make their digital way downstream to reap the rewards of subsequent windows.[51] But this downstream bonanza applies predominantly to blockbusters and consequently can often skew interpretations of the industry. Blockbusters increasingly account for the largest percentage of film revenues, but the fortunes of smaller films, especially foreign art films, depend proportionately more on theatrical returns; often they do not reach the later markets and, even when they do, will not necessarily realize significantly more revenue in subsequent release windows.[52] Such films require longer exposure in theaters to build an audience, and the practice of word-of-mouth can still supply that, as explained in De Vany's discussion of informative cascades (chapter 7).

In France, art films, returning already disproportionately lower box office receipts in theaters than non-art films, fare even more poorly in the DVD market than in theaters. And U.S. art films have an even larger DVD market share in France than French films. In French theaters, U.S. art films, officially designated as such in France, make up only 15 percent of all art films screened, but they earn almost double that percentage, while French films, reaching almost 50 percent of all art film releases, earn about half the art film revenues.[53] On DVD, despite fewer titles and copies, U.S. films take about 56 percent of the market, while French films reach only 23 percent.[54] U.S. art films perform twice as well on DVD than in theaters, while French films do half as well.[55] On average, U.S. art films do 25 percent better in theaters than French art films, but almost four times better in DVD.[56] Thus, French art films would be relatively better off if they could earn more revenue in theaters, where they have a relative advantage, bolstering the case for keeping those French films in theaters for longer runs.[57]

In France, the government has done more than probably any other country to maintain a flourishing film industry in the face of all the dramatic changes that movies have undergone in the last fifty years. Those efforts have included not simply assuring the production of more films but also seeking means of assuring new audiences, indeed, in the best of circumstances, a new generation of cinephile spectators. During the heyday of classical cinephilia in the 1950s and 1960s, when ciné clubs proliferated in France and the art et essai movement took shape, analyses of the national film audience revealed that in 1965, 13 percent of filmgoers were "frequent" (at least once a week) representing 53 percent of all tickets sold; 32 percent "regular" (at least once a month, less than once a week), accounting for 31 percent of admissions.[58] That is, those two groups together, labeled *habitués*, made up over 80 percent of annual attendance. In 2010, "frequent" spectators had dropped to 4 percent (23 percent of admissions), but "regular" admissions held steady at 30 percent (49 percent of admissions). Thus, *habitués* still composed over 70 percent of the annual theatrical audience.[59] At the same time, "frequent" spectators of art et essai films rent twice as many DVDs per week as "frequent" viewers of all films, one reason that analysts often view, perhaps counterintuitively, theater and DVD as complementary, not competitive, for cinephiles.[60] Therefore, one possible strategy for building, or at least retaining, the theatrical audience would be to cultivate cinephilia among young people.

Given the international influence of *Cahiers du cinéma* on filmgoers throughout the world, beginning with the first wave of English-speaking cinephiles in Great Britain and the United States during the 1960s, one might assume that the French were natural cinephiles. Yet in her 1993 study, *French National Cinema*, Susan Hayward asserted that "the cultural myth of the cinephilic French is just that—a myth"; the French were not in fact the cinephiles of auteur legend.[61] She held that the attributions of French cinephilia were not supported by the evidence, pointing out, for example, that the national attendance figures for 1992 in France ranked far below the figures for Great Britain and Italy at their peaks. But as the figures above show, "frequent" spectators, arguably the true cinephiles, still represent almost 25 percent of the French national audience and, as might be expected, more than 40 percent of the art cinema annual admissions.[62] As regards the British comparison, it is true that despite having roughly the same population, total moviegoing attendance in France never reached as high as the peak British audience. It is also true, and obviously of greater moment for the respective fates of their industries, that the theatrical drop-off in the French viewing audience was nowhere near as dramatic as the crash in the British filmgoing public. French attendance reached its postwar high of 400 million in 1957 and stood at 200 million in 1982, losing only half of its audience peak, not nine-tenths as in Great Britain.[63] And since 1993, French attendance has exceeded attendance in all of the other countries cited by Hayward (see figures 8.1–8.4). Furthermore, as French market share over a longer period has outstripped market

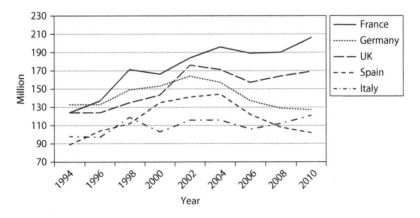

FIGURE 8.1 Cinema attendance in EU5 countries, 1994–2010.

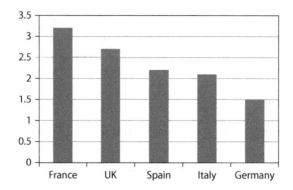

FIGURE 8.2 Cinema attendance per capita in EU5 countries, 2010.

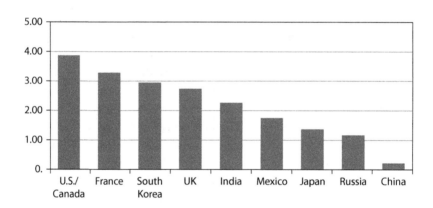

FIGURE 8.3 Cinema attendance per capita, 2010

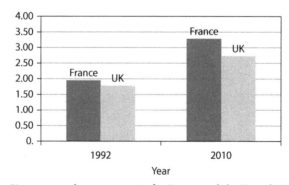

FIGURE 8.4 Cinema attendance per capita for France and the United Kingdom, 1992 and 2010

shares in other European countries, preference for national films becomes even more marked in France.

Rather than concluding that the French became less cinephilic twenty years ago, it is probably more prudent to remain agnostic on the national rankings of "cinephilia," if such crude measures as ticket sales and per capita attendance can vary so significantly in a single generation. Many other factors contribute to national attendance numbers: access to and cost of alternative leisure activities; penetration of television, VCRs, and DVDs; the quality of television fiction; access to broadband Internet; and forms and degree of national support systems, just to name a few. And in France, the status of film towers over that of television, a distinction called by some "quasi-ontological."[64]

During Jack Lang's first tenure as minister of culture in the 1980s, the government had already started examining ways of reviving theatrical attendance, a goal that has since remained as a constant of state policy. Among the proposals considered then was one to teach film as part of the regular school curriculum. Thus, as early as 1983, in Lang's first set of reforms, one can find the first murmurings of cinema education, and early, if episodic, efforts to develop programs in French high schools date from the 1980s.[65] The "near pre-history" of official film education can be traced to various television programs on cinema in the early 1980s, as can the "near pre-history" of French hostility to this form of televised film pedagogy already on offer in 1982: "We are against a television steeped in pedagogy," announced an article in the television journal *Télérama*.[66] The first school experiments took place in 1986, leading to the first bac in 1990.[67] Not everyone welcomed such an idea. The minister of education at the time expressed his horror upon hearing of the plan to introduce film into high schools: "The bac [i.e., diploma] is something serious! We're not going to put film and theater in it."[68]

The educational initiative was taken up again officially in the late 1980s, when Lang was named for the second time to head the Ministry of Culture. The new Lang plan, among many other proposals for the cinema, specifically called for the inclusion of cinema education as an option for schools.[69] Identifying one goal as "winning back a large popular public," the plan proposed the following measures: distribute grants to theaters for renovation, limit increases in ticket prices, and target schools. The first official program, Collège au cinéma (middle school), was installed in the 1989–1990 school year, followed by École et cinéma (for elementary schools) in 1994–1995 and then Lycéens et apprentis au cinéma (high school) in 1998–1999. All programs included a commission to choose the films and an institutional articulation with local governmental entities to help finance it. One of the key, and unusual, characteristics of these programs was the insistence that "it must be done by looking at works in the theater, in the projection conditions for which they were conceived."[70] So despite the increasing penetration of VCRs, and later, DVDs, the program was (and remains) built around the screening of films in regular movie theaters.

The rationale was twofold. First, with screenings arranged in theaters—and for the most part the screenings took place in art cinemas—the initiative would necessarily raise attendance at theaters. Each student would pay for a ticket, at a reduced, subsidized price, and the CNC would arrange for payment of rights for the films.[71] One of the groups participating in the program was the National Association of Theater Owners, who obviously had a vested interest in its success, for it might mean the difference between continuing or going out of business for some theaters. Second, the official documents repeatedly emphasized the importance of creating new cinema spectators for the future, spectators who would continue to watch films in theaters, not exclusively at home on television or video. This second aspect, while complementary to the interests of the theaters, spoke of instilling cinephilia in the students, engaging them in moviegoing.[72] Schools were to be incubators of cinephilia, a way of investing in the future of the cinema industry.

The numbers of participant schools and students have increased steadily since the programs' inception (see figure 8.5).[73] Given the decline in

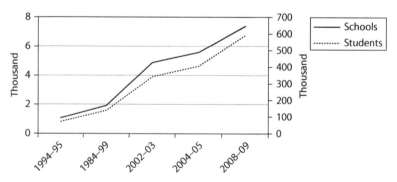

FIGURE 8.5 Elementary schools and students participating in École et cinéma programs, 1994–2009

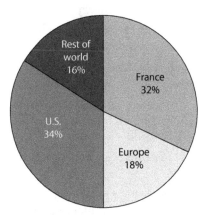

FIGURE 8.6 Percentage by nationality of all films chosen for school cinema programs between 1994 and 2005

theater attendance at French films, one might expect a chauvinistic reaction in the design of the education planning, yet the choice of films to be shown in the school programs exhibits a remarkable ecumenism.[74] Consistently, films were drawn from a wide array of national cinemas (see figure 8.6).[75]

For many years, French critics of their country's cinema policy have attacked the government for hypocrisy, alleging that while proclaiming to support the art of cinema, in reality state policy caters to the corporate cinema lobbies, including powerful groups of theater owners. National pride certainly played a role in the French resistance during the GATT battle of 1993,[76] but French cinema interests just as certainly feared the threat to governmental largesse. One can see playing out, then, even in this apparently noncommercial school arena, familiar tensions between the cinema's dual status as art and industry, specifically around the requirement that all films seen by students must be screened in theaters. Even if attendance of over three million students in these programs (2007) represents a tiny percentage of national audience, perhaps 1.5 percent of the annual attendance, the majority of the theaters participating are art theaters. For these theaters, that small percentage might make the difference between surviving or shutting its doors.

The education programs received a new boost in 2000 when Jack Lang, this time the newly appointed minister of education, devised a joint plan with the minister of culture, Catherine Tasca. Prime Minister Lionel Jospin weighed in: "The national cinema will be that much more alive, creative, and prosperous as it will be rooted in a public of cinephiles—and first of all young cinephiles."[77] Lang called on a filmmaker and critic from *Cahiers du cinéma*, Alain Bergala, to examine and develop plans for carrying out the program. With some ten or fifteen years of experience with the three programs, reaching children from preschool to high school, Bergala wrote a short book laying out the pedagogical thinking behind the plan.[78] Bergala insisted on not installing cinema as a separate course of study, or discipline. There was a fear that such a move would lead to academicizing film in schools, institutionalizing a sclerosis, just as generations of French students had been turned off French literature because of the top-heavy rigidity of the national curriculum.[79] Reflecting this animus, at the annual 1999 industry forum at Beaune devoted to the topic of education, the filmmaker and critic Luc Moullet referred to school as *une pute* (a whore).[80]

Instead, Bergala emphasized the centrality of cinema as an art. Criticizing his own earlier views, he wrote that the traditional orientation to teaching cinema suffered from what he called the "ideological riposte." This approach, rooted in a sociological criticism of the image in a consumer society, sought to warn students, or spectators, of the danger of the image. Thus, one must learn to read it, or decipher it, in order to be adequately inoculated against those threats.[81] It is not clear that others directing the programs shared this rejection of the task of "reading" the image. Bergala published his short treatise in 2002, yet in the ten-year evaluation of the elementary school program, in 2005, one coordinator wrote that she hoped the students will be "enthusiastic and demanding 'children of cinema,'" better equipped to resist turning into "children of advertising."[82]

It would probably be difficult to take issue with the choices of films for the three education programs, but in his book Bergala offered one illustration of his thinking. He took the example of *Moonfleet*, a lesser-known 1955 Fritz Lang picture.[83] For Bergala, this film was a formative one for a number of critics who came of age during the 1960s—all male it might be noted—most emblematically Serge Daney, who took a line from the film for the title of one of his books of criticism.[84] Bergala noted that this film, like several others in the curricula, dealt with questions about the relationship between fathers and sons. As the critics he singled out all had issues with their fathers—abandonment, death—he maintained that this film exerted a particularly powerful influence on future essayists and filmmakers. According to Bergala, these Oedipal issues "make up the part of the enigma of the world of adults on whom [the children] depend: sexuality, betrayal, violence."[85]

Setting aside for the moment recent debates over the rubric of national cinemas, the program of study included a considerable variety of film choices by nationality. Bergala and others also imported a related idea about difference from Daney, that of "alterity." For Daney, cinephilia should entail exposure to difference, even the illegal or illicit. The inclusion of cinema in the official school curriculum risks imposing a stamp of approval on films that contest thematic or formal protocols, effectively stripping them of their alterity. And there is one reported case of an attempt to prohibit the adoption of *Edward Scissorhands*.[86] Another way of thinking about alterity might be to exclude what is not "different" from the curriculum, namely dominant cinema. As the director of the elementary school program put it, "students can see 'dominant cinema' on their own. École et cinéma helps them develop a taste for discovering other things."[87]

Each of the programs includes teaching brochures, for teachers of the youngest students, and for both teachers and students in the later grades. The elementary school students, however, also receive a large postcard with stills on one side and some simple details about the film, like a short press kit, on the other. The brochures present the author's notes on the film, a summary, an analysis of a sequence, a "ricochet-image," and a short bibliography.[88] For the first brochure for École et cinéma, Bergala chose Lang's *Moonfleet* (see figure 8.7a–b).

Though he, like so many others, believed that the cinema theater is the best setting for the initial encounter with films, Bergala recognized that only by repeatedly viewing films and sequences can cinephilia really take root.[89] Thus, Bergala began to produce DVDs to be made available in schools for that purpose. Known as "Eden Cinema," the DVDs normally include, in addition to the film, various complementary materials similar to the bonuses on French DVDs, such as shorts made by the filmmaker, or pedagogical films made by critics, such as Jean Douchet. The brochures typically contextualize the films, such as the one on Jacques Rozier's *Adieu Philippine*, with the fundamental reference to the main character in Bergman's *Monika* looking directly at the camera placed on the same page with stills of other characters looking at the camera in three iconic films from the New Wave.[90] One can find a more extended application of this idea in the study films, such as Douchet's commentary

Les Contrebandiers de Moonfleet,
Fritz Lang, États-Unis, 1955.

 École et cinéma

Avec le soutien de la Direction générale de l'Enseignement scolaire,
et les services Culture Éditions Ressources pour l'Éducation
nationale du SCÉRÉN-CNDP (ministère de l'Éducation nationale,
de l'Enseignement supérieur et de la Recherche) et du Centre
national de la cinématographie, (ministère de la Culture
et de la Communication).
Édité par *Les enfants de cinéma*.

-- ✂ ------

Les Contrebandiers de Moonfleet (Moonfleet)
Fritz Lang

Un film en couleur et en CinémaScope de Fritz Lang, États-Unis, 1955, d'après le roman *Moonfleet* de John Meade Falkner. Durée : 90 minutes.

Les personnages : Jeremy Fox, le chef des contrebandiers : Stewart Granger — John Mohune, le fils d'Olivia : Jon Whiteley — Lord Ashwood, le noble versé dans la piraterie : George Sanders — Lady Ashwood, sa femme : Joan Greenwood — Mrs. Minton, la femme que Fox a ramenée des îles : Viveca Linfors — Grace Maskew, la jeune amie de John : Donna Corcoran.

L'histoire : En pleine nuit, le petit John Mohune arrive à Moonfleet : il veut rejoindre Jeremy Fox, un ancien ami de sa mère, à qui celle-ci, en mourant, a décidé de le confier. Jeremy, aventurier débauché ne veut pas, tout d'abord, s'encombrer de l'enfant, mais celui-ci s'obstine à rester près de lui et a gain de cause...
Tombé par accident dans une crypte, John y trouve le médaillon de son ancêtre le cruel Barberousse et découvre que Jeremy n'est autre que le chef des contrebandiers. Fox défend John que les contrebandiers veulent tuer, puis, ensemble, l'homme et l'enfant découvrent le secret du médaillon et — au fond d'un puits — le diamant de Barberousse. Mais Jeremy Fox abandonne John et part avec Lord et Lady Ashwood, deux nobles qui veulent l'entraîner dans la piraterie. En chemin, il se ravise, mais Lord Ashwood, avant d'être tué par lui, le blesse mortellement; Jeremy rejoint alors John, lui confie le diamant, lui dit adieu et s'éloigne en mer... Plus tard, John laisse grand ouvert le portail des Mohune, car il attend le retour de son ami.

Extrait du film : À la sortie de la taverne, John et Jeremy (habillé en officier) s'apprêtent à chercher le diamant de Barberousse au fond du puits de la forteresse de Hollysbrooke.

Jeremy — Maintenant, écoutez John Mohune : ceci n'est pas un jeu. Comprenons-nous bien : si quelque chose tourne mal ce sera chacun pour soi. Si je dois vous abandonner, je n'hésiterai pas une seconde.
John — Je ne pense pas que vous agiriez ainsi, Monsieur.
Jeremy — Vous vous trompez fortement. Si vous étiez mon fils...
John — Oui, Monsieur ?
Jeremy — Je vous aurais enseigné à ne jamais faire confiance à quiconque !
John — Mais vous êtes mon ami !
Jeremy — Et votre partenaire ! C'est une aventure dangereuse. Est-ce clair ?
John — L'exercice sera profitable.

FIGURE 8.7a Cinéma et l'école handout on *Moonfleet*. Copyright © Les enfants de cinéma

FIGURE 8.7b Stills from *Moonfleet* on the Cinéma et l'école handout. Copyright © Les enfants de cinéma

on the invocation of fetishistic cinephilia exemplified in *The 400 Blows* by the theft of the photograph of Harriet Andersson from *Monika* in the theater display case (see figures 8.8–8.10).

Drawing the arguments of Bergala's "Hypothesis" together with the pedagogical materials, one can sketch what are being proposed as the constituents, or perhaps even the formative elements of cinephilia: capturing children when they are young, a time when they are susceptible to images or sequences that can touch their lives, sometimes echoing those personal enigmas that they are still too young to articulate or make sense of. Repeated viewings in school can respond to these obsessional drives, seeking to connect with desire, soldering the foundations of their cinephilia.

In their recent book on *Cinéphiles et cinéphilies*, Laurent Jullier and Jean-Marc Leveratto deride the idea of incubating cinephilia in school. Even more than Bergala, who argued that cinephilia must be based on alterity, Jullier and Leveratto believe that students want to guard their own autonomy of taste, refusing any official line. Addressing the official education programs, the book includes an account from one teacher of a student who expressed his appreciation of *Steak*, directed by Quentin Dupieux, a film dismissed by most critics at its release. The teacher reported that this student's attitude of rejecting received critical wisdom was one she had encountered on other occasions: "the desire to mark oneself as different, to not give the expected response." She then noted that this film was designated by no less than *Cahiers du cinéma* as "the most singular surprise of 2007" and that the student planned to see the film again . . . at the Cinémathèque française![91] The apparent alterity of judgment is revealed to be precisely the elitist opposite of freedom repudiated by more contemporary critics like Jullier.

Given the aim of fostering cinephilia in these programs, it is probably worth noting that the cinephilia serving as the desired model is what Jullier and Leveratto call "modern cinephilia," the cinephilia practiced and promoted by the *Cahiers* critics of the 1950s.[92] That is perhaps most evident in the emphasis on screening films in theaters. Writing in 2010, and thus in a position to examine the varieties of cinephilia that have drawn academic attention tributary to Susan Sontag's notorious pronouncement of the death of cinema,[93] Jullier and Leveratto labeled the more recent forms of cinephilia "postmodern cinephilia," characterized by the privatization of viewing, the leveling of aesthetic distinction between art and commercial cinema, and in particular, the democratization of taste, an explosion of availability dissolving the hierarchy of accumulated cultural capital.[94]

FIGURE 8.8a Brochure cover for *Adieu Philippine* (directed by Jacques Rozier) for Lycéens et apprentis au cinéma. Copyright © CNC / Cahiers du cinéma

FIGURE 8.8b Stills in the brochure section "The Look–Camera" include (*left, top to bottom*) *The 400 Blows, Breathless, The Umbrellas of Cherbourg, Adieu Philippine*, and (*right*) *Monika*.

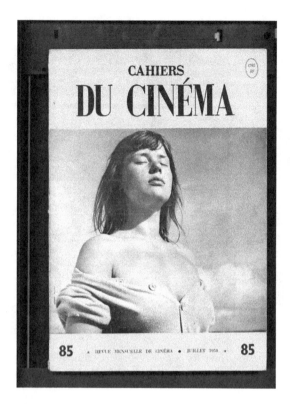

FIGURE 8.9 Harriet Andersson in Ingmar Bergman's *Monika* (1954), on the cover of *Cahiers du cinéma* 85 (July 1958). Copyright © Cahiers du cinéma

FIGURE 8.10 Theft of Harriet Andersson photo in François Truffaut's *The 400 Blows* (1959)

One might see this particular choice of an earlier cinephilia for state education programs as overdetermined. On the one hand, in order to convince the Ministry of National Education to accept cinema in the curriculum, its supporters played the art card. Film would not be taught as a new subject on a par with literature, history, or science but would occupy a separate niche, devoted to art. In addition, by arguing for the importance of ensuring access, the project resurrected the sentiment originally preached by André Malraux, to guarantee access to culture for everyone.[95] On the other hand, and though shunned by pedagogues, the industrial argument comported perfectly with the priorities of the government entity charged with responsibility for regulating the film industry, for schoolchildren offered an additional group of captive spectators to palliate the ills of the exhibition sector.[96]

Amid many commentaries and reports that have addressed these programs, there has as yet been no assessment of the school programs' success in the goal of nourishing cinephiles. Cinephilia does not look like such a "myth" when France is the only country that has pursued its cultivation on such a grand scale, even if the school syllabi anchor the overall approach in an "anachronistic" and maybe even now a mythic idea of cinephilia. Film continues to occupy a special place among the arts, and however fraught the institutionalization of film in schools may be for promoting "alterity," the government appears unwilling to surrender its future to the invisible and implacable hand of the market in the era of accelerating globalization.[97] The national director of École et cinéma explicitly linked the program to the cultural exception: "The school [is] the privileged place to discover that something other than knowledge exists, all that one could truly call the 'cultural exception.'"[98] The European Union may yet follow the French lead, for the European Parliament passed a resolution in 2010 to include cinema education in their national education curricula.[99]

It seems fair to conclude, then, that French cinema since the early 1990s does qualify as a success on multiple measures, whether industrial/commercial or artistic. Regarding the former, indexes of which are easier to quantify, most relevant figures have demonstrated a remarkable recovery (see table 8.1). Critics have noted perverse effects of this productivist emphasis. The glut of films and copies has resulted in shorter exhibition times in theaters, disproportionately limiting the runs of U.S. art films in particular. The shrinking percentage of theatrical receipts in the financing of French films, not to mention the increased weight of television

TABLE 8.1 Recovery of French Cinema Since the 1990s

	Average, 1990–1995	Average, 2005–2010	Percentage of change
Attendance	124	190	+54
Production	102	186	+82
Screens	4,377	5,387	+23
French market share (within France)	32	40	+25

financing, risks creating a certain diffidence about the success of films in theaters, depressing possible receipts in subsequent runs on DVD and television. The larger role for television funding of French cinema threatens the imposition of "formatage" on the films.

Assessments of artistic gains are of course far more difficult to determine. With more countries enjoying their moments in the sun (Taiwan, China, Hong Kong, Romania, Iran), festival prizes are harder to come by for French films. French art films make up an extremely high percentage of annual French production, but most of them are quickly forgotten, as they are in most countries: in the United States, some scholars estimate that 30 percent of annual production never even receives theatrical release, the essential exposure for downstream revenues and critical notice. But rather than tabulating prizes as the sole register of quality, it may be more fruitful to apply a broader view, one that encompasses the three branches of the film industry, since the government has developed support programs for all of them.

As seen in chapter 7, cultural diversity has replaced the cultural exception as one of the core principles motivating the cinema-support programs, and studies of the industry all identify cultural diversity as one of the central goals, for diversity has become a stealth proxy for quality. And the government can still try to quantify diversity. To ensure diversity in production, the rules require that television stations, the largest investors in film, devote a minimum proportion of their investments to independent production, which is presumed to be less standardized. The rules even mandate that stations direct some funding to films with budgets below certain thresholds to prevent concentrating funding on the most expensive films.

The avance sur recettes system, which includes one commission charged with choosing first films to finance, rewards grants exclusively on the basis of quality. Those awards contribute to funding roughly one-third of annual production and could be categorized as the state's annual investment in research and development, since the sometimes difficult art films receiving the avance tend to do worse at the box office. Other production funds are set aside to enable filmmakers in other countries to make films, often in their own countries and languages, which considerably diversifies French national production beyond its own borders.[100]

Over many years, the state has contributed massively to the exhibition sector. It has channeled money from the Compte de soutien to the renovation of theaters, and the multiplex phenomenon often accompanying renovation has drawn spectators back to theaters. Derided by some as the "aircraft carriers of U.S. cinema," the multiplexes do often screen the U.S. blockbusters. For diversity of exhibition, the government supports the subsector of art cinemas, meant to serve as a programming counterweight to the larger commercial theaters. Diversity of programming, evaluated and rewarded according to criteria such as art films screened, debates scheduled, promotion activities, and screenings arranged for schoolchildren all qualify theaters for state funding, in principle at least raising the quality of the theater offerings to spectators. Education initiatives for children at all levels seek to train discerning new viewers by exposing them to a diverse range of films—varying by national origin, by historical period, by genre—in the hope that they will be more likely in the future to demand high-quality films. If most of government support seeks to build supply—of films, filmmakers, theaters—the education initiatives represent efforts to raise demand and the quality of that demand.

Have these concerted efforts to maintain and enrich diversity succeeded in their aims of both raising the quality of French cinema and honing the discrimination of a new generation of spectators? There is no consensus on an answer, and any assessment of recent production in particular would be premature. Seen from the other shore of the Atlantic, there can be little question that talented French directors vastly outnumber the filmmakers from any other country, though one might object that France commits more resources to promotion of its cinema in the United States than any other country. Since 1980, *Cahiers du cinéma*, which has not lost its taste for U.S. film, has placed more French films (102) than U.S. films (75) on its annual ten-best lists, though when adopting the arbitrary divisions of decades, the two ten-year polls of the 1990s and 2000s betrayed a marked preference for U.S. cinema, with eleven U.S. films and only one French film. No other country's cinemas come close in the yearly polls. Such lists, of course, based on votes by critics, almost neces-sarily gravitate toward auteurs, and no doubt Eurocentrism played a sig-nificant role in the skewed geographical results of the polling. In addition, few if any critics can have the linguistic skills, let alone hours in a year, to assess the annual output of world cinema.[101] At the same time, choosing the "best" films from around the world may be a dubious way to evaluate national cinemas. As Court noted in his early attempt to develop a quality test, middle-level production may provide a better stand-in for quality in national cinema production, for many countries of all sizes can point to recognized auteurs, but we have little way of knowing what lies beneath the tips of those industry icebergs. Critics and cinephiles argue endlessly over lists, as the reception to the unseating of *Citizen Kane* by *Vertigo* at the top of the 2012 *Sight and Sound* poll demonstrated, and one has to wonder at the energy expended in such pointless exercises.

It would be more prudent to swear off that type of judgment and instead accept and monitor both the proxies of diversity and the vigilance of the professionals. The support system built on diversity mandates a distribu-tion of required investments from television and state sources. The Compte de soutien still favors automatic aid, linked to box office returns, but it has adjusted the needle to provide a higher percentage of the fund to the selec-tive avances sur recettes. The government has responded to the withdrawal of funding by distributors, now awarding them more state support. Over sixty new filmmakers make their first films each year, with another thirty directing their second. Production has reached all-time highs, with almost 280 films in 2012. The new peaks have given rise to the unexpected ques-tion of whether France now produces too many films, a question that has sparked one of the most controversial debates of recent years. One critic complained in *Libération* that the number of French films produced annu-ally now prevents critics from performing their assessment duties: "Never, in the tangled swamp of releases, has the critical compass been as neces-sary and never . . . has it been so mute. Following a certain parallel logic, criticism finds itself in a situation similar to the excess of films: the films must find their own way to continue to meet the public, criticism must find the words to continue to speak to that public."[102] Many others, including producer Paulo Branco, reject Malthusian-like fears: "To say that there are too many films is a heresy. We must preserve this diversity."[103]

CONCLUSION

The mostly bipartisan support for state aid to the cinema has cracked from time to time, but the many and varied sectors with interests bound up with cinema have rushed to repair the damage. At the end of 2007, the conservative government of Nicolas Sarkozy announced budget reductions for activities known as "cultural action." In response, a new coalition of cultural organizations released a manifesto, "Cinema and Audiovisual, Toward the Dismantling of Cultural Diversity," and announced the formation of the Bureau de liaison de l'action culturelle (BLAC). In February 2008, the minister of culture and communication, Christine Albanel, requested that Alain Auclaire examine various state programs that are often grouped under the rubric "cinematic cultural action." She identified three specific areas in which national and local governments were implicated, including the promotion and distribution of film, the territorial coverage of cinema, and educational initiatives. She noted that governments at different levels provide subsidies in all of these areas and expressed her concern for a "good coordination among the subsidies." In November 2008, Auclaire delivered a report to the Ministry of Culture and Communication titled, "On the Other Hand, Cinema Is Entertainment . . ."[1] Barely two months after its release, BLAC held a two-day conference in Paris where participants attacked the report's neoliberal thrust. Several people singled out the title of the report for special scorn, regarding it as a deliberate and cynical departure from French policy that went back three generations. The title has to be seen as an attention-getting, perhaps even provocative, take on André Malraux's famous line, "On the other hand, cinema is also an industry." At the conference, Auclaire explained that he meant the title as a *boutade*, but the hostile reception to his gesture dramatized not only the sensitivity of the conference attendees but also the attachment still felt by cinema militants to France's "certain idea of cinema." This conception of cinema, attempting to straddle art and industry, has motivated state cinema policy for many decades, and as this book has tried to chronicle, had most recently coalesced under the banner of the cultural exception.

On January 7, 2009, the very day that the BLAC conference opened, President Sarkozy, together with Minister of Culture Albanel, described by *Le Monde* as a "former leftist militant become unshakeable pillar of the seventh art," named Marin Karmitz to chair a new Council for Artistic Creation.[2] The choice of Karmitz was no doubt a clever ploy on Sarkozy's part, for the ex-Maoist Karmitz had always identified himself as an outsider in the cinema profession. Karmitz could therefore serve as a shield against attacks from the left concerning Sarkozy's slashing of funding for culture generally and the cinema in particular.[3] Karmitz had evolved away from his leftist sympathies over time, however, a change underscored by his highly publicized dispute with a small theater just outside of Paris. That contretemps highlights many of the tensions attending a state policy committed to preserving the art and industry of cinema.

In 2007, two theater circuits in Paris sued a small art theater in the Paris suburb of Montreuil. The plaintiffs claimed that the theater's plan to expand from three screens to six constituted "unfair competition" and "abuse of dominant position." The theater, the Méliès, mounted a highly publicized campaign to defend its plan, with a galaxy of internationally renowned directors signing a petition in support of its expansion. The theater published an ad in several papers mimicking the publicity that once accompanied Spielberg's *Jaws*, this time with two large sharks and one small red fish. One of the sharks brought legal action against the papers for defamation. In policy terms, others viewed it as a face-off between legitimate cultural policy and the imperial dictates of liberalization. Would the state commitment to art cinemas prevail over free rein of the market? Once again the state was faced with balancing the industrial and cultural goals of state policy.

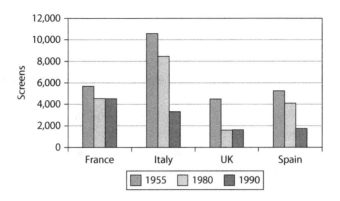

FIGURE CON.1 Number of screens in selected European countries, 1955, 1980, 1990

As attendance declined during the 1980s, cinema theaters all over Europe struggled to remain open. While Italy began the decade with far more theaters than any other European country, thousands of its theaters closed in the following years (see figure Con.1). Italy lost more than 60 percent of its movie houses. Spain saw half of its screens disappear. Britain had experienced that phenomenon long before, with the number of screens shrinking from 4,500 to 1,500 by 1980. As we saw in chapter 6, France had resisted the trend better than the other countries. Even though attendance fell by 50 percent once again during the 1980s, the number of screens fell only slightly.

One of the constants in French support of its film industry has been the maintenance of both the number of theaters and a geographical distribution of screens that would provide reasonable access to films for areas throughout the country, including rural regions with low population density. The state devoted funds to this priority, but state money alone could not stanch the bleeding. A new development intervened, illustrating yet again the challenges facing state policy: towns took possession of theaters when private owners could no longer meet their expenses.

The Bredin report had addressed the problem in 1981, noting that 1,800 theaters in communes with less than twenty thousand residents had closed, representing 40 percent of all theaters. National figures masked this development, for 1,600 theaters had opened in urban centers.

The report emphasized the importance of preventing further erosion of theaters in these zones:

> A first principle must be affirmed: the existing theaters must remain in operation. . . . The Mission [i.e., the report] considers that the CNC must develop a formula that could be called a "contract of cultural and cinematic activity." This contract would have as a goal the establishment of clear reciprocal commitments between the collectivity and the theater. . . . Designated as a collective service, the theater should be run certainly with a concern to contribute to local [cultural] activity but also with the intention to respect as much as possible the demands of the market.[4]

This last sentence goes directly to the crux of the recurrent, by now familiar, tension of a state cultural policy. With attendance plummeting, the report insisted on developing policies to keep theaters open, particularly in the areas hit hardest by closings. Yet the Bredin document did not want market realities ignored. Acting on the report, Lang set up a new organization in 1983 to guide the new decentralization policy promoted by the Socialist Party. Following the first new law for cinema passed in 1982, Lang announced the Agency for the Regional Development of Cinema (ADRC) early in 1983, whose responsibility would be "the reconquest of the popular audience through the creation and renovation of theaters in poorer areas."[5] While the CNC does not track the figures, some estimates indicate that municipalities eventually took over some 1,300 screens, or one-quarter of all French screens, most of which are officially designated as art cinemas.[6]

To judge by the global figures, the number of screens began to grow again in France during the 1990s, owing to the construction of multiplexes. France had renovated theaters regularly over the years, often adding screens to existing theaters, hence the need to distinguish between theaters and screens. Already during the 1980s the CNC listed both the number of screens and the number of theaters, with the number of screens increasing significantly over the number of theaters, but most of the theaters housed fewer than six screens, below the generally accepted minimum of eight used to designate multiplexes.

As multiplex construction proceeded in the 1990s, in a relatively unregulated fashion, critics expressed familiar concerns about concentration and the threat that these new theaters posed to art cinemas.

Attendance at multiplexes steadily rose, accounting for an ever larger percentage of the total number of spectators. By the middle of the first decade of the twenty-first century, when the two circuits lodged their complaints against the Méliès theater in Montreuil, multiplexes, with 31 percent of all screens, drew 52 percent of all spectators in theaters. In earlier years of the multiplex expansion, critics had warned of a bipolarization, with the multiplexes showing blockbusters and the consequent marginalization of art cinemas forced to show only art films. As we have seen, the fear of multiplexes draining audiences from the art cinemas has been a recurrent one. Commentators spoke of the conversion of theatrical exhibition from *salles de quartiers* to *quartiers des salles*, from screens in neighborhoods to neighborhoods of screens.[7] That is, theaters formerly serving local populations in close proximity (*salles de proximité*) were forced to close as spectators were drawn to the large multiplexes built by the large theater circuits.

Smaller theaters, independent of the large circuits, tried to respond with more dynamic programming. Many of those theaters qualified as official art cinemas, which entitled them to a variety of state aids, helping them to hire personnel and renovate their facilities. As French exhibition followed phenomena familiar from practices in other countries, with wider releases of blockbusters, pressures mounted on independent theaters faced with increasing difficulties in obtaining films from distributors. These issues were already the domain of the ADRC, which funded the purchase of additional copies of films that distributors refused to supply, often under pressure from the large circuits. The mediator for cinema, another Lang innovation from the 1980s, also responded to complaints from theaters. Some dynamic art cinemas sought to take advantage of their difference from the multiplexes, accentuating the distinctiveness of their programming through extensive outreach to the most frequent moviegoers, the cinephiles. The Utopia theaters, based originally in Toulouse, thrived in the niche market of art cinema.[8]

In the 1970s, one entrepreneur took the risk of opening new theaters in deteriorating parts of Paris. Marin Karmitz, a Romanian Jew who came to France with his family in 1949, at the age of nine, had attended the French film school (IDHEC) and made radical political films in the early 1970s (*Camarades, Coup pour coup*), but he decided to enter exhibition after the possibilities of a left government faded after 1968. In 1974, Karmitz opened a theater with three screens in the Bastille area, long before its gentrification. Over time, with the success of that theater, Karmitz ventured into other neighborhoods, effectively anticipating and then benefiting from the gentrification of those areas, or what the French call *boboization* (after the term "bobo," for bourgeois bohemian, not unlike "yuppie" in English). He also produced films for well-known auteurs, including the Taviani brothers (*Padre Padrone*), Jean-Luc Godard (*Sauve qui peut, la vie*), and Krzysztof Kieslowski (the Three Colors trilogy), among others, and also developed a catalogue as a distributor, eventually including DVDs. He called his company MK2, which now includes several architecturally striking multiplexes that contributed to reviving various Paris neighborhoods.[9]

From modest beginnings thirty years earlier, Karmitz built a highly successful integrated movie business, anchored by the MK2 circuit in Paris. Though his theaters contain only sixty-one screens in Paris (out of 372 in the city), his mini-circuit was the third largest in Paris, behind Europalaces (Gaumont and Pathé) and UGC. MK2 specializes in art cinema, each theater occupying a rough niche within that category, from the relatively esoteric (Hautefeuille) to the mainstream (Bibliothèque).[10] After building one popular multiplex on the Bassin de La Villette (Nineteenth Arrondissement), Karmitz added another directly on the opposite bank of the canal; to punctuate the art pedigree of the programming, a small boat named "Zéro de conduite" ferries ticketholders back and forth across the narrow waterway. In 2002, Karmitz joined Europalaces in offering fidelity cards, first issued by UGC in 1999, a move that had provoked controversy for various reasons. Aside from the fear that the cards would confer an unfair competitive advantage on UGC, the cards threatened to upset the traditional calculation of the price of a ticket (and the derived rights), for spectators would no longer be paying a fixed price for a particular film. The effective price paid would depend on the number of times a spectator attended a cinema in a month, the price per film dropping as the number of films rose. UGC essentially was betting that more spectators would attend their theaters, but less frequently than the cinephiles, resulting in a net profit for the exhibitor.[11] The CNC examined the numbers in two studies, ultimately allowing the cards under the condition that they must be accepted at art cinemas not belonging to the large circuits offering the cards.[12] One key question was setting a "reference price" in order to determine royalties due to rights holders, which was eventually decided to the satisfaction of the interested parties.

In 2007, after long negotiations, Karmitz could not reach an agreement with the city of Paris for his planned multiplex in Beaugrenelle (Fifteenth Arrondissement). The landlord awarded the franchise to his former fidelity card partner, Pathé.[13] In June of that year, Karmitz renounced his pact with Europalaces and entered a marriage of convenience with UGC, joining UGC's card system.[14] Thus, anyone holding a UGC card could attend MK2 theaters, in addition to other art cinemas in Paris.

UGC had a history of harassing small theaters when Karmitz entered a separate action against the Méliès in Montreuil. UGC had already taken legal action against a theater in Lyon, the Comoedia. UGC had managed the Comoedia, a theater that dated back to the 1920s, but ceded ownership in 2003. The city assumed control of the theater and worked out an arrangement to run it as an officially recognized art cinema. In 2005, the Comoedia applied for and received a grant from the CNC for €600,000 to upgrade the theater, at a total cost of €2 million. In December 2006, UGC took the CNC to court regarding the grant.[15] UGC also filed suit against an expansion plan from six to ten screens by an art cinema in Épinal on the grounds that it would compete with UGC's theater in Ludres, thirty miles away. The new management objected, ultimately prevailing in the legal proceedings. In June, UGC protested the decision approving yet another municipal theater, this time in Noisy-le-Grand, outside Paris.[16]

Like the Comoedia, the Méliès had established a solid record as an art theater catering to the community of Montreuil.[17] Under the guidance of Stéphane Goudet, a young critic, cinephile, and professor, the Méliès built its spectator base, raising attendance by 27 percent in the first year and 38 percent in the second year.[18] In addition to obtaining support from the town of Montreuil (population 100,000), the theater, like all official art theaters, received funding from the CNC according to a variable support system dependent on the degree of extracurricular activities undertaken by the theater, including the kinds of films shown, the number of debates, conferences, printed material developed, special screenings for children, and so forth. Because of the extent of these activities, beyond its designation as an art cinema, the Méliès also qualified for three labels, attesting to its commitment to cultural work: Research and Discovery, Repertory and Patrimony, and Cinema for Children, each label qualifying it for access to additional funding sources at the CNC. As outlined in the Bredin report, theaters run by municipalities normally signed contracts with the cities detailing the responsibilities assumed by the group actually operating the theater.

UGC and MK2 lodged separate complaints at separate times. UGC, which had owned the Méliès until 1986, objected that the plan to expand from three to six screens would take business away from its multiplex located in nearby Rosny-sous-Bois.[19] That multiplex drew some 2.3 million spectators each year, making it the third largest cinema in all of France, compared to the 200,000 annual attendance at the Méliès. MK2 operated two multiplexes (Gambetta and Nation) nearby in Paris, a short subway distance (six stops) from the Méliès. Karmitz, like the head of UGC, Guy Verrecchia, claimed that he had no objection to the Méliès with the current three screens, but the expansion to six screens, which would together hold 1,200 seats (compared to the 400 seats that served the three screens), would draw customers from the two Karmitz theaters.[20] While UGC's legal case protested "unfair competition" and improbably, "abuse of dominant position,"[21] Karmitz filed suit on July 13, 2007, against the decision of the Departmental Council for Cinema Equipment to authorize the expansion to six screens.

The plaintiffs may not have anticipated the pitfalls of taking on the little Méliès. In May, Goudet released an open petition of support for the Méliès with hundreds of signatures, endorsing the call that "we need places of exception." The star-studded list included some of the most prominent filmmakers in world cinema, such as the Dardenne Brothers, Abbas Kiarostami, Hou Hsiao-Hsien, Krzysztof Kieslowski, David Lynch, Carlos Reynadas, Alejandro González Iñárritu, Tsai Ming-Liang, Wim Wenders, Wong Kar-Wai, Abel Ferrara, Jia Zhangke; prestigious French filmmakers, some residents of Montreuil, also affixed their names: Claire Denis, Robert Guédigian, Pascale Ferran, Catherine Breillat, Arnaud Desplechin, Jeanne Moreau, and Agnès Varda.[22] Interviews with the respective combatants appeared in the press. On January 9, 2008, several papers printed the ad taken out by the Méliès with two sharks circling above a small red fish swimming in the water below them. At the top, it announced, "UGC and MK2 Attack the Cinema in Montreuil, the Méliès," with a text accompanying the illustration of the epic sea battle (see figure Con.2).

> The cinema Méliès in Montreuil, a designated Art Cinema, is scheduled soon to move in order to expand from three to six screens.
> But two "big circuits" of distribution, UGC and MK2, are blocking this project and have each lodged legal charges of "unfair competition" and "abuse of dominant position."

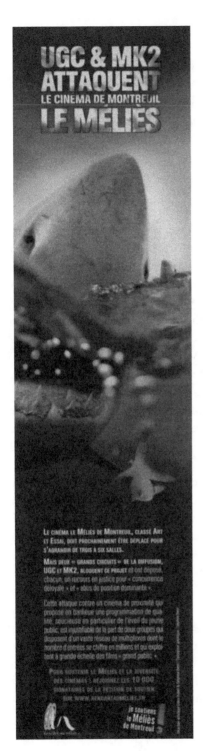

FIGURE CON.2 Advertisement seeking support for the Méliès Theater, January 2008

This attack against a neighborhood cinema which offers in the suburbs a programming of quality, careful in particular to train the young
public, is without foundation on the part of the two groups, which have
at their disposal a vast web of multiplexes with millions of spectators and
which show in large quantities films for popular taste.

To support the Méliès and the diversity of cinemas, join the 10,000
signatures on the petition of support at www.rencartauMéliès.fr

I support the Méliès of Montreuil!!

After Karmitz had initiated legal action, a photo-conscious contingent
from Montreuil (the delegation included the deputy mayor replete with
official tricolor ribbon draped across his chest), forced its way into the
elegant MK2 Bibliothèque on January 26, 2008, carrying helium-filled
balloons imprinted with "the diversity of cinema depends on the diversity
of cinemas." A scuffle broke out as the courageous guardians of MK2
mounted a defense, during which one of the MK2 employees claimed to
have been bitten by the deputy mayor. MK2 subsequently released a med-
ical report on the mark of "5 centimeters" allegedly scarring the left arm
of the employee. It is difficult to know exactly what happened based on
the press reports, with the deputy mayor outraged that his tricolor banner
had been dishonored and Karmitz charging hyperbolically that the attack
"endangers democracy,"[23] for the press appears to have viewed the whole
affair as Grand Guignol.

The former Maoist Karmitz, once called "the anti-Messier," did not
appreciate the broadside.[24] He asserted that he was bringing an action
against the three papers for defamation, adding, "This reminds me of
certain pre-war images where one showed Jews as vultures. I don't like
comparisons between men and animals."[25] Goudet claimed in response
that the ad was a riff on the fact that Karmitz had produced a documen-
tary in defense of sharks.[26] Once the lines were drawn, the war of numbers
followed. UGC counted the screenings listed in one weekly guide to cultural events in Paris, L'Officiel, averring that 45 percent of the screenings
at the two theaters showed the same films.[27] Le Méliès hired a university
student to study the same numbers and concluded that only 4 percent of
the screenings actually overlapped.[28] Ultimately, the confrontation ended
quietly. The court ruled against Karmitz's defamation suit, and apparently Karmitz withdrew his complaint against the Méliès.[29]

On a more sober note, and as the Bredin report foreshadowed implicitly many years earlier, the Méliès drama reflected real structural tensions at the heart of cultural policy. At what point does state support for a culture industry interfere with free competition; should these particular constraints on free completion be viewed differently from other constraints deriving from dominant market positions; and how should the question be resolved?[30] The three screens of an art cinema posed no problem for UGC and MK2 when the Méliès counted 200,000 annual spectators. According to the Méliès, the plan for the expansion to six screens would raise the attendance to 300,000. Apparently, the circuits felt that the additional 100,000 would cut deeply into their businesses, effectively turning the municipality of Montreuil into a competitor. In addition, the Méliès was also contractually bound to charge reasonable prices at its public screenings, to avoid the practice of predatory pricing. Here the "reference price" comes into play, as UGC's Verrecchia pointed out in an interview.[31] If the reference price is €5.40 but the price at the Méliès is €4.50, then rights holders will receive less compensation from the Méliès for all spectators choosing it over UGC or MK2. Goudet pointed out that despite the doubling of the screens, the Méliès would not show more films. Instead, it would take advantage of the additional screening times to keep films in the theater for longer runs, allowing more time for word of mouth to attract spectators to more difficult films.[32]

As this confrontation was unfolding, Jean-Pierre Leclerc, with coauthor Anne Perrot, delivered yet another report on the cinema, this time to the Ministry of Culture and the Ministry of Economy, Industry, and Employment. Minister of Culture Albanel and the vice president of the Council on Competition, Christine Lagarde, had asked them to examine the relation between the current practices of the film industry and the laws of competition, precisely the terrain on which the legal squabble over the Méliès took place. The letter charging them with the assignment began by recalling to them that the French president himself had observed that the mechanism that has "favored the creativity of French cinema and the vitality of its industry, . . . constitutes one of the essential dimensions of the French cultural exception." In their introduction, the authors wrote that contrary to the normal functioning of competition in other industries, "the film industry . . . rests . . . on the consistent commitment to constrain the mechanisms of the market, which [otherwise] would have led to the elimination of French cinematic creation, unable to resist the seductive power of the U.S. cinema."

Leclerc and Perrot devoted one section to issues posed by the existence of municipal theaters, though they do not pass judgment on the merits of the arguments marshaled in the Méliès case. Local governments should be guided always by "public interest," and they cited relevant existing legislation already covering a variety of cases. Municipalities might judge that private theaters were not serving the public interest because of inadequate screening of art films, so public theaters could correct that absence through subsidies. If a private theater did not offer sufficient diversity or quality in its programming, the locality could support a theater to plug those gaps. They found no principled objection to competition between municipal theaters and private ones, so long as the competition was not "unfair." Thus, in their opinion, subsidies should not push ticket prices below the real cost of screenings.[33]

It is perfectly understandable, then, that the BLAC militants took offense at Auclaire's *boutade* twisting Malraux's formulation into a defense of cinema as "entertainment." With one word the Auclaire report had struck at the elaborate edifice patched together over so many years by the CNC and industry professionals to defend the cultural exception. No wonder they called Auclaire's exposition "schizophrenic." If film was just merchandise, state policy could hardly justify the dizzying array of funding streams to support it. Discussants at the BLAC conference railed against Auclaire's application of a "market" discourse to the cinema, which they decried as substituting quantity for quality. In the published proceedings of the conference, one speaker objected to Auclaire's characterization of the choice of films shown to students in the École et cinéma program as "elitist." In keeping with Minister Albanel's call to double the number of students in the school programs, Auclaire had proposed doubling the number of films in the catalogue and more films with which teachers would be more familiar. The speaker opposed this proposal as abject pandering and damned it as a symptom of the market mentality of Auclaire: "Regarding the question of the school programs and the expansion of the catalogues, what you suggest is to transform these programs into simple cultural 'supply.' So that there will be more teachers and thus more spectator students, you propose to make the catalogues less 'difficult.' But this is exactly the logic of the market: effectively reducing the cultural action to a market based on supply and demand."[34]

This tension between the commercial and the cultural, or the industrial and the artistic in Malraux's terms, lies at the heart of the rationale for the cultural exception. Debates over such tensions are unheard of in the United States, for in the absence of government intervention directed at, or at least the lack of public discussion over, such issues as the distribution of theaters across the national territory, access of populations to theaters, the diversity of films on offer, competition between art cinemas and multiplexes, support for first-time filmmakers, and so on, the film industry faces no government interference. Ideas of "quality control" or "public interest" never arise for the film industry in the United States; in France, the government views the health and quality of the cinema as a national priority, whence the incessant adjustments to commercial and cultural logics. At the Cannes Film Festival in 2000, Prime Minister Jospin recalled his own cinephilia, citing his discovery of the "American films noirs, the works of the New Wave, or of the works of Ozu, Mizoguchi, and Kurosawa."[35] President Ronald Reagan had a successful career in Hollywood as an actor before entering politics, yet his tastes ran to the likes of *Dirty Harry* and *Rambo*.[36] When UGC and MK2 asked the government to restrain the expansion of the Méliès art cinema, the minister of culture supported art over industry.[37] On the eve of the Césars ceremony in 2008, several organizations of independent theater owners released a statement conveying their worries over the dismantling of policies of public support for the cinema: "We do not want to see an evolution which would eliminate the principle of the cultural exception and which would succumb to the law of the survival of the fittest."[38]

This book has examined how France has managed this balancing act between art and industry. The studies, books, and debates in France that chronicle these efforts reveal the care devoted to an industry forever described as being in crisis, never more so than when the GATT confrontation threatened to render the efforts moot. The French fought to preserve their prerogative to determine their own cultural policies. With Hollywood taking 80 percent of the European market, Jack Valenti, supported by Spielberg and Scorsese, argued absurdly that spectators should have the "freedom" to choose the films they wanted to see. Some estimates in the United States indicate that 30 percent of all U.S. films produced each year are never released in theaters, but Valenti never objected to that act of commercial repression by the industry paying his million-dollar salary.[39] Legal experts in the United States pore over the texts of trade agreements to denounce French transgressions. Scholars who make no claims to cinema expertise dismiss French films as trifles and mediocrities. The U.S. trade representative threatens the EU with sanctions. Adding insult to injury, the European Commission regularly pulls out its fine-toothed neoliberal comb, searching for dirigiste nits with which to confront the unreconstructed French miscreants.

Yet French cinema has withstood these assaults and even thrived in the process. It has maintained the right to design its own policies, a right that most other countries have ultimately also wanted to preserve, even if they have not necessarily copied French methods. With the partial exception of the United States and perhaps India (as discussed in chapter 1), most countries with functioning film industries provide state support. Within France, many critics fault the support system for encouraging a presumed indifference to theatrical success. With various funding streams available from television and the state, filmmakers can patch together enough prefinancing to cover their costs before the films reach the theaters, the logic of prefinancing having replaced the financing of amortization (in theaters). But studies of state aids show that most European countries provide outright grants to filmmakers wholly unrelated to box office results, while France channels most of the Compte de soutien to films in direct proportion to their performance in theaters, known for that reason as "automatic aid."[40] Less than 30 percent of state funding taken out of theater receipts for production is awarded to films on the basis of quality. As it has done since 1948, state policy favors theatrical success in relation to other EU film industries, thereby actually *giving the market more weight* in its support system than other countries with state support (see figure Con.3).

Critics in France call for adjusting existing dispensations to award more funding to selective aid, on the assumption that selective aid contributes more artistic quality to annual production. Pascal Ferran has supported such redirection, but she also has refused to argue for an indifference to the market. In her call for the importance of *films du milieu*, she was trying to make a case for the centrality of middle-level production for national cinema. Big-budget blockbusters, even on the more modest French financial scale, seek to drive spectators into the maw of multiplexes, which she views as "nightmares."[41] Low-budget art films have little hope of drawing substantial audiences. But for Ferran, the mid-budget films can find popular audiences, and that should be the bedrock goal of a national cinema, one neither spurning box office success as the death of artistic

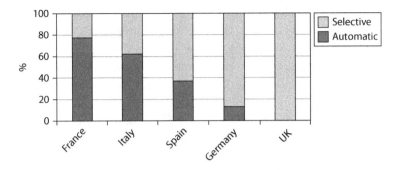

FIGURE CON.3 Selective vs. automatic aid in EU5 countries, 2002

purity nor cynically placing theatrical success as the ultimate measure of value. Films *du milieu* require budgets appropriate to their artistic needs, consigned neither to the ghetto of nombrilistic art films nor the consumer bazaar of multiplexes.[42]

Many commentators, not only in France, claim that national cinemas cannot exist today without state support.[43] Even with the elaborate French system, however, studies have shown that French cinema operates at a loss, yet as these chapters have shown, French cinema outperforms its European partners in virtually any measurable category. One study from 2004 found that only 14 percent of French films made in 1996 showed a combined profit from all windows.[44] But before jumping to conclusions about the miserable performance of French cinema, one might ask about the performance of the vaunted U.S. cinema. Unfortunately, the most accomplished number crunchers in the United States admit that they cannot offer reliable information. De Vany, who found that "profit is a dirty secret in the movie business," estimated that only 22 percent of films are profitable; Epstein, who obtained proprietary studio information for 1999–2004, wrote that only 5 percent of films turn a profit, "according to industry estimates."[45] Vogel concluded that the hype of theatrical release actually distracts from the real sources of profit, the majors' international distribution network.[46] With so much of Hollywood's financing hidden from view, it is difficult to rush to judgment about the purported failures of French cinema, as documented so copiously by the French themselves.

France may not have solved the problems facing national film industries, but as this book has tried to show, the French system has adapted to the successive challenges, of television, of multiplexes, of blockbusters, and of DVDs. Starting with Jack Lang, France has drafted laws, designed policy, lobbied its neighbors, faced up to the European Commission, and fought Hollywood in multiple venues to defend its right to develop its own cultural policies. And it has won that right, one that some countries have emulated. As noted, the Republic of Korea has modeled its own film policy since GATT on the French system. More recently, when Romanian cinema emerged unexpectedly as one of the surprise success stories of European film, inquiry found its policies closely modeled on and aided by the French system.[47]

Most recently, and twenty years after France enunciated the principle of the cultural exception in 1993, René Bonnell led an updated study of the French film industry.[48] Already in his first book, from 1978, Bonnell had criticized French cinema for various failings, and he argued in 1990 that the idea of "European cinema" was an illusion, for films could not melt together cultural differences, a view confirmed by the rejection of subsequent Europuddings by audiences and critics alike. He called instead for building an audience for national cinema productions across political frontiers, given that no European country could match the size and wealth of the U.S. market.[49] Bonnell's 2013 report, like earlier ones, documented the continuing problems of French cinema, which still remained unprofitable globally, but it also showed that 33 percent of French films earned a profit, more than double the percent found ten years earlier, and considerably higher than the best guesses for the U.S. cinema. While Bonnell did not claim the cultural exception as an explanation for the demonstrable successes of the French film industry, he did identify the cultural exception as an "axiom" on the first page of the report:

> For thirty years all the [French] governments, actively supported by the professionals, have defended the axiom of the cultural exception, which poses the inviolable principle that the production and distribution of cultural contents should be exempt from the ordinary laws of free exchange. Respect for this principle has served as a rampart against all attempts to dismantle the French system of support for the seventh art. Many foreign governments have been inspired to support their own film industries. Isolated at the beginning of this combat, France has succeeded in winning over by now thirteen European countries and fourteen Ministers of Culture to this cause increasingly adopted on other continents. In May 2013, the European Parliament voted, at French initiative, its approval of this

principle in demanding that cultural goods and services be exluded from the remit of negotiation of the free trade agreement taking place between Europe and the United States. France has finally succeeded in imposing its point of view in excluding, at this stage, the cultural services, including film, from the field of discussions.[50]

As the voluminous discourse on globalization in recent decades has shown, capitalism continues to extend its penetration of all facets of daily life across the world, whether measured in centuries or decades. Before the 1980s, international, multilateral treaties did not include cultural production. Only when the GATT agreements encompassed services did culture enter the crosshairs. France convinced its EU partners, including free trade believers, and many other countries, that culture deserved a special status in these trade agreements. Few countries may have meticulously copied the French system for its film industry, but the cultural exception has preserved the prerogative of countries to design their own methods of support for culture. More significantly, the ongoing debates over the cultural exception, as in the stalled Trans-Pacific Partnership in 2014, have shown that the form of globalization championed and aggressively pursued by the United States can be resisted. Before the cultural exception was forged as a weapon in trade wars, the French president of the European Commission, Jacques Delors, a man who once dreamed of being a film director, spoke on behalf of all countries when he asked "our American friends . . . Do we have the right to exist?"

APPENDIX A

A Note on Sources

For readers interested in data on the French film industry, the best single location is the Documentation Center of the Centre national du cinéma et de l'image animée (CNC) in Paris. Since 2000, the CNC has made a large number of its reports on all aspects of the industry available online. In particular, the annual *Bilan* is invaluable.

The industry trade papers, *Le Film Français* and *L'Écran Total*, are helpful, but they normally use CNC data.

French newspapers regularly cover the film industry, though they also rely on the CNC for data. Many can be searched in LexisNexis or Factiva, though the start dates vary before 2000.

The Council of Europe created the European Audiovisual Observatory in 1992 to gather data on the European audiovisual industry and report on legal issues. Since 1994, the EAO has published regularly a *Statistical Yearbook* (in several languages), though it is prohibitively expensive for most individuals. The yearbooks include copious information on European countries, often with figures for the United States and Japan, traditionally the two largest national markets, though China replaced Japan as the second largest market in 2012. Unfortunately, few U.S. libraries have it.

The *Bilans* and the *Statistical Yearbooks* have the key advantage of at least attempting consistency over time.

The EAO, with the Council of Europe, also publishes a more compact yearly *Focus: World Market Trends*, with selected data for many countries.

Many scholars have commented on the astonishing inadequacy of data available on the U.S. audiovisual industry. The problem appears to be that the industry is made up of private, even if publicly traded, companies. No doubt the industry compiles copious data for internal use, but it is not available. One need only compare the websites of the official U.S. trade organization, the Motion Picture Association of America, and the CNC. The trade paper *Variety* includes some data, but without references to sources beyond the MPAA. One standard secondary reference with some statistical tables is Harold L. Vogel's *Entertainment Industry Economics*, 7th ed. (New York: Cambridge University Press, 2007).

For an excellent, detailed discussion of sources for data, see the appendices in David Waterman's *Hollywood's Road to Riches* (Cambridge, Mass.: Harvard University Press, 2005).

The basic problem in tracking down data is that no country has devoted the resources to collecting data that France has. This commitment can be traced to the elevated status of cinema in France, where the regulatory system directs large financial flows to the national industry; bilateral co-productions; European production, distribution, and exhibition; and foreign filmmakers. As the government designs the regulations, the size of the flows requires careful tracking to monitor compliance and minimize waste.

APPENDIX B

Calculation of Automatic Aid in France

I n order to calculate for automatic state aid available to producers in France, the government applies two scales (*barèmes*). Points are assigned according to the country of residence of personnel or business.

The first scale is used to determine whether a film is considered European. A fiction feature film must earn 14 out of a possible 18 points to qualify as European.

THE 18 POINTS OF THE EUROPEAN SCALE

6 points for screenwriters and directors
   3 points for director
   2 points for screenwriter
   1 point for other writers
6 points for actors
   3 points for leading role
   2 points for secondary role
   1 point for 50 percent of other roles
4 points for creative collaborators
   1 point for cinematography
   1 point for sound
   1 point for editing
   1 point for designer

2 points for technical work
  Laboratories
  Editing/mix
  Studio shooting

If a film qualifies as European, the amount of aid is assigned on the basis of a 100-point scale used in France.

THE 100 POINTS OF THE AUTOMATIC AID SCALE

10 points for the production company
20 points for the language of shooting
10 points for authors
  5 points for director
  4 points for writers, adaptation, dialogue
  1 point for composer
20 points for actors
  10 points for leading roles (characters in at least 50 percent of scenes)
  10 points for all other roles
14 points for technicians and creative collaborators
  2 points for directing, other than director
  2 points for administration of production
  2 points for cinematography
  2 points for design
  2 points for sound
  2 points for editing
  2 points for makeup
6 points for workers
  4 points for shooting crew
  2 points for construction crew
20 points for shooting and post-production
  5 points for shooting, of which
    3 points for locations
    2 points for laboratory
  5 points for technical materials, of which
    2 points for cinematography
    2 points for lighting
    1 point for equipment

5 points for sound post-production
5 points for image post-production

A film must earn 25 points in order to qualify for automatic aid generated by the exhibition receipts for theaters, television, and video. A film earning 25–70 points will qualify for a percentage of the support fund receipts corresponding to the number of points listed below. A film earning 25 points will receive 25 percent of the funds generated for the support fund from the receipts; a film earning 70 points will receive 70 percent of the receipts generated for the support fund.

Above 70 points, the following coefficients are applied:

71 points: 73%
72 points: 76%
73 points: 79%
74 points: 82%
75 points: 85%
76 points: 88%
77 points: 91%
78 points: 94%
79 points: 97%

If a film earns 80–100 points, it qualifies for 100 percent of the funds in the support fund generated by receipts.

EXAMPLE

The fund for automatic aid is generated by a tax on all tickets (about 11 percent). Following the figures assigned by the CNC, producers qualify for a percentage of that tax, calculated as the product of the number of tickets sold, the price of the ticket, the tax rate on the tickets, and the percentage of TSA available to the producer.

For a film drawing 200,000 spectators, a ticket price of €6, a TSA of 11 percent, and a percentage of 125 percent applied to the sum generated, the potential automatic aid would be €165,000:

Number of tickets sold	×	Price of ticket	×	Rate of tax on price of tickets (TSA)	×	Percentage of TSA available to producer(s)
200,000	×	€6	×	11%	×	125%

Depending on the relevant percentages derived from the automatic aid scale, the film would receive the following amounts of automatic aid:

With 30 points, 30% of €165,000 = €49,500
With 73 points, 79% of €165,000 = €130,350
With 83 points, 100% of €165,000 = €165,000

For automatic aid generated by receipts from television and video, the same coefficient from the automatic aid scale would be applied.

If a film received payment for screening on television of €200,000, with a television tax rate (for the automatic aid) of 10 percent, and a coefficient from the automatic aid scale of 88 percent, the film would receive €17,600:
€200,000 × 10% × 88% = €17,600

APPENDIX C

The Compte de soutien: A Schematic

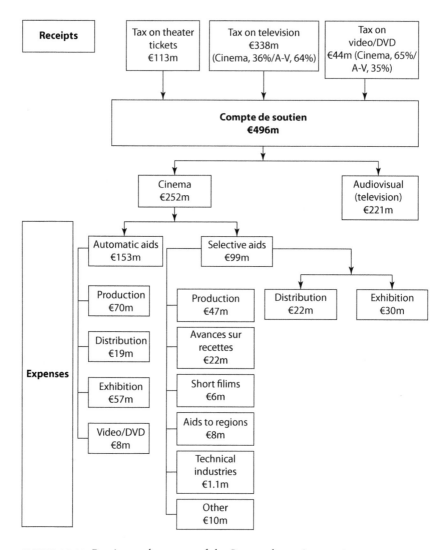

FIGURE AP.C1 Receipts and expenses of the Compte de soutien, 2006

APPENDIX D

Financing French Film: A Schematic

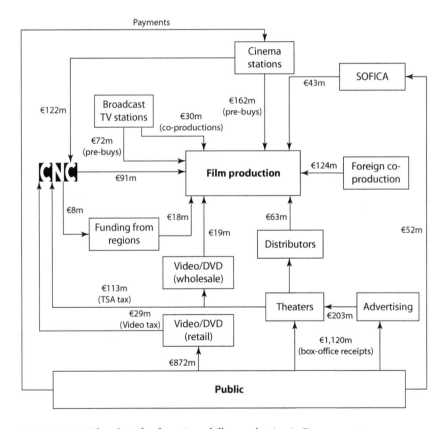

FIGURE AP.D1 Flowchart for financing of film production in France, 2006

APPENDIX E

Grants to Art et essai Theaters

The French commitment to art cinema rests largely on the grants to theaters officially designated art et essai by a CNC commission. The sizes of the grants vary according to multiple criteria, the two most important being the size of the population in the theater's city or town and the percentage of art et essai films (French and foreign) shown during the year. The following figures represent the base grants within each category. They can be increased or decreased according to additional demographic and programming criteria.

Within each category (A, B, C, D), there are four breakdowns according to the annual revenue at each theater (A2, A3, A4, A5; B2, B3, B4, B5; C2, C3, C4, C5; D2, D3, D4, D5). Theaters that promote difficult films or program filmmaker visits, debates, and promotional outreach can receive the supplemental designation of "Research," which can be applied to some of the other categories (A1, RA2, B1, RB2, RC1, RC2, RD1, RD2). Within each category, grants are awarded in amounts that decrease with the size of the box office, inversely correlated with size of the potential local market. In addition to the label "Research," theaters can receive labels of "Young Viewers" and "Patrimony."

CATEGORY A

Paris and towns with population greater than 200,000—minimum 65 percent art et essai screenings:

A2	€10,291
A3	€7,927
A4	€4,726
A5	€1,601

CATEGORY B

Towns with population between 100,000 and 200,000—minimum 50 percent art et essai screenings:

B2	€10,290
B3	€7,927
B4	€4,726
B5	€1,601

CATEGORY C

Towns with population less than 100,000—minimum 40 percent art et essai screenings:

C2	€10,290
C3	€7,927
C4	€4,726
C5	€1,601

CATEGORY D

Towns with population between 20,000–100,000—minimum 30 percent art et essai screenings:

D2	€10,290
D3	€7,927
D4	€4,726
D5	€1,601

CATEGORY RESEARCH

A1	€14,102
RA1	€15,702
RA2	€12,577
B1	€14,102
RB1	€15,702
RB2	€12,577
RC1	€15,702
RC2	€12,577
RD1	€18,751
RD2	€12,577

APPENDIX F

Films Chosen for High School Students
in Lycéens et apprentis au cinéma

Lycéens et apprentis au cinéma is one of three programs designed to educate French elementary, middle, and high school students about cinema (see chapter 8). Program directors chose the following films for 2009–2010 (from "Lycéens et apprentis au cinéma Année scolaire 2011–2012" [Paris: CNC, 2010], http://www.cnc.fr/web/fr/bilans/-/ressources/17595):

Adieu Philippine. Directed by Jacques Rozier. France, 1962.
Ali, Fear Eats the Soul. Directed by Rainer Werner Fassbinder. Germany, 1973.
All About My Mother. Directed by Pedro Almodóvar. Spain/France, 1999.
Army of Shadows. Directed by Jean-Pierre Melville. France, 1969.
The Betrayal. Directed by Philippe Faucon. France/Belgium, 2006.
Bled Number One. Directed by Rabah Ameur-Zaimech. Algeria/France, 2005.
Breathless. Directed by Jean-Luc Godard. France, 1959.
The Celebration. Directed by Thomas Winterberg. Denmark, 1998.
The Ceremony. Directed by Claude Chabrol. France, 1995.
Crouching Tiger, Hidden Dragon. Directed by Ang Lee. USA, 2000.
Dead Man. Directed by Jim Jarmusch. USA, 1995.

Elephant. Directed by Gus Van Sant. USA, 2005.

Freaks. Directed by Tod Browning. USA, 1932.

Fury. Directed by Fritz Lang. USA, 1936.

Grizzly Man. Directed by Werner Herzog. USA, 2005.

Hiroshima Mon Amour. Directed by Alain Resnais. France, 1959.

The Host. Directed by Joon-ho Bong. South Korea, 2006.

Human Resources. Directed by Laurent Cantet. France, 1999.

Kairo. Directed by Kiyoshi Kurosawa. Japan, 2002.

The Little Lieutenant. Directed by Xavier Beauvois. France, 2005.

Man with the Movie Camera. Directed by Dziga Vertov. USSR, 1928.

Man Without a Past. Directed by Aki Kaurismäki. Finland/France, 2002.

Mamma Roma. Directed by Pier Paolo Pasolini. Italy, 1962.

Monika. Directed by Ingmar Bergman. Sweden, 1952.

Noi the Albino. Directed by Dagur Kàri. Germany/Iceland, 2002.

North by Northwest. Directed by Alfred Hitchcock. USA, 1959.

Pickpocket. Directed by Robert Bresson. France, 1959.

The Return. Directed by Andrei Zviaguintsev. Russia, 2003.

The Royal Tenenbaums. Directed by Wes Anderson. USA, 2001.

S21: The Khmer Rouge Killing Machine. Directed by Rithy Panh. France, 2002.

The Shining. Directed by Stanley Kubrick. USA, 1980.

Since Otar Left. Directed by Julie Bertucelli. France/Belgium, 2003.

Sleepy Hollow. Directed by Tim Burton. USA, 1999.

Some Like It Hot. Directed by Billy Wilder. USA, 1959.

Starship Troopers. Directed by Paul Verhoeven. USA, 2007.

Sunrise. Directed by F. W. Murnau. USA, 1927.

Tokyo Eyes. Directed by Jean-Pierre Limosin. France/Japan, 1998.

Touch of Evil. Directed by Orson Welles. USA, 1958.

2046. Directed by Wong Kar-Wai. France/Italy, 2003.

Vertigo. Directed by Alfred Hitchcock. USA, 1958.

Waltz with Bashir. Directed by Ari Forman. Israel, 2008.

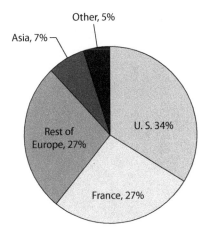

FIGURE AP.F1 Films chosen for the 2009–2010 Lycéens et apprentis au cinéma program by country/region, percentage of total

APPENDIX G

List of Films Aided by Fonds Sud

The Fonds Sud, founded in 1984, was sponsored by the Ministry of Foreign Affairs and the Ministry of Culture. In 2012, the Fonds Sud was folded into the Fonds images de la diversité, founded in 2007, cosponsored by the CNC and the Agence nationale pour la cohésion sociale et l'égalité des chances (Agency for Social Cohesion and Equality of Opportunity).

During its years of operation, the Fonds Sud contributed to the financing (production, completion funds, screenwriting) of more than 500 films by 260 filmmakers from over 70 countries, primarily developing countries:

Africa: 130 films
The Maghreb (Algeria, Morocco, Tunisia): 78 films
Far and Middle East: 70 films
Latin America: 142 films
Asia: 84 films

A partial list includes the following films:

ALGERIA (16 FILMS)

Bab El Oued City. Directed by Merzak Allouache, 1994.
Rachida. Directed by Yamina Bachir, 2002.
Roma wa la n'touma. Directed by Tariq Teguia, 2006.
Le thé au Harem. Directed by Medhi Charef, 1985.

ARGENTINA (40)

La cienaga. Directed by Lucrecia Martel, 2001.
Un crisantemo estalla en cinco esquinas. Directed by Daniel Burman, 1998.
La nube. Directed by Fernando Solanas, 1999.
Ne regarde pas en bas. Directed by Eliseo Subiela, 2007.
Ronda nocturna. Directed by Edgardo Cozarinsky, 2004.

BRAZIL (14)

Central do Brasil. Directed by Walter Salles, 1998.
La 3ème rive du fleuve. Directed by Nelson Peirera dos Santos, 1993.

BURKINO FASO (17)

Yam Daabo. Directed by Idrissa Ouédraogo, 1986.
Zan Boko. Directed by Gaston Kaboré, 1988.

CAMBODIA (4)

Les gens de la rizière. Directed by Rithy Panh, 1994.

CAMEROON (8)

Clando, paroles d'étranger. Directed by Jean-Marie Teno, 1996.
Quartier Mozart. Directed by Jean-Pierre Bekolo, 1992.

CHILE (16)

Americonga. Directed by Helvio Soto, 1987.

CHINA (27)

Jiabiangou. Directed by Wang Bing, 2010.
Platform. Directed by Jia Zhang-Ke, 2001.
Shanghai Triad. Directed by Zhang Yimou, 1995.
The World. Directed by Jia Zhang-Ke, 2004.

CUBA (3)

Aunque estés lejos. Directed by Juan Carlos Tabio, 2003.

EGYPT (13)

Alexandrie encore et toujours. Directed by Youssef Chahine, 1989.

ETHIOPIA (2)

Téza. Directed by Haile Gerima, 2008.

GUINEA-BISSAU (5)

Les yeux bleus de Yonta. Directed by Flora Gomes, 1990.

HAITI (3)

L'homme sur les quais. Directed by Raoul Peck, 1993.
Moloch Tropical. Directed by Raoul Peck, 2009.

INDIA (20)

Genesis. Directed by Mrinal Sena, 1985.
Le serviteur de Khali. Directed by Adoor Gopalakrishnan, 2003.

IRAN (12)

Gabbeh. Directed by Mohsen Makhmalbaf, 1995.

LEBANON (18)

West Beyrouth. Directed by Ziad Doueiri, 1998.

MALI (13)

Bamako. Directed by Abderrahmane Sissako, 2006.
Finzan. Directed by Cheick Oumar Sissoko, 1989.
Yeelen, la lumière. Directed by Souleymane Cissé, 1987.

MAURITANIA (4)

Fatima, l'Aurésienne. Directed by Med Hondo, 1999.

MOROCCO (19)

Les yeux secs. Directed by Narjiss Nejjar, 2003.

MEXICO (12)

Batalla en el cielo. Directed by Carlos Regadas, 2005.
El cobrador. Directed by Paul Leduc, 2007.
Dollar Mambo. Directed by Paul Leduc, 1993.
La niña en la piedra. Directed by Maryse Sistach, 2006.
Le reina de la noche. Directed by Arturo Ripstein, 1994.

PALESTINIAN TERRITORIES (11)

Divine Intervention. Directed by Elia Suleiman, 2002.

PERU (9)

Malabrigo. Directed by Alberto Durant, 1986.

SENEGAL (11)

Hyènes. Directed by Djibril Diop Mambety, 1992.
Moolaadè. Directed by Sembène Ousmane, 2004.

THAILAND (4)

Tropical Malady. Directed by Apichatpong Weerasethakul, 2004.

TUNISIA (36)

Un été à la Goulette. Directed by Férid Boughedir, 1995.

APPENDIX H

First Films in French Film Production

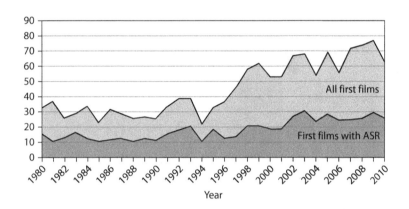

FIGURE AP.H1 Number of first films produced in France with avance sur recettes (ASR), 1980–2010

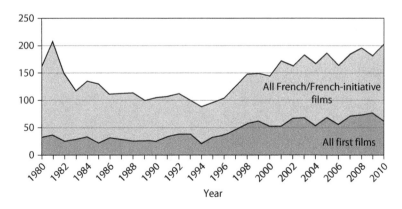

FIGURE AP.H2 Number of first films among all French-initiative productions, 1980–2010

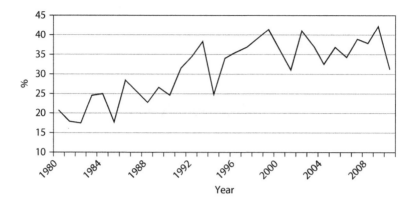

FIGURE AP.H3 First films as a percentage of all French films, 1980–2010

NOTES

INTRODUCTION

1. David Waterman, *Hollywood's Road to Riches* (Cambridge, Mass.: Harvard University Press, 2005), 6.

2. According to LexisNexis, *Le Monde* devoted more than two hundred stories to the cultural exception, in 1993; the *New York Times* carried four.

3. Laurent Creton, *Histoire économique du cinéma français: Production et financement 1940–1959* (Paris: CNRS, 2004), 279. In an earlier book, Creton provided some comparative industry revenue figures for movie theaters: 5 billion francs; French television: 33 billion francs; and Compagnie générale des eaux, parent company of Havas and Canal+: 164 billion francs. Creton, *Cinéma et marché* (Paris: Armand Colin, 1997), 210. In Europe, the entire European film industry accounted for only 7.4 percent of all audiovisual markets. Nils Klevjer Aas, "Challenges in European Cinema and Film Policy" (Strasbourg: European Audiovisual Observatory, October–November 2001), 4.

4. Renaud Donnedieu de Vabres, "La diversité culturelle n'est pas une arrogance," *Le Monde*, October 19, 2005.

5. In 2009, the CNC changed its name to the Centre national du cinéma et de l'image animée (National Center of Cinema and the Moving Image). For an overview of the CNC's history, see "Les articles consacrés aux 60 ans du CNC," http://www.cnc.fr /web/fr/historique-du-cnc, and "Cinquantenaire du CNC, 1946–1996" (Paris: CNC, 1996).

6. According to Leclerc, the CNC doubled the budget and personnel devoted to data gathering between 1991 and 2002. Jean-Pierre Leclerc, "Réflexions sur le dispositif français de soutien à la production cinématographique" (Paris: Ministry of Culture, 2003). *Bilans* since 2000 are available at http://www.cnc.fr/web/fr/bilans.

7. For example, as Harold Vogel, author of one authoritative industry account of showbiz accounting and finance, *Entertainment Industry Economics* (Cambridge: Cambridge University Press, 2007), was quoted in *Variety*, "The lack of access to real numbers in this industry is astounding and it's getting worse all the time. We have no way to judge Hollywood's actual return on equity nor can we accurately assess the year-to-year health of the film business." Meredith Amdur, "H'W'D Burns as Feds Fiddle," *Variety*, July 29–August 4, 2002, cited in Janet Wasko, "Show Me the Money: Challenging Hollywood Economics," in *Toward a Political Economy of Culture: Capitalism and Concentration in the 21st Century*, ed. A. Calabrese and C. Sparks (Lanham, Md.: Rowman and Littlefield, 2004), 135.

8. For some of the French studies, see especially works in the bibliography by Bonnell, Creton, Farchy, Forest, and Frodon. For the more limited discussion in English, see studies by Danan, Hayes, Hayward, and Jäckel.

9. "The government's support for films that won prizes in international film festivals helped to maintain the New Taiwan Cinema, while the mainstream commercial cinema died." Chris Berry, "Full Service Cinema: The South Korean Cinema Success Story (So Far)," in "Text and Context of Korean Cinema: Crossing Borders," ed. Renaud Young-Key Kim, R. Richard Grinker, and Kirk Y. Larsen, Sigur Center Asia Paper no. 17 (Washington, D.C.: Sigur Center for Asian Studies, 2003), 13.

10. Tino Balio, "'A Major Presence in All of the World Markets': The Globalization of Hollywood in the 1990s," in *Contemporary Hollywood Cinema*, ed. Steve Neale and Murray Smith (London: Routledge, 1998), 58–73.

11. Jean-Michel Baer, "L'exception culturelle: Une règle en quête de contenus," *En Temps Réel* 11 (October 2003): 27.

12. By 67 percent in the United States and 47 percent in the EU5 countries (France, Germany, Great Britain, Italy, and Spain), through 2010. *Bilan 1991*, dossiers du CNC no. 241 (Paris: CNC, May 1992); *Bilan 2010*, dossiers du CNC no. 318 (Paris: CNC, May 2011); *Bilan 2011*, dossiers du CNC no. 322 (Paris: CNC, May 2012).

13. Laurent Creton and Anne Jäckel use the phrase "a certain idea of cinema," adapted from de Gaulle's famous invocation of a "certain idea of France," which he used in his memoirs to refer to his sense of French exceptionalism, for better or for worse. "A Certain Idea of the Film Industry," in *The French Cinema Book*, ed. Michael Temple and Michael Witt (London: BFI, 2004): 209–220.

14. Later in the same article, Andrew goes on to say that "indigenous productions may take only a small percentage of the box office, but the critical attention they receive in addressing local issues increases their heat coefficient to a potentially incendiary level." Dudley Andrew, "An Atlas of World Cinema," in *Remapping World Cinema: Identity, Culture and Politics in Film*, ed. Stephanie Dennison and Song Hwee Lim (London: Wallflower, 2006), 26, 28. There is an ever-growing literature on transnational cinema. See, for example, *Transnational Cinema: The Film Reader*, ed. Elizabeth Ezra and Terry Rowden (New York: Routledge, 2006), 1–12; Mette Hjort, *Small Nation, Global Cinema: The New Danish Cinema* (Minneapolis: University

of Minnesota Press, 2005); Nataša Ďurovičová and Kathleen E. Newman, eds., *World Cinemas, Transnational Perspectives* (London: Routledge, 2009); the journal *Transnational Cinemas*; and, especially, Chris Berry, "What Is Transnational Cinema? Thinking from the Chinese Situation," *Transnational Cinemas* 1, no. 2 (2010): 111–127.

15. A short list would include the following names: David Lynch (United States), Jia Zhangke (China), Arturo Ripstein (Mexico), Walter Salles (Brazil), Mohsen Makhmalbaf (Iran), Elia Suleiman (Palestine), Ousmane Sembène (Senegal), Youssef Chahine (Egypt), and Amos Gitai (Israel). For a longer list, see appendix G.

16. John Hill, "The Future of European Cinema; The Economics and Culture of Pan-European Strategies," in *Border Crossings: Film in Ireland, Britain and Europe*, ed. John Hill, Martin McLoone, and Paul Hainsworth (Belfast: Institute of Irish Studies, 1994), 72.

1. INTERNATIONAL DOMINATION BY THE U.S. FILM INDUSTRY

1. René Bonnell called these factors exogenous to the film industry. *Le cinéma exploité* (Paris: Éditions du Seuil, 1978), 260.

2. "Today's 'theatrical window,' despite talk of the impact of cable TV and home video, remains the most important venue to create the blockbusters that can be exploited in other media." Benjamin Compaine and Douglas Gomery, *Who Owns the Media? Competition and Concentration in the Mass Media Industry*, 3rd ed. (Mahway, N.J.: Lawrence Erlbaum, 2000), 380. A study from the European Commission had made the same point several years earlier, as "exhibition in theaters continues to be a crucial element in total revenues." "L'industrie européenne du cinéma en analyse" (Brussels: Commission Européenne DG X, Direction de la politique audiovisuelle et de l'action culturelle, November 12, 1996), 17.

3. According to one source, India limited the number of imported films to one hundred in 2000. Mary E. Footer and Christoph Beat Graber, "Trade Liberalisation and Cultural Policy," *Journal of International Economic Law* 3, no. 1 (2000): 126. On the import side, U.S. films dominate the market for foreign films in India. Around 120 American films are imported annually, which constitutes 2 percent of the total market revenue. Arpita Mukharjee, "India's Trade Potential in Audio-Visual Services and the GATS," Working Paper no. 81 (New Delhi: Indian Council for Research on International Economic Relations, April 2002), 35.

4. "Hindi films have not been able to make a significant dent into Hollywood's territory. It is still rare to find many Westerners, or for that matter, Chinese, queuing up to watch a Bollywood film." Daya Kishan Thussu, "The Globalization of 'Bollywood': The Hype and the Hope," in *Global Bollywood*, ed. Anandam P. Kayoori and Aswin Punathambekar (New York: New York University Press, 2008), 107.

5. Ibid., 111. The 1 percent figure is based on Thussu's data in combination with my own.

6. In 2011, Hindi (Bollywood) films accounted for 16 percent of annual production, followed by Telegu (15 percent), Tamil (15 percent), Kannada (11 percent), Bengali (10 percent). *Annual Report* (Mumbai: Central Board of Film Certification, Ministry of Information and Broadcasting, Government of India, 2011), 33.

7. For reasonably reliable, if limited, figures on world cinema, see the annual "World Film Market Trends" published by the European Audiovisual Observatory.

8. For discussion of approaches to Chinese cinemas, see "Historical Introduction: Chinese Cinemas (1896–1996) and Transnational Film Studies," in *Transnational Chinese Cinemas: Identity, Nationhood, Gender,* ed. Sheldon Hsiao-peng Lu (Honolulu: University of Hawai'i Press, 1997), and Chris Berry and Mary Farquhar, *China on Screen: Cinema and Nation* (New York: Columbia University Press, 2006).

9. "Although the official aim is to raise local market share, the Government agreed to widen the quota of imported films by 14 titles . . . to 34 a year, as well as to allow foreign companies to increase their share of the local BO from a maximum of 13% to up to 25%." *FOCUS 2013: World Film Market Trends* (Cannes: Marché du film, for the European Audiovisual Observatory, 2013), 50–51.

10. "Other things being equal, a country's domestic support base is disproportionately important to maintaining a viable theatrical film industry." David Waterman, *Hollywood's Road to Riches* (Cambridge, Mass.: Harvard University Press, 2005), 203.

11. For a recent discussion of the challenge of "objective criteria" in identifying the nationality of films, see Ian Christie, "Where Is National Cinema Today (and Do We Still Need It)?," *Film History* 25, no. 1–2 (January 2013): 19–30.

12. L. Klady, "Earth to H'wood: You Win," *Variety,* February 13–19, 1995. David Puttnam used this headline as a chapter title in his book about the battle over culture between Hollywood and the rest of the world, *The Undeclared War: The Struggle for Control of the World's Film Industry* (London: HarperCollins, 1997). The U.S. edition bears a less provocative title: *Movies and Money* (New York: Vintage, 2000).

13. For a recent historical overview, see *Cultural Imperialism: Essays on the Political Economy of Cultural Domination,* ed. Bernd Hamm and Russell Smandych (Peterborough, ON: Broadview, 2005).

14. Bill Grantham, "*Some Big Bourgeois Brothel*": Contexts for France's Culture Wars with Hollywood (Luton, UK: University of Luton Press, 2000), 1.

15. *Time,* November 21, 2007.

16. In the subsequently expanded version of the article published as a book, Morrison wrote that he was "rather shocked" about the title change for the European edition. Donald Morrison and Antoine Compagnon, *The Death of French Culture* (Cambridge: Polity Press, 2010), 7.

17. Antoine Compagnon, "Le déclin français vu des États-Unis," *Le Monde*, November 30, 2007.

18. Morrison and Compagnon, *Death of French Culture*, 103.

19. Morrison, for example, wrote that there is a quota on U.S. films exhibited in France. The European Union's Directive on Television Without Frontiers does call for a minimum percentage of European works to be shown on television, but France has no quota on films shown in theaters. This perhaps minor error reflects a persistent readiness in the United States to exaggerate the protectionist reflex in France. A *New York Times* article from June 13, 2013, repeated the same error (though it was subsequently corrected).

20. Frédéric Martel, *De la culture en Amérique* (Paris: Gallimard, 2006), 289.

21. In France, for example, public funding supports the Cinémathèque française in Paris. There is no comparable public institution in the United States. The closest analogue in New York is the film program of the private, nonprofit Museum of Modern Art, which benefits as a nonprofit from considerable financial advantages granted by the government, some of which could certainly be classified as a subsidy.

22. According to Laurent Creton, out of €30 billion spent on culture in France in 2003, public spending accounted for €13 billion, philanthropy for €230,000. *L'économie du cinéma* (Paris: Nathan, 2003), 27. Farchy notes the importance of local, municipal spending on culture, roughly equal to all central state funding; with many ministries supporting culture, the Ministry of Culture is responsible for only one-fifth of all state funding for culture. Joëlle Farchy, *La fin de l'exception culturelle?* (Paris: CNRS, 2002), 178–179.

23. Martel, *De la culture en Amérique*, 550.

24. Christopher Anderson, *Hollywood TV: The Studio System in the Fifties* (Austin: University of Texas Press, 1994).

25. David A. Cook, *Lost Illusions: American Cinema in the Shadow of Watergate and Vietnam. 1970–1979* (Berkeley: University of California Press, 2000), 313–314.

26. By the time Universal president Lew Wasserman lost his copyright suit against Sony in 1979, other studios had already signed agreements with Sony (Betamax) or Matsushita (VHS). Ibid., 5.

27. "I start first by asking who owned, controlled and operated the corporations." Douglas Gomery, *The Hollywood Studio System: A History* (London: BFI, 2005), 3.

28. Ibid., 316.

29. Thomas Schatz, "The Studio System and Conglomerate Hollywood," *The Contemporary Hollywood Film Industry*, ed. Paul MacDonald and Janet Wasko (Malden, Mass.: Blackwell, 2008), 22, citing J. Mickelthwait, "A Survey of the Entertainment Industry," *Economist*, December 23, 1989.

30. Tino Balio, " 'A Major Presence in All of the World's Important Markets': The Globalization of Hollywood in the 1990s," in *Contemporary Hollywood Cinema*, ed. Steve Neale and Murray Smith (London: Routledge, 1998), 62. The failure of Ross's Orlando, Florida, experiment "signalled the end of the Ross era at Time

Warner." Douglas Gomery, "Hollywood Corporate Business Practice and Periodizing Contemporary Film History," in Neale and Smith, *Contemporary Hollywood Cinema*, 53–54.

31. Janet Wasko, "Critiquing Hollywood: The Political Economy of Motion Pictures," in *A Concise Handbook of Movie Industry Economics*, ed. Charles Moul (Cambridge: Cambridge University Press, 2005), 5–31.

32. Toby Miller and Richard Maxwell, "Film and Globalization," In *Communications Media, Globalization and Empire*, ed. Oliver Boyd-Barrett (Eastleigh, UK: John Libbey, 2006), 35. Perhaps overstating the case for the neglect of economic analyses of the film industry by scholars in favor of textual analyses of films, Richard Maltby has written that "the history of the American cinema is not the history of its products any more than the history of railroads is the history of locomotives." Maltby, "'Nobody Knows Everything': Post-classical Historiographies and Consolidated Entertainment," in Neale and Smith, *Contemporary Hollywood Cinema*, 28.

33. Thomas Guback, *The International Film Industry* (Bloomington: Indiana University Press, 1969).

34. Richard Maltby, *Hollywood Cinema*, 2nd ed. (Malden, Mass.: Blackwell, 2003), 175–176.

35. David Cook estimated the value of the government tax advantages to have been $150 million from 1971 to 1976, when the programs ended. *Lost Illusions: American Cinema in the Shadow of Watergate and Vietnam, 1970–1979* (Berkeley: University of California Press, 2000), 11–14. Cook cites as a source Martin Dale, *The Movie Game: The Film Business in Britain, Europe and America* (London: Cassell, 1997), but Dale's book supplies no figures and only a thin list of sources. Harold Vogel describes the mechanism in *Entertainment Industry Economics: A Guide for Financial Analysis* (Cambridge: Cambridge University Press, 2007), 110–111. Toby Miller et al. include a table of tax advantages offered by thirty-three states but do not provide any estimate of their value. *Global Hollywood 2* (London: BFI, 2005), 97–102.

36. Valenti, "Webb-Pomerene," October 15, 1980, reprinted in *Vital Speeches* 47 (1980): 26-28, cited in Kerry Segrave, *American Films Abroad: Hollywood's Domination of the World's Movie Screens* (Jefferson, N.C.: McFarland, 1997), 323, and quoted in Anna Herold, *European Film Policies in EU and International Law: Culture and Trade—Marriage or Misalliance* (Groningen, Neth.: Europa Law Publishing, 2010), 360. On Webb-Pomerene, see Guback, *The International Film Industry*, 91–95.

37. Wasko, "Critiquing Hollywood," 12. For an excellent discussion, see Tom O'Regan, "The Political Economy of Film," in *The Sage Handbook of Film Studies*, ed. James Donald and Michael Renov (London: Sage, 2008), 244–261.

38. "The 1970s were a pre-staging for a renewal of movie exhibition that would make the 'Golden Age' of Hollywood pale in comparison." Cook, *Lost Illusions*, 416.

39. See Waterman, *Hollywood's Road to Riches*, 184–185, for excellent timelines of television adoption and theatrical movie attendance since World War II.

40. The most balanced, concise account from a quantitative scholar can be found in Waterman, *Hollywood's Road to Riches*, 168–204. See also Colin Hoskins, Stuart McFadyen, and Adam Finn, *Global Television and Film: An Introduction to the Economics of the Business* (New York: Oxford University Press, 1997). For a highly nuanced discussion, see Tom O'Regan, "Too Popular by Far: On Hollywood's International Popularity," in *Continuum: The Australian Journal of Media and Culture* 5, no. 2 (1990): 302–351.

41. In Tyler Cowen, *Creative Destruction* (Princeton, N.J.: Princeton University Press, 2002), 73–101.

42. The concept of cultural discount illustrates the murkiness of such measurements. Cultural discount refers to the relative attraction of exported goods in foreign markets. The number of English speakers in foreign countries reduces the foreignness of U.S. films in those countries, giving them a lower cultural discount. But cultural discount then measures only more the impregnation of U.S. culture in other countries than the relative appeal of U.S. exports by virtue of some putative quality of the goods (or services). That is, cultural discount measures the cultural advantage enjoyed by U.S. products, but it is not an independent variable explaining success. Hoskins, McFadyen, and Finn developed the idea to show, persuasively, that the size of the domestic market in the producing country is the primary factor in initial decisions to produce films, even when cultural discounts may be equivalent between two countries, with the United States and Canada serving as the case study. Hoskins, McFadyen, and Finn, *Global Television and Film*, 40–42. Waterman, *Hollywood's Road to Riches*, 155–156, 174–177, adds the crucial variable of the wealth (GDP) of the domestic market. The figures cited above for India and China substantiate the salience of Waterman's emphasis.

43. Cowen, *Creative Destruction*, 95.

44. Fabrice Montebello, "Le cinéma américain est imbattable parce que nous l'aimons," in *Quelle diversité face à Hollywood?*, ed. Thomas Paris, CinémAction, Hors-série (Condé-sur-Noireau, France: CinémAction-Corlet, 2002), 33.

45. To take another example, the lethal effect of state support on French creativity can be found in the assessment of the Paris correspondent for the *New York Times* who reported on "the powerful tradition of French intellectual snobbery, which requires that commercial success in the arts be scorned, particularly if it involves anything remotely linked to American popular culture. . . . Could too much money be the problem? Do Government subsidies stifle creativity?" Alan Riding, "Where Is the Glory That Was France?," *New York Times*, January 14, 1996.

46. Cowen, *Creative Destruction*, 99.

47. In French, "Par ailleurs, le cinéma est une industrie." André Malraux, *Esquisse d'une psychologie du cinéma* (Paris: Nouveau monde, 2003), 77. The essay was originally published in 1940 in *Verve*. Gallimard printed a limited edition in 1946 as a book "for bibliophiles," according to Malraux, cited in the introduction by Jean-Claude Larrat (8).

48.   René Bonnell called this tracking of the tickets the "central nervous system" of the support system, for it ensured a reliable record of ticket sales, which generated the *Compte de soutien* (support account). *La vingt-cinquième image* (Paris: Gallimard, 1996), 523. He added that the functioning of the Compte de soutien constitutes "the metabolism of the system of public intervention in the economy of cinema" (556).

49.   According one historical account, "The introduction of the notion of quality in the criteria for grants to production constitutes one of the novelties of the system in 1953." *1946 cinquentenaire du CNC 1996: 50 ans de soutien au cinéma et à la création audiovisuelle* (Paris: CNC, 1997), 8.

50.   French writers often characterize this economic structure as *oligopolie à frange*, a small group of powerful companies at the center complemented by a large number of micro-companies with insignificant economic mass. Farchy, *La fin de l'exception culturelle?*, 200–201. Farchy cites L. Benzoni and B. Quelin, "La concurrence oligopolistique: Dynamique et instabilité," *Traité d'économie industrielle* (Paris: Économica, 1988), 478–501, and Françoise Benhamou, "Entre économie de marché et économie administrée: La politique du cinéma en question," *Esprit* 328 (October 2006): 63–74.

51.   Joëlle Farchy discusses the treacherous path leading from "national champions" to increased concentration in *Les enjeux de la mondialisation culturelle* (Paris: Éditions Hors Commerce, 2006), 274.

52.   "45 ans d'avances sur recettes" (Paris: CNC, [2006]), n.p.

2. THE LANG YEARS

1.   Laurent Creton, *Histoire économique du cinéma français* (Paris: CNRS, 2004), 186.

2.   Ibid., 186–187. The law was passed on September 16, 1948, then renewed in 1953, with some revisions. According to Creton, "These two laws rest on the same principle which is at the core of the French model of aid to film production: the plan is 'to share among the different recipients a fraction of the receipts of all the films shown in France, the fraction corresponding to the additional tax on the price of seats paid for by spectators.'"

3.   Jean-Michel Frodon describes competing claims between the government and the sectors of the industry on the status of the funds produced by the tax. Frodon, *L'âge moderne du cinéma français: De la Nouvelle Vague à nos jours* (Paris: Flammarion, 1995), 140.

4.   According to René Bonnell, 81 percent of the fund was disbursed as automatic aid, initially favoring production. After the extension of the law in 1953, a larger percentage was devoted to exhibition. Bonnell, *Le cinéma exploité* (Paris: Éditions du Seuil, 1978), 334.

5.   For a recent, richly documented account of this early history, see Dimitri Vezyroglou, ed., *Le cinéma: Une affaire d'État* (Paris: La Documentation française, 2014).

See also Frédérique Gimello-Mesplomb, "Le prix de la qualité: L'État et le cinéma français (1960–1965)," *Politix* 16, no. 61 (2003): 102.

6. Creton, *Histoire économique du cinéma français*, 185–186.

7. Pierre Billard, *L'âge classique du cinéma français: Du cinéma parlant à la Nouvelle Vague* (Paris: Flammarion, 1995), 514. Léon Blum had been Socialist prime minister in France, 1936–1937, during the period known as the French Popular Front. James Byrnes was the U.S. secretary of state.

8. Jean-Pierre Jeancolas, "L'arrangement Blum-Byrnes à l'épreuve des faits: Les rélations (cinématographiques) franco-américaines de 1944 à 1948," *1895* 13 (December 1992): 37. As part of his account of the second, political phase of the protests (which reflected the first signs of the Cold War), Jeancolas cites remarks by the head of the French Communist Party, Maurice Thorez, at a meeting on April 18, 1948, denouncing U.S. films that "invade our screens thanks to Léon Blum . . . and which, not satisfied to throw our technicians out of work, poison literally the souls of our children, of our young people, of our young girls, whom they want to turn into docile slaves of American billionaires." See also Billard, *L'âge classique du cinéma français*, 518.

9. Jacques Portes, "Les origines de la légende noire des accords Blum-Byrnes sur le cinéma," *Revue d'histoire moderne et contemporaine* 33 (1986): 314–329. For the relevant text of the film provisions, see "Arrangement entre le gouvernement provisoire de la République française et le gouvernement des États-Unis d'Amérique au sujet de la projection des films américains en France," *1895* 13 (December 1992): 42–49. A filmed document of the signing, with statements by Byrnes and Blum, on May 28, 1946, can be viewed online at http://www.ina.fr/fresques/jalons/fiche-media/InaEdu01263/la-signature-des-accords-blum-byrnes-1946-?video=InaEdu01263.

10. At least according to Billard, *L'âge classique*, and Colin Crisp, *The Classic French Cinema, 1930–1960* (Bloomington: Indiana University Press, 1997), 415–422. In a masterful genealogy of the term "New Wave," Ginette Vincendeau welcomes the appearance in the 1990s of studies downplaying the discontinuities between "New Wave and mainstream cinema." Vincendeau, "Introduction: Fifty Years of the French New Wave: From Hysteria to Nostalgia," in *The French New Wave: Critical Landmarks*, ed. Peter Graham with G. Vincendeau London: BFI, 2009), 15–21.

11. Décret 59-733, June 16, 1959, drafted and passed under time pressure of the pending expiration of the previous law, was amended many times in subsequent months and years to refine the mechanism. See especially Décret 59-1512, December 30, 1959. "It took only two years for this regime full of good intentions to be shown to be inadequate, such that in March 1963 a new *décret* had to be issued." Catherine Sieklucka, *Les aides à l'industrie cinématographique: Dans la Communauté économique européenne* (Paris: Presses universitaires de France, 1967), 37.

12. "These advances are as a rule awarded after the completion of the film, on the basis in particular of the nature of the subject, of the characteristics and qualities of the film and of the conditions of the production following the decision of a commission

made up of qualified people from the financial, technical and artistic point of view." Article 7, Décret 59-733, June 16, 1959. In fact, almost half of the awards were granted to films before production. In Malraux's view, cinema was a visual medium, and a script gave no indication of the look or quality of the completed work. "One can judge a film only by its images," Malraux testified at the National Assembly, November 25, 1959. Cited in Dimitri Vezyroglou and Gaël Péton, "La politique française du cinéma au moment de rattachement du CNC au ministère des Affaires culturelles, 1957–1962," in Vezyroglou, *Le cinéma: Une affaire d'État*, 47.

13. In 1992, Joëlle Farchy estimated the reimbursement rate at 30 percent in the best years. Farchy, *Le cinéma déchaîné: Mutation d'une industrie* (Paris: CNRS, 1992), 174. A CNC study in 1996 placed the average reimbursement rate at 5–10 percent, leading to reform of the repayment procedure and aid to distributors of first films receiving the avance. "Rapport de la commission de reforme de l'avance sur recettes" (Paris: CNC, July 1, 1996). For a list of recipients from 1960–2004, see "45 ans d'avances sur recettes" (Paris: CNC, [2006]).

14. In the words of one later CNC publication, the selective aids were intended to "temper the mathematically rigorous nature of the aid proportional to the receipts in order to encourage the production of works of quality." *Informations CNC* 206 (June 1985): 11.

15. According to Farchy, the original mission of the avances was "to encourage the production of films whose artistic ambition would take precedence over immediate commercial concerns." Farchy, *Le cinéma déchaîné*, 192.

16. Gimello-Mesplomb, "Le prix de la qualité," 113–115.

17. Farchy, *Le cinéma déchaîné*, 212; Farchy, *L'industrie du cinéma* (Paris: Presses universitaires de France, 2004), 92.

18. Over the years, rates of digressivity have varied. In 1988, theaters received 120 percent of the TSA when receipts were less than 30 million francs; 95 percent with receipts between 30 and 40 million francs; 60 percent with receipts more than 60 million francs. For a history of the automatic aids to production, see "Historique du fonctionnement du soutien automatique à la production cinématographique" (Paris: CNC, November 2007).

19. Bonnell, *Le cinéma exploité*, 311, 334. See also Sieklucka, *Les aides à l'industrie cinématographique*.

20. For an excellent discussion of aids to theaters in the postwar years, see Sylvie Perras, "Logique économique des aides à l'exploitation cinématographique: Une mise en perspective historique, 1946–1993" (Université de Paris I, September 1993), CNC D2949.

21. Commentators have often claimed that the avances sur recettes played a significant role in launching the New Wave. François Truffaut and Claude Chabrol, for example, received primes de qualité (after their films were completed), before the avance sur recettes, and their films were surprisingly successful. Their subsequent films drew few spectators, however. Antoine de Baecque wrote that the New Wave

lost its audience after the autumn of 1960, adding that four good films (*Les bonnes femmes, Tirez sur le pianiste, Les carabiniers,* and *Adieu Philippine*) were attacked by the critics and did poorly at the box office. De Baecque, *La Nouvelle Vague: Portrait d'une jeunesse* (Paris: Flammarion, 2009), 97. Looking more closely at the data, Frédéric Gimello-Mesplomb concluded, "Contrary to what is thought, during the first five years of the avance sur recettes, only six films of the New Wave out of 192 films receiving the [avances sur recettes] benefited from the aid," and only three of those six received the aid before production (the other three receiving the award after completion of the film). Gimello-Mesplomb, "Le prix de la qualité," 117. The avance was not in effect when Godard made *À bout de souffle* (1959), but he was refused the avance for his next three films *Le Petit Soldat* (1960), *Une femme est une femme* (1961), or *Vivre sa vie* (1962). See *Cahiers du cinéma* 161–162 (January 1965), cited in Jean-Marie Charuau, "'Je t'aime, moi non plus': Une histoire d'avance. Les pouvoirs publics, la profession cinématographique et le système des avances sur recettes, de 1959 à nos jours" (Université de Paris I, September 1991), CNC D 288, 101. Apparently *Breathless* did receive a quality award, but not an avance sur recettes, after the film was completed. Vezyroglou, *Le cinéma: Une affaire d'État,* 262. The same book supplies new information on the trajectory of "quality" aids disbursed by the CNC. Jacques Flaud, head of the CNC (1952–1959), pushed hard to both protect the conception of quality awards and to reorient the aids from the "tradition of quality" to the new talents associated with the New Wave. For Vezyroglou and Péton, that "unusual activism of an administrator of a public institution will lead Malraux to dismiss Jacques Flaud." Vezyroglou and Péton, "La politique française du cinéma," 46. See also Gaël Péton, "L'avance sur recettes: Rajeunir la profession (1956–1964)," in *58–68, retour sur une génération,* ed. Laurent Bismuth and Eric Le Roy (Paris: CNC, 2013), 72–86.

22. Farchy pointed out that receipts remained stable between 1957 and 1976 because prices rose over 300 percent even as attendance fell by 60 percent. Farchy, *Le cinéma déchaîné,* 74.

23. Jean-Denis Bredin, "Rapport de la mission de réflexion et de propositions sur le cinéma" (Paris: Ministry of Culture, 1981).

24. Ibid., 48. Bredin is no doubt referring to the incredible roster of auteur films produced by Gaumont during what Jean-Michel Frodon called "the Toscan years," from 1975 to 1984, during which Gaumont, led by Daniel Toscan du Plantier, produced "a virtual who's who of quality European cinema." Frodon, *L'âge moderne du cinéma français,* 525–533.

25. Bredin, "Rapport de la mission," 49.

26. *Groupement d'intérêt économique,* referring to an agreement between two firms to share resources in particular areas while each firm retains autonomy in other areas.

27. Bredin, "Rapport de la mission," 47.

28. Ibid., 7. Bredin is emphatic on this point: "To renounce the artisanal nature of original art would be tantamount to throwing out the film with the bathwater" (8).

A decade later Susan Hayward observed that "artisanal cinema is one specificity of French national cinema." Hayward, *French National Cinema* (London: Routledge, 1992), 28.

29.   "Conférence de presse de Jack Lang, Ministre de la Culture sur les grands principes de la réforme du cinéma," April 1, 1982, CNC D3051, 2–4.

30.   Farchy, *Le cinéma déchaîné*, 187. French statistics appropriately distinguish between screens (*écrans*) and theaters (*salles*).

31.   *Bilan 85, supplément au no. 209* (Paris: CNC, May–June 1986), 24.

32.   For a demonstration of the advantage, see Claude Forest, *Économies contemporaines du cinéma en Europe: L'improbable industrie* (Paris: CNRS, 2001), 177–179.

33.   For more details, see Farchy, *Le cinéma déchaîné*, 198–202.

34.   Bredin cited Samuel Goldwyn's remark that "oral contracts are not worth the paper they are written on." Bredin, "Rapport de la mission," 56.

35.   For an excellent account of the work of the mediator, which "offers general observations on the evolution of the distribution of films, on the types of complaints which affect this distribution and on the value of the institution of the Mediator, after eight years of operation," see "Rapport d'activité, juin 89–juin 91," CNC info no. 236 (August 1991), 20–25.

36.   The later tension between these rescued "municipal" theaters and commercial theaters accusing the former of unfair competition is discussed in the conclusion.

37.   Farchy referred to the education initiative as an effort to complement the traditional emphasis on supply—of films and theaters—with an attempt to build demand. Farchy, *Le cinéma déchaîné*, 328. This initiative took time to mature (see chapter 8).

38.   Apparently, only some two thousand individuals placed funds in SOFICAs, for the real advantage accrued only to those with high incomes. Farchy, *Le cinéma déchaîné*, 208.

39.   P. Willats, "Défense et illustration de l'abri fiscal cinématographique appliqué dans trois pays," *Film Échange* 10 (Spring 1980), cited in Farchy, *Le cinéma déchaîné*, 204.

40.   For one early evaluation of the SOFICAs, see Farchy, *Le cinéma déchaîné*, 204–209. The last sentence of a report by three government bureaucrats provides a clear statement on the new emphasis on industrial concerns: "It is indispensable to develop the thinking of this sector [cinema] so that it adopts a modern and economic approach and that it moves from a mentality of assistance to a capitalist, entrepreneurial logic, commercially aggressive on the world image market." P. Careil, D. Kessler, and F. Werner, "Rapport sur le financement du cinéma et l'avenir des SOFICAs" (Paris: Ministry of Culture, May 1990), CNC D311, 37.

41.   In 1980, advertising provided only 36 percent of television income. Régine Chaniac and Jean-Pierre Jézéquel, *La télévision* (Paris: La Découverte, 2005), 18.

42.   Proposition 94 of the "110 propositions pour la France, avril–mai 1981: Programme de gouvernement préparé par le Parti Socialiste (PS) pour l'élection presidentielle d'avril–mai 1981," declared: "Television and radio will be decentralized and pluralist. . . . A National Audiovisual Council will be created in which the State

representatives will be in the minority." "Histoire des gauches au pouvoir," *Manière de voir* 124 (August–September 2012): 31.

43. Valérie Lecasble, *Le roman de Canal+* (Paris: Grasset, 2001), 76. Plans for a new station had circulated earlier, for the Bredin report (November 1981) referred to a public debate over a pay television channel, noting that the government had "emphatically dismissed a cinema station because it would establish a discrimination based on money." Bredin, "Rapport de la mission," 39.

44. Lecasble, *Le roman de Canal+*, 75–84.

45. "Convention de concession de service public et cahier des charges pour Canal Plus signés entre l'État et l'agence Havas, 6 décembre 1983," in *Les politiques audiovisuelles en France*, ed. Rémi Tomaszewski (Paris: La Documentation française, 2001), 216–217.

46. In the 1950s, the average run of a film was three years, with 90 percent of receipts returned after two years. Fabrice Montebello, *Le cinéma en France, depuis les années 1930* (Paris: Armand Colin, 2005), 49. In 1989, films in theaters earned 82 percent of their theatrical receipts in three months. Farchy, *Le cinéma déchaîné*, 43.

47. The public stations paid a fixed sum of 120,000 francs for films shown on television, based on the amount of TSA that the films would have generated at the box office if they had drawn 70,000 spectators. Farchy, *Le cinéma déchaîné*, 252. According to the Bredin report, television contributed only 50,000 francs ($10,000) per film, "a risible figure," to the Compte de soutien. Bredin, "Rapport de la mission," 36.

48. The tax on television stations was directed to the Compte de soutien, but in 1986 the account was renamed the Compte de soutien financier de l'industrie cinématographique et de l'industrie des programmes audiovisuels (COSIP), with two separate sections: cinema and audiovisual (television). In the view (from 1995) of Pierre Viot, former director of the CNC (1973–1984), the creation of COSIP, "forty years after the creation of the CNC, is the best recent illustration of the economic and cultural role that an organism like the Center can play within the Ministry of Culture as an instrument both of a governmental policy and an understanding with the profession." "Intervention de Pierre Viot, ancien directeur général du Centre national de la cinématographie à la réunion du Comité d'historie du 13 novembre 1995," in Vezyroglou, *Le cinéma: Une affaire d'État*, 209. See also "Cinquantenaire du CNC, 1946–1996" (Paris: CNC, 1996).

49. The CNC divides production into three categories: films financed entirely by French money; films in which the majority of financing comes from French sources; and films with minority French funding. Films with full or majority French financing are considered French, and called French-initiative films (FIF). In 1990, there were eighty-one French-financed films, twenty-six majority French-financed films, and thirty-nine minority French-financed films. *Bilan 1990*, CNC info no. 235 (May 1991): 8.

50. Charles Tesson, "Le goût français," *Cahiers du cinéma* 395–396 (May 1987), cited in Régine Chaniac and Jean-Pierre Jézéquel, *Télévision et cinéma: Le désenchantement* (Paris: Nathan, 1998), 197.

51. Farchy discusses the figures in *Le cinéma déchaîné*, 229–258. The chart uses the TV share of the Compte de soutien that went to the cinema section of the Compte de soutien; a smaller share (35 percent) goes to the audiovisual (television) section.

52. Jean-François Court, "Le cinéma français face à son avenir: Rapport au ministre de la Culture et de la Communication" (Paris: La Documentation française, 1988), 20.

53. Ibid., 40–41.

54. "Il n'y a plus moyen de moyenner." Ibid., 44. Gnomic aphorisms from Godard appear repeatedly in analyses of French cinema. As another now familiar example, Godard, in his acceptance of an honorary César in 1987, lampooned the power players of the film industry by referring to them as "professionels de la profession."

55. Court, "Le cinéma français," 46.

56. In 1985, only 6 percent of French viewers watched films on video. Farchy, *Le cinéma déchaîné*, 64. Only 10 percent of homes owned VCRs in 1986; by 1991, the figure was 48 percent, rising to 61 percent in 1993. Chaniac and Jézéquel, *Télévision et cinéma*, 98–99.

57. Court, "Le cinéma français," 49.

58. Averages for other countries were far lower: Italy (107), Spain (88), Germany (69), UK (50).

59. "Plan d'action en faveur du cinéma," February 7, 1989, CNC SD1175, 2–3.

60. Previously, the digressive scale reduced the return of automatic aid as the size of the audience increased (see n18 above). In a sense, the digressivity penalized the most successful films. After the elimination of the digressive scale, all films would receive the same percentage in automatic aid, independent of the receipts. Thus, for *Les visiteurs* (1993), with 14 million spectators, a ticket price of 44 francs, a TSA of 11 percent, and the automatic aid rate of 120 percent, the film would generate 73 million francs of automatic aid. Cluzel also pointed out that the rate of automatic aid would go down if the domestic market share of French films went up. See Jean Cluzel, "L'efficacité des aides publiques en faveur du cinéma français," Rapport d'information 11 (98-99) (Paris: Office parlementaire d'évaluation des politiques publiques, Senate, July 8, 1988), 75. In addition, the rate is adjusted according to a point system (earned by each film) determined by scores on a number of parameters. Serge Regourd, *L'exception culturelle* (Paris: Presses universitaires de France, 2002), 37. For a detailed history of coefficients, see "Historique du fontionnement du soutien automatique à la production cinématographique" (Paris: CNC, November 2007). That report shows how the coefficient must be reduced when the market share for French films rises, as occurred after 2000.

61. "Paradoxically, the support for French cinema is today financed by its two principal rivals, television since the mid-1980s and U.S. cinema since the beginning of the [support] system." Farchy, *L'industrie du cinéma*, 81.

62. Forest, *Économies contemporaines du cinéma en Europe*, 38.

63. For two French authors of a 1979 study of the film industry, "one cannot say it often enough, the French cinema is neither aided nor subsidized. It benefits from a system

of self-financing that it has invented, for which Parliament has made a law." Jean Roux and René Thévenet, *Industrie et commerce du film en France* (Paris: Éditions scientifiques et juridiques, 1979), 128.

64. "If the contribution of television to cinema seems significant, it is not large in relation to the resources of the stations. Cinema represents only 2–3% of the budgets of stations and 8–12% of their costs of programming. These percentages are weak in relation to the real importance of the Seventh Art for television. In effect, the film is the program which earns the highest audience scores and which burnishes the image of the station. Thus, television benefits more from the advantages of cinema than cinema from the remunerations of television." Jean-Emmanuel Cortade, *La télévision française, 1986–1992* (Paris: Presses universitaires de France, 1993), 83.

65. "Arrangement entre le gouvernement provisoire de la République française et le gouvernement des États-Unis d'Amérique," 43.

66. Frodon, *L'âge moderne du cinéma français*, 655.

67. The combination of the tax on income (5.5 percent) and the obligation to invest (3 percent) totals 8.5 percent.

68. These net numbers fail to indicate the figures for theater closings and openings. The net effect was the loss of 500 screens (not theaters), but some 1,500 screens closed while 1,000 screens opened. *L'activité cinématographique française en 1980*, supplement to CNC info no. 188–189 (Paris: CNC, 1981); *Bilan 1989*, CNC info no. 228 (Paris: CNC, April–May 1990); *Bilan 1990*, CNC info no. 235 (Paris: CNC, May 1991); *Bilan 1991*, CNC info no. 241 (Paris: CNC, May 1992); Claude Forest, *Les dernières séances* (Paris: CNRS, 1995), 135.

3. EUROPEAN FILM POLICY AND TELEVISION WITHOUT FRONTIERS

1. In Europe, "liberal" in this context normally refers to limiting the role of the state in economic affairs.

2. Claude Degand, *Les industries cinématographiques de l'Europe des Six et le Marché Commun*, Notes et études documentaires no. 3271 (Paris: La Documentation française, 1966), 13.

3. Ibid., 22.

4. In English and emphasized in original. Ibid., 14.

5. Catherine Sieklucka, *Les aides à l'industrie cinématographique dans la Communauté économique européenne* (Paris: Presses universitaires de France, 1967).

6. Ibid., 15.

7. Ibid., 83.

8. Ibid., 5, citing M. Lilti in *Communauté européenne*, February 1963. Sieklucka wrote, "The elimination of the aid regimes, without some planned alternative arrangement, would lead to the collapse of the European cinema industries" (66).

9. M. Batz, *À propos de la crise de l'industrie cinématographique* (Brussels: Éditions de l'Institut de sociologie, Université libre de Bruxelles, 1963), cited in Sieklucka, *Les aides à l'industrie cinématographique*, 66.

10. Sieklucka, *Les aides à l'industrie cinématographique*, 86.

11. Joop Voogd, "Exposé des motifs," in "Le cinéma et l'État: Rapport de la commission de la culture et de l'éducation et documents du colloque organisé à Lisbonne du 14 au 16 juin 1978" (Strasbourg: Council of Europe, 1979), v.

12. Ibid., 102.

13. Ibid., 103.

14. Ibid., 101.

15. Ibid., 174.

16. Ibid., 172.

17. Olivier Amiel, *Le financement public du cinéma dans l'Union européenne* (Paris: LGDJ, 2007), 104. The relevant directives all date from the 1960s (see 101–103).

18. Technically, the title of the position was Councilor of State Charged with Cultural Affairs.

19. Many cinephiles will recognize the French term *politique*, for the French film journal *Cahiers du cinéma* had coined and promulgated a *politique des auteurs* during the 1950s and 1960s. See, for example, the texts gathered in J. Hillier, ed., *Cahiers du cinéma, The 1950s: Neo-Realism, Hollywood, New Wave* (Cambridge, Mass.: Harvard University Press, 1985), 4–7. For a succinct definition in French, see Jacques Aumont and Michel Marie, eds., *Dictionnaire théorique et critique du cinéma*, 2nd ed. (Paris: Armand Colin, 2008), 195. In his extended discussion, Antoine de Baecque refers to it as a "political line (an auteur is someone that one *must* love)." De Baecque, *Cahiers du cinéma: Histoire d'une revue*, vol. 1: *À l'assaut du cinéma, 1951–1959* (Paris: Cahiers du cinéma, 1991), 148, 147–179. For a critical discussion in English, see John Hess, "*La politique des auteurs* (part one): World View as Aesthetics," *Jump Cut* 1 (1974): 19–22, and "*La politique des auteurs*, 2: Truffaut's Manifesto," *Jump Cut* 2 (1974): 20–22.

20. Malraux's *La condition humaine* won the Prix Goncourt in 1933, and he wrote and directed *L'Espoir* in 1939/1945. Olivier Amiel suggests that the industrial aspect of cinema had negative connotations for him after his experience with attracting financing for *L'Espoir*. Amiel, *Le financement public du cinéma*, 5.

21. Décret 59-889, July 24, 1959. In a speech at the Chamber of Deputies on October 27, 1966, Malraux stated, "The problem is to do for culture what the Third Republic did for education: every child in France has the [same] right to painting, theater, cinema, as to the alphabet." Cited in Joëlle Farchy, *La fin de l'exception culturelle* (Paris: CNRS, 2002), 175.

22. On Malraux's tenure as minister of culture, see Philippe Urfalino, *L'invention de la politique culturelle* (Paris: Hachette, 2009).

23. Ministers of culture from the following countries attended the meeting: Mexico, Italy, Spain, Portugal, and France. *Le Monde*, July 23, 1982.

24.   *Le Monde*, July 9, 1982.

25.   Ibid.

26.   *Quotidien de Paris*, July 1, 1982.

27.   *Figaro*, September 20, 1982.

28.   For the text of the Mexico City speech, see Philippe Poirrier, ed., *Les politiques culturelles en France* (Paris: La Documentation française, 2002), 391–395. In a detailed brochure, Lang explained, "This reform is cultural in its will to revitalize creation, to enlarge access to the cinema and to develop exchanges with the cinemas of other nations. It is economic by the transformations it makes in the funding mechanisms of the cinema economy for the purpose of developing pluralism and competition." "2 ans de politique culturelle, 1981–1983" (Paris: Ministry of Culture, [1983]), 2.

29.   Robert Wangermée wrote in a report for the Council of Europe in 1988: "The fact that a socialist minister undertook this rehabilitation of the cultural industries was astonishing. The tradition of the Left for a long time had been moralist about this and had viewed with suspicion the role of the power of money. The recognition of the impact of the products of these industries on a large public, more effective than the productions of institutions traditionally subsidized, has contributed to this change in attitude." "Rapport du Groupe d'experts européens," in *La politique culturelle de la France*, ed. Robert Wangermée and Bernard Gournay (Paris: La Documentation française, 1988), 44. In Philippe Poirrier's description, "the intentional linkage of culture with the economy amounted to a Copernican revolution in Socialist thinking." Poirrier, "French Cultural Policy in Question, 1981–2003," in *After the Deluge: New Perspectives on Postwar French Intellectual and Cultural History*, ed. Julian Bourg (Lanham, Md.: Lexington Books, 2004), 302.

30.   Commenting on the list of complaints by Third World countries about the penetration of U.S. television programs, William Pfaff wrote: "There is something in these complaints. Certainly the world would be a better and happier place without most U.S. television programs. U.S. television, 30 years ago inventive, pioneering, even intelligent, has become puerile, apish, and sometimes vicious. Except for its admirable news programming, commercial television has mostly become a corrupt and corrupting force." Pfaff, "France, U.S. Reach for Their Guns Over Culture," *Herald Tribune*, August 8, 1982.

31.   For a partial chronology of these efforts, see Annabelle Littoz-Monnet, *The European Union and Culture: Between Economic Regulation and European Cultural Policy* (Manchester: Manchester University Press, 2007), 48–49.

32.   E. J. Dionne Jr., "Paris, the World's Economy Gets a Dose of Culture," *Herald Tribune*, February 14, 1983. Among the participants were Norman Mailer, Kate Millett, William Styron, Elie Wiesel, Mary McCarthy, Amos Oz, Francis Ford Coppola, Arthur Penn, Alan Pakula, Sidney Lumet, Volker Schlondorff, Peter Brook, Sophia Loren, Gabriel García Márquez, John Kenneth Galbraith, and Wassili Leontief.

33.   Mary Blume, "Sidney Lumet: Jack Lang and Other Cinema," *Herald Tribune*, February 18, 1982.

34.   Dionne, "Paris, the World's Economy Gets a Dose of Culture."

35.   Raymond Sokolov, "Junket of the Year: 'Les Intellos,'" *Wall Street Journal*, February 15, 1982. For an account of the event, and more particularly the diverting commentary following it, including the citation of Sokolov, see Richard Kuisel, *The French Way: How France Embraced and Rejected American Values and Power* (Princeton, N.J.: Princeton University Press, 2012), 56.

36.   B. Poirot-Delpeck, "Vers une réponse européenne au défi audiovisuel," *Le Monde*, November 30, 1983.

37.   *Le Monde*, November 30, 1983. According to *Libération*, April 19, 1984, the announced meeting in May, apparently not held until June, would be the first time in the twenty-four years of the EEC that the Ministers of Culture will meet officially.

38.   E. R., "M. Jack Lang plaide pour un espace européen de la culture," *Le Monde*, April 18, 1984.

39.   Philippe Gavi, "Du Rififi dans l'Europe hertzien," *Libération*, April 19, 1984.

40.   Eric Rohde, "Timides débuts de l'Europe de la culture," *Le Monde*, June 24, 1984.

41.   Philippe Gavi, "Les dix font leur cinéma européen," *Libération*, June 23–24, 1984.

42.   *Libre Belgique*, November 16, 1984. Filmmakers included Antonioni, Comencini, Schlöndorff, Angelopoulos, Loach, Enrico, Costa-Gavras, Bertolucci, Ivens, Kluge, and more.

43.   "Réconcilier l'art et l'argent," interview with Lang, *Cinéma* 337 (January 15, 1986): 5.

44.   "Commission Communication to the Council, the European Parliament and the Economic and Social Committee," COM(86) 320 final, June 3, 1986.

45.   According to the extensive dossier of materials accompanying a major Lang press conference of January 11, 1983, "the minister strongly reminded the EC in 1982 of his concern regarding the cultural industries, especially cinema. The French position on national aid to cinema, valorizing the cultural specificity of this activity which cannot be subjected to the same conditions as other industries to the free international circulation, was reaffirmed on several occasions." "Les mésures d'application de la nouvelle politique du cinéma," press materials (Paris: Ministry of Culture, January 11, 1983), 14.

46.   Jean-Denis Bredin, "Rapport de la mission de réflexion et de propositions sur le cinéma" (Paris: Ministry of Culture, 1981), 16.

47.   Jean-François Court, "Le cinéma français face à son avenir: Rapport au ministre de la Culture et de la Communication" (Paris: La Documentation française, 1988). Depétris notes that the EC did lodge a complaint against Germany, Italy, Great Britain, Denmark, and France in 1979, followed in October 1981 by an *avis motivé* condemning the French system of financial support for the cinema. According to the documentation cited by Depétris, French officials took the EC action seriously, but he does not adduce other evidence that the case was pursued, suggesting that at the time the issue of television had more legal traction. In the only national aid to cinema case to reach the EC during the 1980s (Decision of EC 89/491, December 21, 1988), the commission rejected the aid law of Greece for discrimination against

nonnationals, ruling that such a condition rendered the aids "incompatible with the EEC Treaty since they are linked to a condition of nationality which is discriminatory toward residents of other member states." *Official Journal of the European Community* L208 (July 1989): 38, cited in Amiel, *Le financement public du cinéma*, 217. The EC would, however, return to the question of aids continually in the second half of the 1990s and into the next century. F. Depétris. *L'État et le cinéma en France: Le moment de l'exception culturelle* (Paris: L'Harmattan, 2008), 148–150. According to Herold, this decision is the only official pre-Maastricht decision concerning the film industry. Anna Herold, *European Film Policies in EU and International Law: Culture and Trade—Marriage or Misalliance?* (Groningen, Neth.: Europa Law Publishing, 2010), 131. See also chapter 6.

48.　Jack Lang, *Journal Officiel* 34 S (July 30, 1981): 1205, cited in Yves Surel, *L'État et le livre: Les politiques publiques du livre en France* (Paris: L'Harmattan, 1997), 206.

49.　Y. Galmot and J. Biancarelli, "Les réglementations nationales en matière de prix au regard du droit communautaire," *Revue trimestrielle de droit européen* 21, no. 2 (1985): 304, cited in Surel, *L'État et le livre*, 220.

50.　"You can't imagine what I had to go through for a year to prevent the law being declared not to conform to the treaty [of Rome]. If the decision had been negative, it was a catastrophe." Surel, *L'État et le livre*, 221.

51.　Jean-Michel Frodon, *L'âge moderne du cinéma français: De la Nouvelle Vague à nos jours* (Paris: Flammarion, 1995), 660–661.

52.　*Television Without Frontiers: Green Paper on the Establishment of the Common Market for Broadcasting, Especially by Satellite and Cable*, Communication from the Commission to the Council, COM(84) 300 final (Brussels: Commission of the European Communities, June 14, 1984).

53.　Richard Collins, *Broadcasting and Audio-visual Policy in the European Single Market* (London: Libbey, 1994), 55–63, 144. Depétris claims that the liberal orientation of, and German influence on DG III gathered strength in the early 1980s and corresponded to debates in the German parliament over the future of television. He also observed that DG III was dominated by Northern European states opposed to state intervention: Germany, Great Britain, and the Netherlands. DG X (Culture, Information, Communication) leaned toward a more interventionist position; its head, named in 1986, Jean Dondelinger, with close ties to the Compagnie luxembourgeoise de la télvision (CLT), pushed it closer to the liberal, DG III point of view. Depétris, *L'État et le cinéma en France*, 157–159.

54.　Richard Collins calls that battle "one of the 'grand narratives' of the Community." Collins, *Broadcasting and Audio-visual Policy in the European Single Market*, 23.

55.　Polo attributes the expression to the secretary general of the French professional organization ARP (Association des réalisateurs et producteurs). Jean-François Polo, "La naissance d'une direction audiovisuelle à la commission: La consécration de l'exception culturelle," *Politique Européenne* 11 (Autumn 2003): 24.

56.　*Television Without Frontiers: Green Paper*, 6.

57. Depétris, *L'État et le cinéma en France*, 163–164.

58. The draft directive is preceded by a thirty-eight-page "Explanatory Memorandum."

59. "Chapter II: Promotion of Distribution and Production of Television Programmes," Article 2, in "Proposal for a Council Directive on the Coordination of Certain Provisions Laid Down by Law, Regulation, or Administrative Action in Member States Concerning the Pursuit of Broadcasting Activities," *Official Journal of the European Communities* C179 (July 17, 1986): 7.

60. Despite the apparent validity of this objection, Hoskins, McFadyen, and Finn persuasively reject that characterization, for one of the peculiar features of exported films is the low (or even nonexistent) marginal cost of producing one additional copy, the normal benchmark for assessing charges of "dumping." Colin Hoskins, Stuart McFadyen, and Adam Finn, *Global Television and Film: An Introduction to the Economics of the Business* (New York: Oxford University Press, 1997), 79–80.

61. At a meeting of thirty European directors organized by Lang in Paris on November 13, 1984, Ken Loach lamented that the British are "literally drowned by American influence." Depétris, *L'État et le cinéma en France*, 149.

62. Ibid., 181.

63. The name of this authority changed several times during the 1980s, eventually becoming the Conseil supérieur de l'audiovisuel (CSA) in 1989. As we saw in chapter 2, Canal+ has enjoyed an exception to the chronology of media rules and is subject to only a year's delay. Other stations could reduce the delay to two years for a film they co-produced.

64. Mae Huettig, *The Economic Control of the Motion Picture Industry: A Study in Industrial Organization* (Philadelphia: University of Pennsylvania Press, 1944), 80–86. For a more detailed examination of the system of run, clearance, and prices, based on materials compiled during the legal proceedings leading up to the Paramount decrees in 1948, see Michael Conant, *Antitrust in the Motion Picture Industry: Economic and Legal Analysis* (Berkeley: University of California Press, 1960), 61–83.

65. According to the Paramount findings: "148(e). The percentages of first run theatre ownership and domestic film rentals controlled by the major defendants when coupled with the strategic advantages of vertical integration created a power to exclude competition from the distribution and exhibition markets when desired." Cited in Conant, *Antitrust in the Motion Picture Industry*, 55.

66. The early studies by Huettig and Conant remain fundamental texts for understanding how the studio system actually functioned. They are long out of print, but Tino Balio included some of Huettig's and Conant's work in *The American Film Industry*, rev. ed. (Madison: University of Wisconsin Press, 1985).

67. Michael Conant, "The Paramount Decrees Reconsidered," *Law and Contemporary Problems* 44, no. 4 (Autumn 1981): 79–80. With the commitment to deregulation during the Reagan years, the major Hollywood companies began acquiring theaters again in the late 1980s, in a successful attempt to re-create their power over run and clearance in the changed media environment where subsequent run had migrated

to other delivery systems (video, DVD, broadcast television, cable television, video on demand, and most recently, the Internet). See Amiel, *Le financement public du cinéma*, 196.

68. Régine Chaniac and Jean-Pierre Jézéquel, *La télévision* (Paris: La Découverte, 2005), 28.

69. Jack Ralite, interview with Depétris, March 2002, cited in Depétris, *L'État et le cinéma en France*, 188.

70. Cited in ibid., 188. Declaration published in *La culture française se porte bien pourvu qu'on la sauve* (Paris: Messidor, 1987).

71. "Amended Proposal for a Council Directive on the Coordination of Certain Provisions Laid Down by Law, Regulation or Administrative Action in Member States Concerning the Pursuit of Broadcasting Activities," COM(88) 154 final SYN 52 (Brussels: Commission of the European Communities, March 21 1988), 22.

72. Ibid., 13–14.

73. "A certain degree of protectionism—subject to GATT rules—may prove essential in an exceptional period such as the one now imminent, when there is going to be an enormous increase in the demand for programmes. With some justification the situation of the European audio-visual industry could be compared to that of an 'emergent industry.' " Jacques Barzanti, European Parliament document A 2-0246/87, December 3, 1987, 41. Even the liberal green paper named the United States: "The creation of a common market for television production is thus one essential step if the dominance of the big American media corporations is to be counterbalanced. This is yet another area where the establishment of a Community-wide market will allow European firms to improve their competitiveness." *Television Without Frontiers: Green Paper*, 33.

74. The "Year of Cinema and Television" was to have the following objectives: "end the competition between cinema and television; seek at the European level a concerted response to the crisis of production, distribution, diffusion and exhibition of quality audiovisual works; slow down, before it becomes inevitable, the invasion of our screen by works from 'elsewhere.' " Pervenche Beurier, *Les politiques européennes de soutien au cinéma: Vers la création d'un espace cinématographique européen?* (Paris: L'Harmattan, 2004), 33.

75. Depétris, *L'État et le cinéma en France*, 186.

76. Littoz-Monnet, *The European Union and Culture*, 85.

77. The opening of the letter underlines the gravity of the situation: "The hour is dire. Those committed to the cultural identity of France and to that of the countries of the European Community, see a mortal danger. After great hopes, the French cultural policy [politique culturelle], when it comes to Europe, seems today to be resigned to decline and abandonment." *Le Quotidien de Paris*, April 3, 1989, 7, cited in Jean-Noël Dibie, "Les clefs du marché audiovisuel international." *Cahiers d'actualité et de recherche sur l'audience et la télévision (CARAT)* 1 (September 1990): 104.

78. Ibid.; Littoz-Monnet, *The European Union and Culture*, 86.

79. Leyla Ertugrul, "'TV Without Frontiers' Sparks Fierce Euro-debate," Reuters News, May 24, 1989.

80. Delwit and Gobin suggested that the replacement of the more dirigiste Ojela by the more liberal Dondelinger from Belgium reinforced the position of the opponents of mandatory quotas. P. Delwit and C. Gobin, "Étude du cheminement de la Directive 'TWF': Synthèse des prises de position des institutions communitaires," in *L'espace audiovisuel européen*, ed. G. Vandersanden (Brussels: Éditions de la Université de Bruxelles, 1991), 66.

81. Dibie, "Les clefs du marché audiovisuel international," 104. Dibie provides a useful chronology; see also P. Delwit and C. Gobin, "Étude du cheminement de la Directive 'TWF.'"

82. "Assises européennes de l'audiovisuel: Projet EUREKA Audiovisuel, Paris-La Défense, CNIT, du 30 sept. au 2 oct. 1989" (Paris: Ministry of Foreign Affairs, [1989]), 14.

83. Also, for Mitterrand, culture was not narrowly national: "Hundreds of millions of men, of billions across the world, have been formed by our culture, are sensitive to our culture. Let's not turn in on ourselves: we need others. Our own cultures are often and fortunately mixed [*métissées*] and have benefited from external contributions. Let us continue. Nothing of what I am saying should be interpreted as a sort of closing [in]." Ibid., 22.

84. Speaking at the Rencontres cinématographiques in Beaune (France) almost exactly ten years later, Jack Lang observed, "It was necessary to wait until 1989 or 1990 for the European Union to recognize that a work of the spirit was not the same as merchandise. It was necessary to wait for Jacques Delors, as president of the European Commission, at the Eureka Audiovisual in Paris, to pronounce this almost magical phrase that we were awaiting for so long from the high European authorities." *8èmes Rencontres Cinématographiques de Beaune, 22/25 octobre 1998* (Paris: ARP, 1999), 48.

85. Article 4, Directive on Television Without Frontiers, October 3, 1989, emphasis added.

86. Richard Collins, generally dismissive of bureaucratic doublespeak, calls this phrase "weasel words," for the attempt to have it both ways. Collins, *Broadcasting and Audio-visual Policy*, 161.

87. "The Directive has done little to establish the single market envisaged by the Commission for, even without formal juridical barriers to entry, Community audio-visual markets have remained stratified on largely national and linguistic lines. Changes in regulation and establishment of subsidy programmes have done little to rupture the cultural and linguistic membranes which separate European television viewers." Collins, *Broadcasting and Audio-visual Policy*, 72. In a more recent account, Annabelle Littoz-Monnet concludes, "Fundamentally, France and other dirigiste states opted for a political compromise, because the nature of the status quo, characterized by the de facto intervention of EU institutions and the development of

trans-frontier broadcasting, was less desirable than a 'middle-course' EU–level solution." Littoz-Monnet, *The European Union and Culture*, 90.

88. Following the approval of the directive, Commissioner Dondelinger wrote that the wording of the text had "no juridical meaning" but should be understood as political. Pascal Marchetti, *La production d'oeuvres audiovisuelles dans l'Union européenne* (Paris: Économica, 2007), 263. One article published the day after the approval of the directive quoted Commissioner Bangemann: "It's not a legal obligation, it's a political commitment." Steven Greenhouse, "Europe Reaches TV Compromise; U.S. Officials Fear Protectionism," *New York Times*, October 4, 1989, cited in Herold, *European Film Policies in EU and International Law*, 72–76.

89. Voogd, "Le cinéma et l'État," xvii, emphasis added. In a later intervention, Voogd asked: "Can one imagine a European film? The response must be an emphatic no. How could one combine in a single film French eloquence, British reserve, German obsession with detail, Scandinavian calm, Dutch stinginess?" (106).

90. Wangermée and Gournay, *La politique culturelle de la France*, 45.

91. Collins, *Broadcasting and Audio-visual Policy*, 215, citing Jean Cluzel, *Une autre Bataille de la France* (Paris: LGDJ, 1992), 126.

4. GATT

1. "Simply put, the principle of 'comparative advantage' says that countries prosper first by taking advantage of their assets in order to concentrate on what they can produce best, and then by trading these products for products that other countries produce best. . . . In other words, liberal trade policies—policies that allow the unrestricted flow of goods and services—sharpen competition, motivate innovation and breed success. They multiply the rewards that result from producing the best products, with the best design, at the best price." "The Case for Open Trade," http://www.wto.org/english/thewto_e/whatis_e/tif_e/fact3_e.htm.

2. The question of subsidies is a complex one, which should be kept in mind in any discussion of trade, especially when they are yoked, as they invariably are, to ideological arguments. John H. Jackson, author of the standard work on GATT, warns, "The definition of 'subsidy' has always perplexed policymakers, partly because the word 'subsidy' can mean so many different things." Jackson, *The World Trading System: Law and Policy of International Economic Relations*, 2nd ed. (Cambridge, Mass.: MIT Press, 1997), 293.

3. Jacques Barzanti, European Parliament document A 2-0246/87, December 3, 1987, 41.

4. Article XX includes the following exceptions: (*a*) necessary to protect public morals; (*b*) necessary to protect human, animal, or plant life or health. Article XXI (*b*) exempts measures "necessary for the protection of its essential security interests."

5. Americo Beviglia-Zampetti, "WTO Rules in the Audio-Visual Sector," in *Cultural Diversity and International Economic Integration: the Global Governance of the Audio-Visual Sector*, ed. Paolo Guerrieri, P. Lelio Iapadre, and Georg Koopman (Cheltenham, UK: Edward Elgar, 2005), 271.

6. "If any contracting party establishes or maintains internal quantitative regulations relating to exposed cinematograph films, such regulations shall take the form of screen quotas which shall conform to the following requirements: (*a*) Screen quotas may require the exhibition of cinematograph films of national origin during a specified minimum proportion of the total screen time actually utilized, over a specified period of not less than one year, in the commercial exhibition of all films of whatever origin, and shall be computed on the basis of screen time per theatre per year or the equivalent thereof." Article IV: Special Provisions Relating to Cinematograph Films, General Agreement on Trade and Tariffs, 1947, http://www.wto.org/english /docs_e/legal_e/gatt47_01_e.htm.

7. Emmanuel Cocq and Patrick Messerlin, "French Audiovisual Policy: Impact and Compatibility with Trade Negotiations," HWWA-Report 233 (Hamburg: Hamburg Institute of International Economics, 2003), 3–4, http://ageconsearch.umn .edu/bitstream/26105/1/re030233.pdf, also published in Guerrieri, Iapadre, and Koopman, *Cultural Diversity and International Economic Integration*, 21–51.

8. However, no country could increase the quotas in the future. Paragraph (c) of Article IV states that "any contracting party may maintain screen quotas . . . *Provided* that no such minimum proportion of screen time shall be increased above the level in effect on April 10, 1947."

9. According to one French estimate, for every film shown in a theater, fifty were watched on television. Claude Forest, *L'argent du cinéma: Introduction à l'économie du septième art* (Paris: Belin, 2002), 28. Several U.S. scholars have noted the continuing importance of theatrical release to the ultimate earning potential of films. For example, "Through all the changes during the 1980s, domestic theatrical release remained the launching pad for blockbuster hits and it established a movie's value in virtually all other secondary or ancillary markets." Thomas Schatz, "The New Hollywood," in *Movie Blockbusters*, ed. Julian Stringer (London: Routledge, 2003), 32. See also Douglas Gomery, "The Hollywood Film Industry: Theatrical Exhibition, Pay TV, and Home Video," in *Who Owns the Media? Competition and Concentration in the Mass Media Industry*, ed. Douglas Gomery and B. M. Compaine, 3rd ed. (Mahwah, N.J.: Lawrence Erlbaum, 2000), 380.

10. When the United States tried to include television in the early 1960s, a GATT study panel could not reach a decision, and the European Court of Justice in 1974 determined that television was a service, not a good like film, so television could not be subjected to the rules of GATT, which applied only to goods. Jean-François Polo, "La relance de la politique audiovisuelle européenne: Les ressources politiques et administratives de la DG X," *Pôle Sud* 15, no. 1 (2001): 7. The distinction between goods and services has been debated at length in the international trade literature.

For example, see Christophe Germann, *Diversité culturelle et libre-échange à la lumière du cinéma: Réflexions critiques sur le droit naissant de la diversité culturelle sous les angles du droit de l'UNESCO et de l'OMC, de la concurrence et de la propriété intellectuelle* (Paris: LGDJ; Basel, Switzerland: Helbing Lichtenhahn; Brussels: Bruylant, 2008), 312–313.

11. "The enactment of such a measure is unjustifiable and would almost certainly have a disastrous effect on the U.S. industry's substantial European earnings." "European Group Votes to Restrict U.S. TV Programs," *Wall Street Journal*, May 25, 1989.

12. Farchy has noted the "paradox" of France calling for diversity in foreign trade negotiations in the struggle against cultural homogenization, but domestically "homogenization is transformed into a virtue in the struggle against communitarian pressures." Joëlle Farchy, "Exception culturelle, identité et mondialisation," *Le Monde*, May 29, 2007.

13. These are difficult issues which have received extensive discussion. Germann addresses not only racist tendencies but also inequities inherent in legal arguments built on preserving the prerogatives of nations. Germann, *Diversité culturelle et libre-échange à la lumière du cinéma*, 234–237, 424–428. Richard Collins traced many of the tensions found in the attempts to collapse culture and national identities, in particular the claim of congruence between culture and nation. Countries tended to assert such a congruence, but nations did not necessarily fit within national borders, and subnational groups like the Basques did not accept the imposition of "national" culture. Richard Collins, *Broadcasting and Audio-Visual Policy in the European Single Market* (London: John Libbey, 1993). As for the idea of national identity, Hobsbawm and others have stressed the degree to which national identity has been "invented," not a natural outgrowth of nation formation. Eric Hobsbawm, *The Invention of Tradition* (Cambridge: Cambridge University Press, 1984). For an acknowledgment of these tensions in French cinema policy, see Farchy, "Exception culturelle, identité et mondialisation."

14. In its ruling of April 30, 1974, the ECJ wrote that "in the absence of clear evidence contrary to the Treaty [of Rome], a television program should be considered a service in the sense of the Treaty." Cited in Serge Regourd, *Droit de la communication audiovisuelle* (Paris: Presses universitaires de France, 2001), 98. Regourd comments that the court arrived at this opinion in the historical context when all television was a noncommercial state monopoly, thus exempt from the rules of competition normally used as a criterion. The court did not address the later question of the status of an immaterial, cultural good. Ibid., 98–99. See also Annabelle Littoz-Monnet, *The European Union and Culture: Between Economic Regulation and European Cultural Policy* (Manchester: Manchester University Press, 2007), 76–77. The European Commission green paper on broadcasting explicitly refers to the ECJ's decision in the Sacchi case to justify its treatment of television as a service. *Television Without Frontiers: Green Paper on the Establishment of the Common Market for Broadcasting, Especially by Cable and Satellite*, Communication from

the Commission to the Council, COM(84) 300 final (Brussels: Commission of the European Communities, June 14, 1984), 105.

15. In addition to the agreements on goods (GATT) and services (GATS), the negotiations also included the agreement on intellectual property, Trade-Related Aspects of Intellectual Property Rights (TRIPS).

16. In addition, before the vote on the TWF directive, on October 3, 1989, the U.S. House of Representatives passed a unanimous resolution denouncing the EEC for "adopting a broadcast directive that is trade restrictive and in violation of GATT." See Suzanne Schwartz, "Television Without Frontiers?," *North Carolina Journal of International Law and Commercial Regulation* 16, 2 (1991): 362–363.

17. Steven Greenhouse, "Europe Reaches TV Compromise; U.S. Officials Fear Protectionism," *New York Times*, October 4, 1989.

18. As mentioned, there were few contemporaneous news reports in the United States of the GATT fight. For an early, balanced account of some central issues, see W. Ming Shao, "Is There No Business Like Show Business? Free Trade and Cultural Protectionism." *Yale Journal of International Law* 20 (1995): 105–150. See also a less balanced treatment by Bill Grantham, *"Some Big Bourgeois Brothel": Contexts for France's Culture Wars with Hollywood* (Luton, UK: University of Luton Press, 2000).

19. "1. Cultural industries are exempt from the provisions of this Agreement, except as specifically provided in Article 401 (Tariff Elimination), paragraph 4 of Article 1607 (divestiture of an indirect acquisition) and Articles 2006 and 2007 of this Chapter. 2. Notwithstanding any other provision of this Agreement, a Party may take measures of equivalent commercial effect in response to actions that would have been inconsistent with this Agreement but for paragraph 1." For discussion, see Chi Carmody, "When 'Cultural Identity Was Not at Issue': Thinking About Canada—Certain Measures Concerning Periodicals," *Law and Policy in International Business* 30, no. 2 (Winter 1999): 282; Thiébaut Thory, "L'accord de libre échange américano-canadien," *Annuaire français de droit international* 34 (1988): 549–562, http://www.persee.fr/web/revues/home/prescript/article/afdi_0066-3085_1988 _num_34_1_2855; and Keith Acheson and Christopher Maule, *Much Ado About Culture: North American Trade Disputes* (Ann Arbor: University of Michigan Press, 2001).

20. The United States prevailed in its official protest against Canadian legal attempts to protect its magazines in a dispute over the "split run" publication of *Sports Illustrated* in Canada. See Acheson and Maule, *Much Ado About Culture*, 186–205.

21. "Assises européennes de l'audiovisuel: Projet EUREKA Audiovisuel, Paris–La Défense, CNIT, du 30 sept. au 2 oct. 1989" (Paris: Ministry of Foreign Affairs, [1989]), 23.

22. Several foreign news sources in 1991 reported use of the expression by Carla Hills, but there are no other news references to it in the United States or France before its appearance in *Le Monde* in March 1993. Based on LexisNexis and Factiva searches.

23. Bill Grantham has argued that the U.S. trade officials failed to recognize the future importance of the audiovisual question. "Competing government departments, often short-staffed, failed to monitor the development of the Directive until it had nearly been promulgated. Further, when the administration attempted to mount a campaign against the Directive, it appeared for a long time to substitute bluster for argument as it failed to get a tight grasp on the real economic issues and the extent to which fundamental U.S. issues were implicated." Grantham, *Some Big Bourgeois Brothel*, 130.

24. France passed Loi 86-1067 du 30 septembre 1986 relative à la liberté de communication (Loi Léotard), requiring programming quotas on television. Article 27 required "the broadcasting, in particular in prime time, of minimum proportions of 60 percent European cinema and television works, and minimum proportions of 40 percent French-origin cinema and television works." For the original law, see http://www.legifrance.gouv.fr/affichTexte.do?cidTexte=LEGITEXT000006068930&dateTexte=20090909. The law was modified subsequently to conform to the changing EEC and EU legal regulation of the audiovisual sector, but the quotas were consistently retained.

25. Regourd, *Droit de la communication audiovisuelle*, 108.

26. Schlesinger defines the subsidiarity principle as "the doctrine that no political issues should be decided at a level higher than is absolutely necessary." Philip Schlesinger, "From Cultural Defense to Political Culture," *Media, Culture & Society* 19 (1997): 383.

27. Ivan Bernier, "Trade and Culture," in *The World Trade Organization: Legal, Economic and Political Analysis*, ed. Patrick F. J. Macrory, Arthur E. Appleton, and Michael G. Plummer (New York: Springer, 2005), 2:747–793.

28. Thomas Schatz, "The Studio System and Conglomerate Hollywood," *The Contemporary Hollywood Film Industry*, ed. Paul MacDonald and Janet Wasko (Malden, Mass.: Blackwell, 2008), 22, citing J. Mickelthwait, "A Survey of the Entertainment Industry," *Economist*, December 23, 1989.

29. Douglas Gomery, "Hollywood Corporate Business Practice and Periodizing Contemporary Film History," in *Contemporary Hollywood Cinema*, ed. Steve Neale and Murray Smith, 47–57 (London: Routledge, 1998); Schatz, "The Studio System and Conglomerate Hollywood."

30. "*Jaws* proved to be a genuine industry watershed, marking the birth of the New Hollywood. . . . a prototype for the modern blockbuster." Schatz, "The Studio System and Conglomerate Hollywood," 19. See also Julian Stringer, ed., *Movie Blockbusters* (London: Routledge, 2003).

31. Edward J. Epstein, "Hollywood's Profits Demystified: The Real El Dorado Is TV," *Slate.com*, August 8, 2005, http://www.slate.com/articles/arts/the_hollywood_economist/2005/08/hollywoods_profits_demystified.html. In 2004 theatrical exhibition lost $2.2 billion; DVD and VHS generated a gross profit of $14 billion and television licensing $15.9 billion. Cited in Harold Vogel. *Entertainment Industry*

Economics: A Guide for Financial Analysis (Cambridge: Cambridge University Press, 2007), 158 n73. For a chart on the breakdown of major studio revenue sources from 1948–2003, see Schatz, "The Studio System and Conglomerate Hollywood," 36. See also Charles R. Acland, *Screen Traffic: Movies, Multiplexes and Global Culture* (Durham, N.C.: Duke University Press, 2003), 65.

32.   Schatz, "The Studio System and Conglomerate Hollywood," 31.

33.   While Acland properly questions the reliability of numbers, he refers to "a key turning point that has circulated in the trade periodicals: 1993 was the first year that international rentals for Hollywood films exceeded domestic." Acland, *Screen Traffic*, 26. The point is only that Hollywood viewed international revenues as crucial to its future and pressured the U.S. government to oppose quotas in the GATT talks.

34.   C. Hoskins, S. McFadyen, and A. Finn, *Global Film and Television: An Introduction to the Economics of the Business* (Oxford: Clarendon Press, 1997), 28.

35.   *Bilan 1993* (Paris: CNC, May 1994). With significantly higher ticket prices, Japan box office receipts are disproportionately high compared to the European countries. In 1993, Japan and France had about 130 million spectators, but the Japanese box office was twice as large. But EU5 box office was more than twice as high as the Japanese box office. *Statistical Yearbook, 1994–1995: Cinema, Television, Video and New Media in Europe* (Strasbourg: European Audiovisual Observatory, 1994).

36.   "What's Gone Wrong?," *Media Business School* (1995), 2, cited in Hoskins, McFadyen, and Finn, *Global Television and Film*, 62. It should be understood that the figure of 7 percent is inflated by the high export percentage of films from Great Britain, hard to separate out from U.S. productions.

37.   Anne Jäckel has written often on European co-productions. See following note and other articles in the bibliography.

38.   The MEDIA program (Mésures pour encourager le développement de l'industrie audiovisuelle) was designed primarily for development, distribution, and exhibition, not production. For discussion, see Jäckel, *European Film Industries* (London: BFI, 2003), 65-76, and Herold, *European Film Policies in EU and International Law: Culture and Trade—Marriage or Misalliance?* (Groningen, Neth.: Europa Law Publishing, 2010), 48–68.

39.   Martin Kanzler, with Susan Newman-Baudais and André Lange, "The Circulation of European Co-productions and Entirely National Films in Europe, 2001–2007" (Strasbourg: European Audiovisual Observatory, August 2008).

40.   According to one study, the EU aid in 1996 represented only 0.7 percent of all audiovisual investment in fifteen EU countries. Pierre-Jean Benghozi, "L'Europe de l'audiovisuel n'est pas pour demain," *Sociétal* 25 (June 1999): 76.

41.   The issues are complicated, for there are many varieties of co-productions (bilateral agreements; majority/minority co-productions; EU and COE programs, often complementing national arrangements; financial vs. content definitions; etc.). Anne Jäckel has offered a balanced assessment in *European Film Industries* and other articles (see bibliography). In terms of number of films produced, there is no

question that co-productions are significant and have resulted in the production of excellent films, but it is not clear that co-productions represent an advance in building audiences for European films. While acknowledging successes, critics fault the relative penury of resources devoted to the programs and their failure to establish positive structural changes in the dispersed European support system, "The programs MEDIA and EURIMAGES . . . have tried . . . to redynamise the sector . . . but without succeeding in challenging American hegemony. . . . This failure [is] relative—for MEDIA and EURIMAGES have enabled or contributed to a large number of quality works." Frederic Sojcher, "Cinéma européen et identités culturelles," in *Cinéma européen et identités culturelles* (Brussels: Université de Bruxelles, 1996), 5. For example, in 2013, the French avance sur recettes alone (a tiny part of French film investment), awarded €23 million to fifty-seven films; Eurimages, with thirty-six participating countries, distributed €23 million to fifty-seven films. In 1992, Jacques Renard wrote a (once confidential) report balancing the strengths and weaknesses of Eurimages for the CNC. In it, he commented, "The notion of European film is ambiguous. The films most likely to circulate in Europe are without doubt not the films with an artificial multilateral construction, but those which, rooted in their language and culture, are successful on their national market and can then succeed also in other markets." Renard, "Rapport sur Eurimages" (Paris: CNC, October 2002), 16. For a highly critical assessment of co-productions from a French perspective, see Margaret Ménégoz and René Bonnell, "Rapport de la Commission de réforme de l'agrément" (Paris: Ministry of Culture, November 1996), CNC SD 485. And the definition of national film is itself a subject of contention, as mentioned in chapter 1. For a recent discussion, which calls transnational film "a kind of benevolent counterpart to the perceived evil of globalization," see Ian Christie, "Where Is National Cinema Today (and Do We Still Need It)?," *Film History* 25, no. 1–2 (January 2013): 24.

42. Patrice Vivancos, *Cinéma et Europe: Réflexions sur les politiques européennes de soutien au cinéma* (Paris: L'Harmattan, 2000), 75.

43. *Le Monde*, March 11, 1993. Valenti did not mention that the European share of the U.S. domestic market was less than 5 percent. As for giving citizens what they wanted, Valenti in 1982 warned the House Judiciary Committee in 1982 that "The VCR is to the American film producer and the American public as the Boston strangler is to the woman home alone." Josh Barro, "Thirty Years Before SOPA, MPAA Feared the VCR," *Forbes*, January 18, 2012. Janet Wasko has written an account of the history of home video, including the eight-year legal battle over the introduction of home video in the United States. Wasko, *Hollywood in the Information Age* (Austin: University of Texas Press, 1994), 113–170.

44. Hoskins, McFadyen, and Finn, *Global Television and Film*, 27–28; *Le Monde*, March 11, 1993.

45. *Le Monde*, March 24, 1993.

46. On dumping, see chapter 3, n60.

47. *Le Monde*, March 24, 1993. According to Footer and Graber, the term was introduced at a midterm ministerial meeting in Montréal in December 1988, but no other commentators cite that reference as a precursor. Mary E. Footer and Christoph Beat Graber, "Trade Liberalization and Cultural Policy," *Journal of International Economic Law* 3, no. 1 (March 2000): 119. Their source, Karl F. Falkenberg, did not cite that expression in his article, "The Audiovisual Sector," in *The Uruguay Round Results: A European Lawyers' Perspective*, ed. Jacques H. J. Bourgeois, Frédérique Berrod, and Eric Gippini Fournier (Brussels: European Interuniversity Press, 1995), 429. Valenti responded with more circumspection in May: "As a student of European history, and more particularly of French art and literature, I would be more than happy to contribute to the success of the agreement." *Le Monde*, May 3, 1993.

48. For a sampling of some later accounts, see Shao, "Is There No Business Like Show Business?," 105; Toby Miller, "The Crime of Monsieur Lang: GATT, the Screen, and the New International Division of Cultural Labour," in *Film Policy: International, National and Regional Perspectives*, ed. Albert Moran (London: Routledge, 1996), 76; and Clint Smith, "International Trade in Television Programming and GATT: An Analysis of Why the European Community's Local Program Requirement Violates the General Agreement on Tariffs and Trade," *International Tax and Business Lawyer* 10, no. 97 (1993): 101.

49. Falkenberg, "The Audiovisual Sector," 430.

50. "1. Cultural industries are exempt from the provisions of this Agreement, except as specifically provided in Article 401 (Tariff Elimination), paragraph 4 of Article 1607 (divestiture of an indirect acquisition) and Articles 2006 [on copyright] and 2007 [on print magazines] of this Chapter. 2. Notwithstanding any other provision of this Agreement, a Party may take measures of equivalent commercial effect in response to actions that would have been inconsistent with this Agreement but for paragraph 1." Article 2005: Cultural Industries, Canada–United States Free Trade Agreement, October 4, 1987. This second paragraph allows the United States, which objected to the article, to take retaliatory action.

51. Yves Mamou, "Les ministres européens de la communication réunis en séminaire à Mons: 'L'exception culturelle' définie en six points," *Le Monde*, October 7, 1993. Mamou did not clarify the explicit refusal to commit to future liberalization of the sector.

52. Serge Regourd, *L'exception culturelle* (Paris: Presses universitaires de France, 2002), 81. Regourd contributed to the debate at the time with an article in *Le Monde Diplomatique*, November 1993, in which he argued in favor of the cultural exclusion, as the title of the article clearly announced: "Pour l'exclusion culturelle."

53. According to Marchetti, Germany, Great Britain, the Netherlands, Italy, and the European Commission supported this position; France, Spain, Belgium, and Greece pushed for the cultural exception. Pascal Marchetti, *La production d'oeuvres audiovisuelles dans l'Union européenne* (Paris: Économica, 1997), 288–289. At the same time, *Le Film Français* reported in July that the European Parliament had passed a

resolution on July 14, 1993, calling for a "clause of cultural specificity" in GATT. *Le Film Français* 2464 (July 23, 1993): 1, 6, cited in Ivan Bernier, "Commerce international et cultures nationales: Le débat sur la clause d'exception culturelle dans les négociations de l'Uruguay Round," in *Industries culturelles nationales et mondialisation des marchés*, ed. Mario Beaulac and François Colbert (Montréal: École des hautes études commerciales, 1994), 61.

54. "MM. Mitterrand, Balladur et Toubon défendent la clause d'exception culturelle," *Le Monde*, September 23, 1993.

55. The appeal was published in France, Germany, Great Britain, and Spain. Bernier, "Trade and Culture," 749; Jean-François Polo, "L'Union européenne dans les négotiations internationales sur l'audiovisuel: Une exception culturelle construite par l'action collective," in *L'Union européenne, acteur international*, ed. F. Petiteville and D. Helly (Paris: L'Harmattan, 2005), 245.

56. *Le Monde* published their remarks on October 8, 1993. Both directors' comments were taken from *PR Newswire*, October 4, 1993.

57. Agence France presse, October 20, 1993.

58. Twenty years later, speaking as president of the jury at the Cannes Film Festival in 2013, when awarding the prize for best film (*Blue Is the Warmest Color*), Spielberg remarked, "The cultural exception is the best way of defending the diversity of cinema." Clarisse Fabre, "Comment les Français ont rallié Spielberg et des cinéastes de tous les pays à leur combat," *Le Monde*, June 19, 2013.

59. Ange-Dominique Bouzet, "Le cinéma français sur le qui-vive: Ce week-end, trois ministres et la commissaire européenne à la Culture ont tenté de rassurer la profession," *Libération*, October 26, 1999. More neutrally, Elisabeth Lequeret called Beaune a "valuable barometer of the hopes, states of mind, and worries of the profession." Lequeret, "Vivre sans l'argent des télés?," *Cahiers du cinéma* 574 (December 2002): 33.

60. *Et le cinéma va: Europe–États-Unis. [3e] Rencontres cinématographiques de Beaune, [28-31 octobre] 1993* (Paris: Lieu Commun/Edima, 1994), 17.

61. Ibid., 19.

62. Ibid., 30.

63. Ibid., 40.

64. Ibid., 48.

65. "After all our position is clear. We want culture to benefit from an exception in Article 14 of the General Agreement, along with security, public order, health and citizens' privacy. As far as I know the Commission's legal experts have stated that from the point of view of protection of European interests in film and audiovisual the thesis of the [cultural] exception was more efficient than the thesis of specificity. So they agree with us. . . . Our objective is to obtain inclusion of an exception in Article 14 in the General Agreement, then use this exception to uphold what Europe and the community have achieved. And which, we have to admit, comes to relatively little." Ibid., 50.

66. In attendance at Beaune, Falkenberg acknowledged the danger of panels, but he argued that the panels could also be used against the United States, which did not always prevail: "Even the United States, who most people think can obtain whatever they want from the GATT, were condemned by a panel when they tried to invoke the provision to protect the poor little dolphins." Ibid., 24.

67. Jean-Pierre Jeancolas, "From the Blum-Byrnes Agreement to the GATT Affair," in *Hollywood and Europe: Economics, Culture, National Identity, 1945–95*, ed. Geoffrey Nowell-Smith and Steven Ricci (London: BFI, 1998), 59.

68. Years later, Regourd called the cultural exception a "product of juridico-semantic bricolage." Serge Regourd, "Exception, diversité . . . des instruments de politique culturelle en quête de leur objet: Contribution à un examen critique," *La Pensée* 349 (2007): 52.

5. FROM CANAL+ TO CANAL–

1. The technical plans were developed by a group working for the public France Télévision in anticipation of a new channel, but the idea migrated to Havas under Rousselet when he was developing plans for Canal+. Régine Chaniac and Jean-Pierre Jézéquel, *Télévision et cinéma: Le désenchantement* (Paris: Nathan, 1998), 56–57. Chaniac and Jézéquel contest the "legend" that the conception of Canal+ originated at Havas. For the alternative account, see Nicole Vulser, *André Rousselet: Les trois vies d'un homme d'influence* (Paris: Calmann-Lévy, 2001), 169–205; Valérie Lecasble, *Le roman de Canal+* (Paris: Grasset, 2001), 79–84; and Jacques Buob and Pascal Mérigeau, *L'aventure vraie de Canal+* (Paris: Fayard, 2001), 10–12. Chaniac and Jézéquel repeat their version in *La télévision* (Paris: La Découverte, 2005), 53–54.

2. Serge Regourd, *Droit de la communication audiovisuelle* (Paris: Presses universitaires de France, 2001), 58–59. Lang released a statement expressing astonishment at a leaked report on a new pay station, recalling that "the authorities of the Republic have been elected by the workers and the popular classes to honor the public interest." Chaniac and Jézéquel, *Télévision et cinéma*, 57.

3. "Convention de concession de service public et cahiers des charges pour Canal Plus signés entre l'État et l'agence Havas, 6 décembre 1983," in *Les politiques audiovisuelles en France*, ed. Rémi Tomaszewski (Paris: La Documentation française, 2001), 216–217.

4. French regulations already required that at least 50 percent of films shown on television had to be French. Jean Roux and René Thévenet, *Industrie et commerce du film en France* (Paris: Éditions scientifiques et juridiques, 1979), 269.

5. "Canal Plus, c'est déjà l'échec," *France Soir*, November 4, 1984, cited in Isabelle Repiton, "Canal Plus, vingt ans et un avenir à décrypter," *La Tribune*, November 4, 2004.

6. Some subscribers had not received their decoders; others could not receive the signal because of defective decoders; and for the 11:00 A.M. broadcast on the first day of the popular Belmondo film *L'as des as*, with angry subscribers calling to report they could not view it, the station decided to broadcast the film unscrambled and deal with the rights question later; the rules did not allow Canal+ to broadcast films unscrambled. Buob and Mérigeau, *L'aventure vraie de Canal+*, 41–47.

7. Mitterrand referred to eighty-five new stations, confusing local and national networks, according to Buob and Mérigeau, *L'aventure vraie de Canal+*, 50.

8. Lecasble reports that Rousselet exclaimed, "Mitterrand stabbed me in the back." Lecasble, *Le roman de Canal+*, 101. Canal+ took advantage of the opening to gain other concessions, including the right to show 364 films annually, instead of the original 320.

9. According to Lecasble, the initial authorization for Canal+ prohibited production, but over time Canal+ developed relationships with production companies, which eventually led to participation through StudioCanal to active production. Ibid., 152.

10. Jean François Lacan and René Bonnell, "Canal Plus veut se lancer dans la production: La chaîne cryptée ne veut plus financer le cinéma les yeux fermés," *Le Monde*, May 12, 1990.

11. Canal+ earned most of its revenues from subscriptions. A 1999 report indicated that advertising contributed only 3.3 percent of the group's revenue. "Canal+" (Paris: L'Observatoire des groupes, Eurostaf, 1999), 11. In the following decade, advertising rose slightly, to 5.5 percent of income. "Les chiffres clés de la télévision hertzienne (1998–2007)" (Paris: CNC, February 2009), 11.

12. According to one chronicler, "These are the shows that make the personality of the station. Without them, Canal+ would be simply another pay station, profitable, perhaps, but with no originality." Lecasble, *Le Roman de Canal+*, 27.

13. Jean-Emmanuel Cortade, *La télévision française* (Paris: Presses universitaires de France, 1993), 39.

14. The group included Banque nationale de Paris, Crédit lyonnais, Crédit commercial de France, and Crédit mutuel. Lecasble, *Le roman de Canal+*, 88.

15. Rousselet referred to this political "debt" indirectly in an interview published in Josepha Laroche and Alexandre Bohas, *Canal Plus et les majors américains: Une vision désenchantée du cinéma monde* (Paris: L'Harmattan, 2008), 20.

16. Ownership was divided into Havas (45 percent), BNP group (20 percent), CGE (15 percent), Compagnie du Midi (5 percent), Garantie mutuelle des fonctionnaires (5 percent), a group of regional daily papers (5 percent), and Guy Merlin (5 percent). Lecasble, *Le roman de Canal+*, 91.

17. In addition to authorization to air forty-four additional films per year, Canal+ won the right to show one every night at 8:30 or 9:00 P.M., except Saturday, when it could show one film at 11:00 P.M., and a reduction in the normal value-added tax from 20.5 percent to 5.5 percent. Lecasble, *Le roman de Canal+*, 123–126. See also

René Bonnell, *Mon Cinéma: De Cannes à Canal+, itinéraire d'un distributeur gâté* (Paris: Balland, 2011), 203.

18. According to Lecasble, PSG was, like J.R. in *Dallas*, a lightning rod for public commentary. Lecasble, *Le roman de Canal+*, 151.

19. Ibid., 190–191.

20. Regourd traced the legal history of the "denaturation" of the notion of public service in the formation of new stations, culminating only several years later in the scandal over La Cinq when "the very idea of public service [was] being emptied of all meaning." Regourd, *Droit de la communication audiovisuelle*, 58–60.

21. Benzoni documented the benefits of the monopoly granted Canal+ as the period of its concession from the state was about to end. He noted that the majority (60 percent) of early investors was state-owned, and the concession was supposedly granted as a public service. States may grant such concessions when the state lacks the experience of offering a new service, but if it determines that the concessionaire(s) have earned a monopoly rent beyond the reasonable costs of the new service, "the State may deem it appropriate to reclaim control of the service and call for discussion on the options for renewal of the station." Benzoni proposed several possible scenarios for the state to reclaim the monopoly rent. Laurent Benzoni, "Position dominante et rente de monopole: Une analyse économique de la concession de Canal+," *Revue d'économie industrielle* 66 (1993): 8. According to William Emmanuel, Canal+ tried to suppress this article by an academic. Emmanuel, *Le maître des illusions: L'ascension et la chute de Jean-Marie Messier* (Paris: Économica, 2002), 275.

22. *Le Monde*, February 17, 1994.

23. Rousselet adapted the phrase from the words scrawled in blood at the scene of a notorious murder case, "Omar m'a tuer." The obvious grammatical mistake (instead of the improper use of the infinitive, the correct form of the French verb would be written "Edouard m'a tué," though the pronunciation of each sentence would be identical) and the name Omar suggested that the murderer was a foreigner with limited command of French, a clue intentionally meant to deflect suspicion from the real criminal. Rousselet wrote later that the idea of the title came from his wife and son. The sister of the murdered woman informed Rousselet that she did not appreciate his exploitation of her loss for his personal settling of accounts. Rousselet remarked that the title was so good that people would think it came from the Canal+ satirists, Les Guignols, not Rousselet. Vulser, *André Rousselet*, 282.

24. Actually, Lecasble thinks it impossible that Balladur was behind the unseating of Rousselet and that in fact Balladur was furious that the scandal played out as it did. Lecasble, *Le roman de Canal+*, 157–181. Reporters Martine Orange and Jo Johnson suggested "Jean-Marie m'a tuer." Orange and Johnson, *Une faillite française* (Paris: Albin Michel, 2003), 65.

25. Lecasble, *Le roman de Canal+*, 179.

26. One early assignment in 1989 involved investing in a small U.S. firm, which led to large losses. Orange and Johnson, *Une faillite française*, 61.

27. The ENA is the feeder for top-level managers and civil servants in France. Raoul Peck directed a 2009 miniseries about one cohort of ENA graduates, *L'école du pouvoir*, the 1980 graduating class ("promotion Voltaire") that included François Hollande, Ségolène Royal, and Dominique de Villepin.

28. At the same time, Dejouany was facing possible charges of diversion of funds, which may have sped his decision to leave CGE. Orange and Johnson probed the close, if opaque, relations between CGE and Lazard in *Une faillite française*, 68–77, implying that Lazard, through Messier and others, earned considerable commissions from the CGE–Canal+ connection over the years.

29. When Messier began at CGE in 1994, the company controlled 2,700 subsidiaries; four years later, that number had jumped to 3,300. Ibid., 103–104. After Messier's fall from grace, the former finance director of Vivendi Universal, Guillaume Hannezo, called Vivendi under Messier "a deal machine." Jacques Follorou, "Guillaume Hannezo donne sa version de la chute du groupe; Le Monde révèle le détail de la note remise à la COB par l'ancien directeur financier," *Le Monde*, December 14, 2002. One book on Messier includes a list of Vivendi's holdings referred to as a "catalogue à la Prévert." Emmanuel, *Le maître des illusions*, 313.

30. Lecasble, *Le Roman de Canal+*, 179.

31. Years later, Rousselet credited Lescure's talent for building content at Canal+, but no doubt still nursing wounds from Lescure's later disloyalty, he also emphasized that Lescure did so only under his own paternal vision. "Pierre Lescure . . . was a formidable assistant to me. . . . Even if he disappointed me . . . he remains nonetheless in my eyes the unequalled artisan of the success of this station, when I was its head." Rousselet, "Canal peu banal," *L'Express*, November 5, 2009.

32. Lecasble, *Le roman de Canal+*, 198–201; Martine Orange, "Seize ans pour prendre le contrôle de Canal," *Le Monde*, December 12, 2000.

33. "The industrial genius of Rousselet was to occupy Europe when it was still asleep." Yves Mamou and Guy Dutheil, "Les dix années de Canal+: Mots-clés pour un bilan," *Le Monde*, November 7, 1994. Lescure shared that strategy, as he explained in an interview earlier in 1994: "What counts today is the international." Yves Mamou and Pierre Lescure, "Ce qui compte aujourd'hui, c'est l'international," *Le Monde*, June 7, 1994.

34. Guy Dutheil and Yves Mamou, "Canal Plus fusionne avec le groupe sud-africain NetHold: Ce mariage donne naissance au plus grand groupe européen de télévision à péage," *Le Monde*, September 9, 1996. The industry trade magazine *Stratégies* voted Lescure "man of the year" at the same time. At the time, NetHold was the third largest pay television company in Europe, behind Canal+ and Rupert Murdoch's BskyB. Guy Dutheil, "Difficile choix de décodeur pour TPS; CLT, TF 1 et France Télévision étalaient leurs dissensions sur le futur décodeur, tandis que Viacom et NetHold s'allient," *Le Monde*, April 18, 1996.

35. Lescure predicted early in 1998, wrongly, that Telepiu would turn the corner by the end of 1999. Guy Dutheil, "Les résultats de Canal Plus devraient progresser en 1999,"

Le Monde, March 24, 1998. A year earlier, *Le Monde* reported that Lescure had given himself two years to solve the Telepiu problem. Guy Dutheil and Martine Orange, "La Compagnie générale des eaux officialise l'absorption d'Havas: La fusion permet au groupe de Jean-Marie Messier d'intégrer tous les métiers de la communication," *Le Monde*, March 11, 1998.

36.   Financial analysts later criticized the deal, claiming that Canal+ paid €7.3 billion for a company worth only €4.7 billion. François Clairval, "Canal+: Avis de tempête," *Communication et langages* 115 (1998): 22–23.

37.   Bonnell, *Mon cinéma*, 280. Canal+ then occupied first place in pay television in Europe.

38.   For the problems with cable television development in France, see Hervé Michel and Anne-Laure Angoulvent, *Les télévisions en Europe* (Paris: Presses universitaires de France, 1992), 80–87.

39.   Like the remaining state channels, F2 and F3, the other large private stations, TF1 and M6, were free over-the-air channels.

40.   In 1993, Canal+ had 3.7 million subscribers; in 1994, that figure did not change, and the cancellation rate began to rise, as did the cost of attracting new customers. Lecasble, *Le Roman de Canal+*, 190.

41.   Guy Dutheil, "Pour abus de position dominante, Canal Plus est condamnée par le Conseil de la concurrence," *Le Monde*, December 30, 1998; Dutheil, "Nouvelle saisine du Conseil de la concurrence à l'encontre de Canal+ et des droits de diffusion de films," *Le Monde*, November 18, 2000.

42.   Messier recounted the long process of hiring a company to develop a new name, with Vivendi chosen from a list of two hundred other possibilities. Jean-Marie Messier, *J6M.COM: Faut-il avoir peur de la nouvelle économie?* (Paris: Hachette, 2000). In an incisively prescient analysis of Messier's talent for dissimulation, Nicole Vulser described his success in "anaesthetizing many stockholders, politicians, and even the Paris Court of Appeals with reassuring discourses on the strategy of Vivendi and Havas." Nicole Vulser, "Jean-Marie Messier, le pari de la communication," *Le Monde*, May 16, 1998. Shortly after Rousselet's resignation four years earlier, *Le Nouvel Observateur* had dubbed Messier "Rastignac aux mains propres," *Le Nouvel Observateur* 1567 (November 23–17, 1994).

43.   Laurent Creton, "Filière cinématographique, secteur télévisuel et industries de la communication: Les enjeux de la convergence," in *Le cinéma à l'épreuve du système télévisuel*, ed. Laurent Creton (Paris: CNRS, 2002), 37.

44.   That purchase followed Sony's takeover of Columbia in 1989, a period of accelerating consolidation in media industries, including the U.S. film industry. Thomas Schatz, "The Studio System and Conglomerate Hollywood," in *The Contemporary Hollywood Film Industry*, ed. Paul MacDonald and Janet Wasko, 13–42 (Malden, Mass.: Blackwell, 2008). Warner Bros. had bought Time to form Time Warner in 1989, the largest communications conglomerate in the world. Several years later, with the end of the Financial and Syndication rules in the United States, parent

companies holding the Hollywood majors began buying up television networks in a continuing return of vertical integration, forty-five years after the first Paramount consent decree in 1948. For a global account of the consolidation movement between 1980 and 2000, see Nathalie Coutinet, François Moreau, Stéphanie Peltier, "Les grands groupes des industries culturelles: Fusions, acquisitions, alliances: Les stratégies des années 1980–2000" (Paris: Département des études et de la prospective, Ministry of Culture, 2002).

45. The Dutch owner of Polygram, Philips, had decided to concentrate on equipment, giving up its content (music, cinema) businesses. Joëlle Farchy and Fabrice Rochlandet, "De Polygram à Vivendi Universal: L'impossible constitution d'une 'major européenne,' " in *Quelle diversité face à Hollywood, CinémAction*, Hors series, ed. Thomas Paris (Condé-sur-Noireau, France: Éditions Corlet, 2002), 100.

46. Telephony accounted for some fifty million of those subscribers; Canal+ had 14 million subscribers in Europe (in eleven countries). Regourd, *Droit de la communication audiovisuelle*, 307.

47. Interview with Denis Olivennes, "Un énarque culturellement compatible avec l'esprit Canal," *Film Français* 2832 (June 9, 2000): 14. In the words of an academic observer, "When Canal+ has a cold, all of French production coughs." Daniel Sauvaget, "Le couple cinéma-télévision face aux réglementations Law and Order," in *Le cinéma à l'épreuve du système télévisuel*, ed. Laurent Creton (Paris: CNRS, 2002), 116.

48. *Le Monde*, November 15, 2000.

49. *Le Monde*, November 16, 2000. According to one source, Rousselet reprimanded Lescure even more tartly in person: "I was Pétainist, but you are being Laval!" Buob and Mérigeau, *L'aventure vraie de Canal+*, 401. Rousselet was playing on the (perhaps illusory) distinction between Marshal Pétain and Pierre Laval during the German occupation of France. Pétain accepted the leadership of occupied (Vichy) France, but Laval applied German policies with such vigor that he was perceived as even more traitorous than Pétain. Paxton described Laval as "an ideal scapegoat . . . a symbol of evil incarnate," exaggerations of his true culpability. Robert O. Paxton, *Vichy France: Old Guard and New Order, 1940–1944* (New York: Columbia University Press, 2001), 24–25. In an article the next week, commenting on the relationship between Messier's ascent and Lescure's loss of independence, the journalists referred to them respectively as the suzerain and his vassal. Nathalie Bensahel and Isabelle Roberts, "Le suzérain et son vassal+," *Libération*, November 22, 2000. Lescure wrote an indignant letter in response to Françoise Giroud, claiming that Rousselet had actually said, "Don't worry about being Laval, I myself was Pétainist." *Le Nouvel Observateur*, January 25, 2001.

50. "Danger de mort," *Libération*, November 24, 2000. Signatories included Bertrand Tavernier, Josiane Belasko, Claude Lanzmann, and Cédric Klapisch. Representatives of official French film organizations raised similar questions. Ange-Dominique Bouzet, "Le scénario Canal+ inquiète le cinéma français," *Libération*, November 24, 2000.

51. "Le CSA agrée la fusion Canal+/vivendi/Universal: Communiqué du jeudi 30 novembre 2000" (Paris: CSA), http://www.csa.fr/Espace-Presse/Communiques-de-presse /Le-CSA-agree-la-fusion-Canal-Vivendi-Universal.

52. Diller had built a reputation as a shrewd and tough media businessman, earning the nickname "Killer Diller." In a replay of the NetHold acquisition, Messier paid $10.4 billion for USA Networks, which Seagram had sold to Diller only four years earlier for $4.1 billion.

53. One article listed statements in support of the cultural exception from French presidents, prime ministers, and ministers of culture. "De François Mitterrand à Jacques Chirac, la défense d'une cause," Le Monde, December 29, 2001. Nicole Vulser wrote an inventory of the reactions, counting 250 reports on radio and television. "La petite phrase sur la mort de l'exception culturelle française qui déclencha une tempête," Le Monde, February 8, 2002. President Chirac, though not naming Messier, characterized the idea of considering cultural works as ordinary merchandise as "a deep mental aberration." "Chirac défend la diversité culturelle et le petit commerce," Le Monde, January 12, 2002.

54. Samuel Blumenfeld and Guy Dutheil, "Canal+ veut réduire ses obligations envers le cinéma français," Le Monde, December 22, 2001; "Financement du cinéma— Lescure veut un débat," Libération, December 21, 2001.

55. Denis Olivennes, "La règle du jeu," Le Monde, January 12, 2002.

56. At the time of General Electric's later purchase of Vivendi's U.S. media holdings (Universal Studio, USA Network, etc.), Le Monde approved the deal in an editorial that described the Vivendi empire as having "no real industrial coherence." "Un échec français," Le Monde, September 4, 2003.

57. Isabelle Roberts, "Le CSA se débarrasse de la patate chaude Messier," Libération, January 9, 2002. A later Senate report traced the itinerary of the examination through the Council of State. M. Philippe Marini, "Section B: Le CSA et la crise de Vivendi Universal. Rapport Général no. 68, Annexe au procès verbal de la séance du 21 novembre 2002" (Paris: Senate), 45–54.

58. Nathalie Bensahel and Nicolas Cori, " 'Un vrai compte de fées': Vivendi Universal présente; Malgré 13,6 milliards d'euros de pertes, Jean-Marie Messier l'assure: son groupe 'va mieux que bien,' " Libération, March 6, 2002.

59. Écran Total 413 (April 10–16, 2002).

60. Frédéric Lemaître, "Messier La Buigne," Le Monde, July 3, 2002.

61. Orange and Johnson, Une faillite française, 271–316.

62. In a faux self-deprecating touch used for the title of his book, Messier used the sobriquet coined by Les Guignols, the irreverent satirists at Canal+: Jean-Marie Messier Moi-Même Maître du Monde (Jean-Marie Messier Myself Master of the World). Messier, J6M.COM.

63. For a fair and nuanced view of Messier's fall, see Emmanuel, Le maître des illusions, 284–312. In a 2009 interview, the eighty-seven-year-old André Rousselet presented his largely positive assessment of Canal+ since his resignation in 1994. "Canal peu banal," L'Express, November 5, 2009.

64. *Film Français*, March 14, 2003, reported that Canal+ had reduced its investments in French cinema from €153.11 million (122 films) in 2001 to €122.99 million (109 films) in 2001, and it invested in only 18 percent of French films in 2002, compared to 25 percent in 1999. Similar charges were leveled in *Cahiers du cinéma* 664 (January 2002) and *Libération*, October 24, 2003. A CNC "work group" found that Canal+ had failed to honor the terms of the diversity clause in 2001. "Rapport du groupe de travail sur le financement de la production cinématographique" (Paris: CNC, July 2002), 17.

6. *BILAN(S)*

1. There were significant adjustments, but primarily to conform to EU rules of nondiscrimination, such as the revision of the TWF directive (1992), leading to the reform of the *agrément* rules (1998). For the latter, see n48 below.

2. Beginning in 1986, the newly named Compte de soutien financier de l'industrie cinématographique et de l'industrie des programmes audiovisuels (COSIP) received contributions for both film and television.

3. The status of the taxes on television income varied. If the taxes went first to a special account before transfer to the Compte de soutien, they were known as *parafiscal*; if the taxes entered directly into general tax revenues and then to the Compte de soutien, they were called *fiscal*. Regional (EU) and international (GATT, WTO) trade agreements typically prohibit "state aid," so if the funds devoted to the film industry are set aside, rather than come out of general tax revenues, they may be less likely to be proscribed.

4. Jean-Paul Cluzel and Guillaume Cerutti, "Mission de réflexion et de propositions sur le cinéma français," Rapport no. 92-372 (Paris: Inspection générale des finances, December 3, 1992).

5. Régine Chaniac and Jean-Pierre Jézéquel, *Télévision et cinéma: Le désenchantement* (Paris: Nathan, 1998), 111–115.

6. Jean-François Court, "Le cinéma français face à son avenir: Rapport au ministre de la Culture et de la Communication" (Paris: La Documentation française, 1988), 41.

7. In 1981, theatrical receipts covered 85 percent of production costs. In 1991, that figure had plunged to 30 percent. Cluzel and Cerutti, "Mission de réflexion et de propositions sur le cinéma français," 17.

8. Ibid., 22.

9. Ibid., 23.

10. With the creation of COSIP in 1986, the Compte de soutien dispensed funds to both television and cinema, with about one-third to television and two-thirds to cinema. Cluzel proposed raising the percentage reserved for cinema.

11. The *aide automatique* is the global sum from the Compte de soutien pegged to box office receipts. If the tax on tickets is 11 percent, then producers receive a certain percentage of the money generated by the 11 percent of admissions. Because U.S.

films take such a large share of the theater admissions but do not have access to the *aide automatique* because they are not French productions, the percentage returned to French producers can exceed 100 percent, for receipts from U.S. films are effectively subsidizing French producers. The MPAA objected to this exclusion in the GATT negotiations for it violated national treatment (NT), which requires that nonnationals have access to the same benefits accorded to nationals following the principle of nondiscrimination.

12. In 1983, there were 269 distributors; in 1991, there were 164. These figures should be taken as indicative of a trend, rather than a precise count; Cluzel refers to "active distributors," for there are many distributors that do not necessarily release even one film per year.

13. Cluzel and Cerutti, "Mission de réflexion et de propositions sur le cinéma français," 28.

14. The report refers rarely to writers and directors, for they are not recipients for the most part of state aid. State aid for film projects is awarded to the producing company, not the director. A small fraction of the Compte de soutien is set aside for writers, even if reports regularly pay lip service to the importance of scripts for the quality of production. For example, in 1999, only 1.2 percent of film investment was devoted to development of screenplay. *Bilan 1999*, CNC info no. 276 (Paris: CNC, May 2000), 82.

15. Frodon wrote that the report "murmurs on every page that the real producer [of the majority of French films] is television." Jean-Michel Frodon, *L'âge moderne du cinéma français: De la Nouvelle Vague à nos jours* (Paris: Flammarion, 1995), 669.

16. Cluzel and Cerutti, "Mission de réflexion et de propositions sur le cinéma français," 37, 29–30.

17. Ibid., 51.

18. Specifically, the Bredin report recommended breaking up the agreement (GIE) between two large circuits, Pathé and Gaumont. Jean-Denis Bredin, "Rapport de la mission de réflexion et de propositions sur le cinéma" (Paris: Ministry of Culture, 1981).

19. Cluzel and Cerutti, "Mission de réflexion et de propositions sur le cinéma français," 54.

20. Ibid., 70–71. For discussion of the Besson strategy, see Laurent Creton, "Analyses et options stratégiques pour le cinéma européen," in *Cinéma européen et identités culturelles*, ed. Frédéric Sojcher (Brussels: Université de Bruxelles, 1996), 217.

21. David Cook, *Lost Illusions: American Cinema in the Shadow of Watergate and Vietnam, 1970–1980* (Berkeley: University of California Press, 2000), 350, 404.

22. By 1998, 15 percent of all theaters in Europe were multiplexes, ranging from 50 percent of theaters in Great Britain to only 3 percent in Italy.

23. There is no clear definition of a multiplex, in terms of the number of screens and number of seats. Francis Delon, "Les multiplexes: Rapport au ministre de la culture

et de la communication" (Paris: Ministry of Culture, January 2000), after acknowledging the looseness of the term, uses eight screens as the criterion, as do the annual CNC *Bilans*.

24. Even at that low point of slightly more than 4,200 screens, France still had more screens than any other country in Europe in 1994, including Germany, its closest competitor (3,763); Great Britain had 1,976 screens in 1994, down from more than 4,500 in the mid-1950s.

25. *Bilan 2001*, CNC info no. 283 (Paris: CNC, May 2002), 7.

26. Delon, "Les multiplexes," 8.

27. Ibid., "Lettre de mission."

28. Ibid., section 2.2.1.

29. "Regarding film equipment and not commercial equipment, a representative of spectators would be more likely to defend a perspective based on the construction of multiplexes, even if the procedure for designating one [spectator representative] remains to be specified." Ibid., section 2.2.2.5.4.

30. Ibid., "Lettre de mission."

31. Circulaire de la ministre de la culture du 4 décembre 1998, Annex 5, in Pieyre-Laurent Mailly, "Étude et conséquences de l'implantation des multiplexes en France" (DEA paper, Université de Paris I, Panthéon-Sorbonne, [2000]).

32. Jean-Michel Frodon, "L'observatoire du cinéma français révèle ses premières statistiques," *Le Monde*, May 27, 1996. See also Claude Forest, "Le jour de la dépendance: Exportation cinématographique américaine et positionnement des interventants français de la filière," in *Cinéma & (in)dépendance: Une économie politique*, Théorème no. 5, ed. Laurent Creton (Paris: Presses de la Sorbonne Nouvelle, 1998), 134.

33. For an incisive later analysis, see Graeme Hayes, "Multiplexes et résistance(s): À la recherche d'Utopia," in *Cinéma et engagement*, ed. Graeme Hayes and Martin O'Shaughnessy (Paris: L'Harmattan, 2005), 199–222.

34. The top ten distributors had a market share of 90 percent. Daniel Goudineau, "La distribution des films en salle: Rapport à Mme la ministre de la culture et de la communication" (Paris: Ministry of Culture, May 2000).

35. "It seems to me that the state has less legitimacy in controlling the tissue of companies than concerning itself with the cultural result of their activity." Ibid., 36. At the same time, "the emergence of distributors on a European scale is a goal to encourage" (37).

36. Jean-Pierre Leclerc, "Réflexions sur le dispositif français de soutien à la production cinématographique: Rapport établi à la demande du ministre de la culture et de la communication" (Paris: Ministry of Culture, 2003). Leclerc was well aware of the limited scope of his report, for he discussed it in his conclusion, calling the report "only interim or provisional" (119).

37. See chapter 7 for a discussion of the EC and state aid to cinema.

38. Regions are official geographical/administrative units in France, a bit like U.S. states. A reorganization in 2016 reduced the regions from twenty-two to thirteen.

The CNC has made matching funds available to regions to encourage their participation in film production, contributing one euro for every two euros a region raises.

39.   If television co-productions could receive *aide automatique* from the Compte de soutien based on theater receipts, like any other producer, television would be relieved of a part of its required investment percentage. Emmanuel Cocq estimated that television could reduce its contribution to the Compte de soutien by 7.6 percent through co-production. Cocq, "L'analyse économique de la politique cinématographique française" (Ph.d. thesis, Institut d'études politiques de Paris, 2000), 317, cited in Emmanuel Cocq, Alexis Dantec, and Florence Lévy-Hartmann, "Combien tu m'aimes? Pour une analyse économique de la politique cinématographique française," *Revue de l'OFCE* 97 (April 2006): 318.

40.   "Rapport du groupe de travail sur le financement de la production cinématographique" (Paris: CNC, July 2002).

41.   According to the report, Canal+ signed the agreement with BLIC, BLOC, and ARP. Ibid.

42.   French writers introduced the term *filière* (chain or thread) to refer to the industry as an interlocked system of participants, traditionally split among the categories of production, distribution, and exhibition. Laurent Creton, *Économie du cinéma: Perspectives stratégiques* (Paris: Nathan, 1997), 53–56.

43.   Leclerc recommended €7.5 million for the new threshold. In a 2000 report, Farchy and Kopp wrote that "under the influence of lobbying, the public powers opt often for a solution that is not a remedy of the cause [of the problem] but a re-equilibration of the system by another type of intervention. The intervention is done in the direction of increasing complexity designed to palliate the increasingly numerous problems found in the sector. Rarely have they returned to sources. The cinematic policy . . . then appears to be like a 'piling up' of measures, certain ones having the sole objective of attenuating the secondary effects of previous measures deemed harmful to certain parts of the profession." Joëlle Farchy and Pierre Kopp, "Le soutien public à l'industrie cinématographique et audiovisuelle" ([Paris]: [CNC], February 2000), CNC D 716, 46. Creton referred to this process as a "crushed pastry layering" of measures. Laurent Creton, "Retour sur les origines du système d'aide à la production cinématographique en France," *Quaderni* 54 (Spring 2004): 117.

44.   The details are somewhat more complicated, for the coefficient has often had a digressive scale, reducing the coefficient below one once total attendance passes a specified threshold. While the principle of automatic aid rewards box office success, greater digressivity attenuates the advantage of that success.

45.   Farchy and Kopp, "Le soutien public à l'industrie cinématographique et audiovisuelle," 23.

46.   In principle, a new funding source, TPS, competing with Canal+, would benefit filmmakers. But when TPS took Canal+ to court for unfair competition, 140 filmmakers signed a petition to Prime Minister Lionel Jospin in February 1999 in support of Canal+, which lost the case. See Guy Doutheil, "La deuxième fenêtre

de diffusion des films à la télévision divise le monde du cinéma," *Le Monde*, March 3, 1999. On another occasion, when the troubles of Canal+ began to surface in the press, Robert Guédigian, an independent filmmaker who had made a series of films that failed at the box office before his breakthrough with *Marius et Jeannette* (1997) wrote that "to support the system established by Canal+ is . . . a way of resisting [the threats posed by Vivendi Universal]," *Cahiers du cinéma* 553 (January 2001): 21.

47. Daniel Sauvaget has claimed that the reports commissioned by the Ministry of Finances are increasingly dissatisfied with the CNC reports and the studies conducted by parliamentary cultural commissions. Sauvaget, "Le modèle français de soutien au cinéma: Le désenchantement," *Quaderni* 54 (2004): 83.

48. The CNC commissioned René Bonnell (former head of cinema at Canal+) and Margaret Ménégoz (head of the CNC commission that approved films as French or European) to recommend changes to the rules for receiving the *agrément*, formerly an official recognition as a French film. Under the EU, member states had to apply national treatment to other member states, so France had opened its support system to EU members. Their report tried to take stock of the repercussions of those earlier adjustments and the complexity of the system that had developed over the fifty years since the installation of the first automatic aid. René Bonnell and Margaret Ménégoz, "Rapport de la commission de réforme de l'agrément" (Paris: CNC, November 1996). The CNC revised the *agrément* in 1998.

49. Jean Cluzel, "L'efficacité des aides publiques en faveur du cinéma français," Rapport no. 1107 (National Assembly) / Rapport no. 11 (Senate) (Paris: National Assembly and Senate, October 1998), 11.

50. Ibid., 14.

51. Ibid., 17. Supporters of the French system usually avoided the term "subsidy" in favor of "regulation," for "subsidy" risked being deemed state aid, which the EU treaties proscribed. Thus, Leclerc acknowledged that the low repayment rate (10 percent) of the avance sur recettes turned the avance "in a practical sense into a subsidy." Leclerc, "Réflexions sur le dispositif français de soutien à la production cinématographique," 50.

52. Cluzel, "L'efficacité des aides publiques," 17. While not directly relevant to the health of the film industry, the report also referred to the spiraling cost of part-time workers in the sector, known as *intermittents du spectacle*. Part-time cultural workers enjoyed disproportionately generous unemployment benefits, a situation that exploded in 2003 when the government appeared to support a reduction of those benefits. See Pierre-Michel Menger, *Les intermittents du spectacle: Sociologie du travail flexible*, 2nd ed. (Paris: Éditions de l'École des hautes études en sciences sociales, 2011). For a shorter account in English, see Jonathan Buchsbaum, "The Exceptional *Intermittents du spectacle*: Hyperflexibility as the Avant-Garde of Labor Security in France," in *The Routledge Companion to Labor and Media*, ed. Richard Maxwell (New York: Routledge, 2015).

53. Yves Gaillard and Paul Loridant, "Revoir la règle du jeu: Mieux évaluer l'efficacité des aides publiques au cinéma: Rapport d'information fait au nom de la Commission des finances, du contrôle budgétaire et des comptes économiques de la Nation sur les aides publiques au cinéma en France," Rapport d'information no. 276 (2002–2003) (Paris: Senate, May 2003).

54. Michel Fansten, "Le cinéma français face à l'évolution technologique et à la transformation des marchés" (Paris: Réalisations et recherches audiovisuelles, Senate, November 2002), 7, in Gaillard and Loridant, "Revoir la règle du jeu."

55. "Les modes de financement du film français sont-ils adaptés aux perspectives d'évolution de ses différents marchés?" ([Paris]: Départment d'études stratégiques sur l'audiovisuel et le cinéma [DESAC], January 2003). A year earlier, Cahiers du cinéma had used the same expression, detecting "a movement of tectonic plates— slow, hard to discern, but ineluctable." Elisabeth Lequeret, "Jusqu'ici tout va bien . . . ," Cahiers du cinéma 564 (January 2002): 11.

56. Because each approval applies for only a few years, much hand-wringing accompanies each scheduled renewal procedure (2004, 2007, 2009, 2013). In 2011, the European Film Agency Directors (EFAD) composed a statement, signed by twenty-eight directors, stating their frustration that the implementation "by analogy" to the original 2001 communication created "a growing juridical uncertainty for Member states and funding agencies." "European Film Agencies Directors Contribution to the Consultation of the European Commission on the Issues Paper 'Assessing State Aid for Films and Other Audiovisual Works' " (Brussels: EFAD, September 2011), http://www.efads .eu/wp-content/uploads/2015/02/EFADs-092011.pdf.

57. Gaillard and Loridant, "Revoir la règle du jeu," 32. Emphasis in original.

58. Thus, they note that Leclerc had recognized the problem but had recommended only including figures outside the industry in the professional commissions, and a more rapid turnover of the members of the commissions, which Gaillard and Loridant found inadequate. They proposed to pursue this question "by requesting that the Minister of Culture and Communication explore new methods of management, separating more clearly the responsibilities of the state from those of the actors of the filière." Ibid., 84.

59. French cinema confronting technological change and the transformation of markets.

60. Fansten, "Le cinéma français face à l'évolution technologique et à la transformation des marchés," 3, 9.

61. Others had cited the relevance of the theory of "Baumol's disease" in relation to cultural production. See, for example, Joëlle Farchy, Le cinéma déchaîné: Mutation d'une industrie (Paris: CNRS, 1992), 160–162. In his study of theater, Baumol had theorized that costs in theater production would rise disproportionately to other industries that could benefit from productivity gains, which resulted in reducing costs of production. Theater, and by extension other cultural industries, did not experience productivity gains, so their costs, largely attributed to salaries, would rise more rapidly. William G. Baumol and W. G. Bowen, Performing Arts: The Economic

Dilemma (Cambridge, Mass.: MIT Press, 1966). France was the host of an international conference organized around the analyses of Baumol and Bowen (William Baumol and Hilda Baumol presented the opening talk). The proceedings were published as *L'économie du spectacle vivant et l'audiovisuel* (Paris: Ministry of Culture, Service des études et recherches and Association pour le développement et la diffusion de l'économie de la culture; La Documentation française, 1985).

62. Fansten, "Le cinéma français face à l'évolution technologique et à la transformation des marchés," 50.

63. Others have pointed out that in fact cinema is different from "spectacle" arts with live audiences, for cinema has always benefited from technological innovation, which can reduce costs, whether in videotape/DVD sales or digital projection. Joëlle Farchy, *La fin de l'exception culturelle* (Paris: CNRS, 2002), 14.

64. A CNC report completed at the same time observed that "the regulations in no way oppose the concentration of activities and companies. Up to a point it could be said that they even facilitate it." "Groupe de travail sur le cinéma face à la concurrence" (Paris: CNC, January 2003), 23–25.

65. Consistently critical of the obstructiveness of the European Commission, at one point Fansten characterizes the absurdity of the EC's refusal to take into consideration the domination of U.S. film in the European market in its commitment to free trade in the following way: "The Commission takes the position of a referee who, at a boxing match between a super featherweight and a super heavyweight, judges that the fight is fair because the rules are the same for each." Fansten, "Le cinéma français face à l'évolution technologique et à la transformation des marchés," 43.

66. Jean Cluzel, *Propos impertinents sur le cinéma français* (Paris: Presses universitaires de France, 2003).

67. In his foreword, "Touche pas à mon cinéma," a sarcastic riff on SOS Racisme's slogan, "Touche pas à mon pôte" (Hands off my pal), Cluzel claims that he wants his book to play a "role like that of a François Furet in the construction of a lucid history and freed of its ideological *a prioris*." Ibid., 2. For a different take on Furet's project, in which Perry Anderson asserts, "No modern historian has been so intensely political," see "Dégringolade," *London Review of Books*, September 2, 2004. Not all of these complaints were new. For example, Serge Toubiana, responding to the first Lang plan in 1983, had warned against "an assisted cinema . . . permanently 'under transfusion.' " Toubiana, "Le cinéma en plan large," *Cahiers du cinéma* 344 (February 1983): 37.

68. "Cinéma français et État: Un modèle en question?," *Quaderni* 54 (2004).

69. Sauvaget, "Le modèle français de soutien au cinéma."

70. Creton, "Retour sur les origines du système d'aide"; Laurent Creton, *Économie du cinéma: Perspectives stratégiques*, 3rd ed. (Paris: Nathan, 2003); Joëlle Farchy, "L'exception culturelle, combat d'arrière garde?," *Quaderni* 54, no. 1 (2004): 67–79; and Farchy, *L'industrie du cinéma* (Paris: Presses universitaires de France, 2004).

71. Laurent Creton, "Filière cinématographique, secteur télévisuel et industries de la communication: Les enjeux de la convergence," in *Le cinéma à l'épreuve du système télévisuel*, ed. Creton (Paris: CNRS, 2002), 12.

72. In order to qualify for funds from the Compte de soutien, a film must be approved as a *film* by the CNC. As a rule, films made for television do not receive such approval (known as the *agrément*). Occasionally, films in this category can be released in theaters if the filmmakers return the television funds advanced from the television section of the Compte de soutien, making them eligible then for the *aide automatique*. Robert Guédigian's *Marius et Jeannette* is one successful example, a film made for television (Arte) that turned out to be a success in theaters (his first, after six failures), rewarding his gamble of returning the financing from Arte. Laurent Cantet's *Ressources humaines* (Arte) is another.

73. Creton "Filière cinématographique, secteur télévisuel et industries de la communication," 40–41.

74. On broadcast television, two-thirds of the films have already been shown previously. Claude Forest, "Fréquentation en salles et audience à la télévision," in Creton, *Le cinéma à l'épreuve du système televisual*, 181–182. See also Chaniac and Jézéquel, *Télévision et cinéma*, 103–108. Ten years earlier, Court had referred to the "desacralization of film by overexposure on television." Court, "Le cinéma français face à son avenir," 20.

75. Goudineau recommended limited film advertising on television, but "specific space could be reserved for [it] to show clearly that the cinema is not just a 'product' like any other." Goudineau "La distribution des films en salle," 52. For Benjamin's famous article, see Walter Benjamin, "The Work of Art in the Age of Mechanical Reproduction," in *Illuminations*, ed. Hannah Arendt (New York: Schocken, 1969), 217–252. One reason for the ban on film advertising on television is the negative impact it would have on film advertising in the press.

76. Laurent Creton, *Histoire économique du cinéma français: Production et financement, 1940-1959* (Paris: CNRS, 2004).

77. "The game is if not a zero sum, it is at least a sum growing only weakly." Gaillard and Loridant, "Revoir la règle du jeu," 48. The DESAC report, also from 2003, makes the same point. "Les modes de financement du film français," 41.

78. "The need to maintain cinema and audiovisual companies capable of facing the international competition is basically contradictory with the will to limit concentration." Farchy and Kopp, "Le soutien public à l'industrie cinématographique et audiovisuelle," 45.

79. "Situation économique du cinéma français," *Problèmes Politiques et Sociaux* 381 (February 1980): 5–43.

80. Pascal Mérigeau and Jacques Zimmer, "On ne tire pas sur une ambulance Cinéma TV," *La Revue du Cinéma, Image et Son* 331 (September 1978):77–82. Mérigeau published his own bill of critical charges in 2007, in a book similar in tone to Cluzel's screed: *Cinéma: Autopsie d'un meurtre* (Paris: Flammarion, 2007).

81. Pierre Billard, "1970–1980: Dix ans de cinéma français," *Le Film Français* 1791 (December 1, 1979), extracts reprinted in "La situation économique du cinéma français," *Problèmes Politiques et Sociaux* 381 (February 1980): 6.

82. "*Les raisins de la colère* (*The Grapes of Wrath*), released by the Association de défense du cinéma et de ses spectateurs," quoted in ibid., 5.

83. As Bredin wrote on the first page of his 1981 report, "We dream in France of building cinema empires, French majors whose prestigious films would go off seeking to win Oscars and spectators in the Tucson suburbs." Bredin, "Rapport de la mission de réflexion et de propositions sur le cinéma," 5.

84. Farchy, *Le cinéma déchaîné*, 190. Looking at the problem from another angle, Fansten sees the failure in 2001 of forty-two films with budgets less than €1 million, "representing less than 3.6 percent of film investment, [as] a completely reasonable percentage for research and development." Fansten, "Le cinéma français face à l'évolution technologique et à la transformation des marchés," 76. For a broad discussion of the question, see the report on the conference, "Trop de films? La diversité cinématographique en question: Actes de Colloque," Nineteenth Festival Prémiers Plans (Angers, January 26, 2007), http://www.gncr.fr/sites/default/files/actes_colloque_2007.pdf.

85. "They will swallow Messier after having destroyed the fragile tissue of French cinema," wrote Françoise Giroud in *Le Nouvel Observateur* 1887 (January 2001), cited in Jacques Buob and Pascal Mérigeau, *L'aventure vraie de Canal+* (Paris: Fayard, 2001), 431.

7. FROM CULTURAL EXCEPTION TO CULTURAL DIVERSITY

1. See Anna Herold, *European Film Policies in EU and International Law: Culture and Trade—Marriage or Misalliance?* (Groningen, Neth.: Europa Law Publishing, 2010), 13, 23–26.

2. The French single-price book case, discussed in chapter 2.

3. Article 107 (ex Article 87 TEC): Aids Granted by States. The original Treaty of Rome, approved in 1958, was revised and replaced by the Maastricht Treaty of 1992 (approved in 1993). References usually specify one version, with the relevant numbering in a previous one.

4. Article 167 (TFEU).

5. The criteria were listed in the Decision of the European Commission, N3/98, June 3, 1998, published in *Official Journal of the European Communities* C279/4, September 8, 1998; after similar reviews of aid systems in other countries (Denmark, Germany, Ireland, the Netherlands, and Sweden) between 1998 and 2000, the EC released the Communication from the Commission to the Council, the European Parliament, the Economic and Social Committee and the Committee of the

Regions on Certain Legal Aspects Relating to Cinematographic and Other Audio-visual Works. COM(2001) 534 final. The wording included in the text is taken from the more concise formulation found in the 2001 communication. Herold, *European Film Policies in EU and International Law*, 143. For a discussion of other cases, see Lucia Bellucci, "National Support for Film Production in the EU: An Analysis of the Commission Decision-Making Practice," *European Law Journal* 16, no. 2 (2010): 211–232.

6.   "The doctrine that no political issue should be decided at a level higher than is absolutely necessary." Philip Schlesinger, "From Cultural Defense to Political Culture: Media, Politics and Collective Identity in the European Union," *Media, Culture & Society* 19, no. 3 (1997): 383. For a more legalistic account of subsidiarity, see Serge Regourd, *Droit de la communication audiovisuelle* (Paris: Presses universitaires de France, 2001), 86. A lawyer who has worked for the European Commission has offered a definition based on his experience within the bureaucracy: "In fact, nobody can define subsidiarity a priori. It results from a political negotiation." Jacques Delmoly, "De MEDIA I à MEDIA II, ou Comment dynamiser le secteur audiovisuel européen," in *Cinéma européen et identitiés culturelles*, ed. Frédéric Sojcher (Brussels: Université de Bruxelles), 225.

7.   Anna Herold, "EU Film Policy: Between Art and Commerce," European Diversity and Autonomy Papers EDAP 3/2003 (Bozen, Italy: EURAC, 2003), 13. Herold adds that the European Parliament criticized this 2001 communication of the European Commission, inquiring "whether the Treaty, which puts forward a purely cultural solution, provides the flexibility which is necessary when dealing with the unavoidably dual nature (cultural and industrial) of this sector, even though this highly specific nature is the starting-point of this section. The communication shows that the Commission refuses to take the specific nature of the sector's industrial dimension into account. As for the revision announced for post–June 2004, the rules ought to be relaxed rather than strengthened, given that the European audiovisual industry is far from being internally competitive within the Union, or competing with the industries of third countries. To put things into perspective, American film has a market share of over 70% in the cinemas of our primary market, i.e. that of the European Union." See "Report on the Commission Communication on Certain Legal Aspects Relating to Cinematographic and Other Audiovisual Works," COM(2001) 534 – C5-0078/2002 – 2002/2035(COS) (Brussels: Committee on Culture, Youth, Education, the Media and Sport, European Parliament, June 5, 2002).

8.   Jean-Michel Frodon, *L'âge moderne du cinéma français: De la Nouvelle Vague à nos jours* (Paris: Flammarion, 1995), 660–661.

9.   For text of the decision, see Judgment of the Court of 11 July 1985, *Cinéthèque SA and others v Fédération nationale des cinémas français*, http://eur-lex.europa.eu /LexUriServ/LexUriServ.do?uri=CELEX:61984J0060:EN:NOT.

10.   Article 128 (Culture), Paragraph 4, Amsterdam Treaty of 1997.

11. As with most of the trade pacts, the U.S. press devoted little coverage to MAI, relative to the French press. For an account sympathetic to MAI opponents, see F. Depétris, *L'État et le cinéma en France: Le moment de l'exception culturelle* (Paris: L'Harmattan, 2008), 236–252. For an alternative view, see D. Henderson, *The MAI Affair* (Wellington: New Zealand Business Roundtable, 1999).

12. Jack Lang once again intervened publicly with an article whose title puns on the French acronym AMI for the MAI. "L'AMI, c'est l'ennemi" [The friend is the enemy], *Le Monde*, February 10, 1998. Lang concludes the article, "The MAI is the enemy. The enemy of diversity. The enemy of creation. The enemy of social justice."

13. Catherine Lalumière and Jean-Pierre Landau, "Rapport sur l'Accord multilatéral sur l'investissement (AMI)," Rapport intérimaire, annex to Rapport d'information no. 1150 (Paris: National Assembly, September 1998).

14. "A few European film directors . . . were able to provide the 'coup de grâce' to the . . . MAI." Patrick A. Messerlin and Emmanuel Cocq, "Preparing Negotiations in Services: EC Audiovisuals in the Doha Round," in *The Audiovisual Services Sector in the GATS Negotiations*, ed. Patrick A. Messerlin et al. (Paris: Groupe d'économie mondiale de Sciences Po; Washington, D.C.: AEI Press, 2004), 50.

15. The "positive list" procedure required countries that wished to include parts of their audiovisual industries in the GATS rules to submit declarations to that effect, an option not available under GATT. For a discussion of the procedure and a list of the countries and their commitments, see C. B. Graber, "Audio-visual Policy: The Stumbling Block of Trade Liberalisation?," in *The WTO and the Global Convergence in Telecommunications and Audio-visual Services*, ed. D. Geradin and D. Luff (New York: Cambridge University Press, 2004), 173–176. Full commitments were accepted by only Albania, the Central African Republic, and the United States. Michael Hahn, "A Clash of Cultures? The UNESCO Diversity Convention and International Trade Law," *Journal of International Economic Law* 9, no. 3 (2006): 526.

16. The GATS schedules limited exemptions to ten years, but the French submitted claims for an indefinite amount of time. Voon points to possible ambiguity in the language of GATS, but as with much of her scrupulous textual analysis of the legal terrain, political factors may be more pertinent. Tania Voon, *Cultural Products and the World Trade Organization* (New York: Cambridge University Press, 2007), 116.

17. GATT clause 301 permitted such retaliation through a complaint procedure to establish the damages, precisely the instrument threatened by U.S. trade representative Carla Hills in her letter to the EEC during the debate over the TWF directive (see chapter 3).

18. Manjunath Pendakur, *Canadian Dreams and American Control: The Political Economy of the Canadian Film Industry* (Detroit: Wayne State University Press, 1990), 266.

19. Canada had not invited the United States because the latter had no minister of culture, though the United States was allowed to send observers from its embassy in

Ottawa. Anthony DePalma, "19 Nations See U.S. as Threat to Cultures," *New York Times*, July 1, 1998.

20. *Final Report of the International Meeting on Cultural Policy, Ottawa, Canada: Putting Culture on the World Stage*, June 29 and 30, 1998 (Ottawa: International Relations Directorate, Dept. of Canadian Heritage, 1999), 23–24.

21. Serge Regourd, *L'exception culturelle* (Paris: Presses universitaires de France, 2002), 96–97.

22. Joëlle Farchy and Heritiana Ranaivoson, "La diversité culturelle, soubassements économiques et volonté politique," *Hermès* 40 (November 2004): 36.

23. Hahn, "A Clash of Cultures?," 534.

24. "Déclaration et Plan d'Action," IIIe conférence ministérielle de la Francophonie sur la culture, Cotonou, Benin, June 14–15 (Paris: Agence intergouvernementale de la Francophonie, 2001); Christine Rousseau, "Faire du concept de diversité culturelle une politique: Les ministres francophones de la culture adoptent un plan d'action décennal," *Le Monde*, June 19, 2001.

25. Claire Tréan, "Jacques Chirac décrit les axes de résistance de la France contre un monde unipolaire: Le président de la République a reçu tous les ambassadeurs de France," *Le Monde*, August 28, 1999.

26. "Referring very clearly to the battle for the cultural exception that it is important to defend in the coming WTO negotiations, [Chirac] added: 'The cultural responsibility of the government goes further. As you know, France is leading the battle not just for a cultural exception but also for cultural diversity in the world. It is why we refuse to consider the cultural product, whatever it may be, as a simple piece of merchandise obeying only the law of the market. It is thus legitimate, in my view, that in the audiovisual domain, the rules [should] favor the national production and distribution, and that the public aids be given, nationally and in Europe, to support the export of programs to foreign markets. It is an issue of cultural outreach, but also, of course, a major economic issue.'" *Le Figaro*, October 12, 1999.

27. Catherine Trautmann, "Sur le mandat donné à la Commission européenne pour préserver l'exception culturelle," press conference, November 10, 1999, http://www.culture.gouv.fr/culture/actualites/politique/diversite/point-omc.htm. An abridged version in English can be found in Jeremy Ahearne, ed., *French Cultural Policy and Debates: A Reader* (London: Routledge, 2002), 206–210.

28. C. Edwin Baker, "An Economic Critique of Free Trade in Media Products," *North Carolina Law Review* 78 (June 2000): 1360–1435.

29. Baker takes the distinction between weak and strong protectionism from Oliver R. Goodenough, "Defending the Imaginary to the Death? Free Trade, National Identity, and Canada's Cultural Preoccupation," *Arizona Journal of International and Comparative Law* 15 (Winter 1998): 203–253.

30. Baker was not alone in using the strengthening of democracy as a criterion in the discussion of cultural diversity. Bernier made a similar argument in 1994: "In reality, the only real reason to justify the insertion of a cultural exception clause is the fact

that . . . the audiovisual industries constitute an absolutely essential element of the democratic process at the heart of every State, and even at the heart of a region moving toward integration like Europe." Ivan Bernier, "Commerce international et cultures nationales: Le débat sur la clause d'exception culturelle dans les négotiations de l'Uruguay Round," in *Industries culturelles nationales et mondialisation des marchés: Actes du colloque, Montréal, October 21–23, 1993*, ed. Mario Beaulac and François Colbert (Montréal: École des hautes études commerciales de Montréal, 1993) 72–74.

31. In the words of Jack Valenti, "The audience is king. . . . Let the market forces collide and something better will come out of it." *The Times* (London), May 3, 1993, cited in Lisa Garrett, "Commerce Versus Culture: The Battle Between the United States and the European Union Over Audiovisual Trade Practices," *North Carolina Journal of International Law and Commercial Regulation* 19 (1994): n73.

32. Baker, "An Economic Critique of Free Trade in Media Products," 1387.

33. Ibid. Curiously, while Baker identifies "people's welfare and preference satisfaction" as the "normative goals of economics," he does not revert to the earlier term used to refer once to those goals: "political economy." Janet Wasko, one of the few contemporary media scholars committed to the practice of political economy describes "moral philosophy" as "the distinguishing characteristic of political economy." She defines that characteristic as "not only analysis of the economic system but also discussion of the policy problems and moral issues that arise from it." Wasko, "Critiquing Hollywood: The Political Economy of Motion Pictures," in *A Concise Handbook of Movie Industry Economics*, ed. Charles Moul (Cambridge: Cambridge University Press, 2005), 8.

34. Baker, "An Economic Critique of Free Trade in Media Products," 1366.

35. Ibid., 1431.

36. Peter S. Grant and Chris Wood, *Blockbusters and Trade Wars: Popular Culture in a Globalized World* (Vancouver: Douglas and McIntyre, 2004), 382.

37. According to one Canadian source, France parted ways with Canada ("a subtle divergence") in pushing for an alternative instrument through UNESCO. Gilbert Gagné, René Côté, and Christian Deblock, "Les récents accords de libre-échange conclus par les États-Unis: Une menace à la diversité culturelle" (Montréal: Institut d'études internationales de Montréal, June 18, 2004), 21–22.

38. The headline quotes Jean Musitelli, a former ambassador to UNESCO and one of the authors of the convention. Nicole Vulser, "Diversité culturelle: Un manifeste pour une autre mondialisation," *Le Monde*, October 21, 2005.

39. "The rapidity with which the Convention obtained the required number of ratifications and entered into force in 2007 tends to underline the demand for such a measure." Susan Newman-Baudais, "Public Funding for Film and Audiovisual Work in Europe" (Strasbourg: European Audiovisual Observatory, 2011), 139. According to *Le Monde*, October 21, 2005, Mauritania called the convention "a veritable antidote to globalization." Passage of the convention gives a definitive response to the

claim by two scholars in 2000 that "it is doubtful whether any other countries, aside from Canada and France, support the idea of a specific international instrument on cultural diversity." Mary E. Footer and Christoph Beat Graber, "Trade Liberalization and Cultural Policy," *Journal of International Economic Law* 3, no. 1 (2000): 142.

40. Jean-Michel Frodon criticized the state's failure to convince its European partners to adopt the cultural exception, viewing cultural diversity as an additional weakening of the French position. "Le cinéma en péril," *Le Monde*, December 30, 2000. Similarly, Joëlle Farchy wrote, "Contrary to the 'exception,' negotiated in the context of an international treaty in 1993, [cultural diversity] is not the product of any serious political engagement and it is doubtless for this reason that it has received unanimous approbation." Farchy, "L'exception culturelle, combat d'arrière-garde?," *Quaderni* 4 (Spring 2004): 75.

41. Roland Blum, "Sur les forces et les faiblesses du cinéma français sur le marché international," Rapport d'information no. 3197 (Paris: National Assembly, June 26, 2001), 35–38. In another National Assembly report, Deputy Marcel Rogement wrote that "this notion of 'cultural exception,' viewed as too defensive . . . has been replaced by the more positive 'cultural diversity.' " Marcel Rogemont, "Le cinéma," Rapport d'information no. 3642 (Paris: National Assembly, February 20, 2002), 69–70.

42. Farchy, "L'exception culturelle, combat d'arrière-garde?," 67–79.

43. Jean-Marie Messier, "Vivre la diversité culturelle," *Le Monde*, April 10, 2001, cited in Farchy, "L'exception culturelle, combat d'arrière-garde?," 71.

44. Laurent Creton called this global strategy "glocalisation." Creton, "Filiére cinématographique, secteur télévisuel et industries de la communication: Les enjeux de la convergence," in *Le cinéma à l'épreuve du système télévisuel*, ed. Creton (Paris: CNRS, 2002), 25.

45. Farchy recognized the potential "dangerous distortions" of a narrow focus on national identity when she referred to Jean-Marie Le Pen's support for the cultural exception. "Exception culturelle, identité et mondialisation," *Le Monde*, May 28, 2007.

46. Serge Regourd, "Exception, diversité . . . des instruments de politique culturelle en quête de leur objet: Contribution à un examen critique," *La Pensée* 349 (2007): 57.

47. "Conceptually, this proposed shift of paradigm to be specifically applied to cultural industries would allow clearer identification and assessment of abuses of a dominant position based on culturally discriminatory business practices." Christophe Germann, "Towards a Global 'Cultural Contract' to Counter Trade-Related Cultural Discrimination," in *UNESCO's Convention on the Protection and Promotion of the Diversity of Cultural Expression*, ed. Nina Obuljen and Joost Smiers (Zagreb: Institute for International Relations, 2006), 335. For a more detailed discussion, see Christophe Germann, *Diversité culturelle et libre-échange à la lumière du cinéma: Réflexions critiques sur le droit naissant de la diversité culturelle sous les*

angles du droit de l'UNESCO and de l'OMC, de la concurrence et de la propriété intellectuelle (Paris: LGDJ; Basel: Helbing Lichtenhahn; Brussels: Bruylant, 2008).

48.   Ivan Bernier discusses new bilateral agreements in "The Recent Free Trade Agreements of the United States as Illustration of Their New Strategy Regarding the Audiovisual Sector" (Montréal: Centre études internationales et mondialisation, Institut d'études internationales de Montréal, Université de Québec à Montréal, June 18, 2004). See also Gagné, Côté, and Deblock, "Les récents accords de libre-échange conclus par les États-Unis."

49.   These increases are according to the "2005 National Trade Estimate Report on Foreign Trade Barriers" (Washington, D.C.: Office of the U.S. Trade Representative, 2005), 380, cited in Hahn, "A Clash of Cultures?," 523. For an account of this history, see Jung-Woo Lee, "Analyse comparée des politiques cinématographiques françaises et coréennes: Étude de la formation de la cristallisation de l'exception en France et en Corée" (doctoral thesis, Institut d'études politiques de Paris, March 2003).

50.   *Focus: World Film Market Trends* (Strasbourg: European Audiovisual Observatory, 2005–2009).

51.   Germann, "Towards a Global 'Cultural Contract' to Counter Trade-Related Cultural Discrimination," 297–300.

52.   *Bilan 2011*, CNC info no. 322 (Paris: CNC, May 2012), 184. It is difficult to find relevant figures from other countries.

53.   *Yearbook* (Strasbourg: European Audiovisual Observatory, 2012).

54.   Anne Jäckel, "European Co-production Strategies: The Case of France and Britain," in *Film Policy: International, National and Regional Perspectives*, ed. Albert Moran, *Film Policy* (London: Routledge, 1996); Anne Jäckel, "The Inter/Nationalism of French Film Policy," *Modern Contemporary France* 15, no. 1 (2007): 21–36. On transnational cinema, see introduction, n14.

55.   Clint N. Smith, "International Trade in Television Programming and GATT: An Analysis of Why the European Community's Local Program Requirement Violates the General Agreement on Tariffs and Trade," *International Tax & Business Law* 10 (1993); Garrett, "Commerce Versus Culture"; John David Donaldson, " 'Television Without Frontiers': The Continuing Tension Between Liberal Free Trade and European Cultural Integrity," *Fordham International Law Journal* 90 (November 1996); Suzanne Schwartz, "Television Without Frontiers?," *North Carolina Journal of International Law and Commercial Regulation* 16, no. 2 (1991). Some downplay the effects of the domination: "Policy responses constrained by cognitive bias . . . constitute an overestimation of the American popular culture's threat to cultural identity, and represent a subjective reliance on intuition rather than hard data." Frederick Scott Galt, "The Life, Death, and Rebirth of the 'Cultural Exception' in the Multilateral Trading System: An Evolutionary Analysis of Cultural Protection and Intervention in the Face of American Pop Culture's Hegemony," *Washington University Global Studies Law Review* 909 (2004): 5. While hard data may be

interpreted in different ways, the "hard data" clearly document the domination of U.S. cinema internationally. For a more balanced account, see W. Ming Shao, "Is There No Business Like Show Business? Free Trade and Cultural Protectionism," *Yale Journal of International Law* 20 (1995): 105–150.

56. "Out of respect for the principle of state sovereignty, the use of verbs such as 'must,' 'shall' and 'undertake' with States as subjects, and of expressions implying the obligation to perform specified actions (such as 'States Parties are under the obligation [or have a duty] to . . .' was questioned." "Meetings of Experts (Category VI) on the First Draft of an International Convention on the Protection of the Diversity of Cultural Contents and Artistic Expressions: Report of Second Meeting (30 March–4 April 2004)," 8, cited in Germann, *Diversité culturelle et libre-échange à la lumière du cinéma*, 358.

57. Germann, *Diversité culturelle et libre-échange à la lumière du cinéma*, 360.

58. Germann explicitly articulates this analogy: "In the area of human rights, equal treatment of men and women or black and white people relies on the assumption that men and women or black and white people are 'like' human beings. From the perspective of the rule of law, when using the principle of equality, this analogy makes sense if one considers that gender, race, and culture have in common the challenge of assimilating diversity without causing uniformity. The prohibition of discrimination therefore imposes a similar approach on the normative level between different individuals, communities, and cultures to enable their factual diversity to flourish." Ibid., 27. Others have also proposed moving beyond diversity of supply to "diversity consumed." Emmanuel Cocq, Alexis Dantec, Florence Lévy-Hartmann, "Combien tu m'aimes?: Pour une analyse économique de la politique cinématographique française," *Revue de l'OFCE* 97 (2006): 322.

59. Germann, "Towards a Global 'Cultural Contract' to Counter Trade-Related Cultural Discrimination," 18.

60. Pierre Bourdieu, *La domination masculine* (Paris: Le Seuil, 1998), 69, cited in Germann, *Diversité culturelle et libre-échange à la lumière du cinéma*, 299.

61. Germann, "Towards a Global 'Cultural Contract' to Counter Trade-Related Cultural Discrimination," 11.

62. Herold, *European Film Policies in EU and International Law*, 303 n162; Martin Roy, "Audiovisual Services in the Doha Round: 'Dialogue de Sourds, The Sequel'?," *Journal of World Investment & Trade* 6, no. 6 (2005): 927; Voon, *Cultural Products and the World Trade Organization*, 225–227.

63. "In our view, the concept of the 'cultural exception,' that is, the choice to remove cultural policies completely from the rules of international trade law and thus to legitimize 'cultural nationalism' would have the harmful consequence of excluding the countries and cultures economically weaker from the appreciation of cultural diversity." Germann, *Diversité culturelle et libre-échange à la lumière du cinéma*, 367.

64. Farchy and Ranaivoson, "La diversité culturelle, soubassements économiques et volonté politique," 37.

65. "UNESCO traps itself in not committing to multilateralism as it 'nationalizes' cultural diversity in restricting the relevant competence to States." Germann, *Diversité culturelle et libre-échange à la lumière du cinéma*, 372.

66. For legal EU discussion of relevant market and concentration, see "Commission Notice on the Definition of Relevant Market for the Purposes of Community Competition Law," *Official Journal of the European Communities* C 372/5, December 9, 1997, cited in Herold, *European Film Policies in EU and International Law*, 188.

67. "American films benefit from massive distribution from the first week while French films must prove their success in order to receive better exposure." Daniel Goudineau, "La distribution des films en salle: Rapport à Mme la ministre de la culture et de la communication" (Paris: Ministry of Culture and Communication, May 2000), 11.

68. Arthur De Vany, *Hollywood Economics: How Extreme Uncertainty Shapes the Film Industry* (New York: Routledge, 2004), 122–125.

69. "At some point in the run, private information will take over and break the uninformative cascade and then audiences will choose on the basis of quality rather than quantity signals." Ibid., 124.

70. Germann calls the three prior markets "initial" markets to distinguish them from the secondary markets in which all buyers have box office performance data, which eliminates the information deficit of the initial markets. Thus, all films offered in the secondary markets will then be like products, for their relative values can be known from their performance in theaters, and prices will then vary accordingly. In the initial markets, before reaching theaters, value cannot be estimated with any confidence. Germann, *Diversité culturelle et libre-échange à la lumière du cinéma*, 404–408.

71. Cited by Germann, "Diversité culturelle et cinéma: une vision pour un pays en voie de développement," in *Free Trade vs. Cultural Diversity: WTO Negotiations in the Field of Audiovisual Services*, ed. Christoph Beat Graber, Michael Girsberger, and Mira Nenova (Zurich: Schulthess, 2004), 105–106. The author of one of the definitive texts on the U.S. entertainment industry used this exact analogy: "Ownership of entertainment distribution capability is like ownership of a toll road or bridge. No matter how good or bad the software product (i.e., movie, record, book, magazine, TV show, or whatever) is, it must pass over or cross through a distribution pipeline in order to reach the consumer. And like at any toll road or bridge that cannot be circumvented, the distributor is a local monopolist who can extract a relatively high fee for use of his facility." Harold Vogel, *Entertainment Industry Economics: A Guide for Financial Analysis*, 2nd ed. (Cambridge: Cambridge University Press, 1990), 110, cited in Tino Balio, "Adjusting to the New Global Economy: Hollywood in the 1990s," in Moran, *Film Policy*, 27.

72. Germann, *Diversité culturelle et libre-échange à la lumière du cinéma*, 385.

73. From the decision: "Accordingly, the Arbitrator found that Ecuador may request authorization by the DSB [Dispute Settlement Body] to suspend concessions or

other obligations under GATT 1994 (not including investment goods or primary goods used as inputs in manufacturing and processing industries); under GATS with respect to 'wholesale trade services' (CPC 622) in the principal distribution services; and, to the extent that suspension requested under GATT 1994 and GATS was insufficient to reach the level of nullification and impairment determined by the Arbitrator, under TRIPS in the following sectors of that Agreement: Section 1 (copyright and related rights); Article 14 (on protection of performers, producers of phonograms and broadcasting organisations), Section 3 (geographical indications), Section 4 (industrial designs)." "Dispute Settlement: Dispute DS27 European Communities—Regime for the Importation, Sale and Distribution of Bananas," settled November 8, 2012, http://www.wto.org/english/tratop_e/dispu_e/cases_e/ds27_e.htm.

74. Germann, *Diversité culturelle et libre-échange à la lumière du cinéma*, 386.

75. Ibid., 387.

76. See Michael Conant, *Antitrust in the Motion Picture Industry: Economic and Legal Analysis* (Berkeley: University of California Press, 1960).

77. Germann, "Diversité culturelle et cinéma," 103.

78. Ibid., 426, 388.

79. In the revised second edition (1997) of his standard text on GATT, Jackson wrote that it was possible that "the United States has gradually moved away from its earlier adamant support for MFN and multilateralism toward a more 'pragmatic'— some might say 'ad hoc' approach—of dealing with trading partners on a bilateral basis and 'rewarding friends.' " John H. Jackson, *The World Trading System: Law and Policy of International Economic Relations* (Cambridge, Mass.: MIT Press, 1997), 173.

8. WAS THE EXPERIENCE BENEFICIAL?

1. Quoted in Benoît Delmas, "Cinéma français: La fin d'une epoch," *Le Nouvel Économiste*, May 23, 2003.

2. Aurélien Ferenczi, "Pourquoi le cinéma ne s'est jamais aussi bien porté," *Télérama*, January 14, 2009. The headline refers to the upbeat discourse of the sociologist Gilles Lipovetsky waxing enthusiastic over a "new cinephile public": The erosion of former distinctions between great filmmakers and directors of bombs "gives me great hope! The cinema has become more complex, with what I call the multiplex narrative, which privileges disorder and chaos, the discontinuous and the fragmentary."

3. Jean-Michel Frodon, *Le cinéma sans la télévision* (Paris: Gallimard, 2004).

4. Jean-Michel Frodon, "Crises et mutations," *Cahiers du cinéma* 608 (January 2006): 11. Frodon introduced this description by asking, "What pornographic urge drives this time the film industry? This urge is called the industry of TV programs."

5. Pascale Ferran, "Violence économique et cinéma français: Le discours de la réalisatrice de 'Lady Chatterley,' César du meilleur film français," *Le Monde*, February 27, 2007.

6. "Diversité du cinéma," *Le Monde*, February 27, 2007.

7. Released April 1, 2008, the document was subsequently published as a book: Club des 13, *Le milieu n'est plus un pont, mais une faille* (Paris: Stock, 2008).

8. The one less familiar topic is the long opening discussion encouraging a greater appreciation of the work of the screenwriter, "to better valorize the contributions of the screenwriters, an old story for us."

9. Anne Perrot and Jean-Pierre Leclerc, "Cinéma et concurrence: Rapport remis à Mme Christine Lagarde, ministre de l'économie, de l'industrie et de l'emploi et Mme Christine Albanel, ministre de la culture et de la communication," March 2008, http://www.culture.gouv.fr/culture/actualites/dossiers/Rapport%20 cin%E9%20concurrence/Rapportcin%E9maconcurrence.pdf. A CNC report from 2002 had warned that "the category of middle-budget films risks over time suffering . . . from underfinancing" as low- and high-budget films threatened to drain financial resources formerly reserved for these films. "Rapport du groupe de travail sur le financement de la production cinématographique" (Paris: CNC, July 2002), 17.

10. Because the fidelity cards were purchased to cover an unlimited number of films, the "actual" ticket price would vary with the spectator. To address the question of rights, a "reference price" was set to determine rights payments.

11. The *producteur délégué* is like a hybrid of line producer and executive producer in the U.S. system.

12. On regional support, see chapter 6, n38.

13. As noted in the introduction, Tyler Cowen, *Creative Destruction* (Princeton, N.J.: Princeton University Press, 2002), hedged his equation of more expensive films with higher quality films with the escape clause that he meant only that more expensive films attracted more spectators. David Waterman, hewing more scrupulously to his quantitative commitments, performed a similar dance: "In economic terms, then, a studio's or an individual producer's decision to make a greater negative-cost -investment means higher product 'quality'—a term we use in this book to indicate production values and audience attractiveness, *not* aesthetic quality." Waterman, *Hollywood's Road to Riches* (Cambridge, Mass.: Harvard University Press, 2005), 12 (emphasis in original). Thus, two scholars are tempted to judge quality by size—of box office and/or budget—even as they acknowledge that such a criterion sidesteps the aesthetic dimension, the question of whether the films are any good.

14. Frodon called it "the visual." Jean-Michel Frodon, *L'âge moderne du cinéma français: De la Nouvelle Vague à nos jours* (Paris: Flammarion, 1995), 700–701. For Susan Hayward, "All is style, be it retro-nostalgic or hi-tech." Hayward, *French National Cinema*, rev. ed. (London: Routledge, 2005), 284. Powrie and Reader called it the "cinéma du look." Phil Powrie and Keith Reader, *French Cinema: A Student's Guide*

(London: Arnold, 2002), 41. René Prédal judged it "all for the image." Prédal, *50 ans de cinéma français (1945–1995)* (Paris: Nathan, 1996), 547.

15. The reputation of the New Wave, since its astonishing early success, rested on the shoulders of only a few directors; of the 150 films made by new filmmakers in the first years of the 1960s, most of directors' names dropped out of sight.

16. Michel Marie, *Le jeune cinéma français* (Paris: Nathan, 1998), 4; René Prédal, *Le jeune cinéma français* (Paris: Nathan, 2002), 3. Though less insistent on aesthetic quality, Claude-Marie Trémois (who declares openly that she is "a child of the New Wave and has never completely recovered") has praised "the young French cinema" for its inclusion of political engagement with aesthetic commitments. Trémois, *Les enfants de la liberté* (Paris: Éditions du Seuil, 1997), 11. For an excellent discussion of the politics of this cinema, see Martin O'Shaughnessy, *The New Face of Political Cinema: Commitment in French Film Since 1995* (New York: Berghahn, 2007).

17. Prédal, *Le jeune cinéma français*, 4.

18. Robert Wangermée and Bernard Gournay, *La politique culturelle de la France: Programme européen d'évaluation* (Paris: La Documentation française, 1988), 5.

19. Bernard Gournay, "Rapport national," in ibid., 326.

20. Of course the exercise began with the identification of "quality" directors by the CNC in the first place, so the objective assessment was based on the CNC's subjective choice of "good" directors (not identified).

21. Jean-François Court, "Le cinéma français face à son avénir: Rapport au ministre de la culture et de la communication" (Paris: La Documentation française, 1988). The Balladur government had enlarged the scope of the Ministry of Culture to encompass the growing television sector, hence the change of name of the ministry. An unsigned introductory note concludes with the observation that the report "tries, as Robert Le Vigan says to Jean Gabin in the unforgettable *Quai des brumes* of Marcel Carné 'to see the things behind the things,' confident of the quality and future of French cinema" (13).

22. Ibid., 44.

23. Court added, "And Jean-Luc Godard alone cannot be the French cinema." Ibid., 28. The genuflection before festival prizes belonged to a long tradition within the French Ministry of Culture. André Malraux cited international prizes won by French films in his appearance at the National Assembly on November 5, 1960. Jean-Marie Charuau, "'Je t'aime, moi non plus': Une histoire d'avance" (unpublished paper, 1991), CNC D 288. For the year 1960, Malraux noted the Oscar for *Black Orpheus*, the top prize at Venice for *Le passage du Rhin*, Jeanne Moreau's award for Best Actress (in *Moderato Cantabile*) at Cannes, and the Golden Bear at Berlin for *Les jeux de l'amour* (*The Lovers*). "Présentation du budget des affaires culturelles" (Paris: National Assembly, November 5, 1960), http://www.assemblee -nationale.fr/histoire/andre-malraux/discours/malraux_5nov1960.asp.

24. The discussion in the text is based on Emmanuel Cocq, Alexis Dantec, and Florence Lévy-Hartmann, "Combien tu m'aimes? Pour une analyse économique

de la politique cinématographique française," *Revue de l'OFCE* 97 (April 2006): 273–328, 307–313. See also Patrick A. Messerlin and Emmanuel Cocq, "Preparing Negotiations in the Services: EC Audiovisuals in the Millennium Round," in *The Audiovisual Services Sector in the GATS Negotiations*, ed. Messerlin, Stephen E. Siwek, and Cocq (Washington, D.C.: AEI Press; Paris: Groupe d'économie mondiale de Sciences Po, 2004), and Messerlin, "Regulating Culture: Has It 'Gone with the Wind'?," in *Achieving Better Regulation of Services: Conference Proceedings, Australian National University, Canberra, 26–27 June 2000* (Melbourne: Productivity Commission, 2000).

25. In his short study of the New Wave, Michel Marie suggests that the relative absence of "authentic new auteurs" can be explained by the fact "that the filmmakers of the New Wave of 1958 are still as productive and often as inventive as when they started." Marie, *La Nouvelle Vague: Une école artistique* (Paris: Nathan, 1997), 113–114.

26. Digressive scales returned in 2001 and were revised in 2005. Cocq, Dantec, and Lévy-Hartmann, "Combien tu m'aimes?," 322.

27. Françoise Benhamou, Olivier Gergaud, and Nathalie Moureau, "Le financement du cinéma par la télévision: Une analyse économétrique des investissements des chaines," *Économie & prévision* 188 (2009): 107, 109–110.

28. "50 ans d'amour du cinéma" (Paris: AFCAE, 2006), 9.

29. According to Billard, art theaters over time replaced the ciné clubs. Pierre Billard, *L'âge classique du cinéma français: Du cinéma parlant à la Nouvelle Vague* (Paris: Flammarion, 1995), 658. The AFCAE began with five theaters in Paris: Cinéma des Agriculteurs, Cardinet, Studio de l'Étoile, Studio Parnasse, and Studio des Ursulines. Paul Léglise, *Le cinéma d'art et d'essai*, Notes et études documentaires 4551–4552 (January 10, 1980): 18. For a more recent account, with fresh documentation, see Aurélie Pinto, "L'Art et essai ou la politique de la qualité dans les salles de cinéma (1949-1961)," in *Le cinéma: Une affaire d'État*, ed. Dimitri Vezyroglou (Paris: La Documentation française, 2014).

30. More precisely, the four categories refer to the size of the population agglomerations where the theaters are situated, with lower minimum requirements of art et essai percentages required the smaller the population. See appendix E for a more thorough description. The number of categories has varied over the years, but the principle has not changed.

31. While the number of art cinemas (screens) doubled from 1970 to 1978 (from 328 to 663), the number of seats increased by only 17 percent, reflecting the reduced capacity of the art cinema circuit. Léglise, "Le cinéma d'art et d'essai," 64. To get a sense of the strength of art cinemas at the end of the 1970s, Léglise noted that nineteen of Paris's twenty arrondissements (not the Tenth, Strasbourg/Saint-Denis) in Paris had at least one art cinema, and in five arrondissements, art cinemas were more numerous than other cinemas. In 2010, six arrondissements (First, Second, Twelfth, Fifteenth, Sixteenth, Twentieth) had no art cinemas; the two arondissements of

the Latin Quarter (Fifth, Sixth) contained half of the art cinemas in Paris, only slightly higher than the percentage in 1979. "Géographie du cinéma," Dossier no. 320 (Paris: CNC, 2011), 16.

32.   The Delon report listed the following characteristics of multiplexes: big reception area; stadium seating; air conditioning; comfort; large screens (more than ten meters); high-quality projection; parking if not located in center of city; candy concession stands; possible restaurant; video games; possible child care. Francis Delon, "Les multiplexes: Rapport au ministre de la culture et de la communication" (Paris: Ministry of Culture and Communication, January 2000), 4.

33.   Delon looked briefly at three sites to examine how the arrival of a multiplex affected attendance. He found that the multiplex had not harmed the art cinema attendance, but the single sample was hardly conclusive. Ibid., section 2.1.2.3.1.

34.   "Les missions de l'ADRC," http://www.adrc-asso.org/missions_et_services/missions.php.

35.   Jean-Michel Gévaudan, "Parc de salles et diffusion des films: Évolutions 2003" (Paris: ADRC, 2004), http://www.adrc-asso.org/pdf/salle_de_cinema/Etude_evolutions_2003.pdf. An earlier report from another organization found that the construction of two multiplexes in Tours had significantly depressed the attendance at both the art cinema and the generalist cinemas, though the global attendance for the town had risen steadily. "La diffusion cinématographique en région Centre" (Orléans: DRAC Centre et le Conseil régional du Centre, December, 2001), 50.

36.   "Les salles art et essai," "Le public du cinéma art et essai," "L'exploitation des films recommandés art et essai en salles, à la télévision, en vidéo," and "Perceptions du public des cinémas art et essai" (Paris: CNC, October 2006).

37.   Jean-Pierre Leclerc, "Mission de médiation et d'expertise relative aux conditions actuelles des sorties de films en salles" (Paris: CNC, May 2006).

38.   For discussion of the problems with the designation "independent" in French cinema, see Cinéma & (in)dépendance: Une économie politique, Théorème no. 5, ed. Laurent Creton (Paris: Presses de la Sorbonne Nouvelle, 1998).

39.   Ludovic Lamant, "L'art & essai de Straub à Shrek," Cahiers du cinéma 607 (December 2005): 74.

40.   Serge Toubiana, "Mission de réflexion sur l'art et essai: Nouveaux horizons," January 1990, CNC D 2433, 56.

41.   Le Monde, March 4, 2004. More than two hundred filmmakers signed the statement, including Chantal Akerman, Ali Akika, Mathieu Amalric, Dominique Cabrera, Léos Carax, Laurent Cantet, Alain Guiraudie, Cédric Klapisch, Rithy Panh, Nicolas Philibert, and Bertrand Tavernier.

42.   Responding to criticism of their earlier demand for a minimum of two weeks for the exhibition of less commercial films, they proposed instead "limiting the authorized number of copies, not at the national level—which would penalize the rural or isolated theaters—but by swath of population." "Diffusion des film indépendants en salles: Document du groupe de travail SRF/ACID" (Paris: ACID, September 2005), n.p.

43. "Rapport d'activité" (Paris: ADRC, 2003), 50.

44. "Douze objectifs pour le cinéma en France," *Cahiers du cinéma* 622 (April 2007): 10–13.

45. "Only the CNC can counterbalance, through regulation and an appropriate support policy for theaters, the often devastating effects of the market." "Diffusion des films indépendants en salles," n.p.

46. In his characterization of *(télé)spectators* in 1997, who can now watch films at any hour of the day, Forest called them "devourers of film." Claude Forest, *Les dernières séances* (Paris: CNRS, 1995), 286–287. In an article on festivals, A. Ferenczi distinguished between earlier "univorous" cinephiles and modern omnivore cinephiles. Ferenczi, "Pas de crise pour le ciné," *Télérama*, January 1, 2009.

47. Benoît Delmas, "Les mégaplexes, à la croisée de l'urbanisme et des loisirs," *Le Nouvel Économiste*, March 5, 2004.

48. "The big theaters chains turn spectators not into cinephiles but into cinephages," according to Xavier Blom, a Paris film programmer. Quoted in Marion Truchaud, "L'exploitation 'art et essai' aujourd'hui: Quels enjeux et quelles politiques" (master's thesis, Université de Paris I, Panthéon-Sorbonne, 2005), 105.

49. Frodon, *Le cinéma sans la television*, 208.

50. Antoine de Baecque, *La cinéphilie: Invention d'un regard, histoire d'une culture, 1944–1968* (Paris: Fayard, 2003), 364. Already in 1999 Claude Forest saw during the 1990s "a regression of one fraction of the [cinema] milieu toward a celebration of the 'old' cinema, a coagulation around a nostalgic vision of cinema, a necrophilia." Forest, *Dernières séances*, 260. There is a growing literature on cinephilia, as digital technology is quickly replacing celluloid even in theaters. See, for example, two dossiers on cinephilia: *Framework* 50 no. 1–2 (Spring/Fall 2009): 176–228, and *Cinema Journal* 49, no. 2 (Winter 2010): 130–166. See also Christian Keathley, *Cinephilia and History; or, The Wind in the Trees* (Bloomington: Indiana University Press, 2006); *Movie Mutations: The Changing Face of World Cinephilia*, ed. Jonathan Rosenbaum and Adrian Martin (London: BFI, 2003); and *Cinephilia: Movies, Love, and Memory*, ed. Marijke de Valck and Malte Hegener (Amsterdam: Amsterdam University Press, 2005). By 2013, the percentage of digital screens in theaters had reached 97 percent. *Bilan 2013*, CNC info no. 330 (Paris: CNC, May 2014), 128.

51. According to Joëlle Farchy, "the theater is indispensable not because it guarantees receipts . . . but because it remains the site of valorisation of the film." Farchy, *Le cinéma déchaîné: Mutation d'une industrie* (Paris: CNRS, 1992), 320.

52. One study indicated that of four thousand films available on video in 2000, 37 percent were French and 47 percent from the United States; but the U.S. films took more than 70 percent of the market, and French films only 20 percent. "Rapport du groupe de travail sur le financement de la production cinématographique" (Paris: CNC, July 2002), 21.

53. "L'exploitation des films recommandés art et essai en salles, à la télévision, en vidéo," 51.

54. Ibid., 15.

55. Of course the art film label does not exist in the United States, even if reviewers may often use the term, a term of art as it were. But the CNC applies the label to both domestic and foreign films shown in France, which is why the CNC can track the theatrical performance of all art films in the markets of theater, television, and DVD/video. The CNC idea of a U.S. "art film" would stupefy North American moviegoers. Three of the top ten art films in terms of attendance between 2000 and 2005 were U.S. films: *Shrek*, *Million Dollar Baby*, and *American Beauty*. The practice of labeling caused yet another controversy in France, when one writer noted that showing the multimillion dollar *Shrek* would earn the same amount of CNC support as the screening of a Straub film. Didier Péron, "À la rescousse de l'art et essai français," *Libération*, September 14, 2005. See also Lamant, "L'art & essai de Straub à *Shrek*."

56. "L'exploitation des films recommandés art et essai en salles, à la télévision, en video," 15.

57. U.S. art films earn more of their theatrical receipts in the first five weeks of exhibition than French films. Ibid., 57.

58. Farchy, *Le cinéma déchaîné*, 50–52. The Gournay report in 1988 indicated that 11,000 cine-clubs, with one million members, received financial support from the Ministry of Culture. Gournay, "Rapport national," 347.

59. "Évolution du public des salles de cinéma, 1993–2011" (Paris: CNC, July 2012).

60. "Le public du cinéma art et essai."

61. Susan Hayward, *French National Cinema*, 1st ed. (New York: Routledge, 1993), 48, The 2005 second edition retains the same claim. Farchy offers a more nuanced analysis of viewers based on various studies from the 1980s. Farchy, *Le cinéma déchaîné*, 144–147.

62. "Le public des cinémas Art et essai," 25.

63. Since then, average attendance in France has almost doubled. Are the French now cinephiles? Perhaps with the explosion of alternate viewing sites, the statistic has lost its illustrative relevance, but it also demonstrates the hazards of assessing national characteristics. A recent comparison between cultural practices in the United States and France showed that for the decade between 1997 and 2008, the number of spectators attending the cinema once a year has risen in France and declined in the United States. Angèle Christin and Olivier Donnat, "Pratiques culturelles en France et aux États-Unis: Éléments de comparaison, 1981–2008," Étude no. 2014-1 (Paris: Ministry of Culture and Communication, March 2014), 6.

64. "The French cinephilic tradition, culturally distinguished by a quasi-ontological separation between cinematic works and telefilms, explains, in part, the permanence of a formal distinction between their respective juridic regimes while in material terms they are identical." Serge Regourd, *Droit de la communication audiovisuelle* (Paris: Presses universitaires de France, 2001), 253. Laurent Creton described a "symbolic hierarchisation: for cinema, art, aura, nobility; for television, the profane, even the vulgar." Creton, *Cinéma à l'épreuve du système télévisuel* (Paris: CNRS, 2002), 19.

65. "2 ans de politique culturelle 81–83" (Paris: Ministry of Culture, 1983). See also "La politique culturelle 1981–1985, Bilan de la législature: Le cinéma et l'audiovisuel" (Paris: Ministry of Culture, 1986), 14. The idea did not originate entirely under Lang. The Luneau report several years earlier had proposed that the "initiation to the riches of French cinema should have a more important place in school curricula, next to theater and literature." Maurice Luneau, "Les perspectives des industries françaises du cinéma" (Paris: Conseil économique et social, May 23, 1979), 77. There are similar glancing references to cinema in school in the Council of Europe study from 1978. Joop Voogd, "Le cinéma et l'État: Rapport de la commission de la culture et de l'éducation" (Strasbourg: Council of Europe, 1979), xxix, 106.

66. Francis Mayor, "Allumez vos caméras" (editorial), *Télérama*, February 10, 1982, cited in Francis Desbarats, "Les sections cinéma en lycée, signes de tendances nouvelles dans le système éducatif," *Images Documentaires* 39 (2000): 68, 70. In the context of ciné clubs, Philip Watts described André Bazin's reservations many years earlier about imposing interpretations on viewers: "the deft teacher should give the public the feeling of 'critical freedom,' that is, the freedom to judge the film." Watts, "The Eloquent Image: The Postwar Mission of Film and Criticism," in *Opening Bazin: Postwar Film Theory and Its Afterlife*, ed. Dudley Andrew (New York: Oxford University Press, 2011), 220.

67. The bac is the rigorous exit exam for French high schools; every year newspapers print the names of all students who passed the bac. The first cinema bac, requiring an oral and written exam, on the topic "telephone," called for writing an outline for a short film, an explanation of its goals, and a detailed shot breakdown (*découpage*) of one sequence. Desbarats, "Les sections cinéma en lycée," 74 . The films included in the curriculum were *M*, *La règle du jeu*, and *Citizen Kane*. Pierre Forni, "Historique des dispositifs nationaux d'éducation au cinéma," in "Géographie de l'éducation au cinéma. 20 ans d'action culturelle cinématographique, 1989–2009" (Paris: CNC, 2009), 7.

68. Francis Desbarats, "Les sections cinéma en lycée," 73.

69. In a brochure from the Minister of Culture in 1985/1986, one short section referred to a special budget item devoted to arranging screenings in theaters for schoolchildren. "La politique culturelle 1981–1985," 13. See also "Plan d'action en faveur du cinéma: Conférence de presse de Jack Lang, Ministre de la culture, de la communication, des grands travaux et du bicentaire" (press conference), February 7, 1989."

70. "Plan d'action en faveur du cinéma," 8.1. Even before the programs began officially, Court had insisted, "For the film to be fully film, it must be seen in the dark theater, in the act of maieutics which provides its true essence." Court, "Le cinéma français face à son avenir," 61. In his contribution to "Cinéma et école," a special issue of *Images Documentaires* in 2000, Jean-Pierre Daniel wrote that "we attach great importance to the discovery by the children of film in a 'real cinema theater.' " Daniel, "Éloge du partenariat entre création artistique et enseignement," *Images Documentaires* 39 (2000): 18.

71.   For example, in 2004, the average ticket price for France was €5.84; students paid €2.30, a subsidy of 61 percent. "Cahier des charges du dispositif Collège au cinéma" (Paris: Ministry of Culture and Communication and Minister of National Education, 2004), 6.

72.   Fédération nationale des cinémas français. The organizers of the program emphasized, in an editorial of an annual evaluation, that "First and foremost, 'École et cinéma' is not a support mechanism for the theater sector." Eugène Andréanszky, "L'édito du délégué général: L'enfant doit rester au coeur du projet!," in "Évaluation nationale d'École et cinéma: Année scolaire 2005/2006" (Paris: Les enfants de cinéma, April 2007), 7.

73.   In his 2008 report, Auclaire wrote that the number of spectators for the three education programs was roughly equivalent to the attendance at cine-clubs thirty years earlier. Alain Auclaire, "Par ailleurs le cinéma est un divertissement . . . Propositions pour le soutien à l'action culturelle dans le domaine du cinéma: Rapport à Madame Christine Albanel, Ministre de la culture et de la communication" (Paris: Ministry of Culture, November 2008), 18.

74.   One of the early catalogues of the middle-school program stresses the importance of discovering pleasure at the cinema, "a moment of shared dream with others, toward other horizons and other cultures." "Catalogue, Collège au cinéma, 1992–1993" (Paris: CNC, 1992), 7. The more formal "Cahiers des charges du dispositif Collège au cinéma" (Paris: CNC, 2004) lists among the criteria for the choice of films "an openness to other cultures" (4).

75.   Sara Chatel, "Dictionnaire de l'enseignement du cinéma," *Cahiers du cinéma* 591 (June 2004): 46.

76.   One early protocol for the programs overtly made the connection with the cultural exception: "All these artistic domains . . . make part of the heritage to transmit to future generations if we wish to safeguard one's own cultural identity, at a moment when the phenomena of globalization are accelerating." "Signature du protocole d'accord relatif à l'éducation artistique" Paris: Palais de l'Institut de France, November 17, 1993).

77.   *Le Monde*, May 11, 2000, cited in Daniel, "Éloge du partenariat entre création artistique et enseignement," 9. For discussion, see Maryvonne de Saint Pulgent, "Mondialisation et politiques publiques: Le cas de la culture en France," in *Mondialisation et diversité culturelle: Le cas de la France*, ed. Maryvonne de Saint Pulgent, Pierre-Jean Benghozi, and Thomas Paris, Notes de l'IFRI 51 (Paris: Institut français des relations internationales, 2003): 15–54. Jospin made his remarks, "Le cinéma à venir," at the closing ceremony at Cannes, May 10, 2000; available at http://discours .vie-publique.fr/notices/003001179.html.

78.   Alain Bergala, *L'hypothèse cinéma: Petit traité de transmission du cinéma à l'école et ailleurs* (Paris: Cahiers du cinéma, 2002).

79.   Catherine Blangonnet cites Philippe Meirieu's warning about the danger of "sterile scholasticism." Blangonnet, introduction to "Cinéma et école," special issue,

Images Documentaires 39 (2000): 10. "School risked alienating for life the students of cinema just as it has turned off generations of students of French literature." Charles Tesson, "La fin de la méfiance," *Cahiers du cinéma* 552 (December 2000): 17. In his 2008 report, Auclaire also warned of the risk of a new "academicism," though he was referring to choosing films considered esoteric by the teachers. Auclaire, "Par ailleurs le cinéma est un divertissement," 61.

80. "Éducation et cinéma," in *9èmes Rencontres cinématographiques de Beaune: 21/24 Octobre 1999* (Paris: ARP, 2000), 66.

81. "A whole culture of distrust and defiance toward the image is used to inoculate students with anti-toxin needed 'to learn to read images' (horrible expression)." Charles Tesson, "La fin de la méfiance," *Cahiers du cinéma* 573 (December 2000): 17.

82. Eugène Andréansky, "Évaluation des 10 ans d'École et cinéma, 1994/1995–2004/2005" (Paris: SCÉRÈN-CNDP, April 2006), 28.

83. *Moonfleet* receives barely a passing mention in Tom Gunning's *The Films of Fritz Lang: Allegories of Vision and Modernity* (London: BFI, 2008).

84. Serge Daney, *L'exercise a été profitable, Monsieur* (Paris: POL, 1993). The first credit sequence for the Midnight Cinema (Cinéma de minuit) program on the France 3 television station in 1976 included a still from *Moonfleet* (see http://www.dailymotion.com/video/x1547s_cinema-de-minuit-premier-generique_shortfilms#.UdXRDOv1v9g). U.S. writer and cinephile extraordinaire Jonathan Rosenbaum has commented on the obscurity of this title, even for U.S. cinephiles: "I can't begin to imagine how one could translate the title of *L'exercise a été profitable, Monsieur* into a context that would make much sense to American cinephiles except as an exotic emblem of French cinephilia. Even starting with the English line spoken in the Lang film by Stewart Granger—'The exercise was beneficial'—would get one nowhere." Rosenbaum, "Daney in English: A Letter to *Trafic*," http://www.jonathanrosenbaum.net/2001/04/daney-in-english-a-letter-to-trafic-tk/, originally published in French in *Trafic* 37 (Spring 2001).

85. "This film spoke to them better than any other of their relation to the world." Bergala, *L'hypothèse cinéma*, 55.

86. While the film had passed through the normal approval procedure, some teachers objected to its violence. Perrine Boutin, "Le 7e art aux regards de l'enfance: Les médiations dans les dispositifs d'éducation à l'image cinématographique" (doctoral thesis, Université d'Avignon et des pays de Vaucluse, 2010), 215–219.

87. Andréansky, "Évaluation des 10 ans d'École et cinéma," 29.

88. Many of these *dossiers pédagogiques* are available at the CNC website.

89. One of the first animators of the education initiative cited Godard's observation that "Video cassette provides a reproduction of the film, and not the film itself." Ginette Dislaire, "Quelques extraits des rapports demandés par le CNC à Ginette Dislaire chargée de Mission," June 18–19, 1996, CNC D 1068, 11.

90. A still of the actress Harriet Andersson appeared on the cover of *Cahiers du cinéma* 85 (July 1958), and it is that same still that Antoine Doinel steals in *The 400 Blows*.

"This image, once understood, is the virtual matrix of the New Wave: the body, nature, provocation, youth." Antoine de Baecque, *La Nouvelle Vague: Portrait d'une jeunesse* (Paris: Flamarion, 2009), 26–30.

91. Laurent Jullier and Jean-Marc Leveratto, *Cinéphiles et cinéphilies* (Paris: Armand Colin, 2010), 215–216. The authors take a critical view of the continuing influence of *Cahiers du cinéma*, which they view as an elitist journal that has always championed its own alterity, as the anecdote in the text illustrates. Former *Cahiers* editor Antoine de Baecque's claim in his 2003 book that cinephilia died in 1968 embalms that *Cahiers* cinephilia, insulating it, as it were, against later, more populist critics like Jullier and Leveratto.

92. In his history of *Cahiers du cinéma*, de Baecque wrote that there was a "political line (an auteur is someone one must love)." De Baecque, *Cahiers du cinéma: Histoire d'une revue* (Paris: Cahiers du cinéma, 1991), 1:148.

93. Sontag seemed to worry more about the end of cinephilia than that of cinema itself: "Perhaps it is not cinema that has ended but only cinephilia—the name of the very specific kind of love that cinema inspired." Susan Sontag, "The Decay of Cinema," *New York Times*, February 25, 1996.

94. Jullier and Leveratto, *Cinéphiles et cinéphilies*, 157–160.

95. For Bergala, the goal of the project is the same as that of "the republican school which guarantees equality of access to culture." Jean-Sebastien Chavin, "Éducation: Jack Lang prépare l'entrée du cinéma à l'école primaire," *Cahiers du cinéma* 552 (December 2000): 15.

96. The 2005–2006 evaluation of École et cinéma insists that the program "is not a support program for theaters." Andréansky, "Évaluation nationale d'École et cinéma, 2005/2006," 7. Then, again, the report did note that the program "generates more than a million spectators for the cinema industry" (16). More than twenty years ago, Joëlle Farchy supported the pursuit of both goals: "We have to build demand, not just for a leisure activity but for a cultural habit. Government action then takes on new meaning without harming the necessary economic transformation of the sector." Farchy, *Le cinéma déchaîné*, 328. Sensitive to the industry argument, Farchy also wrote that the goal is "not to support an industry, but to promote the taste for cinema in the population (especially sensitizing the young public)" (221).

97. "Signature du Protocole d'Accord relatif à l'éducation artistique," 6.

98. Andréansky, "Évaluation nationale d'École et cinéma, 2005/2006," 8. Bergala, who has written a book on Godard, has cited yet another Godard formulation: "There is the rule, and there is the exception. There is culture, which is the rule, and there is the exception, which is art." Bergala, *L'hypothèse cinéma*, 20.

99. Manon Oostveen, "Politique de l'UE," in "L'avenir des aides d'État," IRIS plus 2012-3 (Strasbourg: European Audiovisual Observatory, April 2012), 28.

100. The Fonds ECO (1989–1996) invested heavily in Eastern European countries after the breakup of the Soviet Union (10 million francs annually, contributing

to a total of sixty-five feature films), and the Fonds Sud (1984) supported hundreds of filmmakers from seventy countries before being folded into the new Aide aux cinémas du monde in 2011. Laurent Creton and Anne Jäckel, "A Certain Idea of the Film Industry," in *The French Cinema Book*, ed. Michael Temple and Michael Witt (London: BFI, 2004), 215. See appendix G for a partial list of filmmakers and countries aided by the Fonds Sud and the Aide aux cinémas du monde.

101. One French scholar, Françoise Benhamou, frustrated at what she viewed as the excessive annual production of French cinema, said that the only solution was to increase the number of weeks in the year. Benhamou in "Trop de films? La diversité cinématographique en question: Actes de Colloque" (Nineteenth Festival Prémiers Plans, Angers, January 26, 2007), 18, http://www.gncr.fr/sites/default/files/actes _colloque_2007.pdf.

102. Olivier Séguret, "Obésité ordinaire," *Libération*, January 25, 2006.

103. Nicole Vulser, "L'inflation des films provoque un embouteillage en salles," *Le Monde*, April 13, 2005.

CONCLUSION

1. Alain Auclaire, "Par ailleurs le cinéma est un divertissement . . . Propositions pour le soutien à l'action culturelle dans le domaine du cinéma: Rapport à Madame Christine Albanel, Ministre de la culture et de la communication" (Paris: Ministry of Culture, November 2008).

2. Daniel Psenny, "L'art de la dialectique," *Le Monde*, January 22, 2009.

3. According to a friend of his, Alain Minc, Karmitz "believes that the whole world is against him . . . He needs to see himself as a victim. It's his fuel." Étienne Garnelle, "Karmitz, l'emmerdeur," *Le Point*, September 6, 2007.

4. Jean-Denis Bredin, "Rapport de la mission de réflexion et de propositions sur le cinéma" (Paris: Ministry of Culture, 1981), 68.

5. "Déclaration de Jack Lang, Ministre de la Culture, sur la mise en oeuvre de la nouvelle politique du cinéma," 1983, CNC D 1141. According to one later source, the Ministry of Culture provided help for 150 municipalities to finance the purchase of the theaters. The same source lists the options available for municipalities interested in saving their theaters. *Journal des Maires*, February 1999.

6. One document from 1993 lists 832 municipal theaters. André Bourdale-Dufau, "Les salles de cinéma" (Paris: Inspecteur général de l'administration, 1993), CNC D 248, 8. A decree of April 14, 1989, allowing grants to towns to buy their last theater resulted in saving 255 theaters in 159 cities. Sylvie Petras, "Logique économique des aides à l'exploitation cinématographique: Une mise en perspective historique, 1946–1993" (master's thesis, Université de Paris I, September 1993), CNC D 2949, 49. A Ministry of Culture and Francophonie document from 1993

asserted that 18.9 percent of all screens were owned or run by municipalities. Christian Pattyn (Chef du service de l'Inspection générale de l'administration), "Note," 1993, CNC D 248, 3. Daniel Sauvaget made the same claim ten years later in "Le modèle français de soutien au cinéma: Le désenchantement," *Quaderni* 54 (2004): 91.

7. René Bonnell used this formulation in *Le cinéma exploité* (Paris: Éditions du Seuil, 1978), 242.

8. For Anne-Marie Faucon, a founder of Utopia, "Utopia is the choice between the large groups and the municipal theater, very aided [by the state], which opened its new site with *Pirates of the Caribbean*!" *Télérama*, October 31, 2007.

9. The November 2007 monthly programming brochure published by MK2 included the following description of the circuit: "For thirty years we have been precursors in various domains: implanting theaters in neighborhoods [arrondissements] abandoned by cinema, neighborhood work in the neighborhoods, subtitled films, screenings of unknown directors, cycles for children."

10. One study measured the percentage of art films shown by Parisian theaters MK2 Hautefeuille (98 percent) and MK2 Bibliothèque (54 percent). Sandrine Cerda, "Le cinéma d'auteur dans les multiplexes: Un exemple d'ouverture dans la médiation des produits culturels" (master's thesis, 2004), 64, cited in Marion Truchaud, "L'exploitation 'art et essai' aujourd'hui: Quels enjeux et quelles politiques?" (master's thesis, Université de Paris I, Panthéon-Sorbonne, 2005), 63.

11. Interview with UGC head Guy Verrecchia, *Le Film Français*, November 16, 2007.

12. "Les cartes d'abonnement illimité au cinéma" (Paris: CNC, December 2001); "Les cartes d'abonnement illimité au cinéma: Évaluation de l'impact financier des dispositions de mise en oeuvre du décret 'cartes' " (Paris: CNC, December 2002).

13. According to Karmitz, the landlord, as part of the construction of a mall, wanted to raise the rent for a new MK2 theater (after the razing of the current MK2 theater) from €180,000 per month to €1.2 million per month. Karmitz offered 800,000 but the proprietor signed with another company (Pathé). Karmitz went to court to contest the proprietor's decision, winning a judgment of €7.4 million as compensation. A spokesperson for the mayor of Paris expressed surprise at the complaints of Karmitz, as Karmitz had already received €1.5 million in subsidies from Paris for two multiplexes, La Bibliothèque and the Quai de Loire. Jean-Luc Douin, "Marin Karmitz polémique avec la Mairie de Paris sur l'aide au cinéma," *Le Monde*, March 13, 2007; Paule Gonzales, "Marin Karmitz négocie ses emplacements," *Figaro*, October 17, 2007; Karmitz opened the theater at Beaugrenelle in 1982.

14. Nicole Vulser, "UGC et MK2 lancent leur carte commune d'abonnement illimité," *Le Monde*, September 6, 2007.

15. Frank Dupoux, "UGC multiplie les recours," *Écran Total*, September 12, 2007.

16. Nicole Vulser, "UGC en conflit avec des cinémas municipaux: Pour le groupe, il y a concurrence déloyale," *Le Monde*, September 19, 2007.

17. George Méliès built his famous all-glass studio in Montreuil in 1897. It featured prominently in Martin Scorsese's homage to Méliès, *Hugo* (2011).

18. Antoine de Baecque, "Le Méliès renait multiplexe," *Libération*, June 8, 2005.

19. Vulser, "UGC en conflit avec des cinéma municipaux." It's possible that UGC and MK2 were influenced by the mediator's recommendation earlier in the year that the Cinémathèque Française *raise* its prices following a complaint by Parisian art cinemas that the state-owned Cinemathèque was engaging in unfair competition. Nicole Vulser. "Les difficultés croissantes des salles d'art et d'essai," *Le Monde*, January 11, 2007. See also "Rapport annuel: Août 2005–juillet 2006" (Paris: Médiateur du cinéma, 2006), http://www.lemediateurducinema.fr/Mediateur/Includes /Pdf/rapport_2005_2006.pdf, for discussion of the decision.

20. Verrecchia wondered whether this situation of subsidizing some theaters but not private ones would lead to "a sort of Goskino à la française." Nicole Vulser, "Les cinémas municipaux agacent de plus en plus les circuits privés," *Le Monde*, November 22, 2007.

21. UGC's legal complaint stipulated that "the utilization of public money using subsidized prices . . . constitutes on the part of the commune an abuse of dominant position and violations of the rules of competition." Didier Péron, "UGC, un appétit décomplexé," *Libération*, September 25, 2007.

22. The petition can be found in *Libération*, September 27, 2007, and *Cahiers du cinéma* 628 (November 2007).

23. Juliette Bénabent, "Les dents du maire: La politique incisive de l'élu de Montreuil face à MK2 et UGC," *Télérama*, February 2, 2008. The title of the article puns on the French title of *Jaws*, *Les dents du mer*. A flash in *Libération* reported that Montreuil had released a statement downplaying the carnage, and that the editor of *Le Film Français* in an editorial had "flown to the aid of the weak and the oppressed in protesting against all this 'violence.'" Dider Péron, "SOS requins," *Libération*, February 2, 2008.

24. Benoît Delmas, "Art et essai en VO," *Le Nouvel Économiste*, November 24, 2005.

25. "Je ne suis pas un raquin," *Paris Obs*, February 7–13, 2008.

26. Goudet noted that "when Karmitz linked this parody to his own Jewishness to suggest that it is anti-Semitic, I find that absolutely scandalous." "En attendant Dominique Voynet," *Paris Obs*, March 27, 2008. In his autobiography, Karmitz related that he never heard the expression "dirty Jew" until he moved to France. Karmitz, *Marin Karmitz: Profession producteur* (Paris: Hachette, 2003), 25.

27. Interview with Guy Verrecchia, *Le Film Français*, November 16, 2007.

28. Juliette Bénabent. "Bataille entre le cinéma Méliès et UGC: On a les vrais chiffres!" *Télérama*, February 13, 2008. According to one newspaper article, both sides were right in their fashion, but each used a different metric. The Méliès for example, counted total numbers of screenings of all films over the course of the year while UGC looked only at screenings of the same films in both theaters. Frank Dupoux, "MK2–Méliès: La guerre des chiffres," *Écran Total*, February 13, 2008.

29. Mehdi Pfeiffer, "Les cinémas enterrent la hache de guerre," *Le Parisien*, March 9, 2010. Goudet speculated that the lawyers for UGC and Karmitz realized after studying the figures that they would lose the court decision and that UGC had convinced Karmitz that the bad publicity of pursuing the case was not worth it. Goudet interview with author, August 11, 2009.

30. These questions were not new. They can be found in the dossier "Cinéma et municipalités" (Paris: Fédération nationale des cinémas français, 1978).

31. "J'ai toujours respecté la concurrence pour autant qu'elle soit loyale," *Le Film Français*, November 16, 2007.

32. The petition of May 2007 calling for support of the new project stated that the expanded theater would "not show more films than today" and planned to fight "against the accelerated rotation of films . . . at the expense of word of mouth and the most demanding cinema."

33. *Le Monde* published a short release from AFP on the noncommittal opinion of the Conseil de la concurrence, July 14, 2008. In *Écran Total*, July 17, 2008, Goudet found that "the Méliès has nothing to fear" from the opinion. The mayor of Montreuil announced the next year that the town had reached an agreement, and the circuits had withdrawn their complaints. Thomas Sotinel, "UGC et MK2 renoncent à poursuivre le cinéma Le Méliès," *Le Monde*, March 11, 2010.

34. "Prémiers états généraux de l'action culturelle cinématographique et audiovisuelle" (Paris: BLAC, January 8–9, 2009), 36. In another part of the account, the text objects to the "concentration on the quantitative evaluation of the cultural action, according to a purely accounting logic, and thus the overvaluation of the single criterion of attendance disregarding the qualitative evaluation of the actions" (9).

35. "Lionel Jospin plaide vigoureusement pour le cinéma d'auteur," *Le Monde*, May 11, 2000.

36. Reagan liked to take macho posturing of rogue cops like Dirty Harry or disaffected veterans like Rambo as models, lifting signature dialogue lines as tag lines for policy. He taunted opponents of his tax reductions: "I have only one thing to say to the tax increasers: Go ahead and make my day." See "Quotation of the Day," *New York Times*, March 14, 1985. Following the release of U.S. hostages in Lebanon, he said, "After seeing *Rambo* last night, I'll know what to do next time." Martin Tolchin, "How Reagan Always Gets the Best Lines," *New York Times*, September 9, 1985.

37. According to the minister of culture, Christine Albanel, "As I see it, the Méliès is not in competition with these groups." Nicole Vulser, "Mme Albanel défend le cinéma Méliès," *Le Monde*, October 24, 2007.

38. Didier Péron, "Des Césars sous pression," *Libération*, February 22, 2008.

39. In France, virtually every film produced effectively must be shown in theaters, for qualification for potential automatic aid requires theatrical release as a condition for the *agrément*, even if some films receive only a short "technical release" to meet the rules.

40. André Lange and Tim Westcott, "Les aides publiques aux oeuvres cinématographiques et audiovisuelles en Europe: Une analyse comparative" (Strasbourg: European Audiovisual Observatory, 2004).

41. Interview with author.

42. This position is not new. Many cinema professionals, scholars, and journalists have warned of the dangers of what is often called "bipolarization" between expensive commercial films and low-budget art films. Even before the 1980s, the Malécot report on cinema noted that "cinema activity has been drawn toward two extremes: a commercial cinema (large budget films avoiding creative ambition and aimed at the mass public) and an other cultural cinema (dependent essentially on State aid and tending to distance itself from the mass public), a separation leading eventually to the mediocrity of both extremes." Rapport Malécot, "Le financement du cinéma" (Paris: Secrétariat d'État à la culture, January 1977), cited in Joop Voogd, "Le cinéma et l'État: Rapport de la commission de la culture et de l'éducation" (Strasbourg: Council of Europe, 1979), 29.

43. For example, Anne Jäckel claims that "state funding continues to be crucial to the existence of world cinema." Jäckel, "State and Other Funding for Migrant, Diasporic and World Cinemas in Europe," in European Cinema in Motion: Migrant and Diasporic Film in Contemporary Europe, ed. Daniela Berghahn and Claudia Sternberg (New York: Palgrave Macmillan, 2010), 76.

44. The study looked at one hundred films produced in 1996 over seven years in order to measure total receipts on all release platforms. "La rentabilité des films" (Paris: CNC, February 2004).

45. Arthur De Vany, Hollywood Economics: How Extreme Uncertainty Shapes the Film Industry (New York: Routledge, 2004), 214. See also Edward J. Epstein, The Big Picture: The New Logic of Money and Power in Hollywood (New York: Random House, 2005), 122. Martin Dale, with no sources, asserted that "only one in ten films break even on production revenues." Dale, The Movie Game: The Film Business in Britain, Europe and America (London: Cassell, 1997), 36.

46. Harold Vogel, Entertainment Industry Economics: A Guide for Financial Analysis, 2nd ed. (Cambridge: Cambridge University Press, 1990), 135.

47. "The Cinema Fund was modeled after its European counterparts (especially the French one). . . . First of all, the importance of France and French companies for Romanian cinema cannot be overestimated." Ioana Uricaru, "Follow the Money: Financing Contemporary Cinema in Romania," in A Companion to Eastern European Cinemas, ed. Aniko Imre (Malden, Mass.: John Wiley & Sons, 2012), 433.

48. Réné Bonnell, "Le financement de la production et de la distribution cinématographiques: À l'heure du numérique" (Paris: CNC, December 2013).

49. Bonnell developed some of these ideas in "Le nouvel âge audiovisuel," Le Monde, April 6, 1994.

50. Bonnell, "Le financement de la production et de la distribution cinématographiques," 15.

BIBLIOGRAPHY

Aas, Nils Klevjer. "Challenges in European Cinema and Film Policy." Strasbourg: European Audiovisual Observatory, October–November 2001.

Acheson, Keith, and Christopher Maule. *Much Ado About Culture: North American Trade Disputes*. Ann Arbor: University of Michigan Press, 2001.

——. "Shadows Behind the Scenes: Political Exchange and the Film Industry." *Millennium Journal of International Studies* 20, no. 2 (1991): 287–307.

Acland, Charles R. *Screen Traffic: Movies, Multiplexes, and Global Culture*. Durham, N.C.: Duke University Press, 2003.

Ahearne, Jeremy, ed. *French Cultural Policy and Debates: A Reader*. London: Routledge, 2002.

Aksoy, Asu, and Kevin Robins. "Hollywood for the 21st Century: Global Competition for Critical Mass in Image Markets." *Cambridge Journal of Economics* 16, no. 1 (1992): 1–22.

Alexandre, Olivier. *Utopia: À la recherche d'un cinéma alternatif*. Paris: L'Harmattan, 2007.

Amiel, Olivier. *Le financement public du cinéma dans l'union européenne*. Paris: LGDJ, 2007.

Anderson, Christopher. *Hollywood TV: The Studio System in the Fifties*. Austin: University of Texas Press, 1994.

Anderson, Perry. "Dégringolade." *London Review of Books* 26, no. 17 (September 2, 2004): 3–9.

Andréanszky, Eugène. "L'édito du délégué général: L'enfant doit rester au coeur du projet!" In "Évaluation nationale d'École et cinéma: Année scolaire 2005/2006." Paris: Les Enfants de cinéma, April 2007.

Andrew, Dudley. "An Atlas of World Cinema." In *Remapping World Cinema*, edited by Stephanie Dennison and Song Hwee Lim, 19–37. London: Wallflower, 2006.

Appadurai, Arjun, ed. *Globalization.* Durham, N.C.: Duke University Press, 2001.

"Assises européennes de l'audiovisuel: Projet EUREKA audiovisuel, Paris–La Défense, CNIT, du 30 sept. au 2 oct. 1989." Paris: Ministry of Foreign Affairs, [1989].

Atkinson, Dave. "De 'l'exception culturelle' à la 'diversité culturelle': Les relations internationales au coeur d'une bataille planétaire." *Annuaire français des relations internationales* 1 (2000): 663–675.

Atkinson, Dave, Ivan Bernier, and Florian Sauvageau, eds. *Souveraineté et protectionnisme en matière culturelle: La circulation internationale des émissions de télévision à la lumière de l'expérience canado-américaine.* Sainte-Foy, Québec: Centre québécois de relations internationales, 1991.

Auclaire, Alain. "Par ailleurs le cinéma est un divertissement. . . . Propositions pour le soutien à l'action culturelle dans le domaine du cinéma: Rapport à Madame Christine Albanel, Ministre de la culture et de la communication." Paris: Ministry of Culture, November 2008.

L'audiovisuel et le GATT: Actes des 7ème journées d'actualitité du Droit de l'audiovisuel. Poitiers, November 19–20, 1993. Paris: Presses universitaires de France, 1995.

Augros, Joël. *L'argent d'Hollywood.* Paris: L'Harmattan, 1996.

Augros, Joël, and Kira Kitsopanidou. *L'économie du cinéma américaine: Histoire d'une industrie culturelle et de ses stratégies.* Paris: Armand Colin, 2009.

Austin, Guy. *Contemporary French Cinema.* Manchester: Manchester University Press, 1996.

"L'avenir de l'audiovisuel et des médias en Europe." Brussels: Club de Bruxelles, 1994. CNC D 299.

"L'avenir des aides d'État." IRIS plus 2012-3. Strasbourg: European Audiovisual Observatory, 2012.

Axford, Barrie, Daniela Berghahn, and Nick Hewlett, eds. *Unity and Diversity in the New Europe.* Oxford: Peter Lang, 2000.

Baecque, Antoine de. *Cahiers du cinéma: Histoire d'une revue.* Vol. 1, *À l'assaut du cinéma, 1951–1959.* Paris: Cahiers du cinéma, 1991.

——. *La cinéphilie: Invention d'un regard, histoire d'une culture, 1944–1968.* Paris: Fayard, 2003.

——. *La Nouvelle Vague: Portrait d'une jeunesse.* Paris: Flammarion, 2009.

Baer, Jean-Michel. "L'exception culturelle: Une règle en quête de contenus." *En Temps Réel* 11 (October 2003): 1–31.

Baker, C. Edwin. "An Economic Critique of Free Trade in Media Products." *North Carolina Law Review* 78 (June 2000): 1360–1435.

Balassa, Carol. "America's Image Abroad: The UNESCO Cultural Diversity Convention and U.S. Motion Picture Exports." Nashville: Curb Center for Art, Enterprise & Public Policy at Vanderbilt, 2008.

Balio, Tino, ed. *The American Film Industry.* Madison: University of Wisconsin Press, 1985.

——, ed. *Hollywood in the Age of Television.* Boston: Unwin Hyman, 1990.

——. *Hollywood in the New Millennium.* London: BFI, 2013.

Bathail, Christian. *Cinéma et exception culturelle*. Paris: Dualpha, 2005.

Batz, Jean-Claude. *L'audiovisuel européen: Un enjeu de civilization*. Paris: Séguier, 2005.

Batz, M. *À propos de la crise de l'industrie cinématographique*. Brussels: Éditions de l'Institut de sociologie, Université libre de Bruxelles, 1963.

Baumol, William G., and W. G. Bowen. *Performing Arts: The Economic Dilemma*. Cambridge, Mass.: MIT Press, 1966.

Beaulac, Mario, and François Colbert, eds. *Industries culturelles nationales et mondialisation des marches: Actes du colloque*. Montréal: École des hautes études commerciales de Montréal, 1993.

Bellucci, Lucia. "National Support for Film Production in the EU: An Analysis of the Commission Decision-Making Practice." *European Law Journal* 16, no. 2 (2010): 211–232.

Benezet, Erwan, and Barthélémy Courmont. "Washington et Hollywood: L'arme fatale?" *La Revue international et stratégique* 55 (Autumn 2004): 19–26.

Benghozi, Pierre-Jean. "Le cinéma." In *La mondialisation immatérielle*, edited by Daniel Cohen and Thierry Verdier, 117–134. Paris: La Documentation française, 2008.

———. "L'Europe de l'audiovisuel n'est pas pour demain." *Sociétal* 25 (June 1999): 71–76.

Benghozi, Pierre-Jean, and Christian Delage, eds. *Une histoire économique du cinéma français (1985–1995): Regards croisés franco-américains*. Paris: L'Harmattan, 1997.

Benhamou, Françoise. "Entre économie de marché et économie administrée: La politique du cinéma en question." *Esprit* 328 (October 2006): 63–74.

Benhamou, Françoise, and Joëlle Farchy. *Droit d'auteur et copyright*. Paris: La Découverte, 2009.

Benhamou, Françoise, Gergaud Olivier, and Nathalie Moureau. "Le financement du cinéma par la télévision: Une analyse économétrique des investissements des chaînes." *Économie &Prévision* 2 (2009): 101–112.

Benzoni, Laurent. "Entre exception culturelle et culture de l'exception." *Revue* 124 (November–December 2001): 10–14.

———. "Position dominante et rente de monopole: Une analyse économique de la concession de Canal+." *Revue d'économie industrielle* 66 (1993): 7–32.

Bergala, Alain. *L'hypothèse cinéma: Petit traité de transmission du cinéma à l'école et ailleurs*. Paris: Cahiers du cinéma, 2002.

Bergfelder, Tim. "National, Transnational, or Supranational Cinema? Rethinking European Film Studies." *Media, Culture, and Society* 27, no. 3 (2005): 315–331.

Berghahn, Daniela, and Claudia Sternberg, eds. *European Cinema in Motion: Migrant and Diasporic Film in Contemporary Europe*. Basingstoke, UK: Palgrave Macmillan, 2010.

Bermek, Hasan. "The Impact of EC Law on the Taxation of the European Audiovisual Industry." IRIS Plus 2007-7. Strasbourg: European Audiovisual Observatory, November 2007.

———. "Tax Incentives for Films and Audiovisual Works in France." Strasbourg: European Audiovisual Observatory, October 2007.

Bernier, Ivan. "Audiovisual Media and the Law of the WTO." In Graber, Girsberger, and Nenova, *Free Trade vs. Cultural Diversity*, 15–64.

——. "Les clauses d'exception culturelle dans les accords commerciaux internationaux." Presented at the Colloque recherche Culture et Communications, 64ème Congrès de l'ACFAS, Montréal, May 15–16, 1996.

——. "Commerce international et cultures nationales: Le débat sur la clause d'exception culturelle dans les négotiations de l'Uruguay Round." In Beaulac and Colbert, *Industries culturelles nationales*, 45–76.

——. "Content Regulation in the Audio-visual Sector and the WTO." In Geradin and Luff, *The WTO and Global Convergence*, 215–242.

——. "La dimension culturelle dans le commerce international: Quelques réflexions en marge de l'accord de libre-échange Canada/États-Unis du 2 janvier 1988." *Canadian Yearbook of International Law* 25, no. 25(1987): 243–262.

——. "Les exigences de contenu local au cinéma, à la radio et à la télévision en tant que moyen de défense de la diversité culturelle: Théorie et réalité." *Chronique* 3 (2003): 1–13.

——. "Un nouvel instrument sur la diversité culturelle. Questions et réponses." Presented at the Second Conference of the International Network for Cultural Diversity, Lucerne, September 21–23, 2001

——. "Les politiques culturelles du Canada et du Québec, l'Organisation mondiale du commerce (OMC) et l'Accord de libre-échange nord-américain (ALENA)." In *Les politiques culturelles à l'épreuve, La culture entre l'État et le marché*, edited by Florian Sauvageau, 13–71. Québec: Institut québécois de recherche sur la culture and Presses de l'Université Laval, 1996.

——. "La préservation de la diversité linguistique à l'heure de la mondialisation." *Les Cahiers de Droit* 42 no. 4 (December 2001): 913–960.

——. "Préserver et développer la diversité culturelle: Nécessité et perspectives d'action." Presented at the Première rencontre internationale des associations professionnelles du milieu de la culture, Montréal, September 2001.

——. "The Recent Free Trade Agreements of the United States as Illustration of Their New Strategy Regarding the Audiovisual Sector." Montréal: Centre études internationales et mondialisation, Institut d'études internationales de Montréal, Université de Québec à Montréal, June 18, 2004.

——. "Les subventions aux services audiovisuels dans le cadre du GATS: Situation actuelle et impact des négociations." *Chronique* 6 (2003): 1–11.

——. "Trade and Culture." In *The World Trade Organization: Legal, Economic, and Political Analysis*, edited by Patrick F. J. Macrory, Arthur E. Appleton, and Michael G. Plummer, 2:747–793. New York: Springer, 2005.

——. "A UNESCO International Convention on Cultural Diversity." In Graber, Girsberger, and Nenova, *Free Trade vs. Cultural Diversity*, 65–76.

——. "L'utilisation des données statistiques dans les négociations sur un nouvel accord international sur la diversité culturelle à l'UNESCO." *Chronique* 7–8 (2003): 1–18.

Bernier, Ivan, and Dave Atkinson, "L'avenir de l'intervention gouvernementale en faveur des industries culturelles." *Les Cahier-médias*, no. 7. Québec: Centre d'études sur les médias, July 1998.

——. "Mondialisation de l'économie et diversité culturelle: 'Les arguments en faveur de la préservation de la diversité culturelle.'" October 2000. Document de réflexion, 2e concertation intergouvernementale, Agence intergouvernementale de la Francophonie, Paris, December 12, 2000.

Bernier, Ivan, and Hélène Ruiz Fabri. "Évaluation de la faisabilité juridique d'un instrument international sur la diversité culturelle." Québec: Groupe de travail franco-québécois sur la diversité culturelle, 2002. http://www.diversite-culturelle.qc.ca/fileadmin/documents/pdf/106145_faisabilite.pdf.

Bernier, Ivan, and Jean-François Lamoureux. "Les politiques culturelles du Canada et du Québec, l'Organisation mondiale du commerce (OMC) et l'Accord de libre-échange nordaméricain (ALÉNA)." In Les politiques culturelles à l'épreuve, la culture entre l'État et le marché, edited by Florian Sauvageau. Sainte-Foy, Québec: Institut québécois de recherche sur la culture, 1996.

Berry, Chris. "Full Service Cinema: The South Korean Cinema Success Story (So Far)." In Renaud, Grinker, and Larsen, "Text and Context of Korean Cinema," 7–16.

——. "What Is Transnational Cinema? Thinking from the Chinese Situation." Transnational Cinemas 1, no. 2 (2010): 111–127.

Berry, Chris, and Mary Farquhar. China on Screen: Cinema and Nation. New York: Columbia University Press, 2006.

Bertin, Priscilla. "La production cinématographique française: Le financement en question." Paper completed for UFR Cinéma et Audiovisuel, Université de Paris III, Sorbonne Nouvelle, December 2003.

Betz, Mark, ed. "Dossier: Cinephilia." Cinema Journal 49, no. 2 (2010): 130–166.

Beuré, Fanny, Benoît Danard, Sophie Jardillier, and Caroline Jeanneau. "L'économie des films français." Paris: CNC, December 2013.

Beurier, Pervenche. Les politiques européennes de soutien au cinéma: Vers la création d'un espace cinématographique européen? Paris: L'Harmattan, 2004.

Beviglia-Zampetti, Americo. "WTO Rules in the Audio-Visual Sector." In Guerrieri, Iapadre, and Koopman, Cultural Diversity and International Economic Integration, 261–284.

Billard, Pierre. L'âge classique du cinéma français: Du cinéma parlant à la Nouvelle Vague. Paris: Flammarion, 1995.

Binh, N. T., José Moure, and Frédéric Sojcher. Paris-Hollywood, ou Le rêve français du cinéma américain. Paris: Archimbaud/Klincksieck, 2013.

Bizern, C., and A.-M. Autissier. "Public Aid Mechanisms for the Film and Audiovisual Industry in Europe: Comparative Analysis of National Aid Mechanisms." Strasbourg: European Audiovisual Observatory, 1998.

Blangonnet, Catherine, ed. "Cinéma et école." Special issue of Images Documentaires 39 (2000).

Bomsel, Olivier, and Cécile Chamaret. "Rentabilité des investissements dans les films français." Paris: Centre d'économie industrielle (CERNA), October 2, 2008.

Bonnell, René, Le cinéma exploité. Paris: Éditions du Seuil, 1978.

——. "Le cinéma face à la mondialisation." In *Qu'est-ce que la culture: L'esprit du temps,* edited by Yves Michaud, 404–411. Paris: Odile Jacob, 2001.

——. "Le financement de la production et de la distribution cinématographiques: À l'heure du numérique." Paris: CNC, December 2013.

——. *Mon cinéma: De Cannes à Canal+, itinéraire d'un distributeur gâté.* Paris: Balland, 2011.

——. *La vingt-cinquième image.* 4th ed. Paris: Gallimard, 2006.

Bordat, Françis. "Évaluation statistique de la pénétration du cinéma américain en France." *Revue Française d'Études Américaines* no. 24–25 (May 1985): 226–248.

Bossi, Gaëlle. "Les conditions juridiques de la création d'une politique européenne du cinéma." *Revue du Marché commun et de l'Union européenne* 478 (May 2004): 312–320.

Bourdale-Dufau, André. "Les salles de cinema." Paris: Inspecteur général de l'administration, 1993. CNC D 248.

Bourdieu, Pierre. *La domination masculine.* Paris: Le Seuil, 1998.

Bourgatte, Michaël. "L'exploitation cinématographique dite d'art et essai: Une proposition alternative entre indépendance et dépendance." Presented at "Mutations des industries de la culture, de l'information et de la communication," international colloquium, La Plaine Saint-Denis, France, September 25–27, 2006.

Bourgeois, Jacques H. J., Frédérique Berrod, and Eric Gippini Fournier, eds. *The Uruguay Round Results: A European Lawyers' Perspective.* Brussels: European Interuniversity Press, 1995.

Boutin, Perrine. "Le 7e art aux regards de l'enfance: Les médiations dans les dispositifs d'éducation à l'image cinématographique." Doctoral thesis, Université d'Avignon et des pays de Vaucluse, 2010.

Boyd-Barrett, Oliver, ed. *Communications Media, Globalization and Empire.* Eastleigh, UK: John Libbey Publishing, 2006.

Braun, Michael, and Leigh Parker. "Trade in Culture: Consumable Product or Cherished Articulation of a Nation's Soul?" *Denver Journal of International Law and Policy* 22 (Fall 1993): 155–191.

Bredin, Jean-Dénis. "Rapport de la mission de réflexion et de propositions sur le cinéma." Paris: Ministry of Culture, 1981.

Briançon, Pierre. *Messier story.* Paris: Grasset, 2002.

Broche, Jérôme, Obhi Chatterjee, Irina Orssich, and Nóra Tosics. "State Aid for Films—A Policy in Motion?" *Competition Policy Newsletter* 1 (2007): 44–48.

Bron, Christian M., and Peter Matzneller. "Governance of Film Aid in South-East Europe: Legal Basis, Structural Elements, Aid Criteria." In "An Insight into Selected Film Funding Systems," edited by Susanne Nikoltchev, 7–15. IRIS Plus 2011-2. Strasbourg: European Audiovisual Observatory, 2011.

Browne, Dennis. *The Culture Trade Quandary: Canada's Policy Options.* Ottawa: Centre for Trade Policy and Law, 1998.

Buchsbaum, Jonathan, and Elena Gorfinkel. "Dossier: What Is Being Fought for by Today's Cinephilia(s)?" *Framework* 50, no. 1–2 (2009): 176–228.

Buob, Jacques, and Pascal Mérigeau. *L'aventure vraie de Canal+*. Paris: Fayard, 2001.

Burin des Roziers, Laurent. *Du cinéma au multimedia: Une brève histoire de l'exception culturelle*. Notes de l'IFRI 5. Paris: Institut français des relations internationales, 1998.

Cabannes, Xavier. Le financement public de la production cinématographique. Paris: L'Harmattan, 2006.

Calmel, Jean-Pierre, and Mireille Nouvel. "Le système français d'aide au cinéma et à l'audiovisuel." Paris: CNC, 2000. CNC SD 1459.

"Canal+." L'Observatoire des groupes. Paris: Eurostaf, 1999.

Careil, P., D. Kessler, and F. Werner. "Rapport sur le financement du cinéma et l'avenir des SOFICAs." May 1990. CNC D 311.

Carmody, Chi. "When 'Cultural Identity Was Not at Issue': Thinking About Canada—Certain Measures Concerning Periodicals." *Law and Policy in International Business* 30, no. 2 (Winter 1999): 231–320.

"Les cartes d'abonnement illimité au cinéma: Évaluation de l'impact financier des dispositions de mise en oeuvre du décret 'cartes.'" Paris: CNC, December 2002.

Cathodon [pseud.]. "La legislation de l'audiovisuel en France. Au cours des vingt dernières années: Lignes de force, faux pas et questions en suspens." *Réseaux* 59 (1993): 25–51.

Cerda, Sandrine. "Le cinéma d'auteur dans les multiplexes: Un exemple d'ouverture dans la médiation des produits culturels." Master's thesis, CELSA Paris-Sorbonne, 2004.

Chaniac, Régine, and Jean-Pierre Jézéquel. *Télévision et cinéma: Le désenchantement*. Paris: Nathan, 1998.

——. *La télévision*. Paris: La Découverte, 2005.

Chao, Tina W. "GATT's Cultural Exemption of Audiovisual Trade: The United States May Have Lost the Battle but Not the War." *University of Pennsylvania Journal of International Economic Law* 17 (Winter 1996): 1127–1153.

Chapier, Christohe, Marianne Dalloz, and Albane Flahault. *Le cinéma en France et en Europe: Enjeux territoriaux, nationaux et européens*. Les Cahiers de l'administration territoriale no. 16. Reims: Presses universitaires de Reims, 1999.

Charuau, Jean-Marie. "'Je t'aime, moi non plus': Une histoire d'avance. Les pouvoirs publics, la profession cinématographique et le système des avances sur recettes, de 1959 à nos jours." Université de Paris I, Panthéon-Sorbonne, September 1991. CNC D 288.

Chevalier, Pierre. "Les SOFICAs: Rapport de mission." Paris: CNC, July 2008. http://www.ladocumentationfrancaise.fr/var/storage/rapports-publics/084000633.pdf.

Chiang, Edmund H. "The UNESCO Convention on the Protection and Promotion of the Diversity of Cultural Expressions: A Look at the Convention and Its Potential Impact on the American Movie Industry." *Washington University Global Studies Law Review* 6 (2007): 379–403.

"Les chiffres clés de la télévision hertzienne (1998–2007)." Paris: CNC, February 2009.

Christin, Angèle, and Olivier Donnat. "Pratiques culturelles en France et aux États-Unis: Éléments de comparaison, 1981–2008." Étude no. 2014-1. Paris: Ministry of Communication, March 2014.

"Le cinéma: Crise ou mutation?" *Problèmes politiques et sociaux* 381 (February 1980): 5–42.

"Cinéma et municipalités." Paris: Fédération nationale des cinémas français, 1978. CNC D 1989.

"Cinéma français: Avis de tempête: État des lieux et propostions des réalisateurs pour révitalizer un système à bout de souffle." Paris: Société des réalisateurs de films, 2008. http://www.pole-cinema-paca.org/messagerie/IMG/pdf/SRF-AVISdeTEMPETE.pdf.

"Cinéma français et l'État." Dossier. *Quaderni: La revue de la communication* 54 (Spring 2004).

"Le cinéma français: Ses problèmes, son avenir." Paris: Confédération nationale du cinéma français, September 1949. CNC D 587.

"Cinéma sans frontières." Paris: Le club des producteurs européens, February 6, 1996. CNC D 426.

"Cinema, TV and Radio in the EU: Statistics on Audiovisual Services, Data 1980–2002." Brussels: European Commission, 2003. http://ec.europa.eu/eurostat/documents/3217494/5648553/KS-BT-03-001-EN.PDF/3758081d-5ae4-4e21-9d78-fca7bcc68d5c?version=1.0.

"50 ans d'amour du cinéma: 50ème anniversaire des cinémas d'art et d'essai. Festival du Octobre 2005 au Mars 2006." Paris: AFCAE, 2006.

Clairval, François, "Canal+: Avis de tempête." *Communication et langages* 115 (1998): 22–23.

Clément, Jérôme. "Industries culturelles nationales et mondialisation des marchés." In Beaulac and Colbert, *Industries culturelles nationales*, 13–41.

Cluzel, Jean. *Une autre Bataille de France*. Paris: LGDJ, 1992.

——. "L'efficacité des aides publiques en faveur du cinéma français." Rapport d'information no. 11 (1998–1999). Paris: Office parlementaire d'évaluation des politiques publiques, Senate, July 8, 1988. http://www.senat.fr/rap/r98-011/r98-011_mono.html.

——. *Propos impertinents sur le cinéma français*. Paris: Presses universitaires de France, 2003.

——, ed. *La télévision a-t-elle tué le cinéma?* Paris: Presses universitaires de France, 2005.

Cocq, Emmanuel, Alexis Dantec, and Florence Lévy-Hartmann. "Combien-tu m'aimes? Pour une analyse économique de la politique cinématographique française." *Revue de l'OFCE* 97 (2006): 273–328.

Cocq, Emmanuel, and Patrick Messerlin. "French Audiovisual Policy: Impact and Compatibility with Trade Negotiations." HWWA Report 233. Hamburg: Hamburg Institute of International Economics, 2003. http://ageconsearch.umn.edu/bitstream/26105/1/re030233.pdf.

Coe, Neil, and Jennifer Johns. "Beyond Production Clusters: Towards a Critical Political Economy of Networks in the Film and Television Industries." In *The Cultural Industries and the Production of Culture*, edited by Allen Scott and D. Power, 189–204. London: Routledge, 2004.

Cohen, Elie. "Économie de l'exception culturelle." Occasional paper 2004/2. New York: United Nations Development Programme, 2004. http://hdr.undp.org/sites/default/files/hdr2004_elie_cohen.pdf.

Collins, Richard. *Broadcasting and Audio-visual Policy in the European Single Market.* London: John Libbey, 1994.

——."National Culture: A Contradiction in Terms?" *Canadian Journal of Communication* 16, no. 2 (1991): 1–7.

——."The Screening of Jacques Tati: Broadcasting and Cultural Identity in the European Community." *Cardozo Arts & Entertainment Law Journal* 11 (1993): 361–385.

——. "Television and National Identity on Both Sides of the Atlantic." *Round Table* 318 (April 1991): 173–178.

——. "Trading in Culture: The Role of Language." *Canadian Journal of Communication* 19, no. 3 (1994): 377–399.

"Comment va le cinéma français." *Revue des deux mondes* (May 2006): 67–155.

"Commission Communication to the Council, the European Parliament and the Economic and Social Committee." COM(86) 320 final. June 3, 1986.

Compaine, Benjamin, and Douglas Gomery. *Who Owns the Media? Competition and Concentration in the Mass Media Industry.* Mahway, N.J.: Lawrence Erlbaum, 2000.

Conant, Michael. *Antitrust in the Motion Picture Industry: Economic and Legal Analysis.* Berkeley: University of California Press, 1960.

——."The Paramount Decrees Reconsidered." *Law and Contemporary Problems* 44, no. 4 (1981): 79–107.

Conley, Janet L. "Hollywood's Last Hurrah?: 'Television Without Frontiers' Directive May Close Borders to the European Community's Broadcast Market." *University of Pennsylvania Journal of International Business Law* 14, no. 1 (1993): 87–117.

Cook, David A. *Lost Illusions: American Cinema in the Shadow of Watergate and Vietnam, 1970–1979.* Berkeley: University of California Press, 2000.

Cortade, Jean-Emmanuel. *La télévision française: 1986–1992.* Paris: Presses universitaires de France, 1993.

Cournil, Christel. "Salles de cinéma et concurrence: 'Les liasons contentieuses.'" *La Semaine juridique—Enterprise et affaires*, March 12, 2009, 1–19.

Cournil, Christel, and Fabrice Renaud. "Réflexions sur le soutien automatique à la production cinématographique." *Revue Lamy de droit de l'immatériel* 10 (November 2005): 49–59.

Court, Jean-François. "Le cinéma français face à son avenir: Rapport au ministre de la culture et de la communication." Paris: La Documentation française, 1988.

Coutinet, Nathalie, François Moreau, and Stéphanie Peltier. "Les grands groupes des industries culturelles—Fusions, acquisitions, alliances: Les stratégies des années 1980–2000." Paris: Département des études et de la prospective, Ministry of Culture, 2002.

Cowen, Tyler. *Creative Destruction.* Princeton, N.J.: Princeton University Press, 2002.

Creton, Laurent, ed. *Le cinéma à l'épreuve du système télévisuel.* Paris: CNRS, 2002.

——, ed. *Cinéma & (in)dépendance: Une économie politique.* Théorème no. 5. Paris: Presses de la Sorbonne Nouvelle, 1998.

——, ed. *Le cinéma et l'argent.* Paris: Nathan, 1999.

——. *Cinéma et marché.* Paris: Armand Colin, 1997.

——. *Économie du cinéma: Perspectives stratégiques.* Paris: Nathan, 1994.

——. *Historie économique du cinéma français: Production et financement, 1940–1959.* Paris: CNRS, 2004.

——. "Retour sur les origines du système d'aide à la production cinématographique en France." *Quaderni* 54 (Spring 2004): 109–118.

Creton, Laurent, Yannick Dehée, Sébastien Layerle, and Caroline Moine, eds. *Les producteurs: Enjeux créatifs, enjeux financiers.* Paris: Nouveau monde, 2011.

Creton, Laurent, and Claude Forest. "Évolution des structures et options stratégiques de l'exploitation cinématographique française." *Cinémathèque* 1 (1992): 60-68.

Creton, Laurent, and Anne Jäckel. "A Certain Idea of the Film Industry." In Temple and Witt, *The French Cinema Book*, 209–220.

Creton, Laurent, and Kira Kitsopanidou, eds. *Les salles de cinéma: Enjeux, défis et perspectives.* Paris: Armand Colin, 2013.

Crisp, Colin. *The Classic French Cinema, 1930–1960.* Bloomington: Indiana University Press, 1997.

Dabenne, Olivier, Fadila Boughanemi, Jean-Baptiste Escudier, Laurent Le Ny, and Jean-Francois Polo. "L'Européanisation des politiques publiques." In *Les États membres de l'Union européenne: Adaptations—Mutations—Résistances*, edited by Joel Rideau, 459–475. Paris: LGDJ, 1997.

Dagnaud, Monique. *Les artistes de l'imaginaire: Comment la télévision fabrique la culture de masse.* Paris: Armand Colin, 2006.

——. "L'exception culturelle profite-t-elle vraiment à la création?" *En Temps Réel, Les Cahiers* 17 (October 2004).

——. "Exception culturelle: Une Politique peut en cache une autre." *Le Débat* 134 (March–April 2005): 115-128.

——. "Grandeurs et misères de la politique de l'exception culturelle." *Politiques et Management Public* 21, no. 3 (June 2003): 21–38.

——, ed. *Médias: Promouvoir la diversité culturelle.* Paris: La Documentation française, 2000.

Dagnaud, Monique, and Kristian Feigelson. "Indian Cinema as a Cultural Exception." http://global.asc.upenn.edu/fileLibrary/PDFs/Dagnaud_Feigelson.pdf.

Dale, Martin. *The Movie Game: The Film Business in Britain, Europe and America.* London: Cassell, 1997.

Danan, Martine. "French Cinema in the Era of Media Capitalism." *Media, Culture & Society* 22 (2000): 355–364.

Daney, Serge. *L'exercice a été profitable, monsieur.* Paris: POL, 1993.

Dantec, Alexis, and Florence Lévy. "Le marché cinématographique français en 2004: Parts de marché vs diversité." Policy discussion paper. Paris: Groupe d'economie mondiale de Sciences Po, 2005.

Darre, Yanne. *Histoire sociale du cinéma français.* Paris: La Découverte, 2000.

Davis, Darrell William, and Emilie Yueh-yu Yeh. *East Asian Screen Industries.* London: BFI, 2008.

Degand, Claude. *Les industries cinématographiques de l'Europe des Six et le Marché Commun.* Notes et études documentaires no. 3271. Paris: La Documentation française, 1966.

——. "Où en est l'intégration du cinéma européen?" *Revue du Marché Commun* 124 (June 1969): 312–316. CNC 626.

Delmas, Benoît, and Eric Mahé. *Bal tragique chez Vivendi: La chute de la maison Messier.* Paris: Denoël, 2002.

——. *Western médiatique ou les mésaventures du cinéma au pays de Vivendi.* Paris: Mille et une nuits, 2001.

Delwit, P., and C. Gobin. "Étude du cheminement de la Directive 'TWF': Synthèse des prises de position des institutions communitaires." In *L'espace audiovisuel européen*, edited by G. Vandersanden, 55–74. Brussels: Université de Bruxelles, 1991.

Dennison, Stephanie, and Song Hwee Lim. *Remapping World Cinema: Identity, Culture and Politics in Film.* London: Wallflower, 2006.

Depétris, F. *L'État et le cinéma en France: Le moment de l'exception culturelle.* Paris: L'Harmattan, 2008.

Desbarats, Francis. "Les sections cinéma en lycée, signes de tendances nouvelles dans le système éducatif." *Images documentaires* 39 (2000): 59–82.

"Deux ans de politique culturelle, 1981–1983." Paris: Ministry of Culture, 1983. CNC D 2074.

De Valck, Marijke, and Malte Hagener. *Cinephilia: Movies, Love and Memory.* Amsterdam: Amsterdam University Press, 2005.

De Vany, Arthur. *Hollywood Economics: How Extreme Uncertainty Shapes the Film Industry.* New York: Routledge, 2004.

De Witte, Bruno. "Trade in Culture: International Legal Regimes and EU Constitutional Values." In *The EU and the WTO: Legal and Constitutional Issues*, edited by I. G. de Burca and J. Scott, 237–255. Oxford: Hart, 2001.

Dhooge, Lucien J. "No Place for Melrose: Channelsurfing, Human Rights, and the European Union's 'Television Without Frontiers' Directive." *New York Law School Journal of International and Comparative Law* 16 (1996): 279–335.

Dibie, Jean-Noël "Les clefs du marché audiovisuel international." *Cahiers d'Actualité et de Recherche sur l'Audience et la Télévision (CARAT)* 1 (September 1990).

——. *Les mécanismes de financement du cinéma et l'audiovisuel en Europe.* Paris: Dixit, 1992.

Dislaire, Ginette."Quelques extraits des rapports demandés par le CNC à Ginette Dislaire chargée de Mission." Réunion d'évaluation de Marseille, June 18-19, 1996. École et Cinéma, les Enfants du deuxième siècle. June 18, 19, 1996. CNC D 1068.

"10 propositions pour l'avenir des salles de cinéma." Paris: Fédération nationale des cinémas français, October 1995.

Donaldson, John David. " 'Television Without Frontiers': The Continuing Tension Between Liberal Free Trade and European Cultural Integrity." *Fordham International Law Journal* 20, no. 1 (November 1996): 90–180.

Donnat, Olivier. *Les pratiques culturelles des français: Enquête 1997.* Paris: La Documentation française, 1998.

Donnedieu de Vabres, Renaud. "La diversité culturelle n'est pas une arrogance." *Le Monde*, October 19, 2005.

Doutrelepont, Carine, ed. *L'Europe et les enjeux du GATT dans le domaine de l'audiovisual.* Brussels: Bruylant, 1994.

Drijber, Berend Jan. "The Revised Television Without Frontiers Directive: Is It Fit for the Next Century?" *Common Law Market Review* 36 (1999): 87–122.

Drummond, Philip, Richard Paterson, and Janet Willis, eds. *National Identity and Europe: The Television Revolution.* London: BFI, 1993.

Dubet, Éric. *Économie du cinéma européen: De l'interventionisme à l'action entrepreneuriale.* Paris: L'Harmattan, 2000.

Dupont, Nathalie. "Le cinéma américain: Un impérialisme culturel?" *Revue LISA* 5, no. 3 (2007): 112–132.

Dupuy-Busson, Séverine. "Le cinéma européen: Quelles options stratégiques pour assurer sa perennité?" *Medijska istraživanja* 11, no. 2 (2005): 81–99.

Ďurovičová, Nataša, and Kathleen Newman, eds. *World Cinemas, Transnational Perspectives.* New York: Routledge, 2010.

"The Economic Impact of Television Quotas in the European Union: A Report for Sony Entertainment Prepared by London Economics." June 1994. CNC D 327.

L'économie du spectacle vivant et l'audiovisuel: Colloque Internationale, Nice, October 15–16, 1984. Paris: La Documentation française, 1985.

"Éléments d'évolution du parc des salles de cinéma et de la diffusion du film en Europe." Paris: ADRC, November 24, 1994.

Emmanuel, William. *Le maître des illusions: L'ascension et la chute de Jean-Marie Messier.* Paris: Économica, 2002.

Epstein, Edward J. *The Big Picture: The New Logic of Money and Power in Hollywood.* New York: Random House, 2005.

——. *The Hollywood Economist.* Hoboken, N.J.: Melville House, 2011.

——. "Hollywood's Profits Demystified: The Real El Dorado Is TV." *Slate.com*, August 8, 2005. http://www.slate.com/articles/arts/the_hollywood_economist/2005/08/hollywoods _profits_demystified.html.

Esmein, Bernard. "Les politiques de l'Union européenne dans le domaine de la culture, de l'éducation et des langues." *Journal of European Integration History* 5, no. 2 (1999): 75–105.

"Étude sur le public des cinémas art et essai." Paris: CNC, May 1999. CNC D 584.

"European Union Cinema Day, November 13, 2001: Speeches, Workshops, Reports, Interventions, and Conclusions." 6e Forum du Cinéma européen, Strasbourg, November 8–13, 2001. CNC D 1411.

"Évaluation des 10 ans d'École et cinéma, 1994/1995–2004/2005." Paris: SCEREN-DNDP, April 2006. CNC D 3935.

"Évaluation nationale d'École et cinéma: Année scolaire 2005/2006." Paris: Les Enfants de cinéma, April 2007. CNC D 4295.

Everett, Wendy, ed. *European Identity in Cinema.* Exeter: Intellect, 1996.

"Évolution du public des salles de cinéma 1993–2011." Paris: CNC, July 2012.

"L'exploitation des films recommandés art et essai en salles, à la télévision, en vidéo." Paris: CNC, October 2006.

Ezra, Elizabeth, and Terry Rowden, eds. *Transnational Cinema: The Film Reader.* London: Routledge, 2006.

Fabri, Hélène Ruiz. "Analyse et commentaire critique de l'avant-projet de convention sur la protection de la diversité des contenus culturels et des expressions artistiques dans la version soumise pour commentaires et observations aux gouvernements des États membres de l'UNESCO." Paris: Agence intergouvernementale de la Francophonie, August 2004.

——, ed. *La convention de l'UNESCO sur la diversité culturelle: Premier bilan et defis juridiques.* Unité mixte de recherche de droit comparé de Paris no. 21. Paris: Société de législation comparée, 2010.

Falkenberg, Karl F. "The Audiovisual Sector." In Bourgeois, Berrod, and Fournier, *The Uruguay Round Results,* 429–434.

Fansten, M. "Le cinéma français face à l'évolution technologique et à la transformation des marchés." Paris: Réalisations et recherches audiovisuelles, Senate, November 2002.

Farchy, Joëlle. *Le cinéma déchaîné: Mutation d'une industrie.* Paris: CNRS, 1992.

——. *La fin de l'exception culturelle.* Paris: CNRS, 2002.

——. *L'industrie du cinéma.* Paris: Presses universitaires de France, 2004.

——. "La politique de soutien au cinéma." *Les Notices* 18 (2005): 110–113.

——. "Promouvoir la diversité culturelle: Les limites des formes actuelles de régulation." *Questions de Communication* 13 (2008): 171–195.

Farchy, Joëlle, and Pierre Kopp. "Le soutien public à l'industrie cinématographique et audiovisuelle." February 2000. CNC D 716.

Farchy, Joëlle, and Stéphanie Peltier. "Marchés des oeuvres audiovisuelles et protection nationales." In *Convergence et diversité à l'heure de la mondialisaiton,* edited by Jean-Pierre Faugère et al., 53–62. Paris: Économica, 1997.

Farchy, Joëlle, and Heritiana Ranaivoson. "La diversité culturelle, soubassements économiques et volonté politique." *Hermès* 40 (November 2004): 33–38.

Farchy, Joëlle, and Fabrice Rochlandet. "De Polygram à Vivendi Universal: L'impossible constitution d'une 'major européenne.'" In Paris, *Quelle diversité face à Hollywood,"* 96–103.

Farchy, Joëlle, and Dominique Sagot-Duvauroux. *Économie des politiques culturelles.* Paris: Presses universitaires de France, 1994.

Fautrelle, Séverine. "Le cadre juridique européen de la Télévision sans Frontières." *Medijska istraživanja* 11, no. 2 (2005): 33–48.

Featherstone, Mike, ed. *Global Culture: Nationalism, Globalization, and Modernity.* London: Sage, 1990.

Feigenbaum, Harvey B. "Hegemony or Diversity in Film and Television? The United States, Europe, and Japan." *Pacific Review* 20, no. 3 (September 2007): 371–396.

——. "Public Policy and the Private Sector in Audiovisual Industries." *UCLA Law Review* 49, no. 6 (2001): 1767–1781.

Ferenczi, Aurélien. "Pourquoi le cinéma ne s'est jamais aussi bien porté." *Télérama*, January 14, 2009.

Ferran, Pascale, "Violence économique et cinéma français: Le discours de la réalisatrice de 'Lady Chatterley,' César du meilleur film français." *Le Monde*, February 27, 2007.

Ferri, Delia. "EU Participation in the UNESCO Convention on the Protection and Promotion of the Diversity of Cultural Expressions: Some Constitutional Remarks." European Diversity and Autonomy Papers, EDAP 3/2005. Bozen, Italy: EURAC, 2005.

Filipek, Jon. " 'Culture Quotas': The Trade Controversy Over the European Community's Broadcasting Directive." *Stanford Journal of International Law* 28 (Spring 1992): 323–370.

Final Report of the International Meeting on Cultural Policy, Ottawa, Canada: Putting Culture on the World Stage, June 29 & 30, 1998. Ottawa: International Relations Directorate, Dept. of Canadian Heritage, 1999.

Finney, Angus. *The State of European Cinema*. London: Cassell, 1996.

Footer, Mary E., and Christoph Beat Graber. "Trade Liberalization and Cultural Policy." *Journal of International Economic Law* 3, no. 1 (March 2000): 115–144.

Forest, Claude. *L'argent du cinéma: Introduction à l'économie du septième art*. Paris: Belin, 2002.

——. *Les dernières séances*. Paris: CNRS, 1995.

——. *Économies contemporaines du cinéma en Europe: L'improbable industrie*. Paris: CNRS, 2001.

——. *L'industrie du cinéma en France: De la pellicule au pixel*. Paris: La Documentation française, 2013.

——. *Quel film voir? Pour une socioéconomie de la demande de cinéma*. Paris: Septentrion, 2010.

Forrest, Alan. "La politique audiovisuelle de l'Union européenne."*Revue du Marché Commun et de l'Union Euorpéenne* 412 (November 1997): 595–610.

Fougea, Jean-Pierre. *Les aides au financement*. Paris: Dixit, 1998.

Fowler, Catherine. *The European Cinema Reader*. London: Routledge, 2002.

France, the Coproduction Guide: The French Movie Support System. Paris: Film France/CNC, 2009.

Frau-Meigs, Divina. "La convention sur la diversité culturelle: Un instrument obsolète pour une réalité en expansion." *Annuaire Français de Relations Internationales* 8 (2007): 895–909.

——. " 'Cultural Exception,' National Policies and Globalization: Imperatives in Democratisation and Promotion of Contemporary Culture." *Quaderns del CAC* 14 (September–October 2002): 3–16.

Frodon, Jean-Michel. *L'âge moderne du cinéma français: De la Nouvelle Vague à nos jours*. Paris: Flammarion,1995.

——. *Le cinéma sans la télévision*. Paris: Gallimard, 2004.

——. *Horizon cinéma: L'art du cinéma dans le monde contemporain à l'âge du numérique et de la mondialisation*. Paris: Cahiers du cinéma, 2006.

——. *La projection nationale: Cinéma et nation.* Paris: Odile Jacob, 1998.

Gagné, Gilbert, René Côté, and Christian Deblock. "Les récents accords de libre-échange conclus par les États-Unis: Une menace à la diversité culturelle: Rapport soumis à l'Agence intergouvernementale de la Francophonie." Montréal: Institut d'études internationales de Montréal, June 18, 2004.

Gaillard, Y., and P. Loridant. "Revoir la règle du jeu: Mieux évaluer l'efficacité des aides publiques au cinéma." Rapport d'Information no. 276(2002–2003). Paris: Senate, May 2003.

Galmot, Y., and J. Biancarelli. "Les réglementations nationales en matière de prix au regard du droit communautaire." *Revue trimestrielle de droit européen* 21, no. 2 (1985): 396–413.

Galperin, Hernan. "Cultural Industries Policy in Regional Trade Agreements: The Cases of NAFTA, the European Union, and MERCOSUR." *Media, Culture & Society* 21, no. 5 (1999): 627–648.

Galt, Frederick Scott. "The Life, Death, and Rebirth of the 'Cultural Exception' in the Multilateral Trading System: An Evolutionary Analysis of Cultural Protection and Intervention in the Face of American Pop Culture's Hegemony." *Washington University Global Studies Law Review* 3 (2004): 909–935.

Galt, Rosalind. *The New European Cinema: Redrawing the Map.* New York: Columbia University Press, 2006.

Galt, Rosalind, and Karl Schoonover, eds. *Global Art Cinema: New Theories and Histories.* Oxford: Oxford University Press, 2010.

Garrett, Lisa. "Commerce Versus Culture: The Battle Between the United States and the European Union Over Audiovisual Trade Practices." *North Carolina Journal of International Law and Commercial Regulation* 19 (1994): 533–577.

Gentil, Geneviève, and Philippe Poirrier, eds. *La politique culturelle en débat: Anthologie, 1955–2005.* Paris: La Documentation française, 2006.

Geradin, Damien, and David Luff, eds. *The WTO and the Global Convergence in Telecommunications and Audio-visual Services.* New York: Cambridge University Press, 2004.

Germann, Christophe. "Culture in Times of Cholera: A Vision for a New Legal Framework Promoting Cultural Diversity." *ERA-Forum* 1 (2005): 109–130.

——. "Diversité culturelle et cinéma: Une vision pour un pays en voie de développement." In Graber, Girsberger, and Nenova, *Free Trade vs. Cultural Diversity*, 78–108.

——. *Diversité culturelle et libre-échange à la lumière du cinéma: Réflexions critiques sur le droit naissant de la diversité culturelle sous les angles du droit de l'UNESCO et de l'OMC, de la concurrence et de la propriété intellectuelle.* Paris: LGDJ; Basel: Helbing Lichtenhahn; Brussels: Bruylant, 2008.

——. "Towards a *Global Cultural Contract* to Counter Trade Related Cultural Discrimination." In *UNESCO's Convention on the Protection and Promotion of the Diversity of Cultural Expression: Making It Work,* edited by Nina Obuljen and Joost Smiers, 279–335. Zagreb: Institute for International Relations, 2006.

Gevaudan, Jean-Michel. "Parc de salles et diffusion des films: Évolutions 2003." Paris: ADRC, 2004. http://www.adrc-asso.org/pdf/salle_de_cinema/Etude_evolutions_2003 .pdf.

Gimello-Mesplomb, Frédéric. "The Economy of 1950s Popular French Cinema." *Studies in French Cinema* 6, no. 2 (2006): 141–150.

———. "Le prix de la qualité: L'État et le cinéma français (1960–1965)." *Politix* 16, no. 61 (2003): 95–122.

Godin, Emmanuel, and Tony Chafer, eds. *The French Exception*. New York: Berghahn, 2005.

Gomery, Douglas. "Economic and Institutional Analysis: Hollywood as Monopoly Capitalism" (2005). In Miller, *The Contemporary Hollywood Reader*, 27–36.

———. *The Hollywood Studio System: A History*. London: BFI, 2005.

———. "Toward a New Media Economics." In *Post-Theory: Reconstructing Film Studies*, edited by David Bordwell and Noël Carroll, 407–413. Madison: University of Wisconsin Press, 1996.

Goodenough, Oliver R. "Defending the Imaginary to the Death? Free Trade, National Identity, and Canada's Cultural Preoccupation." *Arizona Journal of International and Comparative Law* 15 (Winter 1998): 203–253.

Gordon, Philip H., and Sophie Meunier. *The French Challenge: Adapting to Globalization*. Washington, D.C.: Brookings Institution Press, 2001.

Goudineau, Daniel. "La distribution des films en salle: Rapport à Mme la ministre de la culture et de la communication." Paris: Ministry of Culture, May 2000. http://www .ladocumentationfrancaise.fr/var/storage/rapports-publics/004000986.pdf.

Gournay, Bernard. *Exception culturelle et mondialisation*. Paris: Presses de Sciences Po, 2002.

Graber, Christoph Beat. "Audiovisual Media and the Law of the WTO." In Geradin and Luff, *The WTO and Global Convergence*, 15–64.

———. "Audio-visual Policy: The Stumbling Block of Trade Liberalisation?" In Geradin and Luff, *The WTO and Global Convergence*, 165–214.

———. "WTO: A Threat to European Films?" In *Actas del v. Congreso Cultura Europea*, edited by Enrique Banús and Beatriz Elío, 865–878. Pamplona: Aranzadi, 2000.

Graber, Christoph Beat, Michael Girsberger, and Mira Nenova, eds. *Free Trade vs. Cultural Diversity: WTO Negotiations in the Field of Audiovisual Services*. Zurich: Schulthess, 2004.

Graham, Peter, and Ginette Vincendeau, eds. *The French New Wave: Critical Landmarks*. London: BFI, 2009.

Grant, Jonas M. "'Jurassic' Trade Dispute: The Exclusion of the Audiovisual Sector from the GATT," *Indiana Law Journal* 70, no. 4 (Fall 1995): 1333–1365.

Grant, Peter S., and Chris Wood. *Blockbusters and Trade Wars: Popular Culture in a Globalized World*. Vancouver: Douglas and McIntyre, 2004.

Grantham, Bill. *"Some Big Bourgeois Brothel": Contexts for France's Culture Wars with Hollywood*. Luton, UK: University of Luton Press, 2000.

Greenwald, Stephen, and Paula Landry. *The Business of Film*. New York: Lone Eagle, 2009.

Grodin, Emmanuel, and Tony Chofer. *The French Exception*. London: Berghahn, 2005.

Guback, Thomas. "Film and Cultural Pluralism." *Journal of Aesthetic Education* 5, no. 2 (April 1971): 35–51.

——. "Government Financial Support to the Film Industry in the United States." In *Current Trends in Research: Audience, Economics, and Law*, edited by Bruce Austin, 88–104. Norwood, N.J.: Ablex, 1987.

——. *The International Film Industry*. Bloomington: Indiana University Press, 1969.

Guerrier, Julien. "Négociations commerciales: La position de l'Union européenne quant aux services audiovisuels." In Graber, Girsberger, and Nenova, *Free Trade vs. Cultural Diversity*, 127–132.

Guerrieri, Paolo, P. Lelio Iapadre, and Georg Koopman, eds. *Cultural Diversity and International Economic Integration: The Global Governance of the Audio-Visual Sector*. Cheltenham, UK: Edward Elgar, 2005.

Guy, Jean-Michel. *La culture cinématographique des français*. Paris: La Documentation française, 2000.

Gyory, Michel. "Making and Distributing Films in Europe: The Problem of Nationality." Strasbourg: European Audiovisual Observatory, 2001.

Hahn, Michael. "A Clash of Cultures? The UNESCO 'Diversity Convention' and International Trade Law." *Journal of International Economic Law* 9, no. 3 (2006): 515–552.

Halle, Randall. *German Film After Germany: Toward a Transnational Aesthetic*. Champaign: University of Illinois Press, 2008.

——. "German Film, *Aufgehoben*: Ensembles of Transnational Cinema." *New German Critique* 87 (2002): 7–46.

——. "German Film, European Film: Transnational Production, Distribution and Reception." *Screen* 47, no. 2 (Summer 2006): 242–251.

Hamm, Bernd, and Russell Smandych, eds. *Cultural Imperialism: Essays on the Political Economy of Cultural Domination*. Peterborough, Ontario: Broadview Press, 2005.

Hancock, David. "La production cinématographique mondiale." Working paper presented at EURO-MEI conference, Venice, August 1998.

Harcourt, Alison. *The European Union and the Regulation of Media Markets*. Manchester: Manchester University Press, 2005.

Harris, Sue, and Elizabeth Ezra, eds. *France in Focus*. Oxford: Berg, 2000.

Harvey, Sylvia. *Trading Culture: Global Traffic and Local Cultures in Film and Television*. Eastleigh, UK: John Libbey, 2006.

Hayes, Graeme. "Regulating Multiplexes. The French State Between Corporatism and Globalization." *French Politics, Culture & Society* 23, no. 3 (Winter 2005): 14–33.

Hayes, Graeme, and Martin O'Shaughnessy, eds. *Cinéma et engagement*. Paris: L'Harmattan, 2005.

Hayward, Susan. *French National Cinema*. 1993. Rev. ed., London: Routledge, 2005.

——. "State, Culture and the Cinema: Jack Lang's Strategies for the French Film Industry, 1981–93." *Screen* 34, no. 4 (1993): 380–391.

Henderson, D. *The MAI Affair*. Wellington: New Zealand Business Roundtable, 1999.

Henning, Victor, and Andre Alpar. "Public Aid Mechanisms in Feature Film Production: The EU MEDIA Plus Programme." *Media, Culture & Society* 27, no. 2 (2005): 229–250.

Herold, Anna. "EU External Policy in the Audio-visual Field: From 'Cultural Exception' to 'Cultural Diversity.'" *ERA Forum* 6, no. 1 (2005): 93–108.

——. "EU Film Policy: Between Art and Commerce." European Diversity and Autonomy Papers, EDAP 3, 2004.

——. *European Film Policies in EU and International Law: Culture and Trade—Marriage or Misalliance?* Groningen, Neth.: Europa Law Publishing, 2010.

——. "European Public Film Support Within the WTO Framework." IRIS Plus 2003-3. Strasbourg: European Audiovisual Observatory, June 2003.

——. Review of *Cultural Diversity and International Economic Integration: The Global Governance of the Audio-visual Sector*, edited by Paolo Guerrieri, P. Lelio Iapadre, and Georg Koopman. *Journal of Cultural Economics* 30, no. 3 (December 2006): 233–235.

Hervé, Michel, and Anne-Laure Angoulvent. *Les télévisions en Europe*. Paris: Presses universitaires de France, 1992.

Hess, John, "*La politique des auteurs* (part one): World View as Aesthetics." *Jump Cut* 1 (1974): 19–22.

——. "*La politique des auteurs*, part 2: Truffaut's Manifesto." *Jump Cut* 2 (1974): 20–22.

Higbee, Will. "Beyond the (Trans)national: Towards a Cinema of Transvergence in Postcolonial and Diasporic Francophone Cinema(s)." *Studies in French Cinema* 7, no. 2 (May 2007): 79–91.

Higbee, Will, and Sarah Leahy, eds. *Studies in French Cinema: UK Perspectives, 1985–2010*. Bristol, UK: Intellect, 2011.

Hill, John, and Pamela Church Gibson, eds. *The Oxford Guide to Film Studies*. Oxford: Oxford University Press, 1998.

Hill, John, Martin McLoone, and Paul Hainsworth, eds. *Border Crossing: Film in Ireland, Britain and Europe*. Belfast: Institute of Irish Studies, Queen's University of Belfast, in association with the University of Ulster and the British Film Institute, 1994.

Hillier, J., ed. *Cahiers du cinéma, The 1950s: Neo-Realism, Hollywood, New Wave*. Cambridge, Mass.: Harvard University Press.1985.

Hjort, Mette, ed. *Film and Risk*. Detroit: Wayne State University Press, 2012.

——. *Small Nation, Global Cinema: The New Danish Cinema*. Minneapolis: University of Minnesota Press, 2005.

Hjort, Mette, and Scott Mackenzie, eds. *Cinema and Nation*. London: Routledge, 2000.

Hjort, Mette, and Duncan Petrie. *The Cinema of Small Nations*. Bloomington: Indiana University Press, 2007.

Hoarau, Jacques, Michel Maric, and Dominique Sagot-Duvauroux. "Menaces sur la diversité culturelle." Dossier. *Mouvements* 37 (January–February 2005).

Hobsbawm, Eric. *The Invention of Tradition*. Cambridge: Cambridge University Press, 1984.

Hoffman-Riem, Wolfgang. "The Broadcasting Activities of the European Community and Their Implications for National Broadcasting Systems in Europe." *Hastings International and Comparative Law Review* 16, no. 4 (1993): 599–617.

Hoskins, Colin, Stuart McFadyen, and Adam Finn. *Global Television and Film: An Introduction to the Economics of the Business*. New York: Oxford University Press.1997.

——. *Media Economics: Applying Economics to New and Traditional Media*. Thousand Oaks, Calif.: Sage, 2004.

Houcken, Robin. *The International Feature Film Industry: National Advantage and International Strategies for European Film Companies*. Potsdam: Verlag für Berlin-Brandenburg, 1999.

Huettig, Mae. *The Economic Control of the Motion Picture Industry: A Study in Industrial Organization*. Philadelphia: University of Pennsylvania Press, 1944.

Hunter, Mark. *Les jours les plus Lang*. Paris: Odile Jacob, 1990.

Ilott, Terry. *Budgets and Markets: A Study of the Budgeting of European Film*. London: Routledge, 1996.

Imre, Aniko, ed. *A Companion to Eastern European Cinemas*. Chichester, UK: John Wiley and Sons, 2012.

"L'incantation de Delphes." *Les dossiers de l'audiovisuel* 35 (January–February 1991): 53–55.

"L'industrie européenne du cinéma en analyse." Brussels: Commission Européenne Direction Générale X, Direction de la politique audiovisuelle et de l'action culturelle, November 12, 1996.

Iordanova, Dina, David Martin-Jones, and Belen Vidal, eds. *Cinema at the Periphery*. Detroit: Wayne State University Press, 2010.

Jäckel, Anne. "Dual Nationality Film Production in Europe After 1945." *Historical Journal of Film, Radio and Television* 23, no. 3 (2003): 231–243.

——. "European Co-production Strategies: The Case of France and Britain." In Moran, *Film Policy*, 85–97.

——. *European Film Industries*. London: BFI, 2003.

——. "The Inter/Nationalism of French Film Policy." *Modern Contemporary France* 15, no. 1 (2007): 21–36.

——. "State and Other Funding for Migrant, Diasporic and World Cinemas in Europe." In Berghahn and Sternberg, *European Cinema in Motion*, 76–95.

Jackson, John H. *The World Trading System: Law and Policy of International Economic Relations*. Cambridge, Mass.: MIT Press, 1997.

Jansen, Christian. "The Performance of German Motion Pictures, Profits and Subsidies: Some Empirical Evidence." *Journal of Cultural Economics* 29 (2005): 191–212.

Jarvie, Ian. "The Postwar Economic Foreign Policy of the American Film Industry: Europe, 1945–1950." *Film History* 4 (1990): 277–288.

Jeancolas, Jean-Pierre. "L'arrangement Blum-Byrnes à l'épreuve des faits: Les relations (cinématographiques) franco-américaines de 1944 à 1948." *1895* 13 (December 1992): 3–41.

——. "The confused image of le jeune cinéma." *Studies in French Cinema* 5, no. 3 (2005): 157–161.

——. "From the Blum-Byrnes Agreement to the GATT Affair." In Nowell-Smith and Ricci, *Hollywood and Europe*, 47–60.

——. *Histoire du cinéma français*. 2nd ed. Paris: Armand Colin, 2007.

Jin, Dal Yong. "A Critical Analysis of U.S. Cultural Policy in the Global Film Market: Nation-States and FTAs." *International Communication Gazette* 73, no. 8 (2011): 651–669.

——. "Cultural Politics in Korea's Contemporary Films under Neoliberal Globalization." *Media, Culture & Society* 28, no. 1 (2006): 5–23.

Joeckel, Sven. *Contemporary Austrian and Irish Cinema*. Stuttgart: Edition 451, 2003.

Johnson, Randal. *The Brazilian Film Industry: Culture and the State*. Austin: University of Texas Press, 1987.

Jullier, Laurent, and Jean-Marc Leveratto. *Cinéphiles et cinéphilies*. Paris: Armand Colin, 2010.

Kanzler, Martin, with Susan Newman-Baudais and André Lange. "The Circulation of European Co-productions and Entirely National Films in Europe, 2001–2007." Strasbourg: European Audiovisual Observatory, August 2008.

Kaplan, Laurence G. C. "The European Community's 'Television Without Frontiers' Directive: Stimulating Europe to Regulate Culture." *Emory International Law Review* 8, no. 1 (Spring 1994): 255–346.

Kapur, Jyostna, and Keith B. Wagner, eds. *Neoliberalism and Global Cinema: Capital, Culture, and Marxist Critique*. New York: Routledge, 2011.

Karmitz, Marin. *Bande à part*. Paris: Grasset, 1994.

——. *Profession Producteur*. Paris: Hachette, 2003.

Katsirea, Irini. "Why the European Broadcasting Quota Should Be Abolished." *European Law Review* 28 (2003): 190–209.

Keathley, Christian. *Cinephilia and History, or The Wind in the Trees*. Bloomington: Indiana University Press, 2006.

Kessler, Kirsten L. "Protecting Free Trade in Audiovisual Entertainment: A Proposal for Counteracting the European Union's Trade Barriers to the U.S. Entertainment Industry's Experts." *Law and Policy in International Business* 26, no. 2 (1995): 563–611.

Kim, Carolyn Hyun-Kyung. "Comment: Building the Korean Film Industry's Competitiveness: Abolish the Screen Quota and Subsidize the Film Industry." *Pacific Rim Law and Policy Journal* 9, no. 353 (May 2000): 353–378.

Kim, Joongi. "The Viability of Screen Quotas in Korea: The Cultural Exception Under the International Trade Regime." *Korean Journal of International and Comparative Law* 26 (1998): 199–242.

Kindem, Gorham, ed. *The American Movie Industry: The Business of Motion Pictures*. Carbondale: Southern Illinois University Press, 1982.

——, ed. *The International Movie Industry*. Carbondale: Southern Illinois University Press, 2000.

Klein, Christina. "Why American Studies Needs to Think About Korean Cinema; or, Transnational Genres in the Films of Bong Joon-ho." *American Quarterly* 60, no. 4 (December 2008): 871–898.

Kordanian, Guillaume. "Comparaison des principaux tax-shelters européens et critique du système français des SOFICAS." Paris: CNC, April 2002.

Kruse, Jörn. "The EC–US Trade Conflict Over Film and Television Software." *Intereconomics* 29, no. 6 (1994): 284–291.

Kuisel, Richard. *The French Way: How France Embraced and Rejected American Values and Power*. Princeton, N.J.: Princeton University Press, 2012.

Kunz, William M. *Culture Conglomerates: Consolidation in the Motion Picture and Television Industries*. Lanham, Md.: Rowman and Littlefield, 2007.

Lagny, M., M.-C. Ropars, and P. Sorlin, eds. "L'école—Cinéma." Special issue, *Hors Cadre* 5 (Spring 1987).

Lalevée, Fabrice, and Florence Lévy-Hartmann. "The Support for the French Cinematographic Production: Who Benefits from the French 'Cultural Exception?'" Working paper. Groupe d'économie mondiale, January 2007.

Lalumière, Catherine, Jean-Pierre Landau, and Emmanuel Glimet. "Rapport sur l'Accord multilatéral sur l'investissement (AMI): Rapport intérimaire." Annex to Rapport d'information 1150. Paris: National Assembly, September 1998.

Lange, André, and Susan Newman-Baudais. "Film Distribution Companies in Europe." Strasbourg: European Audiovisual Observatory, 2007.

Lange, André, and Tim Westcott. "Les aides publiques aux oeuvres cinématographiques et audiovisuelles en Europe: Une analyse comparative." Strasbourg: European Audiovisual Observatory, 2004.

Lant, John. *The Asian Film Industry*. Austin: University of Texas Press, 1990.

Laroche, Josepha, and Alexandre Bohas. *Canal Plus et les majors americains: Une vision désenchantée du cinéma monde*. Paris: L'Harmattan, 2008.

Lavocat, Eric. "La diffusion cinématographique en région Centre." DRAC Centre et le Conseil régional du Centre: Hexacom, December 2001. CNC D 2035.

Lecasble, Valérie. *Le roman de Canal+*. Paris: Grasset, 2001.

Leclerc, Jean-Pierre. "Réflexions sur le dispositif français de soutien à la production cinématographique: Rapport établi à la demande du ministre de la culture et de la communication." Paris: Ministry of Culture, 2003.

Lee, Jung-Woo. "Analyse comprarée des politiques cinématographiques françaises et coréennes: Étude de la formation de la cristallisation de l'exception culturelle en France et en Corée." Doctoral thesis, l'Institut d'études politiques de Paris, March 2003. CNC D 1608.

Lee, Sang-Woo. "Film Trade in Japan Since the 1950s: Government Policies and Media Development." *Keio Communication Review* 26 (2004): 53–76.

Lee, Shi Young, et al. "The Effect of the Korean Screen Quota System on Box Office Performance." *Journal of World Trade* 42, no. 2 (2008): 335–346.

Léglise, Paul. *Le cinéma d'art et d'essai*. Notes et études documentaires nos. 4551–4552. Paris: Le Documentation française, 1980.

Lemesle, Marie-Cerise. "L'évolution de la distribution des films en salles entre 2000 et 2009: La place de la 'l'indépendance.'" Mémoire de Master 2, Université de Paris III, Sorbonne-Nouvelle, 2009.

Lescure, Jean, and Claude Degand. "Création et production cinématographiques face à l'État en Europe." Council of Europe, 1982. CNC D 2053.

Lewis, Jon. *American Film: A History*. New York: Norton, 2008.

——, ed. *The End of Cinema as We Know It: American Film in the Nineties*. New York: New York University Press, 2001.

——, ed. *New American Cinema*. Durham, N.C.: Duke University Press, 1998.

——. "Trust and Anti-Trust in the New New Hollywood." *Michigan Quarterly Review* 35, no. 1 (1997): 85–105.

Litman, Barry R. *The Motion Picture Mega-Industry*. Boston: Allyn and Bacon, 1998.

Littoz-Monnet, Annabelle. "European Cultural Policy: A French Creation?" *French Politics* 1 (2003): 255–278.

——. *The European Union and Culture: Between Economic Regulation and European Cultural Policy*. Manchester: Manchester University Press, 2007.

"Le livre blanc de la distribution indépendante: Préserver la diversité de l'offre cinématographique." Distributeurs indépendants réunis européens (DIRE), 2011.

Lo, Kwai-Cheung. "Double Negations: Hong Kong Culutral Identity in Hollywood's Transnational Representations." *Cultural Studies* 15, no. 3–4 (2001): 464–485.

Looseley, David L. *The Politics of Fun: Cultural Policy and Debate in Contemporary France*. Oxford: Berg, 1997.

Lu, Sheldon Hsiao-peng, ed. *Transnational Chinese Cinemas: Identity, Nationhood, Gender*. Honolulu: University of Hawai'i Press, 1997.

Luneau, Maurice. "Les perspectives des industries françaises du cinéma." Conseil économique social et environnemental, May 23, 1979. CNC D 1975.

Lupinacci, Timothy M. "The Pursuit of Television Broadcasting Activities in the European Community: Cultural Preservation or Economic Protectionism?" *Vanderbilt Journal of Transnational Law* 24, no. 1 (1991): 113–154.

MacDonald, Paul, and Janet Wasko, eds. *The Contemporary Hollywood Film Industry*. Malden, Mass.: Blackwell, 2008.

Malraux, André. *Esquisse d'une psychologie du cinéma*. Paris: Nouveau monde, 2003.

Maltby, Richard. *Hollywood Cinema*. 1995. Reprint, Malden, Mass.: Blackwell, 2003.

——. "'Nobody Knows Everything': Post-classical Historiographies and Consolidated Entertainment." In Neale and Smith, *Contemporary Hollywood Cinema*, 21–44.

Maltby, Richard, and Ruth Vasey. "'Temporary American Citizens': Cultural Anxieties and Industrial Strategies in the Americanisation of European Cinema." In Fowler, *The European Cinema Reader*, 180–193.

Marchetti, Pascal. *La production d'oeuvres audiovisuelles dans l'Union européenne*. Paris: Économica, 2007.

Marie, Michel. *Le jeune cinéma français*. Paris: Nathan, 1998.

——. *La Nouvelle Vague: Une école artistique*. Paris: Nathan, 1997.

Martel, Frédéric. *De la culture en Amerique*. Paris: Gallimard, 2006.

——. *Mainstream: Enquête sur cette culture qui plait tout le monde*. Paris: Flammarion, 2010.

Martin, Reed, "A Crisis of Art and Commerce." *Columbia Journal of World Business* 30, no. 4 (Winter 1995): 6–17.

Mattelart, Armand. *Diversité culturelle et mondialisation*. Paris: La Découverte, 2005.

Mattelart, Armand, Xavier Delcourt, and Michelle Mattelart. *International Image Markets: In Search of an Alternative Perspective*. Trans. David Buxton. London: Comedia, 1984.

Mattelart, Armand, and Michele Mattelart. *Histoire des théories de la communication*. Paris: La Découverte, 1995.

Maule, Christopher. "Rhetoric and Reality: The Debate Over Trade and Culture." *Carleton Economic Papers*, January 21, 2002.

Mayer-Robitaille, Laurence. "L'application de la politique communautaire de concurrence aux accords et aux aides d'État rélatifs à l'audiovisuel." IRIS Plus 2005-10. Strasbourg: European Audiovisual Observatory, November 2005.

McClintick, David, and Anne Faircloth. "The Predator: How an Italian Thug Looted MGM, Brought Credit Lyonnais to Its Knees, and Made the Pope Cry." *Fortune*, July 8, 1996.

McDonald, Kevin M. "How Would You Like Your Television—With or Without Borders and With or Without Culture: A New Approach to Media Regulation in the European Union." *Fordham International Law Journal* 22 (1991): 1991–2023.

McMahon, Darrin. "Echoes of the Recent Past: Contemporary French Anti-Americanism in Historical and Cultural Perspective." International Security Studies, Yale University, January 1995.

Meneu, Olivier. "Le cinéma d'Art et d'Esssai." D.E.A. Économie de l'Industrie, des Services et de la Culture, Université de Paris I, Panthéon-Sorbonne, October 1995. CNC D 431.

Menger, Pierre-Michel. *Les intermittents du spectacle: Sociologie du travail flexible*. Paris: Éditions de l'École des hautes études en sciences sociales, 2011.

——. *Le travail créateur: S'accomplir dans l'incertain*. Paris: Le Seuil/Gallimard, 2009.

Mentré, Paul. "Situation du cinéma français." *Commentaire* 105 (Spring 2004): 169–178.

Mérigeau, Pascal. *Autopsie d'un meurtre*. Paris: Flammarion. 2007.

Mérigeau, Pascal, and Jacques Zimmer. "On ne tire pas sur une ambulance Cinéma TV." *La Revue du Cinéma, Image et Son* 331 (September 1978): 77–82.

Messerlin, Patrick A. "France and Trade Policy: Is the 'French Exception' Passé?" *International Affairs* 72, no.2 (1996): 293–309.

——. "La politique française du cinéma: 'L'arbre, le maire et la médiathèque.' " *Commentaire* 71 (1995): 591–601.

——. "Regulating Culture: Has It 'Gone with the Wind'?" In *Achieving Better Regulation of Services: Conference Proceedings, Australian National University, Canberra, 26–27 June 2000*, 287–318. Melbourne: Productivity Commission, 2000.

Messerlin, Patrick A., and Emmanuel Cocq. "Preparing Negotiations in Services: EC Audiovisuals in the Doha Round." In Messerlin, Siwek, and Cocq, *The Audiovisual Services Sector in the GATS Negotiations*, 32–55.

Messerlin, Patrick A., Stephen E. Siwek, and Emmanuel Cocq. *The Audiovisual Services Sector in the GATS Negotiations*. Washington, D.C.: AEI Press; Paris: Groupe d'économie mondiale de Sciences Po, 2004.

Messier, Jean-Marie. *J6M.COM: Faut-il avoir peur de la nouvelle économie?* Paris: Hachette, 2000.

Meunier, Sophie. "The French Exception." *Foreign Affairs* 79, no. 4 (2000): 104–116.

Michalet, Charles-Albert. *Le drôle de drame du cinéma mondial*. Paris: La Découverte, 1987.

———. *Mondialisation, la grande rupture*. Paris: La Découverte, 2007, 2009.

Miller, Toby, ed. *The Contemporary Hollywood Reader*. London: Routledge, 2009.

———. "The Crime of Monsieur Lang: GATT, the Screen, and the New International Divison of Cultural Labour." In Moran, *Film Policy*, 72–84.

Miller, Toby, et al. *Global Hollywood 2*. London: BFI, 2005.

Mirrlees, Tanner. *Global Entertainment Media: Between Cultural Imperialism and Cultural Globalization*. London: Routledge, 2013.

"Les modes de financement du film français sont-ils adaptés aux perspectives d'évolution de ses différents marchés?" Départment d'études stratégiques sur l'audiovisuel et le cinéma (DESAC), January 2003.

Montebello, Fabrice. "Le cinéma américain est imbattable parce que nous l'aimons." In Paris, *Quelle diversité face à Hollywood?*, 30–35.

———. *Le cinéma en France, depuis les années 1930*. Paris: Armand Colin, 2005.

Moran, Albert, ed. *Film Policy: International, National and Regional Perspectives*. London: Routledge, 1996.

Moreau, François, and Stéphanie Peltier. "Cultural Diversity in the Movie Industry: A Cross-National Study." *Journal of Media Economics* 17, no. 2 (2004): 123–143.

Moretti, Franco. "Planet Hollywood." *New Left Review* 9 (2001): 90–101.

Morgan de Rivery, Eric. "Unresolved Issues in the Audiovisual Sector and the US/EC Conflict." In Bourgeois, Berrod, and Fournier, *The Uruguay Round Results*, 435–443.

Morrison, Donald, and Antoine Compagnon. *The Death of French Culture*. Cambridge: Polity Press, 2010.

Moul, Charles, ed. *A Concise Handbook of Movie Industry Economics*. Cambridge: Cambridge University Press, 2005.

Mukharjee, Arpita. "India's Trade Potential in Audio-Visual Services and the GATS." Working Paper no. 81. New Delhi: Indian Council for Research on International Economic Relations, April 2002.

Musitelli, Jean. "L'invention de la diversité culturelle." *Annuaire français de droit international* 51 (2005): 512–523.

Nagib, Lucia, Chris Perriam, and Rajinder Dudrah, eds. *Theorizing World Cinema*. London: I. B.Taurus, 2012.

Neale, Steve, and Murray Smith, eds. *Contemporary Hollywood Cinema*. London: Routledge, 1998.

Nettelbeck, Colin. "Keeping It All in the Family? French Cinema and the Rencontres de Beaune, 2000–2004." *Modern and Contemporary France* 14, no. 1 (February 2006): 85–99.

Neupert, Richard. *A History of the French New Wave*. Madison: University of Wisconsin Press, 2002.

Newman-Baudais, Susan. "Public Funding for Film and Audiovisual Work in Europe." Strasbourg: European Audiovisual Observatory, 2011.

Nikoltchev, Susanne, ed. *Les obligations des radiodiffuseurs d'investir dans la production cinématographique*. IRIS special. Strasbourg: European Audiovisual Observatory, 2006.

Nikoltchev, Susanne, and Francisco Javier Cabrera Blázquez. "Aides nationales à la production cinématographique: Caractéristiques et tendances juridiques." IRIS Plus 2001-4. Strasbourg: European Audiovisual Observatory, 2001.

Nowell-Smith, Geoffrey, ed. *The Oxford History of World Cinema*. Oxford: Oxford University Press, 1997.

Nowell-Smith, Geoffrey, and Steven Ricci, eds. *Hollywood and Europe: Economics, Culture, National Identity, 1945–95*. London: BFI, 1998.

O'Connell, Shaun P. "Television Without Frontiers: The European Union's Continuing Struggle for Cultural Survival." *Case Western Reserve Journal of International Law* 28 (Spring 1996): 501–530.

O'Regan, Tom. *Australian National Cinema*. London: Routledge, 1996.

——. "The Political Economy of Film." In *The Sage Handbook of Film Studies*, edited by James Donald and Michael Renov, 244–261. London: Sage, 2008.

——. "Too Popular by Far: On Hollywood's International Popularity." *Continuum: The Australian Journal of Media and Culture* 5, no. 2 (1990): 302–351.

Orange, Martine, and Jo Johnson. *Une faillite française*. Paris: Albin Michel, 2003.

Ostrowska, Dorota, and Graham Roberts, eds. *European Cinemas in the Television Age*. Edinburgh: Edinburgh University Press, 2007.

Padis, Marc-Olivier. "France and Cultural Globalisation." *Political Quarterly* 73, no. 3 (2002): 273–278.

Pager, Sean A. "Beyond Culture vs. Commerce. Decentralizing Cultural Protection to Promote Diversity Through Trade." *Northwestern Journal of International Law and Business* 31 (2011): 63–135.

Pallier, Aline, et al. "Menaces sur le cinéma européen." *Liber* 30 (March 1997): 1–8.

Palmer, Michael. "Transnationales de la communication et industries culturelles." In Graber, Girsberger, and Nenova, *Free Trade vs. Cultural Diversity*, 77–104.

Pardo, Carlos. "Au-delà du festival de Cannes: Hollywood contre la diversité culturelle." *Le Monde Diplomatique*, May 2000.

——. "Grande détresse pour le film européen." *Le Monde Diplomatique*, May 1997.

Paris, Thomas, ed. *Quelle diversité face à Hollywood?* CinémAction, Hors-série. Condé-sur-Noireau, France: Éditions Corlet, 2002.

Pauwels, Caroline. "Integrating Economies, Integrating Policies: The Importance of Anti-trust and Competition Policies Within the Global Audiovisual Order." *Communications and Strategies* 30 (1998): 103–132.

Pauwels, Caroline, and Jan Loisen. "The WTO and the Audiovisual Sector: Economic Free Trade vs. Cultural Horse Trading?" *European Journal of Communication* 18 (2003): 291–313.

Paxton, Robert O. *Vichy France: Old Guard and New Order, 1940–1944.* New York: Columbia University Press, 1972.

Pells, Richard. "From Modernism to the Movies: The Globalization of American Culture in the Twentieth Century." *European Journal of American Culture* 23, no. 2 (2004): 143–155.

Peltier, Stéphanie. "Les industries culturelles: Une exception économique?" *Cahiers français* 312 (January–February 2003): 31–36.

——. "La question de l'inefficacité des restrictions quantitatives: Le cas des quotas télévisuels." *Communications & Stratégies* 35, no. 3 (1999): 111–159.

Pendakur, M. *Canadian Dreams and American Control: The Political Economy of the Canadian Film Industry.* Detroit: Wayne State University Press, 1990.

Perras, Sylvie. "Logique économique des aides à l'exploitation cinématographique: Une mise en perspective historique, 1946–1993." D.E.A. paper, University of Paris I, Panthéon-Sorbonne, September 1993. CNC D 2949.

Perrot, Anne, and Jean-Pierre Leclerc. "Cinéma et concurrence: Rapport remis à Mme Christine Lagarde, ministre de l'économie, de l'industrie et de l'emploi et Mme Christine Albanel, ministre de la culture et de la communication." Paris: Ministry of Finance and Ministry of Culture, March 2008.

Péton, Gaël. "L'avance sur recettes: Rajeunir la profession (1956–1964)." In *58–68, retour sur une génération,* edited by Laurent Bismuth and Eric Le Roy, 72–86. Paris: CNC, 2013.

Petrie, Duncan, ed. *Screening Europe: Image and Identity in Contemporary European Cinema.* London: BFI, 1992.

Poirrier, Philippe. "French Cultural Policy in Question, 1981–2003." In *After the Deluge: New Perspectives on Postwar French Intellectual and Cultural History,* edited by Julian Bourg. Lanham, Md.: Lexington Books, 2004.

——, ed. *Les politiques culturelles en France.* Paris: La Documentation française, 2002.

"La politique culturelle: Le cinéma, 1981–1991." Paris: Ministry of Culture, 1991.

"La politique culturelle, 1981–1985: Bilan de la législature: Le cinéma et l'audiovisuel." Paris: Ministry of Culture, n.d. CNC SD 1177.

"Une politique française du cinéma, 1974–1981." Paris: Ministry of Culture, 1981. CNC SD 2010.

Polo, Jean-François. "L'audiovisuel européen: Un enjeu culturel." *Hermès* 23–24 (1999): 65–71.

——. "La naissance d'une direction audiovisuelle à la commission: La consécration de l'exception culturelle." *Politique européenne* 11 (Autumn 2003): 9–30.

———. "La politique audiovisuelle européenne: De l'incantation de l'identité européenne à la défense de la diversité culturelle." *Médiamorphoses* 12 (2004): 82–86.

———. "La politique cinématographique de Jack Lang: De la réhabilitation des industries culturelles à la proclamation de l'exception culturelle." *Politix* 16, no. 61 (2003): 123–149.

———. "La politique cinématographique française face à la mondialisation." *Web Journal of French Media Studies* 5, no.1 (2002), http://wjfms.ncl.ac.uk/poloWJ.htm.

———. "La relance de la politique audiovisuelle européenne: Les ressources politiques et administratives de la DG X." *Pôle Sud* 15, no. 1 (2001): 5–17.

———. "L'Union européenne dans les négotiations internationales sur l'audiovisuel: Une exception culturelle construite par l'action collective." In *L'Union européenne, acteur international*, edited by F. Petiteville and D. Helly, 238–252. Paris: L'Harmattan, 2000.

Portes, Jacques."Les origines de la légende noire des accords Blum-Byrnes sur le cinéma." *Revue d'Histoire Moderne et contemporaine* 33 (1986): 314–329.

Pouchard, David, "Les systèmes de prix fixe du livre dans les zones linguistiques transnationales au regard du droit communautaire." *Revue Trimestrielle de Droit européen* 37, no. 1 (2001): 49–62.

Powrie, Phil, ed. *French Cinema in the 1990s: Continuity and Difference*. Oxford: Oxford University Press, 1999.

Powrie, Phil, and Keith Reader. *French Cinema: A Student's Guide*. London: Arnold, 2002.

Prédal, René. *50 ans de cinéma français (1945–1995)*. Paris: Nathan.1996.

———. *Le jeune cinéma français*. Paris: Nathan, 2002.

"Premiers états généraux de l'action culturelle cinématographique et audiovisuelle." Paris: BLAC, January 8–9, 2009. CNC D 4462.

Prince, Steven. *A New Pot of Gold: Hollywood Under the Electronic Rainbow, 1980–1989*. Berkeley: University of California Press, 2000.

The Promotion and Diffusion of European Cinema: Proposals for a Debate. Proceedings of the European Union Conference, October 28–29, 1997, Valladolid, Spain. Valladolid: Semana Internacional de Cine de Valladolid, 1998.

Prowda, Judith Beth. "U.S. Dominance in the 'Marketplace of Culture' and the French 'Cultural Exception.'" *New York University Journal of International Law and Politics* 29, no. 1–2 (1997): 193–210.

Psychogiopoliou, Evangelia. "The Cultural Criterion in the European Commission's Assessment of State Aids to the Audio-Visual Sector." *Legal Issues of Economic Integration* 37, no. 4 (2010): 273–291.

"Le public du cinéma art et essai." Paris: CNC, October 2006.

Puttnam, David. *The Undeclared War: The Struggle for Control of the World's Film Industry*. London: HarperCollins, 1997.

Quintero, Diana. "American Television and Cinema in France and Europe." *Fletcher Forum of World Affairs* 18, no. 2 (1994): 115–128.

Ralite, Jack. *La culture française se porte bien pourvu qu'on la sauve*. Paris: Messidor, 1987.

———. "Cultures à vendre." *Le Monde Diplomatique*, February 1997.

Ramonet, Ignacio. "Apocalypse médias." *Le Monde Diplomatique*, April 1997.

"Rapport d'activité." Paris: ADRC, 2003.

"Rapport du groupe de travail sur le cinéma face au droit de la concurrence." Paris: CNC, January 2003.

"Rapport du groupe de travail sur le financement de la production cinématographique." Paris: CNC, July 2002. CNC D 1427.

Regourd, Serge. "Le commerce et la culture au sein du GATS, et au-delà." *ERA Forum 6*, no. 1 (2005): 87–92.

——, ed. "De l'exception à la diversité culturelle." Special issue. *Problèmes Politiques et Sociaux 904* (September 2004).

——. *Droit de la communication audiovisuelle*. Paris: Presses universitaires de France, 2001.

——. *L'exception culturelle*. Paris: Presses universitaires de France, 2002.

——. "Exception, diversité . . . des instruments de politique culturelle en quête de leur objet contribution à un examen critique." *La Pensée 349* (2007): 51–65.

——. "Pour l'exclusion culturelle." *Le Monde Diplomatique*, November 1993.

——. *La télévision des européens, vivre en Europe*. Paris: La Documentation française, 1992.

Renaud, Young-Key Kim, R. Richard Grinker, and Kirk W. Larsen, eds. "Text and Context of Korean Cinema: Crossing Borders." Sigur Center Asia Paper no. 17. Washington, D.C.: Sigur Center for Asian Studies, 2003. https://www.gwu.edu/~sigur/assets/docs/scap/SCAP17-KoreanCinema.pdf.

Renault, Charles-Edouard. "Financement et distribution des oeuvres cinématographiques: Quel avenir pour les aides publiques au niveau européen?" *Gazette du Palais*, May 15, 2007.

Renouard,Gilles. *Le cinéma français dans le monde*. Paris: Klincksieck, 2012.

"La rentabilité des films." Paris: CNC, February 2004.

"Report on the Commission Communication on Certain Legal Aspects Relating to Cinematographic and Other Audiovisual Works." COM(2001) 534 – C5-0078/2002 – 2002/2035(COS). Brussels: Committee on Culture, Youth, Education, the Media and Sport, European Parliament, June 5, 2002.

"Le respect de la directive Télévision sans frontières dans les grands pays européens." Paris: Fédération de la production TéléVisuelle, February 2001. CNC SD 1199.

Richardson, Bonnie J. K. "Hollywood's Vision of a Clear, Predictable Trade Framework Consistent with Cultural Diversity." In Graber, Girsberger, and Nenova, *Free Trade vs. Cultural Diversity*, 111–126.

Rigaud, Jacques. *L'exception culturelle: Culture et pouvoirs sous la Ve République*. Paris: Grasset, 1995.

——. "L'exception culturelle: Singularité française ou modèle européen?" *Études 3876* (December 1997): 599–608.

——. *Libre culture*. Paris: Gallimard, 1990.

——. "Pourquoi une politique culturelle?" Paris: Commission d'étude de la politique culturelle d'État, October 1996. CNC D 650.

——. "Pour une refondation de la politique culturelle." Paris: La Documentation française, 1996.

Rioux, Jean-Pierre, and Jean-François Sirinelle, eds. *La culture de masse en France de la Belle Époque à aujourd'hui.* Paris: Fayard, 2002.

Robins, Kevin, and David Morley. "Euroculture: Communications, Community, and Identity in Europe." *Cardozo Arts and Entertainment Law Journal* 11 (1993): 387–410.

Rockett, Kevin, Luke Gibbons, and John Hill. *Cinema and Ireland.* London: Routledge, 1987.

Rojanski, Vladimir. "The European Union's Audiovisual Policy." Question d'Europe no. 48. Paris: Fondation Robert Schuman, December 11, 2006.

"Le rôle de l'État vis-à-vis des industries culturelles: Documents de la conférence organisée à Strasbourg, 28–30 avril 1980." Strasbourg: Conseil de la cooperation culturelle, Council of Europe. CNC D 2007.

Rose, Ian M. "Barring Foreigners from Our Airways: An Anachronistic Pothole on the Global Information Highway." *Columbia Law Review* 95 (June 1995): 1188–1231.

Rosenbaum, Jonathan. *Movie Wars: How Hollywood and the Media Limit What Films We Can See.* Chicago: A Capella, 2000.

Rosenbaum, Jonathan, and Adrian Martin, eds. *Movie Mutations: The Changing Face of World Cinephilia.* London: BFI, 2003.

Ross, George, Stanley Hoffmann, and Sylvia Malzacher, eds. *The Mitterrand Experiment: Continuity and Change in Modern France.* London: Oxford University Press, 1987.

Rousseau, Christine. "Faire du concept de diversité culturelle une politique: Les ministres francophones de la culture adoptent un plan d'action décennal." *Le Monde,* June 19, 2001.

Rousselet, André. "Canal peu banal." *L'Express,* November 5, 2009.

Roux, Jean, and René Thévenet. *Industrie et commerce du film en France.* Paris: Éditions scientifiques et juridiques, 1979.

Roy, Martin. "Audiovisual Services in the Doha Round: 'Dialogue de Sourds, The Sequel'?" *Journal of World Investment and Trade* 6, no. 6 (2005): 923–952.

Saint Pulgent, Maryvonne de, Pierre-Jean Benghozi, and Thomas Paris. Mondialisation et diversité culturelle: Le cas de la France. Notes de l'IFRI 51. Paris: Institut français des relations internationales, 2003.

"La salle de cinéma, lieu de culture et de loisir: Guide à l'usage des collectivités." Paris: Ministry of Culture and CNC, 1998. CNC D 3092.

Schatz, Thomas. *The Genius of the System: Hollywood Filmmaking in the Studio Era.* Minneapolis: University of Minnesota Press, 2010.

——. "The Studio System and Conglomerate Hollywood." In MacDonald and Wasko, *The Contemporary Hollywood Film Industry,* 13-42.

Schlesinger, Philip. "Changing Spaces of Political Communication: The Case of the European Union." *Political Communication* 16 (1999): 263–279.

——. "Europe's Contradictory Communicative Space." *Daedalus* 123, no. 2 (Spring 1994): 25–52.

———. "From Cultural Defence to Political Culture: Media, Politics, and Collective Identity in the European Union." *Media, Culture & Society* 19, no. 3 (July 1997): 369–391.

———. "On National Identity: Some Conceptions and Misconceptions Criticized." *Social Science Information* 26, no. 2 (1987): 219–264.

Schwarz, Suzanne Michele. "Television Without Frontiers?" *North Carolina Journal of International Law and Commercial Regulation* 16, no. 2 (1991): 351–375.

Scott, Allen J. "French Cinema: Economy, Policy and Place in the Making of a Cultural-Products Industry." *Theory, Culture & Society* 17, no. 1 (2000): 1–38.

———. "A New Map of Hollywood: The Production and Distribution of American Motion Pictures." *Regional Studies* 36, no. 9 (2002): 957–975.

———. *On Hollywood: The Place, the Industry*. Princeton, N.J.: Princeton University Press, 2005.

Scriven, Michael, and Monia Lecomte, eds. *Television Broadcasting in Contemporary France and Britain*. New York: Berghahn, 1999.

Sellier, Geneviève. "Le précédent des Accords Blum-Byrnes." *Le Monde Diplomatique*, November 1993.

Semati, M. Mehdi, and Patty J. Sotirin. "Hollywood's Transnational Appeal: Hegemony and Democratic Potential." *Journal of Popular Film and Television* 26, no. 4 (1999): 177–188.

Shao, W. Ming. "Is There No Business Like Show Business? Free Trade and Cultural Protectionism." *Yale Journal of International Law* 20 (1995): 105–150.

Sieklucka, Catherine. *Les aides à l'industrie cinématographique dans la Communauté économique européenne*. Paris: Presses universitaires de France, 1967.

"Signature du protocole d'Accord relatif à l'éducation artistique." Palais de l'Institut de France, November 17, 1993. CNC D 1182.

Sinha, Amresh, and Terence McSweeney, eds. *Millennial Cinema: Memory in Global Film*. New York: Columbia University Press, 2011.

Siroen, Jean-Marc. "Le cinéma, une industrie ancienne de la nouvelle économie." *Revue d'Économie Industrielle* 91 (2000): 93–118.

Smith, Clint N. "International Trade in Television Programming and GATT: An Analysis of Why the European Community's Local Program Requirement Violates the General Agreement on Tariffs and Trade." *International Tax & Business Law* 10 (1993): 97–137.

Sojcher, Frédéric, ed. *Cinéma européen et identités culturelles*. Brussels: Université de Bruxelles, 1996.

Sojcher, Frédéric, and Pierre-Jean Benghozi, eds. *Quel modèle audiovisual européen?* Paris: L'Harmattan, 2003.

Sorlin, Pierre. *European Cinemas, European Societies, 1939–1990*. London: Routledge, 1991.

Stafford, Roy. *The Global Film Book*. London: Routledge, 2014.

Statistical Yearbook, 1994/1995. Strasbourg: European Audiovisual Observatory, 1995.

Stringer, Julian, ed. *Movie Blockbusters*. London: Routledge, 2003.

Strode, Louise. "France and EU Policy-Making on Visual Culture: New Opportunities for National Identity." In Harris and Ezra, *France in Focus*, 61–78.

Surel, Yves. *L'État et le livre: Les publiques du livre en France, 1957–1993*. Paris: L'Harmattan.1997.

Tardif, Jean, and Joëlle Farchy. *Les enjeux de la mondialisation culturelle*. Paris: Hors Commerce, 2006.

Tarr, Carrie, ed. "Introduction: French Cinema—'Transnational' Cinema?" *Modern and Contemporary France* 15, no. 1 (2007): 3–7.

Television Without Frontiers: Green Paper on the Establishment of the Common Market for Broadcasting, Especially by Cable and Satellite. Communication from the Commission to the Council, COM(84) 300 final. Brussels: Commission of the European Communities, June 14, 1984.

"Télévisions Transfrontières en Europe." Inventaire et perspectives no. 34. L'Observatoire de la communication, May 1989. CNC D 0149.

Temple, Michael, and Michael Witt, eds. *The French Cinema Book*. London: BFI, 2004.

Thanouli, Eleftheria. "Narration in World Cinema: Mapping the Flows of Formal Exchange in the Era of Globalization." *New Cinemas: Journal of Contemporary Film* 6, no. 1 (2008): 5–15.

Theiler, Tobias. "Viewers Into Europeans?: How the European Union Tried to Europeanize the Audiovisual Sector, and Why It Failed." *Canadian Journal of Communication* 24 (2001): 1–29.

Thory, T. "L'accord de libre échange américano-canadien." *Annuaire français de droit international* 34 (1988): 549–562. http://www.persee.fr/web/revues/home/prescript/article/afdi_0066-3085_1988_num_34_1_2855.

Thussu, Daya Kishan. "The Globalization of 'Bollywood': The Hype and the Hope." In *Global Bollywood*, edited by Anandam P. Kavoori and Aswin Punathambekar, 97–113. New York: New York University Press, 2008.

Toggenburg, Gabriel N. "The Debate on European Values and the Case of Cultural Diversity." European Diversity and Autonomy Papers, EDAP 1/2004. Bozen, Italy: EURAC, 2004.

Tomaszewski, Rémi, ed. *Les politiques audiovisuelles en France*. Paris: La Documentation française, 2001.

Toubiana, Serge. "Mission de réflexion sur l'Art et Essai: Nouveaux horizons." January 1990. CNC D 2433.

Trémois, Claude-Marie. *Les enfants de la liberté*. Paris: Éditions du Seuil, 1997.

"Trop de films? La diversité cinématographique en question: Actes de Colloque." Nineteenth Festival Prémiers Plans, Angers, January 26, 2007. http://www.gncr.fr/sites/default/files/actes_colloque_2007.pdf.

Truchaud, Marion. "L'exploitation 'art et essai' aujourd'hui: Quels enjeux et quelles politiques?" Master's thesis, Université de Paris I, Panthéon-Sorbonne, 2005. CNC D 3893.

Trumpbour, John. *Selling Hollywood to the World: U.S. and European Struggles for Mastery of the Global Film Industry, 1920–1950*. Cambridge: Cambridge University Press, 2002.

Ulff-Møller, Jens. "The Origin of the French Film Quota Policy Controlling the Import of American Films." *Historical Journal of Film, Radio and Television* 18, no. 2 (1998): 167–182.

Urfalino, Philippe. "De l'anti-imperialisme américain à la dissolution de la politique culturelle." *Revue Française de Science Politique* 43, no. 5 (1993): 823–849.

——. *L'invention de la politique culturelle.* Paris: Hachette, 2004.

Uricaru, Ioana. "Follow the Money: Financing Contemporary Cinema in Romania." In Imre, *A Companion to Eastern European Cinemas*, 427–452.

Van Hemel, Annemoon, Hans Mommaas, and Cas Smithuijsen, eds. *Trading Cuture: GATT, European Cultural Policies and the Transatlantic Market.* Amsterdam: Boekman Foundation, 1996.

Veron, Luc. "Hollywood and Europe: A Case of Trade in Culutral Industries, the 1993 GATT Dispute." School of International Studies, University of Southern California, March 1999.

Vezyroglou, Dimitri, ed. *Le cinema: Une affaire d'État.* Paris: La Documentation française, 2014.

Vitali, Valentina, and Paul Willemen, eds. *Theorising National Cinema.* London: BFI, 2006.

Vivancos, Patrice. *Cinéma et Europe: Réflexions sur les politiques européennes de soutien au cinéma.* Paris: L'Harmattan, 2000.

Vogel, Harold. *Entertainment Industry Economics: A Guide for Financial Analysis.* Cambridge: Cambridge University Press, 2007.

Voogd, Joop. "Le cinéma et l'État: Rapport de la commission de la culture et de l'éducation." Strasbourg: Council of Europe, 1979.

——. "Exposé des motifs." In "Le cinéma et l'État: Rapport de la commission de la culture et de l'éducation (Rapporteur: M. Joop Voogd) et documents du colloque organisé à Lisbonne du 14 au 16 juin 1978." Strasbourg: Council of Europe, 1979.

Voon, Tania. *Cultural Products and the World Trade Organization.* Cambridge: Cambridge University Press, 2007.

Wall, Irwin M. "Les Accords Blum-Byrnes: La modernisation de la France et la guerre froide." *Vingtième Siècle* 13 (January–March 1987): 45–62.

——. "From Anti-Americanism to Francophobia: The Saga of French and American Intellectuals." *French Historical Studies* 18, no. 4 (1994): 1083–1100.

Wang, Ting. "Hollywood's Crusade in China Prior to China's WTO Accession." *Jump Cut* 49 (Spring 2007). http://www.ejumpcut.org/archive/jc49.2007/TingWang/.

Wangermée, Robert. "Rapport du Groupe d'experts européens." In Wangermée and Gournay, *La politique culturelle de la France.*

Wangermée, Robert, and Bernard Gournay. *La politique culturelle de la France: Programme européen d'évaluation.* Paris: La Documentation française, 1988.

Warnier, Jean-Pierre. *La mondialisation de la culture.* Paris: La Découverte, 2007.

Wasko, Janet. "Critiquing Hollywood: The Political Economy of Motion Pictures." In Moul, *A Concise Handbook of Movie Industry Economics*, 5–31.

———. *Hollywood in the Information Age: Beyond the Silver Screen.* Austin: University of Texas Press, 1994.

———. *How Hollywood Works.* Los Angeles: Sage, 2003.

———. *Movies and Money.* Norwood, N.J.: Ablex, 1982.

———. "Show Me the Money: Challenging Hollywood Economics." In *Toward a Political Economy of Culture: Capitalism and Conncentration in the 21st Century*, edited by A. Calabrese and C. Sparks, 131–150. Lanham, Md.: Rowman and Littlefield, 2004.

Wasser, Frederick. *Veni, Vidi, Video: The Hollywood Empire and the VCR.* Austin: University of Texas Press, 2001.

Waterman, David. *Hollywood's Road to Riches.* Cambridge, Mass.: Harvard University Press, 2005.

Waterman, David, and Krishna P. Jayakar. "The Competitive Balance of the Italian and American Film Industries." *European Journal of Communication* 15, no. 4 (2000): 501–528.

Watts, Philip. "The Eloquent Image: The Postwar Mission of Film and Criticism." In *Opening Bazin: Postwar Film Theory and Its Afterlife*, edited by Dudley Andrew, 215–224. New York: Oxford University Press, 2011.

"White Book of the European Exhibition Industry: A Report by London Economics and BIPE Conseil for MEDIA Salles." 1994. CNC D 401.

Wildman, Steven S., and Stephen E. Siwek. *International Trade in Film and Television Programs.* Washington, D.C.: American Enterprise Institute, 1988.

Willats, P. "Défense et illustration de l'abri fiscal cinématographique appliqué dans trois pays." *Film Échange* 10 (Spring 1980): 29–40.

Williams, Alan, ed. *Film and Nationalism.* New Brunswick, N.J.: Rutgers University Press, 2002.

———. *Republic of Images: A History of French Filmmaking.* Cambridge, Mass.: Harvard University Press, 1992.

Wong, Cindy Hing-Yuk. *Film Festivals: Culture, People and Power on the Global Screen.* New Brunswick, N.J.: Rutgers University Press, 2011.

Wright, Claire. "Reconciling Cultural Diversity and Free Trade in the Digital Age: A Cultural Analysis of the International Trade in Content Items." *Akron Law Review* 41 (2009): 399–505.

INDEX

Page numbers in italics refer to figures and tables.

FILM AND CULTURE

A series of Columbia University Press
Edited by John Belton